D1571287

The Behaviour of Fiscal Authorities

The Behaviour of Fiscal Authorities

Stabilization, Growth and Institutions

Edited by

Marco Buti
Jürgen von Hagen
and
Carlos Martinez-Mongay

The articles in this book are reproduced from a number of papers on 'The Behaviour of Fiscal Authorities' which were commissioned by the European Commission's Directorate General for Economic and Financial Affairs. They do not, however, express the Commission's official views. Responsibility for the information and views set out in the papers lies entirely with the authors.

First published 2002 by
PALGRAVE
Houndmills, Basingstoke, Hampshire RG21 6XS and
175 Fifth Avenue, New York, N.Y. 10010
Companies and representatives throughout the world

PALGRAVE is the new global academic imprint of
St. Martin's Press LLC Scholarly and Reference Division and
Palgrave Publishers Ltd (formerly Macmillan Press Ltd).

ISBN 0–333–98495–1

This book is printed on paper suitable for recycling and made from fully managed and sustained forest sources.

A catalogue record for this book is available from the British Library

Library of Congress Cataloging-in-Publication Data
The behaviour of fiscal authorities : stabilization, growth, and institutions / edited by M. Buti, J. von Hagen, and C. Martinez-Mongay.
    p. cm.
    Includes bibliographical references and index.
    ISBN 0–333–98495–1
      1. Fiscal policy – European Union countries. 2. Monetary policy – European Union countries. 3. Economic and Monetary Union.
4. Economic stabilization – European Union countries. I. Buti, Marco.
II. Hagen, Jürgen von. III. Martinez-Mongay, Carlos.
HJ1000 .B43 2002
336.3'094–dc21   2001059052

10 9 8 7 6 5 4 3 2 1
11 10 09 08 07 06 05 04 03 02

Printed and bound in Great Britain by
Antony Rowe Ltd, Chippenham, Wiltshire

Contents

**Part III Monetary and Fiscal Policy
Interactions in EMU**

List of Tables

List of Figures

Foreword

The institutional framework of the European Economic and Monetary Union (EMU) is firmly rooted in monetary as well as fiscal discipline. The creation of EMU not only entails the adoption of a single currency but represents also a fundamental change in the overall policy-setting of the participating countries. This new policy regime involves radical changes in the way public and private agents behave.

EMU poses unique challenges for the management of fiscal policy. Most particularly, policy-makers in EMU have to maintain budgetary discipline, ensure cyclical stabilization and step up economic efficiency, as well as achieving an appropriate mix between monetary and fiscal policies.

To face such challenges and ensure a smooth functioning of EMU, member states agreed on a set of institutional arrangements and procedures in the Treaty of Maastricht and in the Stability and Growth Pact. The Treaty laid down the fiscal criteria for joining EMU and established the Excessive Deficit Procedure with a view to restraining budget deficits and curb public debt. The Pact was adopted to clarify the Treaty provisions and ensure the continuation of fiscal discipline in EMU. To guarantee that the 3 per cent of GDP deficit ceiling is not breached, government budgets should be 'close to balance or in surplus' in the medium term.

The rationale of EMU's fiscal rules can largely be found in the 'fiscal failures' in Europe in the last three decades: a lack of fiscal discipline resulting in persistent deficits and mounting stock of debt; a pro-cyclical bias in the conduct of fiscal policy which has accentuated business cycle swings, rather than smoothing them out; and a rising share of the public sector in the economy coupled with a steadily increasing tax burden which has hampered efficiency and job creation.

Correcting these failures is important *per se*. It is also a condition for a smooth functioning of EMU. Sound public finances are required to prevent the independence of the European Central Bank from becoming an empty shell. Fiscal stabilization is needed to respond to temporary country-specific disturbances. Finally, a less pervasive, more efficient welfare state and a less distortive tax system would enhance the economy's response to permanent shocks.

EMU's institutional framework can help in correcting earlier failures. It not only concerns fiscal prudence, but also recognizes that a degree of flexibility for automatic stabilizers is needed in EMU. The recent attention to the 'quality' of budgetary adjustment and the long-term sustainability of public finances will help promote welfare and structural reforms ensuring a better functioning of product and labour markets.

Within this evolving economic and institutional framework, this book analyses recent advances in the economics of fiscal policy and budgetary behaviour. Particular attention is devoted to some of the outstanding challenges policy-makers face in EMU: the interplay of fiscal discipline and stabilization, the long-run implications of fiscal policy and the relationships between fiscal and monetary authorities.

These are issues of particular relevance for the European Commission, in general, and for the Directorate General for Economic and Financial Affairs, in particular. The publication of this volume is an indication of the active role that the European Commission wants to play in the debate on EMU, not only through its official policy statements, but also, as in this book, by bringing together the contributions of academic scholars and economists from international organizations and national administrations, including the central banks. This intellectual effort is particularly important in the current juncture when the endeavour of policy-makers in Europe is shifting from implementing the 'Maastricht blueprint' to drafting the new policy agenda of EMU.

All in all, this book is a valuable contribution to the ongoing debate on economic policy in Europe and will help to improve our understanding of the effects, role and limitations of budgetary policy and public finances in EMU.

KLAUS REGLING
Director-General for Economic and Financial Affairs
European Commission
Brussels

List of Contributors

Olivier De Bandt	Banque de France
Ali Bayar	Professor of Economics, Free University of Brussels
Anne Brunila	Adviser to the Board of Governors, Bank of Finland
Marco Buti	Head of Unit, Directorate General for Economic and Financial Affairs, European Commission
Nigel Chalk	International Monetary Fund
Paul M. C. de Boer	Professor of Econometrics and Statistics, Erasmus University of Rotterdam and Free University of Brussels
Andrew Hughes Hallett	Professor of Economics, Strathclyde University
Jan in't Veld	Directorate-General for Economic and Financial Affairs, European Commission
Carlos Martinez-Mongay	Head of Unit, Directorate-General for Economic and Financial Affairs, European Commission
Jacques Mélitz	Professor of Economics, Strathclyde University
Philippe Mills	Adviser, Directorate-General for Economic and Financial Affairs, European Commission
Francesco Paolo Mongelli	Directorate-General of Economics, European Central Bank
Alain Quinet	Professor of Economics, Ecole Nationale de la Statistique et de l'Administration Economique (ENSAE)
Werner Roeger	Deputy Head of Unit, Directorate General for Economic and Financial Affairs, European Commission
Rolf Strauch	European Central Bank
Vito Tanzi	Secretary of State, Italian Ministry of Finance

Paul van den Noord	Head of Euro Desk, Economics Department, Organization for Economic Cooperation and Development
Nicola Viegi	Lecturer in Economics, University of Strathclyde
Jürgen von Hagen	Professor of Economics and Director at the Centre for European Integration Studies at the University of Bonn
Hans Wijkander	Professor of Economics, University of Stockholm

1
The Behaviour of Fiscal Authorities: An Overview[1]

Marco Buti, Jürgen von Hagen and Carlos Martinez-Mongay

1.1 Fiscal policy and macroeconomics: an evolving debate

Positive and normative views on the behaviour of budgetary authorities and the effects of fiscal policy have been at the centre of macroeconomics and the analysis of economic policies since the early post-war period. Every turning point in macroeconomic thinking has led to a change in economists' views about what fiscal authorities do or should do.

The traditional Keynesian view of the 1960s and early 1970s saw fiscal policy as an effective tool for cyclical stabilization. The Mundell–Fleming extension of the IS-LM paradigm to open economies linked by fixed exchange rates, which reflected the situation of the Bretton Woods system, strengthened this conviction. Moreover, Blinder and Solow (1973) suggested that fiscal policy would be effective not only in the short run but also in the long run. Given the relatively low levels of public debt and deficits of a cyclical nature, no conflict seemed to exist between the goals of cyclical stabilization and long-term sustainability of public finances. At the same time, the expansion of the modern welfare state in industrialized countries, which aimed at correcting market failures by providing insurance against unemployment, sickness and old-age risks, strengthened the working of automatic stabilizers. Given the low levels and largely cyclical nature of unemployment, no trade-off was perceived between the allocation and the stabilization functions of public finances.[2]

The consensus on the usefulness of fiscal policy for stabilization purposes collapsed in the second half of the 1970s, following the end of the fixed exchange rate era and the stagflationary consequences of the first oil price shocks. Budget deficits in European Union (EU) economies rose from around balance in the 1960s to above 3 per cent of GDP and did not come back below this figure until the consolidation of the 1990s. The subsequent, rapid accumulation of public debts threatened the sustainability of public finances. Moreover, the emergence of a trade-off between output and inflation stabilization following the oil price hike set the scene for a radical reassessment of the role and powers of fiscal policy. The reborn concept of Ricardian equivalence (Barro, 1974) held that deficit spending is ineffective for stimulating output as economic agents anticipate the future increase in taxes to pay back the public debt and cut back consumption accordingly. While the demand-stimulating effects of fiscal policy were called into question, Sargent and Wallace (1981) showed that the 'fiscal roots' of high inflation lye in persistent budgetary imbalances.[3] With the advancement of models based on the paradigm of forward-looking, intertemporally optimizing agents in macroeconomic analysis, the focus on discretionary policies gave way to rules in fiscal as well as in monetary behaviour, and tax smoothing rather than an active fiscal policy became the benchmark for budgetary behaviour (Barro, 1979).

In Europe, more than elsewhere, awareness of the limitations of fiscal policy and the existence of a 'deficit bias' in the behaviour of fiscal authorities gained ground. The project of creating a monetary union built on strong macroeconomic stability and the need to protect the independence and the anti-inflationary credibility of a soon-to-be-created European Central Bank (ECB) led to the convergence criteria enshrined in the Excessive Deficit Procedure (EDP) of the Maastricht Treaty. The fiscal criteria stipulate that budget deficits as a share of GDP should not exceed 3 per cent and the public debt should be on a decreasing path as long at it exceeds 60 per cent of GDP. The Stability and Growth Pact (SGP), subsequently agreed at the European Council in Amsterdam in 1997, set the objective of budget balances in equilibrium or in surplus in the medium run and established a thorough monitoring system at the EU level to prevent or sanction 'excessive deficits'. The Union's need for monitoring the fiscal performance of its members provided a rationale for a very straightforward set of rules based on the control of aggregate macroeconomic variables (limits on budget deficits and debt).[4] Formal models of an independent monetary authority faced with multiple fiscal authorities provide some justification for imposing constraints on national fiscal policies (see, e.g., Beetsma and Uhlig, 1999). Faced with looming unsustainability pressures and, in some cases, given the political priority to qualify for EMU, European countries embarked on a consolidation process which allowed the aggregate budget deficit for EU countries to be brought from a historical high of 5.5 per cent of GDP in 1993 to less than 3 per cent of GDP in 1997 towards a balanced budget in 2000. The adjustment, however, was in most cases heavily tilted on the revenue side. Tax burdens, which are much higher in Europe than in the US and Japan, started to come down only as of 2001 (European Commission, 2000a and 2001).

While the Maastricht cum SGP arrangement was born in the intellectual environment of mistrust of fiscal policy as a flexible policy tool of the late 1980s, the past decade has witnessed a gradual reassessment of the effects and effectiveness of fiscal policy. The picture emerging from the theoretical and empirical analysis in the 1990s is less clear-cut than the 'polar views' of the previous decades. The new debate emphasizes that fiscal policy works through multiple channels which include supply-side effects that under certain circumstances might lead to so-called non-Keynesian effects.[5] An increasing body of empirical evidence pointed to the importance of the composition of budgetary adjustments for the success of fiscal consolidations. This was accompanied by an increasing awareness of the importance of institutions as determinants of budgetary behaviour, which was shown in a growing empirical and theoretical literature.[6] In the European context, the stabilization function of fiscal policy came back to the fore. Since monetary policy in EMU is tailored to suit the euro area as a whole, fiscal policy is the 'natural' candidate to provide cyclical stabilization at the national level and to respond to country-specific shocks. As discretionary fiscal policy had been largely discredited as an instrument to fine-tune the economy, automatic stabilizers came to be regarded as the 'norm' for budgetary behaviour in EMU. This is acknowledged by the SGP, which not only seeks to assure fiscal prudence but also recognizes that a certain degree of flexibility and room for manoeuvre for fiscal stabilization is needed in EMU. In fact, the SGP embodies some degree of state contingency by singling out exceptional circumstances such as severe recessions, under which the deficit ceiling can be temporarily exceeded without putting a country into an 'excessive deficit' according to the Treaty.[7]

With this economic and institutional background, the central goal of this book is to analyse the implications of the recent advances in economic thinking on fiscal policy and budgetary behaviour with a particular focus on fiscal discipline and stabilization, the long-run impact of fiscal policy, and the relationships between fiscal and monetary policies.

The first part of this book is mainly devoted to the empirical evidence on fiscal behaviour and the importance of budgetary institutions for fiscal performance. Part II focuses on the role of fiscal policy for macroeconomic stabilization and growth. Part III of this book, finally, discusses the interplay between fiscal and monetary policies. The rest of this introductory chapter provides an overview of the book and presents its main conclusions. The last section of this chapter summarizes some important lessons to be taken from the studies presented in this volume.

1.2 How do fiscal authorities behave?

The legal and institutional framework of EMU is built on the requirement of strong budgetary prudence. Now that the 'carrot' of EMU membership has been eaten, it is important to ask whether a sufficient degree of fiscal discipline will be maintained in the future. Recent research has demonstrated the importance of the 'quality' of fiscal adjustments for the success and durability of government budget consolidations.

Jürgen von Hagen (ZEI University of Bonn), Andrew Hughes Hallett (Strathclyde University) and Rolf Strauch (ZEI University of Bonn) build on this approach in Chapter 2 to analyse the importance of the economic conditions in which fiscal consolidations are started for their success. Estimating probit models for the start and the success of consolidation episodes, the chapter analyses how the composition of the adjustment affects the likelihood of governments to start consolidations under given economic, monetary, and fiscal policy conditions. In particular, the authors show that the cyclical positions of the domestic and the international economy and the initial debt level are all important determinants of the likelihood of fiscal consolidations. These variables also affect governments' choice of consolidation strategy, making them important determinants of the success of fiscal consolidations. The analysis confirms earlier results, that consolidations relying on expenditure cuts are more likely to last than consolidations that begin with raising additional revenues, and adds important insights about how the circumstances under which fiscal consolidations are started and carried out affect their chances of success. The authors find that consolidations are more likely to begin when the domestic economy is strong, but more likely to last and be successful when the economy is weak.

The authors also test for any 'Maastricht effect' on the choice of consolidation strategies during the 1990s. Such effect is weak and occurred particularly during the first half of the decade. Finally, the authors develop an empirical model of monetary and fiscal policy interaction. The model suggests that the Maastricht process de-linked the strength of the consolidation efforts from macroeconomic fundamentals and mitigated their economic cost.

The fact that fiscal rules in EMU are essentially numerical has focused the debate around the size of government deficits and debt. However, there is not much research on deficit *dynamics*. A way to analyse the likelihood of maintaining fiscal discipline in EMU is to look at the issue of entering into and exiting from excessive deficits. This is of great relevance for the SGP since it rules out deficits larger than 3 per cent of GDP, except under strictly defined conditions.

In Chapter 3, Ali Bayar (Université Libre di Bruxelles) and Paul de Boer (Erasmus University) provide a transition data analysis of the dynamics of public deficits in the 15 member states of the European Union for the period 1970–96. Transition data methods are particularly well suited for the analyses of deficit dynamics since they are concerned with the duration of a state (being or not being in excessive deficit) and with the final state (excessive deficit or not) attained by the system. By using this method, the authors analyse the determinants of entry and exit dynamics of excessive deficits and estimate the hazard rates for each one of the EU countries. They conclude that government receipts and economic growth play a crucial role in the exits, whereas for the entries into excessive deficits the dominant role is played by primary expenditures. In other words, strong control over public expenditures is the way to avoid excessive deficits. Therefore, as in the analyses in the previous chapter, the composition of fiscal policy is key for deficit dynamics, while there exists a clear asymmetry in the way different components of the budget affect such dynamics. On the basis of such models, it is possible to estimate the probability of entering into and exiting from excessive deficits for each one of the member states of the European Union since 1970. Although no member state had an excessive deficit in 2001, the analysis suggests that many of them are in a fragile position and the risk of breaching the 3 per cent of GDP deficit threshold is not forsaken.

However, it is important to note that the computed probability of entering into and exiting from excessive deficits has been obtained on the basis of a parametric structure estimated with a sample over the period ending in 1996. It can legitimately be argued that EMU represents a genuine regime change, so that such relatively low transition rates out of excessive deficits could represent a historically dated propensity rather than a concrete possibility in EMU.

It is therefore important to see whether EMU could have induced a regime change, increasing the 'value' of fiscal prudence. Although this cannot be tested directly, an indirect way to become aware of such regime change is to look at the changes that have taken place in fiscal policy indicators over time. In Chapter 4, Olivier De Bandt (Banque de France) and Francesco Paolo Mongelli (ECB) aim at determining whether economic, financial and monetary integration, on the one hand, and institutional factors, on the other hand, may have led to gradual convergence in key fiscal variables across the euro area. In this case, the process would bring fiscal positions closer together. According to the authors, a natural question arising from this new institutional framework is whether the 'euro-area fiscal position' has a clear empirical content and significance. The alternative scenario would be that the euro zone is still characterized by largely idiosyncratic national fiscal policies.

The convergence of fiscal policies in the euro area is assessed by using, where available, cyclically adjusted fiscal variables. The authors look first at the correlation in cyclical differences with respect to trends in fiscal behaviour. Although this correlation across the euro area is not always very high, it is in most cases positive. Moreover, it has increased steadily over the sample period, especially for net lending and for expenditures over the 1993–8 sub-period.

This correlation analysis is of a short-term nature. To understand whether the underlying longer-term evolution of these selected fiscal variables is also moving closer together, the authors carry out dispersion and cointegration analyses. The former analyses support the 'disciplinary effect argument'. Overall, the decline in fiscal dispersion among euro area countries is more distinguishable in the case of current revenue and current expenditure particularly after the onset of the Exchange Rate Mechanism of the European

Monetary System. Cointegration analyses between fiscal indicators at country and at aggregate level lead to less clear-cut evidence. Yet, jointly interpreted, the battery of tests applied tend to indicate that fiscal policy in euro area countries has significantly converged.

Convergence of fiscal policies within the euro area seems a reasonable hypothesis. In particular, the provisions of the SGP should lead to a high degree of convergence across member states in terms of budget balances. However, where the size of the public sector is concerned, the effect of EMU's fiscal rules is less clear-cut. Although it is true that a number of tax harmonization and coordination processes are taking place across the EU, they affect a relatively small share of total tax revenues. Moreover, the long trend of tax revenues is mainly determined by the developments in total expenditures, which, given the high weight of social spending, could be largely determined by factors not directly related to short-run aspects of fiscal policy.

In Chapter 5, Carlos Martinez-Mongay (European Commission) studies the effects of fiscal policy on cross-country differences in the size of the public sector, as measured by the shares of total and primary expenditures and tax revenues in GDP. The author shows that while there has been a general upward trend in the size of governments, the relative position of countries in terms of the share of total expenditures in the GDP has recorded important changes. Taking stock of relevant literature on the determinants of the size of public sectors, the author concludes that between two-thirds and three-quarters of the variability of government size across countries and over time is explained by differences in income, dependency and openness. The fact that government size has kept pace with income, dependency and trade does not mean that no other factor can play a role in determining the shares of expenditures and taxes in GDP. When analysing the unexplained part of such a regression, the author concludes that cross-country differences in the size of public sectors also depend on fiscal policy and, in particular, on the reaction of fiscal authorities to the level of public debt. High debt levels in the past are associated with lower primary expenditures and taxes in the medium to long run. However, the response of taxes to lagged debt levels is smaller in absolute value than that of expenditures. Therefore, as also confirmed by the analysis in Chapter 12, the overall fiscal policy reaction to debt seems to be stabilizing.

Chapters 2 to 5 emphasize the role of budgetary rules and institutions in fiscal outcomes. The analyses suggest that the institutions governing the budget process are relevant determinants of a country's fiscal performance. In Chapter 6, Jürgen von Hagen, Andrew Hughes Hallett and Rolf Strauch review the importance of budgetary institutions for achieving and maintaining sustainable public finances in European countries. According to the authors, budgetary institutions encompass the formal and informal rules governing the drafting of the budget law, its passage through the legislature, and its implementation. Under such an institutional approach, high deficits and debt are the result of an externality problem, involving a co-ordination failure among the relevant decision-makers. Overall, deficits are higher the more fragmented the budget is. Therefore, from a budgetary process point of view, the solution is to increase the degree of centralization.

According to the authors, the introduction of the EDP and the SGP represents an important step towards centralization. However, such an institutional approach focusing on numerical targets might not suit all euro area members equally well. To ensure the continued effectiveness of the institutional apparatus created by the EU fiscal rules, the authors suggest linking the procedures under the EDP and the SGP more closely to the national budgetary procedures. In addition, they consider that the scope of the stability and convergence programmes should be broadened to include targets for government spending and revenues, as deficit ceilings have little commitment value in times of budget surpluses or balance.

After this overview of the behaviour of fiscal authorities, the rules and their institutions governing fiscal policy, the book turns to the analysis of the effects of fiscal policy in both the short run (cyclical stabilization) and the long run (impact on economic growth).

1.3   Fiscal policies for stabilization and growth

It is commonly argued that, given the loss of national monetary independence in EMU, budgetary policy needs to play a more significant role in smoothing the impact of country-specific shocks on real output and inflation. To this end, automatic stabilizers should be allowed to operate freely in both upturns and downturns, while discretionary policies are the exception (see, e.g., European Commission, 2001). Still, a number of open questions remain. How can cyclical stabilization and discretionary fiscal policy be distinguished in practice? What kind of rules are there to improve the operation of automatic stabilizers? Is there a trade-off between stabilization and efficiency? Is there an important difference between the long-run and the short-run effects of fiscal policy? How do persistent budget deficits and high debt affect long-run growth?

In Chapter 7, Philippe Mills (European Commission) and Alain Quinet (ENSAE) analyse the role of fiscal stabilization in a monetary union, with a particular focus on the work of automatic stabilizers. Letting the automatic stabilizers play freely in EMU raises two difficulties from a policy-making point of view. First, as the SGP does not 'reward virtue' during good times, there may be a risk that the automatic improvement in the budget during upswings is compensated by a discretionary relaxation of fiscal policy. Second, policy-makers have limited knowledge of the incidence of the shocks and structural changes affecting European economies. Therefore, setting fiscal policy by relying exclusively on cyclically adjusted balances (which requires an estimate of the output gap) may lead to wrong decisions. On this basis, the authors ask what fiscal rule could usefully complement the SGP so as to overcome these difficulties. They conclude that for practical reasons a spending rule could allow the automatic stabilizers to operate fully and enhance the credibility of the SGP by correcting its asymmetric bias. A spending rule could ensure compliance with the requirements of the SGP and especially provide the right incentives for budgetary authorities to avoid pro-cyclical behaviour in good times.

In Chapter 8, Paul van den Noord (OECD) analyses the impact of automatic stabilizers on fiscal positions and assesses the effects of fiscal stabilization over the business cycle and on economic performance in the longer term. He first reviews the OECD method for disentangling the effects of the cycle on fiscal variables (various tax categories, expenditures, budget balances) from those arising from discretionary policy actions. The author concludes that for the OECD as well as for the EU average, an output gap of one per cent of GDP will raise the budget balance by half a per cent of GDP. However, such an average figure conceals large differences across countries. Overall, the cyclical sensitivity of the budget depends on the size of the public sector, the tax structure, the progressivity of taxes, the generosity of unemployment benefits and the cyclical sensitivity of unemployment. The analysis shows that automatic fiscal stabilizers generally reduced cyclical volatility of output in the 1990s. However, in some countries the need to undertake fiscal consolidation in order to improve public finances has forced governments to take discretionary actions that have reduced, or even offset, the effect of automatic fiscal stabilizers. The chapter also shows that, by preventing sharp economic fluctuations and frequent changes in expenditures or tax rates, fiscal stabilizers may raise long-term economic performance.

According to the SGP, automatic stabilizers should be allowed to work symmetrically over the cycle in order to avoid public debt accumulation. This requires a prudent judgement of potential growth. Last but not least, automatic stabilization has to be consistent with an efficient functioning of markets. This latter warning discloses a potential trade-off between the stabilizing role of fiscal policy and efficiency. If, as mentioned before, the degree of cyclical stabilization is linked to the degree of tax progressivity and generosity of benefits systems, the smoothing power of fiscal policy could result in undesirable effects on economic incentives, lower long-run growth and sluggish job creation.

In Chapter 9, Hans Wijkander (Stockholm University) and Werner Roeger (European Commission) address this potential trade-off between stabilization and efficiency. The authors argue that, since monetary and exchange rate policies are no longer available at the national level in EMU, euro area countries will need to make fiscal policy a more powerful tool for cyclical stabilization. The question is how to achieve this without jeopardizing work and investment incentives. The chapter analyses the differences between

Germany's and France's budgets in terms of the stabilizing potential of various components of the budget, namely corporate taxes, labour taxes, transfers to households, government purchases and government wages. In particular, the effects on GDP of discretionary changes in policy instruments leading to an increase of the deficit to GDP ratio by 0.2 percentage points are analysed. An interesting conclusion of this exercise is that increasing the degree of progressivity of income tax schemes and increasing transfers to households does not seem to be very efficient from a stabilization point of view. This reduces the potential conflict between stabilization and efficiency. Conversely, consumption taxes, especially VAT, appear to be efficient stabilizers: consumers would increase their purchases of goods and services in times of low rates at the expense of purchases at other times. Public employment also seems to have a high stabilizing potential. However, changing VAT may involve considerable time lags, while public employment does not seem flexible enough to operate symmetrically over the cycle, since layoffs in upturns may not be politically feasible.

The contribution by Anne Brunila (Bank of Finland) in Chapter 10 also looks at the efficiency of fiscal policy as a tool for economic stabilization. In particular, she analyses the effects of public deficits and debts on private consumption in ten EU countries from the early 1960s to the mid-1990s. The benchmark model is fully Ricardian, where expansionary fiscal policy has no impact on economic activity because private agents anticipate future tax liabilities implied by current government borrowing. Departures from the benchmark model are parameterized on the basis of a permanent income model with finite horizons, in which the Ricardian equivalence fails. Econometric analyses indicate that debt neutrality can only be rejected in Germany. However, such conclusions are highly model-dependent. By incorporating financial market imperfections, which prevent consumers from smoothing consumption over transitory fluctuations in income, it is found that aggregate consumption responds to changes in current disposable income and, thus, to changes in taxes and transfers. Therefore, fiscal policy may play a stabilizing role. From the point of view of policy-making in the euro area, the results presented in this chapter give much support to the institutional arrangements of EMU: should Ricardian equivalence hold, constraints on budget deficits would be unnecessary because the latter would not have any effect on interest rates or economic activity.

While the analyses so far of the effects of debt and deficits on economic activity are of a short-run nature, in Chapter 11 Vito Tanzi (Italian Treasury) and Nigel Chalk (IMF) are concerned with the impact of debt on long-run growth. They discuss the channels through which public debt may affect growth and test some of them against past evidence. In the theoretical section, the authors analyse six potential channels through which a link between debt and growth can be established. First, high public debt puts pressure on interest rates, which reduces private investment and, then, growth.

Second, high debt increases public deficits through higher interest expenditures, which sooner or later will raise taxes and lower investment and growth. Third, if the total debt ratio is constant, a rising public debt crowds out private debt, which leads to a fall in private accumulation and growth. Fourth, preferential tax treatment of public debt leads to sub-optimal allocation of investment, which negatively affects growth. Fifth, compulsory acquisition of public debt distorts the functioning of financial markets lowering growth. Finally, rising public debt may be associated with shorter debt maturity which complicates the working of monetary policy and may lead to an inadequate policy mix. Lack of data only allows for formal testing of the first and second channel.

Although the evidence at the country level is not very robust, treating the EU as a group of countries allows the authors to find a stable and positive relationship between interest rates and public debt. If higher debt is associated with rising real interest rates, this may have negatively affected investment and growth. Building on the empirical literature on the long-term effects of fiscal policy, the authors conclude that the increase of public debt leads to higher direct taxes, which have distortionary effects on investment, and lead to lower growth in the long run. This result is relevant in EMU, where declining debt ratios, brought about by budgetary consolidation, might enhance potential growth in the future.

1.4   Monetary and fiscal interactions in EMU

The behaviour of fiscal authorities cannot be analysed comprehensively without taking into account the behaviour of their monetary policy counterparts and, more generally, the existing monetary regime. The following three chapters focus on the interactions between fiscal and monetary policies.

In Chapter 12, Jacques Mélitz (Strathclyde University) presents an empirical model of the interaction of fiscal and monetary policies. The results indicate that fiscal and monetary policies have often tended to move in opposite directions in the past, i.e., fiscal expansions led to tighter monetary policy, while monetary contractions promoted more expansionary fiscal policies. This suggests that the monetary and fiscal instruments were used as strategic substitutes rather than complements. On this basis the author dismisses the conflict hypothesis which holds that a persistently loose fiscal policy eventually triggers a monetary expansion. However, the contractionary response of monetary policy to an expansionary fiscal policy is sample-dependent. While it holds for the whole sample, it is much less clear in a sample only including EU countries without Germany. Other results in this chapter refer to the stabilizing reaction of fiscal policy to debt and the empirical weakness of automatic stabilizers. Regarding the interactions between fiscal and monetary policy, the author concludes that EMU will change the behaviour of national fiscal authorities, so that it is difficult to use past patterns to infer the working of the system in the future. Therefore, it should not be taken for granted that the monetary–fiscal coordination that has occurred in the past would also take place in the new monetary regime.

The issue of complementarity or substitutability between monetary and fiscal policies is also dealt with in Chapter 13. Marco Buti, Werner Roeger and Jan in't Veld (European Commission) analyse the influence of an SGP-like framework on the behaviour of fiscal authorities and their interactions with an inflation-conservative central bank. The authors consider a game between a central bank with an inflation goal and a fiscal authority constrained by an upper limit on the budget deficit. The model is solved under cooperation and non-cooperation. The analysis shows that if the government attempts to stimulate output beyond its natural level, a 'deficit bias' emerges under non-cooperation while, in equilibrium, the central bank will always meet its inflation target; under cooperation, however, the equilibrium is characterized by both a 'deficit bias' and an 'inflation bias' because the central bank will encompass, at least partly, the objective of a positive output gap by fiscal authorities. The theoretical and empirical analysis indicates that the substitutability or complementarity between monetary and fiscal policies depends on the type of shocks hitting the economy. In the event of supply shocks which push output and inflation in opposite directions, there is a clear conflict, since policies ensuring output stabilization are inflation destabilizing. However, although there is no such a conflict in the case of demand shocks, there is a distributional one because it is necessary to determine how both policies share the burden of stabilization. The chapter concludes that if fiscal policy targets the natural level of output (i.e. an output gap equal to zero, in equilibrium) and if monetary policy aims at price stability, in the absence of shocks, there is no need for coordination between fiscal and monetary authorities. However, provided that fiscal authorities only pursue 'pure' fiscal stabilization, there are gains from coordination in response to shocks, especially shocks emanating from the supply side.

In the final chapter, Andrew Hughes Hallett and Nicola Viegi (Strathclyde University) study monetary delegation in a model with political uncertainty. The authors show that the existence of an independent central bank reduces the importance of inflation in the objective function of governments. As a consequence, once the median voter is certain about the control of inflation, which has been delegated to an independent institution, there will be an increase of the demand for a more active fiscal policy to boost output. This will favour political parties more willing to use fiscal instruments to achieve 'real' as opposed to nominal economic goals. The authors predict that the creation of an independent central bank aiming at price stability will produce a political bias towards governments fiscally active and prone to output stabilization. This provides particular support to one of the scenarios considered in the previous chapter, namely that in which there is a clear policy assignment between the monetary (inflation) and the fiscal (output) authorities. One important implication of the analysis is that a radicalization of policy preferences between the government and the central bank would lead to policy divergences if a contradiction emerges between output and inflation stabilization. The authors conclude that the higher likelihood of policy conflicts raises the potential benefits of monetary–fiscal coordination.

1.5   Final remarks

This book reviews much of the academic and political debate on the role and effectiveness of fiscal policy. While the focus is on the behaviour of fiscal authorities, an important theme of the book is the assessment of potential conflicts and trade-offs between the goals of budgetary discipline, cyclical stabilization and economic efficiency that may arise in the implementation of fiscal policy (European Commission, 2001).

1.5.1   Discipline and stabilization

The trade-off between discipline and stabilization, which was raised in the early stage of the debate on EMU, was more than a mere intellectual construct in many EU member states during the run-up to EMU. In those years, the necessity of rebuilding fiscal discipline sometimes conflicted with cyclical stabilization. However, the review of the theoretical and empirical literature, as well as the evidence presented in the first part of the book, suggests that discipline and stabilization are mutually supporting in the longer run.

Backward-looking analyses of the behaviour of fiscal authorities indicate that sound fiscal rules, which ensure discipline without jeopardizing stabilization, have been applied by different countries in different periods. Additionally, governments' reactions to debt have been stabilizing in the sense that primary expenditures and taxes have moved in a deficit-reducing direction.

However, this has not been done on a systematic basis, so that the episodes of pro-cyclical behaviour have been relatively frequent, particularly in the EU (Brunila and Martinez-Mongay, 2001). EMU should be expected to force euro area members to apply sound, common rules, according to which fiscal policy in EMU will play its stabilizing role while avoiding lasting structural imbalances. Within this framework, fiscal behaviour and performance will tend to converge across EMU. There are already some preliminary signs that EMU fostered convergence of fiscal policies in the euro area in the 1990s.

Several contributions in this book have highlighted the importance of spending control. Consolidations relying on expenditure cuts are more likely to last than consolidations starting with raising additional revenues. In particular, spending control is crucial to avoid entering into excessive deficits once a balanced budget position has been achieved. Moreover, as EU countries become more similar in terms of income and demographic structure, the size of their governments, as measured by the share of primary expenditures in GDP, should tend to converge. Respect of the close-to-balance rule of the SGP, complemented with spending restraint, would make sure that convergence does not lead to an increasing share of the public sector in the economy.

1.5.2 Discipline and efficiency

A potential trade-off has also been identified between budgetary discipline and an efficient allocation of resources. For instance, the constraint of a balanced budget might prevent governments from lowering the tax burden and hence reducing the distortions induced by a high level of taxes.

However, such a potential trade-off seems to be more relevant in the short run than in the longer term. Fiscal discipline, by ensuring low debt and deficits, is the precondition for guaranteeing permanent reductions in the tax burden. The lowering of distortionary taxes has positive effects on economic efficiency by boosting investment and promoting employment. Moreover, to the extent that public debt has a negative impact on growth in the long run, maintaining fiscal discipline will enhance potential growth in the euro area.

On the basis of analyses presented in this book, one can conclude that fiscal discipline is also important in preventing sharp economic fluctuations. Relying essentially on the work of automatic stabilizers may also enhance economic performance, as it would avoid frequent changes in expenditures or tax codes thereby reducing uncertainties and fostering an efficient allocation of resources.

1.5.3 Stabilization and efficiency

Arguably, there can be a potential trade-off between stabilization and a flexible functioning of markets, especially the labour market: high progressivity and overly generous welfare systems may indeed result in high automatic stabilizers, but may harm a smooth functioning of the labour market and result in real wage rigidity. While this is a potentially serious trade-off in EMU, some of the analysis in the book points to ways in which the stabilizing role of fiscal policy could be enhanced without jeopardizing work and investment incentives. While progressive taxation and large transfers to households seem not to be very efficient from a stabilization point of view, consumption taxes, especially VAT, appear to be efficient stabilizers.

Overcoming or lessening these policy trade-offs depends not only on the behaviour of fiscal authorities, but also on the interplay with monetary authorities. Empirical analyses reveal that fiscal and monetary policies have tended to be substitutes, and even when both policies moved in the same direction, a relatively tighter fiscal stance was associated with looser monetary stance. However, the institutional framework of EMU may induce a different behaviour in the future. The interactions between multiple fiscal authorities and a single monetary authority makes the policy 'game' in EMU much more complex, with a higher risk of policy conflicts and correspondingly higher gains from successful coordination.

To sum up, the analysis of the behaviour of budgetary authorities and the role of fiscal policy is closely intertwined with actual institutional developments and policy challenges. The economics and political economy of fiscal behaviour have gained new dimensions with the creation of EMU, which has established a new framework for the conduct of fiscal policies. While new rules of behaviour ensuring long-term budgetary prudence have been agreed upon, their effectiveness and impact on actual policy-making remain largely to be tested. This book, which includes contributions by leading academics and policy-makers, attempts to shed some light on these issues and raise new ones. We hope that it will provide a rigorous and thought-provoking input to the current debate.

Notes

1. The views expressed in this chapter are those of the authors and should not be attributed to the European Commission.
2. On the insurance rationale of the modern welfare state, see Buti *et al.* (1999).
3. A later, more sophisticated, version of the 'unpleasant arithmetic' is provided by the so-called Fiscal Theory of the Price Level, according to which monetary authorities would not be able to control the price level if fiscal plans did not satisfy the government budget constraint. For a policy-oriented review, see Canzoneri and Diba (1998).
4. See Buti and Sapir (1998).
5. The empirical case for such effects, however, remains weak at best.
6. On these various aspects, see von Hagen (1992), von Hagen and Harden (1994a), Alesina and Perotti (1995a), Perotti (1999)and Poterba and von Hagen (1999).
7. For a comprehensive analysis of the working of the SGP, see Brunila *et al.* (2001).

Part I

How Do Fiscal Authorities Behave?

2
Quality and Success of Budgetary Consolidations

Jürgen von Hagen, Andrew Hughes Hallett and Rolf Strauch[1]

2.1 Introduction

There is a growing literature on the success of fiscal consolidations in industrialized economies. A consensus among economists and policy-makers has emerged that the success of efforts to consolidate the government budget depends importantly on the quality of the budgetary adjustments undertaken. In this context, the 'quality' of fiscal adjustments refers to the relative contribution of different budgetary items to the adjustment effort. 'Good quality' fiscal adjustments are defined as adjustments marked by a strong emphasis on expenditure cuts rather than increased revenues, and on tackling those expenditures that are politically most sensitive such as transfers, subsidies, and wage expenditures (Perotti *et al.*, 1998). Success is defined in terms of the persistence and size of the consolidation effort and their economic effect. Firstly, a consolidation effort is regarded as successful if the reduction in the budget deficit achieved after a certain number of years reaches a certain minimum size and, as a consequence, contributes to a considerable reduction of the debt level. Secondly, consolidations are successful if they induce a non-Keynesian effect avoiding an economic contraction or even producing an expansion of output. The key insight is that, based on the historical experience with fiscal consolidations in the past 30 years, the quality of fiscal adjustment, i.e. their composition, is an important determinant of the effectiveness of consolidation efforts and their economic consequences (Alesina and Perotti, 1995b, 1997; Alesina and Ardagna, 1998; Perotti, 1999; Perotti *et al.*, 1998; see also European Commission, 2000a).

In section 2.2 we study budgetary adjustments of OECD countries from the 1960s to the 1990s with a view towards the quality of the adjustments. We replicate the analysis of earlier papers concerning the importance of the quality of fiscal adjustments for the success of budgetary consolidation efforts. We do this to verify that we obtain the same results as they do with a larger and somewhat different data set. In section 2.3 we extend the earlier analysis to investigate the importance of quality for success. Specifically, we study the impact of the adjustment strategy on the likelihood of governments persistently pursuing consolidations. We do so by controlling for a number of other macroeconomic factors and assess the consolidation efforts undertaken during the Maastrich convergence process in light of these findings. In section 2.4 we focus on the interaction between fiscal policy and output development. While the previous section investigates the relation between the macroeconomic environment and policy choice, as a discrete strategic variable, we now assess the degree of consolidation achieved and the size of the macroeconomic impact. Applying this analysis to the Maastricht process indicates that the previous consolidation pattern vanished and the economic consequences were mitigated, although an outright non-Keynesian effect cannot be found for consolidations conducted in European countries after 1992. Section 2.5 concludes.

2.2   Quality and success of fiscal adjustments

This section summarizes and updates the evidence presented in Perotti *et al.* (1998). It is based on government budget data for 20 OECD countries spanning the years 1960–98. Here, we focus on fiscal consolidations defined as episodes in which either the cyclically adjusted (total) government budget balance increased by at least 1.25 per cent of cyclically adjusted GDP in two consecutive years; or the cyclically adjusted budget balance increased by at least 1.5 per cent of cyclically adjusted GDP in one year, and was positive but perhaps less than 1.25 per cent in both the preceding and the subsequent year. While the percentage criteria are arbitrary, our procedure helps us to concentrate on episodes in which governments made strong and deliberate efforts to reduce the budget deficit. There are 65 such episodes in the data set. We estimate cyclically adjusted GDP based on country-specific, linear-quadratic trends.

We take the episodes of fiscal consolidations thus defined and classify them into *successful* and *unsuccessful* ones. A consolidation is deemed successful if two years after the initial adjustment the government budget balance has lowered the initial consolidation effort by, at the most, 25 per cent. Otherwise, it is called unsuccessful. Unsuccessful consolidations are short-lived, as the initial improvement in the government budget balance could not be maintained.[2]

Table 2.1 reports the contributions of various budget items to the fiscal consolidations in this sample. The table characterizes consolidations by taking averages and standard deviations across all consolidation episodes in our sample. Let S_t be the structural budget balance relative to potential output in the year before a consolidation started, and S_T the structural balance relative to potential output in the year when the consolidation ended. Similarly, let X_t and X_T be the ratio of budget item X to potential output in the same years, respectively. The difference $S_T - S_t$ indicates the size of the fiscal adjustment

Table 2.1 Composition of fiscal adjustments

Budget item (relative to potential output)	All consolidations	Successful consolidations	Unsuccessful consolidations	Difference
Structural surplus	2.29 (23.61)	2.37 (18.30)	2.17 (14.96)	0.20
Total expenditures	−0.84 (−5.00)	−1.23 (−5.57)	−0.26 (−1.18)	−0.97***
Total revenues	1.45 (10.24)	1.13 (6.24)	1.91 (9.83)	0.78***
Current expenditures	−0.45 (−3.69)	−0.70 (−4.58)	−0.07 (−0.41)	−0.63**
Capital expenditures	−0.39 (−3.88)	−0.53 (−3.34)	−0.18 (−2.56)	−0.35*
Subsidies, transfers	−0.22 (−2.70)	−0.35 (−3.31)	−0.02 (−0.17)	−0.33**
Social transfers	−0.07 (−1.34)	−0.09 (−1.42)	−0.03 (−0.38)	−0.06
Government consumption	−0.23 (−3.91)	−0.35 (−4.70)	−0.05 (−0.61)	−0.30**
Spending on goods and services	−0.11 (−3.96)	−0.10 (−3.02)	−0.12 (−3.52)	0.02
Wage expenditures	−0.12 (−2.65)	−0.25 (−4.93)	0.06 (0.85)	−0.31***
Tax revenues	1.38 (10.71)	1.10 (6.71)	1.79 (9.86)	−0.69**
Non-tax revenues	0.07 (1.16)	0.03 (0.38)	0.12 (1.86)*	−0.09

Note: Numbers in parentheses are *t*-ratios.***, **, and * indicate that the difference between the two averages is statistically significant at a level less than 1 per cent, between 1 and 5 per cent, and between 5 and 10 per cent, respectively.

in terms of the improvement in the ratio of the structural balance to potential output achieved. The difference $X_T - X_t$ shows by how much the budget item X changed relative to potential output during the consolidation episode. Finally, the ratio $(X_T - X_t)/(S_T - S_t)$ indicates the contribution of this budget item to the consolidation effort.

The first row of Table 2.1 shows that the average fiscal consolidation in this sample amounted to a deficit reduction of 2.29 per cent of GDP. The average size is statistically the same for successful and unsuccessful consolidations. Thus, the simple notion that large consolidations are more successful than small ones is dismissed by the data.

However, the *composition* of the adjustments is drastically different between successful and unsuccessful consolidations. Successful consolidations come with expenditure cuts of an average size of 1.23 per cent of GDP, while expenditure cuts in unsuccessful consolidations are not even statistically significant on average. Expenditure cuts contribute 52 per cent (i.e. 1.23 per cent in 2.37 per cent of cyclically adjusted GDP) to the adjustment in successful consolidations, compared to only 12 per cent in unsuccessful consolidations. In contrast, total revenues increase by an average 1.13 per cent of cyclically adjusted GDP in successful consolidations, compared to 1.91 per cent in unsuccessful ones. That is, additional revenues account for 48 per cent of the adjustment effort in successful consolidations, but for 88 per cent in unsuccessful ones. Unsuccessful consolidations thus rely almost exclusively on increasing revenues, while successful ones put heavy emphasis on cutting government spending.

A further message of Table 2.1 concerns the composition of the expenditure cuts. On average, cutbacks in current expenditures account for 57 per cent (0.45 per cent in 0.84 per cent of cyclically adjusted GDP) of the average spending reduction and for 30 per cent of the total deficit reduction in successful consolidations. In contrast, they account for only 27 per cent of the average spending and only 3 per cent of the total deficit adjustment in unsuccessful consolidations. Correspondingly, cuts in capital expenditures account for 43 per cent of the average spending cuts in successful consolidations, compared to about 70 per cent of the average spending cuts in unsuccessful consolidations. Thus, successful consolidations put much less emphasis on cutting public investment than unsuccessful ones.

Cuts in subsidies and transfers contribute 50 per cent on average to the reduction in current spending during successful consolidations, but only 29 per cent in unsuccessful ones. Cutbacks in government wage expenditures contribute an average 36 per cent to the reduction in current government spending during successful consolidations, while they do not fall significantly in relation to GDP during unsuccessful ones. Since reductions in transfers, subsidies, and wage expenditures are politically more difficult than cutting other spending items including public investment, these results suggest that tackling politically sensitive budgetary items is a characteristic of successful consolidations. In contrast, avoiding significant adjustments in these items is a characteristic of unsuccessful consolidations.

In sum, the evidence shown above forcefully confirms the results of earlier research. Specifically, successful consolidations on average put more emphasis on spending cuts than unsuccessful ones, and less emphasis on raising more revenues. Successful consolidations also involve larger cutbacks of current government spending and smaller cutbacks of investment spending than unsuccessful ones. In the same vein, successful consolidations tackle politically sensitive spending items such as transfers, subsidies, and government wages more forcefully than unsuccessful ones.

Table 2.2 provides more evidence by studying the post-consolidation performance of governments in the same time period. Specifically, we compute

Table 2.2   Post-consolidation performance

Budget item (relative to potential output)	Successful consolidations	Unsuccessful consolidations	Difference
Structural balance	0.84 (5.62)	−1.43 (−7.00)	2.27***
Total expenditures	−0.22 (−1.37)	1.08 (4.87)	−1.30***
Total revenues	0.62 (4.93)	−0.35 (−1.47)	0.97***

Note: Numbers in parentheses are *t*-ratios. ***, **, and * indicate that the difference between the two averages is statistically significant at a level less than 1 per cent, between 1 and 5 per cent, and between 5 and 10 per cent, respectively.

the average change in each budgetary item in the two years after the end of a consolidation episode.

The important result is that, on average, successful consolidations are characterized by continued improvements in the budget balance in the third and fourth year after the initial budgetary adjustment, although these improvements are mainly the result of increasing revenues. In contrast, unsuccessful consolidations are followed by years of significant deterioration of the budget balance, reflecting rising expenditures and declining revenues relative to cyclically adjusted GDP. Tables 2.1 and 2.2 together indicate that successful consolidations on average lead to a reduction in the ratio of government spending to trend output, while unsuccessful ones ultimately lead to an increase in this ratio.

2.3   Quality of adjustments and the success of consolidation efforts

In the previous section, we have shown that the quality of fiscal adjustments is an important determinant of the success of consolidation efforts. Now we will look at the evidence presented above using probit estimates. This allows us to control for the impact of other exogenous variables which may have decisively forged the consolidation choice. For the probit model, we define a dummy variable being 'one' if a fiscal consolidation that was successful starts in a given period, and zero otherwise. Moreover, we characterize the economic environment at the start of the fiscal consolidations in four aspects. One is the cyclical position of the domestic economy in the year before and during the start of the consolidation episode. The literature on economic reform argues that policy changes are more likely when 'things go badly' (Drazen and Grilli, 1993) and therefore fiscal consolidations may not be distributed evenly across the business cycle. We use the output gap, i.e., the relative difference between aggregate demand and potential output, as defined by the OECD for this purpose. The second aspect is the stance of monetary policy. Here, we construct a *monetary conditions index* for each country. The index is the sum of the ex-post short-term real interest rate and the real exchange rate, each weighted by its sample standard deviation. The real interest rate is computed using a three-month interest rate and annual rates of CPI (consumer price index) inflation. The effective real exchange rate data are taken from the OECD. An increase in the monetary conditions index thus indicates either a rise in the short-term real interest rate or a real appreciation of the currency. Both can be interpreted as a tightening of the stance of monetary policy. The index allows us to address the proposition that the success of a fiscal consolidation depends critically on a simultaneous easing of monetary policy (see Lambertini and Tavares, 2000), as well as political arguments that laxer monetary policy would facilitate fiscal consolidation. Third, we use the debt-to-GDP ratio to describe the sustainability of the government's financial position.[3] Fourth, we describe the stance of the international economic environment using the OECD average output gap.[4] This again relates to the reform willingness mentioned above. Finally, we use the OECD average structural government budget balance to characterize the international fiscal policy environment. Including this variable, in addition to the aggregate output gap, should control for factors such as direct fiscal coordination, and non-cooperative mechanisms like tax competition and political 'yardstick' competition induced by electoral institutions (Besley and Case, 1995).

Table 2.3 reports the results of a set of probit regressions explaining the likelihood of a consolidation episode being successful in terms of the quality of the adjustment and the initial conditions.

The regressions reported in Table 2.3 use the contribution of government expenditures to the total consolidation achieved over an entire episode as an explanatory variable together with various indicators of the initial economic conditions. Results for the remaining variables describing the quality of the fiscal adjustments are very similar and are not reported here, for brevity. The first column of Table 2.3 reproduces what we already know from section 2.2. Increasing the contribution of spending cuts to the consolidation effort raises the likelihood of a consolidation to be successful significantly. The following columns pair the contribution of government spending with various indicators of the initial and accompanying conditions. We find that a weak economy, both at home and in the OECD, raises the likelihood of a consolidation effort being successful. Furthermore, a large debt-to-GDP ratio raises the probability of a consolidation being successful. Neither the

Table 2.3   Quality, initial conditions, and success of consolidation efforts

Indicator						
Contribution of	0.88	0.68	−0.79	0.95	0.84	0.89
spending	(2.73)***	(1.87)*	(1.99)**	(2.44)**	(2.85)***	(2.77)***
(average over						
consolidation episode)						
Output gap		−0.19				
(current level)		(−2.16)**				
Debt–GDP ratio			0.024			
(lagged level)			(3.32)***			
Monetary conditions				0.16		
index (current level)				(1.31)		
OECD output gap					−0.55	
(current level)					(−2.70)***	
OECD structural balance						−0.15
(current level)						(−0.79)

Note: Dependent variable is the probit for a successful fiscal consolidation. Number of observations is 65. ***, **, * indicate significance at levels below 1 per cent, between 1 and under 5 per cent, and between 5 and under 10 per cent, respectively.

stance of domestic monetary policy nor the average fiscal stance in the OECD, however, contribute to explaining the probability of success of fiscal consolidations. In sum, both the quality of the adjustment and the economic environment in which it occurs are important determinants of the success of fiscal consolidations.

2.3.1 Economic conditions and the choice of adjustment strategy

So far, we have treated the adjustment strategy and the economic conditions of fiscal consolidations as two separate explanatory variables. It is possible, of course, that the choice of the adjustment strategy itself depends on the economic environment. For example, governments might be more likely to rely on raising additional revenues to consolidate the budget when a strong economy promises large revenue effects of an increase in tax rates. To test this suggestion empirically, we estimate models explaining the probability of a consolidation based primarily on expenditure cuts given the prevailing economic conditions. More specifically, we estimate a probit model where the dependent variable is a dummy that takes the value of one when an expenditure-based consolidation is started, and zero elsewhere. We call a consolidation expenditure-based when expenditure cuts contribute at least half of the total deficit reduction achieved during the consolidation episode. Thus, the model explains the probability of a consolidation relying primarily on expenditure cuts given that a consolidation is started.

Table 2.4 has the results. Here, we see that a low output gap, both domestic and international, and a high debt-to-GDP ratio raise the likelihood of consolidations being expenditure-based. Furthermore, a tight stance of fiscal policy

Table 2.4 Initial conditions and choice of consolidation strategy

Indicator	Current level		Lagged level		First difference	
	Univariate	*Multivariate*	*Univariate*	*Multivariate*	*Univariate*	*Multivariate*
Output gap	−0.19	−0.12	−0.12	−0.03	−0.19	−0.15
	(−2.28)**	(−1.23)	(−1.58)	(−0.31)	(−1.71)*	(−1.20)
Debt-to-GDP$_{t-1}$	0.02	0.01	0.02	0.02	0.05	0.04
	(3.57)***	(1.69)*	(3.51)***	(2.10)**	(1.09)	(0.90)
Monetary conditions (real)	−0.04	−0.21	−0.08	−0.36	0.03	−0.08
	(−0.36)	(−1.42)	(−0.65)	(−1.78)*	(0.25)	(−0.56)
OECD output gap	−0.20	−0.67	−0.24	−0.80	0.16	0.13
	(−1.31)	(2.07)**	(−2.03)**	(−2.58)**	(1.13)	(0.48)
OECD structural balance	0.09	0.99	−0.02	1.08	0.28	0.32
	(.52)	(2.79)***	(−0.14)	(2.34)**	(1.00)	(0.58)

Note: Dependent variable is the probit for an expenditure-based fiscal consolidation to occur. Number of observations is 65. ***, **, * indicate significance at levels below 1 per cent, between 1 and under 5 per cent, and between 5 and under 10 per cent, respectively.

in the OECD raises the likelihood of a consolidation being expenditure-based. The picture emerging from this is that, in a relatively weak economic environment and under strong pressures from a large debt burden, governments tend to rely more on expenditure cuts than on increasing revenues to consolidate their budgets. Similarly, a tight fiscal stance in the OECD makes governments opt for expenditure cuts, if they wish to achieve a lasting consolidations. Thus, the economic conditions summarized in these indicators influence the success of fiscal consolidations in part by determining governments' choice of consolidation strategy.

One might argue that this result could be driven by the consolidations occurring in the EU during the 1990s, which took place in a general environment of low growth, and that therefore this result reflects the effects of the Maastricht process more than the typical policy choices of OECD governments. However, the results of these estimates do not change much when we limit the sample to the period ending in 1991.

Finally, monetary policy has only a weakly significant effect on the choice of the adjustment strategy. Tight monetary policy reduces the likelihood of an expenditure-based consolidation in the following year, but the effect is not very strong. As we have seen before, it is too weak to make monetary policy a determinant of the success of fiscal consolidations.

2.3.2   Fiscal policy in the 1990s: was there a Maastricht effect?

The 1990s witnessed strong efforts to consolidate government budget deficits in most European Union member states.[5] During this decade, one group of countries, notably Austria, Finland, Sweden and the United Kingdom, pursued exclusively expenditure-based consolidations. Another group, prominently Greece, Portugal and Germany, followed revenue-based consolidation strategies, but the consolidations were preceded or interrupted by spending-induced fiscal expansions. A third group, notably Belgium, Denmark Ireland, Italy and the Netherlands, followed a strategically more mixed pattern. They started with primarily revenue-based consolidations leading into fiscal expansions due to a reduction of revenues. These expansionary episodes were succeeded by expenditure-based consolidation efforts.

The need and political willingness to undertake such efforts were clearly written into the Maastricht Treaty, which required countries who wanted to participate in the European monetary union to comply with maximum levels of government deficits and debts. These limits implied significant fiscal adjustments for most European Union member states. But the Treaty requirement alone does not warrant the conclusion that the prospect of monetary union created political forces pressuring the governments to undertake consolidations they would not have delivered otherwise. The counter-hypothesis is that governments in any case saw the necessity of fiscal adjustments arising from large debt burdens and persistently weak economic performance. Thus, the Maastricht Treaty and its obligations for fiscal policy only affirmed what was perceived to be necessary anyway. In fact, the argument that the fiscal adjustments were required even without monetary union was often used to attenuate political opposition against the latter. In this view, the fiscal criteria in the Treaty were at best a warning for weak governments to deliver the necessary adjustments in time.

We can test the validity of this hypothesis on the basis of the analysis developed so far. For this purpose, we proceed as follows. First, we estimate probit models for the likelihood of fiscal consolidations to be expenditure-based. In this exercise, we define a consolidation effort as a decline in the cyclically adjusted deficit of at least 0.5 per cent of GDP in one year. Similarly, we define a year of an increase in the cyclically adjusted deficit as a fiscal expansion.[6] The explanatory variables in these models are the economic conditions prevailing in that year. To obtain parsimonious models and improve their predictive abilities, we choose the specifications reported in Table 2.5. This model summarizes the fiscal performance of OECD governments in the years from 1960 onwards. To check whether the Maastricht process had any special influence on the parameter estimates, we estimated the same models cutting the sample in the 1990s. The results were not substantially different from those reported below.

We look at the probabilities of choosing an expenditure-based consolidation as estimated by our empirical models. Table 2.6 reports these probabilities for each year that a consolidation episode was started by one of the EU member states during the 1990s. We say that the model predicts an expenditure-based strategy when the estimated probability is at least 50 per cent; it predicts a revenue-driven consolidation effort otherwise. Comparing this predicted strategy choice with the actual choice, we can determine whether there was a 'Maastricht effect' on the choice of fiscal adjustment strategy.

Table 2.5 Model specification for the start of expenditure-based fiscal consolidations in OECD countries, 1960–99

Variable	Coefficient	Standard errors
Constant	−1.57	0.30***
Debt (lag)	0.018	0.005***
Domestic output gap	−0.13	0.08*
Change of monetary conditions	0.01	0.14
OECD output gap	−0.02	0.13
Change in OECD budget balance	1.63	0.54***
Log-Likelihood=−38.62		Wald Chi^2=18.93***

Note: The number of observations is Nobs = 75. Standard errors are adjusted for clustering on countries. Asterisks indicate significance below the 10 (*), 5 (**) and one (***) per cent level.

Table 2.6   Probabilities of using an expenditure-based strategy, deficit and debt reductions in EU member states during the Maastricht process

Country	Year	Probability of an expenditure-based strategy	Actual strategy	Change in primary surplus	Change in debt level
Austria	1995	0.69	E	3.0	−1.1
Belgium	1992	0.38	R	3.8	5.9
	1996	0.99	E	1.3	−15.7
Denmark	1993	0.62	R	0.7	13.1
	1996	0.78	E	4.0	−18.5
Finland	1993	0.64	E	2.0	18.0
	1996	0.84	E	4.1	−13.2
France	1994	0.54	R	3.1	13.6
Germany	1992	0.01	R	4.1	22.5
Greece	1996	0.96	R	3.7	−4.9
Ireland	1991	0.49	R	2.5	−4.5
	1996	0.85	E	1.3	−36.9
Italy	1995	0.91	E	4.7	−3.6
Netherlands	1993	0.45	R	2.3	1.1
	1995	0.70	E	2.5	−0.2
Portugal	1992	0.05	R	2.4	−7.4
	1994	0.62	R	1.5	−1.0
Spain	1992	0.02	R	1.6	2.6
	1994	0.61	E	4.5	7.0
Sweden	1995	0.77	E	12.4	−4.6
United Kingdom	1994	0.52	E	7.5	−2.1

Note: The abbreviations of the strategy indicate an expenditure-based (E) or revenue-based (R) fiscal consolidation. Strategies are termed expenditure-based if public spending contributed more than 50 per cent to the consolidation effort and revenue-based if revenues contributed more than 50 per cent to the consolidation effort.

Table 2.6 shows that the model fails to predict the actual choice correctly only in four instances. In these cases, the governments adopted revenue-based strategies when our model predicted an expenditure-based strategy. It is interesting to note that three of these four errors are in the early 1990s; all but one of the choices after 1995 are predicted correctly. Thus, if there was a 'Maastricht effect' inducing governments to undertake fiscal consolidations in the early 1990s, the same effect may also have tilted the strategy choice towards a revenue-based strategy, perhaps because governments hoped to achieve visible results more quickly in this way.

Moreover, Table 2.6 provides evidence that the expenditure-driven consolidations were more effective in producing the reduction of the deficit and debt level required by the Maastricht treaty. At an aggregate level, nine of the consolidations included in the table led to a reduction of the debt level, and only two were accompanied by an increasing debt burden. In comparison, four of the ten revenue-based consolidation episodes led to a reduction of the debt to GDP ratio while the majority was accompanied by increasing debt. Concomitantly, the average size of the change in the primary fiscal balance for expenditure-based consolidations is 4.3 and the average reduction of the debt level is −6.4 percentage points of GDP. If we remove Sweden from the sample, which is an outlier due to its improvement of the primary balance by 12.9 per centage points, the values are 3.5 and −6.6 respectively. In comparison, the average improvement of revenue-driven consolidations is only 2.6 percentage points of GDP and the debt level increases on average by 4.1 percentage points of GDP. However, within the framework of these simple descriptive statistics it cannot be determined to what extent this adjustment pattern presents a general characteristic or may be attributed to a specific Maastricht effect. The quantitative impact of the convergence process on fiscal policy behaviour therefore will be analysed more rigorously in the following section.

2.4 The macroeconomics of fiscal consolidations

In section 2.3 we have shown that the macroeconomic environment, both externally and at home, affects the choice between making fiscal adjustments that are primarily revenue-based and making adjustments that are primarily expenditure-based. While this is important in understanding government choices over alternative fiscal policies, nothing in that analysis says that these choices were efficient, i.e., that the results could not have been obtained more easily a different way, or that the governments could not have achieved better results in the 1990s than they did.

In this section, we turn to the macroeconomic aspects of fiscal consolidations. Here, we are interested in the macroeconomic impact of the 1990s fiscal consolidations. Specifically, we wish to know whether there was any special 'Maastricht effect' in this direction, i.e., a change in the effect of fiscal policy on real output. Such a 'Maastricht effect' might be due to the fact that the fiscal consolidations were part of very visible programmes pursued by the governments of the EMU member states to prepare for Stage III of EMU. It would be consistent with the arguments that fiscal contractions can have 'non-Keynesian effects', i.e., that their cost in terms of output lost can be reduced due to favourable expectations effects on private consumption and investment.

Furthermore, we study in more detail the effects of real output changes on fiscal policy, again with the question in mind whether we can detect any 'Maastricht effect.' Here, the special effect would be that, due to the commitment power of the Maastricht programme, the fiscal adjustments of the 1990s were stronger than the macroeconomic environment would have otherwise suggested. In addition, we study the implications of the fiscal restraints implied by the Stability and Growth Pact on fiscal policy in the EMU member states.

The analysis we intend to carry out in this section requires a comparison of what happened in the 1990s with what might have happened under different policy choices and different circumstances. That is, it requires an empirical macroeconomic model describing the effect of policy on the economy, of the impact of changes in real output on policy choices, and of the interaction between monetary and fiscal policy. We estimate a simple, simultaneous equation model for a panel of OECD countries, using data from 1970 to 1998. This approach can only produce a rough picture of the interactions and this limitation must be kept in mind when the results are interpreted.

2.4.1   A macroeconomic model of monetary and fiscal policy interaction

The interaction of fiscal policy and real output and the interaction with monetary conditions are analysed in a system consisting of three endogenous variables: fiscal policy, monetary policy and real GDP growth. Fiscal policy is described by the change in the cyclically adjusted primary deficit, monetary policy by the real monetary conditions index, and real output by the annual real GDP growth rate. As a starting point, we assume that these variables are interdependent. The two policy variables are defined in exactly the same way as they were in sections 2.2 and 2.3 of this chapter.

We estimate this model for a panel of 20 OECD countries and the period from 1973 to 1998, for which the necessary data are available for most countries included. As we are dealing with an unbalanced panel, we allow for country fixed effects in the initial estimations. We take a simple partial reduced form system to determine these three variables. The GDP growth equation (Δy) is characterized by output being dependent only on lagged fiscal or monetary policies, lagged output growth, and the change in the OECD output gap (*GAP*). The monetary policy equation has the real monetary conditions index (*M*) depend on its own lag, the change in the domestic structural balance (ΔF) and its lag, output growth, and the lagged long-term interest rate (*i*). Finally, the fiscal policy equation describes the change in the domestic structural balance as a function of its own lag, current monetary policy, current and lagged domestic output growth, the OECD output gap, and the debt–GDP ratio (*d*). The model can be summarized as follows:[7]

$$\Delta F_t = f\left(\Delta F_{t-1}, M_{t-1}, \Delta Y_t, \Delta Y_{t-1}, \Delta GAP_t^{oecd}, d_t, dummies\right) \tag{2.1}$$

$$M_t = m\left(M_{t-1}, \Delta F_t, i_{t-1}, \Delta Y_t, \Delta F_{t-1}\right) \tag{2.2}$$

$$\Delta Y_t = y\left(\Delta Y_{t-1}, \Delta F_{t-1}, M_{t-1}, \Delta GAP_t^{oecd}\right) \tag{2.3}$$

The baseline estimation of this model uses data from the 20 countries in a sample period ending in 1989. This leaves us with enough data for comparison with a second sub-sample to check for possible 'Maastricht effects.' Table 2.7 has the results. For a better exposition, we do not report the country-dummies.

All three equations have significant explanatory power, although the pseudo R-squares are low – as is usual in models for growth rates and for panel data estimates. Moreover, strictly speaking the R-squares do not have their ordinary meaning since we are using 3SLS estimates. Nevertheless, the *t*-ratios are quite high, indicating significant statistical power. In addition, the coefficients of the three equations conform to conventional predictions. We find output growth is positively related to its own lag and very strongly affected by the change in the cyclical conditions in the OECD area. Output growth falls in reaction to a tightening of both monetary and fiscal policy, with a reaction lag of one year in both cases. Specifically, since current output does not react to a fiscal contraction, the (results indicates that an increase in the fiscal surplus equal to one per cent of GDP causes a drop in

Table 2.7 Baseline estimates

1. *Dependent variable: GDP growth rate*	Coeff.	t-ratio
GDP growth rate (-1)	0.234	4.50
Monetary conditions (-1)	-0.168	2.01
Δ output gap (OECD)	0.733	9.37
Δ fiscal surplus ratio to GDP (-1)	-0.117	1.93
Constant	1.967	9.16
$R^2 = 0.321$, Chi-sq = 120.6, df = 261		
2. *Dependent variable: Δ fiscal surplus ratio to GDP*		
Δ fiscal surplus ratio (-1)	-0.330	5.60
GDP growth	0.179	1.96
Monetary conditions (-1)	-0.284	3.08
GDP growth (-1)	0.076	1.50
Debt/GDP ratio (-1)	0.055	6.41
Constant	-2.450	1.95
$R^2 = 0.245$, Chi-sq = 82.23, df = 240		
3. *Dependent variable: Monetary conditions index*		
Monetary conditions index (-1)	0.531	9.92
GDP growth	-0.098	1.52
Long interest rate (-1)	0.032	1.63
Δ fiscal surplus ratio to GDP	0.281	3.06
Δ fiscal surplus ratio (-1)	0.158	3.85
Constant	-0.613	1.76
$R^2 = 0.245$, Chi-sq = 139.6, df = 260		

Note: R^2 denotes the corrected R^2 coefficient. Δ denotes a one-period change.

the GDP output growth rate by 0.1 per cent in the following year. The long-run impact is a drop in the growth rate of 0.15 per cent. But the effects do not stop here. The decline in domestic output caused by a fiscal contraction has a negative effect on output growth in the other countries. This effect feeds back to the domestic economy and amplifies the impact effect of the fiscal contraction. An increase in the monetary conditions index produces similar effects on output growth.

The fiscal policy variable reacts negatively to its own lag, and positively to current and lagged increases in output growth. This indicates that governments have used structural balances to some extent for anti-cyclical purposes, although the effect is not very strong. Importantly, the fiscal surplus reacts positively to an increase in the debt ratio, which indicates that fiscal policies were, on average, dynamically sustainable. Finally, fiscal policy tends to relax when monetary conditions become tighter. This is consistent with the idea that monetary easing can induce governments to reduce budget deficits (Mélitz, 1997; Wyplosz, 1999).

Monetary policy depends positively on its own lag and on the long-term interest rate. The latter is consistent with monetary tightening as a reaction to rising inflation expectations. The effect of output growth on the monetary conditions index is negative and not statistically significant, meaning that active output stabilization was not an important element of monetary policy, on average, for the countries and period considered. Finally, monetary conditions react positively to an increase in the fiscal surplus, i.e., monetary policy tends to tighten when fiscal policy tightens. Thus, the reaction of monetary policy to fiscal policy has the opposite sign from the reaction of fiscal policy to monetary policy. The implication of this is, first, that the reaction of fiscal policy to a negative shock to monetary conditions (e.g., a monetary expansion undertaken by the central bank to induce an improvement in the deficit) is less in equilibrium than the fiscal policy reaction function itself indicates. Being uncoordinated, fiscal and monetary policy measures have partially offset each other. A second implication is that the output cost of fiscal consolidations consists partly of the growth effects of a tighter monetary policy stance. Those costs may therefore be larger than the changes in fiscal policy alone would indicate.

These estimates have been obtained using data from 20 OECD countries. Since, ultimately, we are interested in policy conclusions for the EMU member states, an important question is, to what extent are these estimates also representative of this subgroup of countries. To see this, we re-estimate our model, dropping all countries not belonging to the EMU from the sample. Table 2.8 has the results.[8]

Dropping the non-EMU states from the sample leaves the coefficients qualitatively unchanged. Thus the picture described above remains broadly the same. However, in the smaller sample, the parameter estimates are less precise. We conclude that the baseline model describes the interaction of

Table 2.8 The model for the EMU member states only, 1972–89

1. *Dependent variable: real output growth rate*	*Coeff.*	*t-ratio*
Real output growth rate (−1)	0.262	3.96
Monetary conditions index (−1)	−0.224	1.89
Δ output gap (OECD)	0.679	7.07
Δ fiscal surplus ratio (−1)	−0.099	1.40
Constant	1.714	6.14
$R^2 = 0.300$, Chi-sq = 70.6, df = 160		

2. *Dependent variable: Δ fiscal surplus ratio*		
Δ fiscal surplus ratio (−1)	−0.398	5.52
Real output growth	0.149	1.14
Monetary conditions index (−1)	−0.247	1.74
Real output growth (−1)	0.049	0.74
Debt/GDP ratio (−1)	0.052	4.67
Constant	−1.548	2.65
$R^2 = 0.240$, Chi-sq = 53.4, df = 139		

3. *Dependent variable: monetary conditions index*		
Monetary conditions index (−1)	0.425	5.51
Real output growth	−0.121	1.45
Long-run interest rate (−1)	0.009	0.36
Δ fiscal surplus ratio	0.361	2.96
Δ fiscal surplus ratio (−1)	0.192	3.28
Constant	−0.485	1.18
$R^2 = 0.000$, Chi-sq = 58.7, df = 159		

Note: R^2 denotes the corrected R^2 coefficient. Δ denotes a one-period change.

real output, fiscal, and monetary policy well. Thus, we continue to use the broader sample for our subsequent analysis.

2.4.2 Fiscal adjustments in the 1990s

We now turn to the question, were the fiscal adjustments undertaken in the EU special compared with the baseline sample of country? We answer this in two steps. First, we take a closer look at the country-specific dummies in the fiscal policy reaction equation. The model has dummies for all countries except Australia, which, hence, is the reference case.

Table 2.9 reports the country-specific effects for the EU countries in the two sample periods. During the 1970s and 1980s, fiscal surpluses in all EU member states were systematically lower than in the reference country. The country-specific effects were significant for Ireland, Italy and Belgium, i.e., for the countries with the largest debt–GDP ratios at the end of the 1980s. The

Table 2.9   Country-specific effects

	1972–89 Sample		1990–98 Sample		Increase over[+]
	Coeff.	t-ratio	Coeff.	t-ratio	First sample
Austria	−1.42	1.37	2.66	1.41	4.08
Belgium	−3.69	2.56**	−1.47	2.60**	2.22
Germany	−0.78	0.98	−1.16	1.64	3.62
Denmark	−1.89	1.62	2.07	1.84*	4.06
Spain	−0.84	1.01	2.78	1.31	3.62
Finland	−0.11	0.60	3.98	0.01	4.09
France	−1.21	1.22	3.48	0.60	4.69
Britain	−0.67	0.78	2.89	1.23	3.56
Greece	−1.31	1.31	1.75	1.53	2.08
Ireland	−3.73	2.56**	−1.09	5.25**	2.64
Italy	−2.73	2.09**	0.11	2.04**	2.84
Netherlands	−2.18	1.79	1.79	1.99**	3.97
Portugal	−1.73	1.55	2.29	2.02**	4.02
Sweden	−0.56	0.82	2.81	1.08	3.37
St. deviation	1.12		1.80		0.68

Note: *= significant at the 10 per cent level; ** = significant at the 5 per cent level; [+] = difference between the second and the first sample coefficients.

1990s, however, brought a general shift in the country-specific effects which turn out to be positive for all EU countries except Germany, Belgium, and Ireland. Thus, relative to the reference country, fiscal policy was generally tighter during the 1990s. Note, also, that six of the country-specific effects gained statistical significance in the 1990s sample. In statistical terms, the country-specific effects have in fact increased significantly in the high-debt countries, i.e., Italy, Ireland, and Belgium, as well as in Denmark, the Netherlands, and Portugal, which experienced large increases in the debt ratios in the first sub-sample. Table 2.9 supports the notion that, controlling for the effects of the business cycle, monetary policy, and debt burdens, fiscal policy in the EU countries was characterized by larger surpluses on average over the 1990s than in the 1970s and 1980s. But the standard deviations of the country effects in Table 2.9 indicate that fiscal policy showed a lower degree of conformity across EU member states in the 1990s compared with the 1970s and 1980s.

For a second look at what the 'Maastricht effects' might contain, we re-examine the fiscal policy reaction function estimated for the EU countries in the 1990s. Table 2.10 has the results.

Table 2.10 indicates that there is indeed evidence for a structural break in the reaction function for the EU countries during the 1990s. First, the intercept is significantly positive now, compared to a significantly negative intercept in the first sub-sample. Second, fiscal surpluses now show no reaction to past

Table 2.10 The EU fiscal policy reaction function in the 1990s

1. *Dependent variable:* Δ *fiscal surplus to GDP ratio*	Coeff.	t-ratio
Δ fiscal surplus ratio (−1)	0.003	0.03
GDP growth	0.299	0.91
monetary conditions index (−1)	−0.128	0.60
GDP growth (−1)	0.130	0.90
Debt/GDP ratio (−1)	0.064	2.82
Constant	4.931	4.42
$R^2 = 0.376$, Chi-sq = 84.1, df = 94		
2. *Dependent variable: monetary conditions index*		
Monetary Conditions Index (−1)	−0.04	0.33
GDP growth	0.02	0.28
Long Run Interest Rate	0.17	5.08
Change in Fiscal Surplus Ratio	0.04	0.36
Change in Fiscal Surplus Ratio (−1)	0.02	0.22
Constant	−2.26	5.10
$R^2 = 0.208$, Chi-sq = 35.4, df = 114		

fiscal surpluses. Similarly, their reaction to output growth and to monetary policy, became much weaker during this period, although the sign of the coefficient did not change. The only explanatory factor remaining significant with a similar coefficient is the debt-to-GDP ratio. Overall, the table supports the notion that, on average fiscal policy in EMU member states in the 1990s reacted less to cyclical fluctuations of output and changes in monetary policy than it had in earlier times, but was more influenced by an exogenous shift towards surpluses represented in the intercept term. In other words, fiscal policy in the 1990s was clearly led by the discipline needed by the Maastricht criteria for entry into EMU – to the exclusion of concerns about output and employment stabilization, or the attempt to match fiscal moderation with monetary tightening (or vice versa) to balance the policy mix in Europe. Hence our concern that this fiscal discipline might be lost after EMU started and the Maastricht sanction was lifted. One ray of hope, however, is that the national policy-makers seem to have focused on the debt ratio rather than the deficit ratio, in which case their fiscal consolidations may be longer lasting than the short-term backsliding on deficit reductions would otherwise imply. However, if this is true, the Stability Pact, designed as it was to protect the deficit ratio, may have been directed at the wrong target.

2.4.3 The cost of fiscal consolidation in the 1990s: were there non-Keynesian effects?

Conventional macroeconomics holds that fiscal retrenchment can only be achieved at the cost of reduced output and employment. Tight fiscal policy reduces aggregate demand for goods and services. With rigid prices, the decline in nominal demand results in a fall in real output. If a fiscal consolidation relies primarily on increased taxes, additional supply-side effects may kick in due to the increased cost of labour resulting from higher tax rates.

This conventional view was challenged in the early 1980s by the so-called 'German view' (Hellwig and Neumann, 1987). According to this view, the private sector realizes that a budgetary consolidation implies less taxes in the future, as the government will face a lower debt service in future years. Assuming that consumption depends on permanent income and that investment demand is forward-looking, consumption and investment will rise relative to the levels that would have prevailed without the fiscal consolidation. Note that this assumes that the pre-consolidation stance of fiscal policy is non-sustainable in the sense that is does indeed require higher taxes in the future to serve the public debt. In essence, then, budgetary consolidations can have expectation effects which have a positive impact on output and employment. In the extreme case, consolidations have positive pay-offs rather than a cost.

The German view gained considerable academic interest following the paper by Giavazzi and Pagano (1990a), which argued that the fiscal consolidations in Denmark and Ireland caused an increase in private sector demand. Giavazzi and Pagano (1995a) and Giavazzi, Jappelli and Pagano (2000) provide further evidence suggesting positive output effects of fiscal consolidations.

In this section, we consider the output cost of the fiscal consolidations in the EU during the 1990s. Our model estimated with data from the 1970s and 1980s suggests that consolidations had a significant, though small, output cost. This is indicated by the coefficients on the fiscal variable in the output equation reported in Table 2.8. Recall that the total output cost of a fiscal consolidation in a country is given by the impact effect on output growth in this country and the feedback effects which arise from the fact that a declining output gap in this country due to a fiscal contraction results in a smaller output gap in the OECD, which in turn has a negative growth effect in the first country. In addition, tighter fiscal policy will not trigger looser monetary policy (as it did in the 1980s; see section 5.1), adding to the output costs.

Using the estimates reported in Table 2.8 as our baseline, we re-estimate the output equation for the EU countries based on data from the 1990s alone. Table 2.11 has the results.

The interesting observation from this estimate is that the coefficient on the fiscal policy variable is now very close to zero and statistically not significant. Comparing this with the estimates using data from the earlier sample period suggests that the output cost of fiscal contractions declined in the 1990s. There is neither a traditional Keyneisan, nor a 'non-Keynesian' effect in the aggregate. To make sure that this result is not due only to the smaller

Table 2.11   The output equation for EU countries, 1990–8

Dependent variable: growth rate in GDP	Coeff.	t-ratio
Explanatory variable, growth rate (−1)	0.581	7.88
monetary conditions (−1)	−0.404	2.74
Change in OECD output gap	0.834	3.45
Change in fiscal surplus ratio (−1)	−0.050	0.47
Constant	1.016	3.90
R^2 = 0.455, Chi-sq = 103.0, df = 115		

number of degrees of freedom in the second sample, we also estimated the output equation for the entire OECD group using data only for the 1990s. In this estimate, the coefficient on the fiscal policy variable also becomes statistically insignificant.

As a further robustness check on our results, we estimate the model using cyclically adjusted fiscal surplus figures rather than their cyclically *un*adjusted counterparts. This change makes virtually no difference to the results, with the exception that the impact of fiscal consolidations on output growth is now a bit stronger – as one might expect. The coefficient on the fiscal variable rises from a statistically significant value of (−0.13) pre-1990 to an insignificant (−0.07) post-1990. Also as one might expect, the impact of growth on the surplus/deficit ratio also rises (from 0.18 to 0.32 in the short term). Otherwise everything else remains almost identical, including significance levels. Thus, the output cost of fiscal consolidations may be somewhat larger than those estimated before. However, the evidence suggests that the cost of fiscal consolidations was smaller in the 1990s than in earlier periods.[9]

In sum, our results indicate a structural break in the output equation, implying a reduced cost of fiscal consolidations in the 1990s. This result is, indeed, consistent with the notion of non-Keynesian effects, but not strong enough to imply that the fiscal contractions were actually expansionary.[10] Specifically, the negative output effects from the fiscal consolidations of the 1990s that were to be expected given that the experience of OECD countries in the 1970s and 1980s may have been balanced by positive demand effects due to improved private sector expectations of future fiscal policies. This interpretation assumes that the public perceived the debt and deficit developments of the EU countries during the 1970s and 1980s to be non-sustainable. The assumption is plausible given the emphasis which the Maastricht Treaty, and the public debate surrounding it, put on the need for fiscal adjustments in the future member states of the monetary union. One implication of this interpretation is that fiscal consolidations may again have significant output effects in the future, when the high visibility of the adjustment efforts due to the Maastricht process no longer prevails.

2.5   Conclusions

In this chapter, we have studied the importance of the composition of the fiscal adjustment, and the initial and accompanying conditions for the success of budgetary consolidations, in terms of their persistence and effectiveness to reduce the deficit and debt level. Our results show that the quality of fiscal adjustments is an important determinant of success. In particular, the likelihood of success rises when governments tackle politically sensitive items on the budget, such as transfers, subsidies, and government wages. Furthermore, economic conditions in the year during or preceding the start of a fiscal consolidation matter. They help explain the probability of success. Specifically, consolidations are more likely to be successful when they start under bleak domestic and international economic circumstances. Economic conditions also influence the choice of governments between revenue and expenditure-based consolidations. The latter are more likely to occur in a weak economy.

We have used the analysis to assess the role of the Maastricht process for achieving fiscal consolidations in the 1990s. The empirical results do not point to a strong Maastricht effect inducing governments to adopt a more stringent fiscal policy and reduce deficits. The consolidations in the second half of the 1990s were all predictable on the basis of the economic conditions prevailing during that period. We find evidence for a Maastricht effect only in the first years of that decade. But this effect led governments to adopt revenue-based consolidation strategies which were predictably short-lived and relatively ineffective in producing the desired reduction of debt levels. The implication is that the reference values set in the Maastricht Treaty are incomplete instruments to guide governments' policy choices. In the future, surveillance of public finances in EU member states should also take into account the 'quality' of the consolidation effort.

In addition we have used a small econometric model to quantitatively investigate the role of the Maastricht process for achieving fiscal consolidations in the 1990s and to asses the macroeconomic effects of these adjustment efforts. Again, we found a 'Maastricht effect'. Here, this means that the fiscal policy reaction function changed in the 1990s. Fiscal policy in the EU member states became more isolated from output and monetary policy developments than the earlier reaction function had indicated. This suggests that fiscal policy was more focused on achieving the Maastricht criteria. Another 'Maastricht effect' suggested by our results is that the cost of consolidations in terms of reduced output growth was lower in the 1990s than in earlier years. This is consistent with the notion of some 'non-Keynesian effects' (the idea that fiscal corrections of non-sustainable policies have positive expectation effects on aggregate demand), but not as far as implying that the fiscal consolidations were actually expansionary.

These results have several implications for the operation of fiscal policy under EMU. Our empirical results suggest that the 1990s were 'special' in several ways. Fiscal discipline was promoted by the goal to achieve monetary union under rules of the Maastricht Treaty, and they were less costly than expected. Now that Stage III of EMU has begun, it is likely that the behaviour of fiscal policy and its effects on the economy will become more 'normal' again. Thus, it is important to ensure that governments will not backslide and allow deficits to emerge again, as they did in the 1970s and 1980s. One should also expect the cost of fiscal consolidations to be higher again in the future, as the signalling and commitment power of the Maastricht criteria is no longer existent. As a consequence, member states should be pressed to stick to the restraint set in the Stability and Growth pact once they have achieved the medium-term position close to balance and/or in surplus. A persistent 'deficit bias' or strong fiscal misalignments due to governments' inability to cope with the problems arising from ageing societies would force them to drastically adjust fiscal policy at some point in the future at a much higher cost.

Notes

1. We thank Roberto Perotti for providing us with the data used in this chapter, and Bernd Hayo for valuable research assistance. This chapter is based on our report entitled 'Fiscal Consolidations in EMU', European Commission Economic Paper 148, March 2001. The report was written while Rolf Strauch was working at the Deutsche Bundesbank. The opinions expressed are those of the authors and do not necessarily reflect views of those institutions to which they are affiliated.
2. Alesina and Perotti (1995b, 1997) and Perotti *et al.* (1998) discuss the robustness of these results with regard to the definition of strong adjustments and their success.
3. We also used a nominal monetary conditions index using the nominal interest rate and the nominal exchange rate. The empirical results were qualitatively the same and are not reported below.
4. OECD aggregates are, of course, computed as averages excluding the country under consideration.
5. For detailed accounts, see von Hagen, Hughes Hallett and Strauch (2001).
6. Using a weaker criterion for the definition of fiscal adjustments than in the preceding analysis is useful for analytical reasons. Here, the task is to describe country histories, and we need an analytical concept that is sufficiently fine-grained to gauge most or all developments. The alternative possibility is to call each improvement of the budget balance a consolidation, and each deterioration an expansion. But this would not be useful in describing episodes during which a specific fiscal strategy prevailed, since small developments can be caused by small, short-term exogenous changes or unexpected consequences of policy measures. For a strategic analysis such a measure would have introduced excessive 'noise'.
7. We use a three-stage least-squares estimator in order to take into account any cross-correlation between the various residuals which may reflect some of the behaviour of the variables which had to be omitted from the panel estimation. Robust standard errors were estimated to account for heteroskedasticity and any remaining serial correlation. Our preferred specification of this model was obtained after applying

a general-to-specific testing-down process to the model we started off with. Country-specific dummies remain in the fiscal policy equation only.

8. Note again that the low R^2 do not mean much for our 3SLS estimates. The t-ratios still indicate significant statistical power.

9. Another possibility is that these costs may be asymmetrically distributed across countries. We have here only the estimates of the costs, Keynesian or otherwise, in terms of aggregate European performance.

10. This result is consistent with the theoretical analysis of Barry and Devereux (1995) or Bradley, Whelan and Wright (1993), and suggests that the Giavazzi–Pagano (1990a) results showing expansions were overdone. For a discussion of why, see Hughes Hallett and McAdam (1998).

3
Entry and Exit Dynamics of Excessive Deficits

Ali H. Bayar and Paul M.C. de Boer[1]

3.1 Introduction

Fiscal discipline and fiscal restructuring have been one of the most debated issues in recent years, more particularly in relation to the European monetary union (EMU) process and to the balanced-budget rule in the US. Three major questions have been at the heart of this debate:

- If discretion in policy-making may lead to high public deficits and debt, should policy-makers be subject to strict fiscal constraints? What are the costs and benefits of fiscal rules?
- What role do economic, political and institutional variables and processes play in the public finance outcomes?
- What are the macroeconomic effects of fiscal adjustments?

A growing theoretical and empirical literature is devoted to the analysis of these questions. Buiter *et al.* (1993) and Roubini (1995) examine the relevance of fiscal constraints and claim that rigid fiscal rules deprive the policy-maker of an important tool to stabilize output and smooth tax distortions over time. Roubini and Sachs (1989), Grilli *et al.* (1991), Alesina and Perotti (1995a), and Alesina and Perotti (1996a) show the importance of political and institutional factors in public finance outcomes. Von Hagen (1992), Alesina and Perotti (1996a and 1996b), and Poterba (1996) consider the role of institutions and procedures involved in the process of preparing and approving the budget. Corsetti and Roubini (1996) compare the European and American fiscal rules. Poterba (1996), Bohn and Inman (1996), and Ahmed (1996) discuss the effectiveness of balanced-budget rules in the US states. Bartolini *et al.* (1995), Bayar *et al.* (1997), Hughes Hallett and McAdam (1997), and Cour *et al.* (1996) evaluate the macroeconomic impacts of fiscal adjustments and rules using econometric models. Alesina and Bayoumi (1996), and Bayoumi and Eichengreen (1995) explore the implications of fiscal rules on economic stabilization. Bertola and Drazen (1993), Giavazzi and Pagano (1990a and 1995a), Barry and Devereux (1995), McDermott and Wescott (1996) discuss whether contractionary policies may have expansionary effects. Alesina and Perotti (1995c and 1997), and Perotti (1996a) show that the composition of fiscal consolidation matters for the success of fiscal adjustments. Heylen (1997) discusses the effectiveness of fiscal consolidation policies in 19 OECD countries since the mid-1970s.

The recent macroeconomic literature on fiscal policy is remarkably rich and provides a much better understanding of the determinants of public deficits. However, the debate has, until now, focused on the *magnitude* of government deficits and debt. An important issue is still largely unexplored:[2] the *dynamics* of deficits.

The dynamics of government deficits will be of utmost importance in the monetary union because the European Stability and Growth Pact,[3] which guides fiscal discipline among the member states since the introduction of the euro on 1, January 1999, explicitly rules out deficits above 3 per cent of GDP, except under precisely defined unusual circumstances. Since the Stability Pact establishes a legal definition of excessive deficit[4] that the member states should avoid, it is important to examine *the entry and exit dynamics* of excessive deficits. How do countries enter into deficits qualified as being excessive, or, if a country has excessive deficits, how does it exit from such a situation? What are the risks of entry and exit for different member states? These questions are essential for the European monetary union because the member countries will lose the exchange rate as a macroeconomic adjustment mechanism and will have to rely on fiscal instruments.[5] The dynamics of excessive deficits and its determinants are therefore a vital issue.

The objective of this chapter is to provide a transition data analysis (Lancaster, 1990) of the dynamics of budget deficits in the 15 member countries of the European Union. The econometric methods of transition data analysis are particularly well suited for this issue because, here, we are concerned both with the duration of a state[6] and the destination[7] that is entered at its end. Transition data refers not only to how long a state lasts but also what happens when it ends.

Using data for the period 1970–96, we examine in this chapter the economic determinants of entry and exit dynamics of excessive deficits and estimate the hazard rates for each one of the member states. The remainder of the chapter is organized as follows. The model is presented in section 2. Section 3 provides the econometric results, whereas section 4 concludes.

3.2   A transition model

The evolution of nominal government deficits (*DEF*) can be expressed by the accounting relation:

$$DEF_t = D_t - D_{t-1} = E_t + iD_{t-1} - TAX_t \tag{3.1}$$

where D is the stock of public debt, E is government primary expenditure, i is the nominal interest rate on the debt and TAX is total government receipts.

Expressing the nominal deficit in terms of GDP gives:

$$\frac{DEF_t}{Y_t} = \frac{E_t}{Y_t} + \frac{1}{(1+g)(1+\pi)}\frac{iD_{t-1}}{Y_{t-1}} - \frac{TAX_t}{Y_t} \tag{3.2}$$

where Y is GDP, g is the growth rate of real GDP, and π is the inflation rate.

Equation (3.2) clearly shows that the deficit-to-GDP ratio increases with government expenditure, nominal interest rate and debt stock, whereas it decreases with the growth rate, the inflation rate and government revenue. Equation (3.2) can be used to analyse how various economic variables determine the evolution of the deficit-to-GDP ratio.

One of the critical questions which arise with the criterion of 3 per cent of the Maastricht Treaty and the Stability and Growth Pact is how the deficit-to-GDP ratio evolves with respect to this threshold of 3 per cent. In order to examine this question let us define two states s_1: the state of being in excessive deficit (deficit-to-GDP ratio > 0.03), and s_2 the state of not being in excessive deficit (deficit-to-GDP ratio ≤ 0.03). Now, the question is: How do countries enter into and exit from such states? What are the effects of various economic variables on these entry and exit dynamics?

Let us think of time to exit the state s_i ($i=1$, 2) as a continuous random variable T. T can be considered as the duration of stay in the state s_i if we set the clock to zero at the moment a country enters into the state in question. Then, the probability of exiting the state s_i in the time interval from t to t', given that the country has been in that state up to time t, can be defined as:

$$P_i(t \leq T < t'|T \geq t) \quad t < t' \tag{3.3}$$

This is the probability that an event (entry or exit) occurs in the time interval from t to t', given that no event (transition) has occurred before in the interval from 0 to t. The definition refers to each point in time and can therefore describe the temporal evolution of the process.

If we divide this probability by $(t'-t)$, we get the average probability of leaving per unit time period over a short interval after t. By considering this average over shorter and shorter intervals we get the hazard function $h_i(t)$ of dynamics for state s_i:

$$h_i(t) = \lim_{t' \to t} \frac{P_i(t \leq T < t'|T \geq t)}{t' - t} \tag{3.4}$$

The interpretation of the hazard function is that $h_i(t)(t'-t)$ is approximately the probability of exit from the state s_i in the short interval after t, given that the country has still been in state s_i at t.

Having defined the hazard functions for the states s_i, we have to evaluate the transition rates between the states and the effects of the relevant economic variables on these rates. The models[8] to be estimated can be written as:

$$h_i(t, X_i, \alpha_i, \beta_i) = h_{0i}(t, \alpha_i)e^{X_i(t)\beta_i} \tag{3.5}$$

where $h_{0i}(t, \alpha_i)$ is the baseline hazard function with parameter α_i, and X_i is a row-vector of covariates associated with the coefficients β_i.

It is impossible to establish the shape of the hazard function h_i of excessive and non-excessive deficits on any theoretical grounds. Therefore, in order to estimate the effects of the relevant economic variables on the hazard rates it is preferable to use the Cox model. Unlike the parametric hazard models, Cox's method does not require any prior choice of a particular probability distribution to represent the survival times. As a consequence, Cox's semiparametric method is considerably more robust.

The initial approach proposed by Cox (1972) is commonly referred to as the proportional hazard model. That name is nevertheless misleading, because the model can be generalized to allow for non-proportional hazards, which is the case with our model. Given that this model incorporates time-dependent covariates which change at different rates for different countries, the model is no longer proportional and the baseline hazard cannot be derived from the estimated Cox model. It is therefore necessary to estimate a parametric model in order to calculate the hazard function for the different constellation of covariates for the different countries. The most attractive specification for this is the complementary log-log function for grouped durations which provide *identical* estimates as in the Cox model for the effects of the covariates on the hazard rate.[9]

3.3   Results

Two models are estimated for exits from and entries into excessive deficits using data for the period 1970–96 for all the fifteen member states of the EU. The following economic covariates are considered:

DEBTL   Debt-to-GDP ratio, lagged by one year
EXPEND   Government primary expenditure-to-GDP ratio
RECEIPT   Government receipts-to-GDP ratio
GROWTH   Growth rate
REALINL   Real long-term interest rate, lagged by one year

Tables 3.1 and 3.2 provide the coefficient estimates for the complementary log-log function. The likelihood-ratio chi-square statistics show that the global null hypothesis that the covariates are jointly not significant, is rejected for both models. This means that at least one of the coefficients is significantly different from 0. We observe that the coefficient for the real interest rate is not significantly different from zero in both models. The

Table 3.1   Estimates for exits from excessive deficits

Variable	Coefficient	Standard error	p-value	Effect in %
INTERCEPT	−4.3866	1.4557	0.0026	
DEBTL	−0.0524	0.0141	0.0002	−5.1
EXPEND	−0.2939	0.0945	0.0019	−25.5
RECEIPT	0.3888	0.0975	0.0001	47.5
GROWTH	0.3805	0.1319	0.0039	46.3
REALINL	0.0378	0.0744	0.6113	
χ^2 36.652 with 5 DF p-value = 0.0001				

Table 3.2   Estimates for entries into excessive deficits

Variable	Coefficient	Standard error	p-value	Effect in %
INTERCEPT	−3.5551	1.5460	0.0215	
DEBTL	0.0546	0.0153	0.0003	5.6
EXPEND	0.6928	0.1738	0.0001	99.9
RECEIPT	−0.6586	0.1681	0.0001	−48.2
GROWTH	−0.3294	0.0931	0.0004	−28.1
REALINL	0.0461	0.0648	0.4767	
χ^2 50.269 with 5 DF p-value = 0.0001				

other estimates are highly significant and the signs of the coefficients are what we expect theoretically.

The numerical magnitudes of the coefficients are not very informative on their own but a simple transformation leads to a very intuitive interpretation. The effects of a covariate can easily be interpreted if we examine the percentage change in the hazard rate when the covariate changes its value by one unit. These effects (in percentage) are given in the last column (*Effect*) of each table.

We observe that the influence of the debt stock (lagged by one year) on the dynamics of excessive deficits is quite low. Its impact on the hazard rate is −5.1 per cent for exits and 5.6 per cent for entries.

It is interesting to note that government receipts play similar roles (in absolute terms) in the exit and entry dynamics, whereas the effects of public expenditures are significantly different in the entries and exits. An increase of one point in the government receipts-to-GDP ratio increases the exit rate from excessive deficits by 47.5 per cent, and decreases the entry risk by 48.2 per cent. An increase by one percentage point in the primary expenditure-to-GDP ratio decreases the exit rate by 25.5 per cent, but increases the entry rate by 100 per cent! This means that, in the monetary union, the focus should be on the expenditure side in order to prevent any entry into excessive deficits.

Economic growth also plays an asymmetric role in the entry and exit dynamics. An increase by one point in the growth rate decreases the entry rate by 28.1 per cent, but it increases the exit rate by 46.3 per cent if the country is in excessive deficit.

In summary, government receipts and economic growth play a capital role in the exits, whereas for the entries into excessive deficits the dominant role is played by the primary expenditures. This implies that even if growth and government receipts play a major role in exiting, fiscal policy should then take over and keep a strong control over public expenditures to secure a lasting budgetary consolidation.

It is also important to note that the effects of the covariates are not independent of each other. They are related multiplicatively. For example, all other things being equal, a simultaneous increase in government primary expenditure-to-GDP ratio by two points and a decrease in the growth rate by one point will increase the hazard of entry into excessive deficit by 455 per cent:

$$(e^{0.6928*2}.e^{-0.3294*(-1)} - 1).100 = 455 \text{ per cent !}$$

This implies that some small but simultaneous changes in the economic situation and government policy may induce major changes in the state of public finances.

As we have already seen above, the transition rate from the origin state j to the destination state k varies with different constellations of covariates in time. In other words, the transition rates are country and time specific. Consequently, we can use the different constellations of covariates in time in the different EU countries in order to compute the evolution of the conditional probabilities of transitions in each one of the EU member states.

Table 3.3 provides the results of these backward simulations for entry into and exit from excessive deficits. The table presents only the average transition rates for various periods. The complete evolution in time between 1971 and 1996 is provided in appendix 3.A.1. The last two columns of Table 3.3 give the average exit and entry probabilities computed for mutually exclusive states. For example, a figure in the last column represents the average of the entry probabilities when the country was in a non-excessive deficit situation. Similarly, a figure in the column before the last one represents the average of the exit probabilities when the country was in an excessive deficit situation.

Table 3.3 and the figures in appendix 3.A.1 clearly show that *Belgium*, *Greece*, and *Italy* had very low transition rates out of excessive deficits until 1996. These countries are the ones which may face the excessive deficit procedure in the future because they easily *get stuck* in excessive deficits once they enter into such a situation. This is why it is so important for them to avoid entering into excessive deficits by keeping a strong control on government expenditures.

Table 3.3 Conditional probabilities (in percentage)

Country	1971–1989 Exit	1971–1989 Entry	1990–1996 Exit	1990–1996 Entry	1996 Exit	1996 Entry	Split states Exit	Split states Entry
Belgium	6.1	93.2	1.5	98.9	1.5	99.8	4.4	52.7
Denmark	75.3	21.0	58.3	26.6	65.6	20.3	38.8	8.2
Germany	41.5	35.4	27.9	56.8	8.5	93.1	21.0	25.9
Greece	16.4	51.2	0.6	96.4	1.4	79.3	0.8	7.5
Spain	22.6	35.5	9.1	74.9	6.0	73.6	7.3	9.6
France	58.0	22.5	26.2	74.1	15.7	94.6	20.1	21.2
Ireland	4.4	80.9	19.2	14.9	34.6	4.4	4.2	14.5
Italy	1.8	98.7	1.0	99.5	8.0	100.0	1.6	100.0
Luxembourg	85.7	9.2	99.5	1.6	99.5	1.4	34.1	4.3
Netherlands	35.9	57.7	15.5	73.6	16.2	49.1	19.5	29.5
Austria	45.6	43.2	18.8	72.6	6.9	99.2	18.5	32.0
Portugal	22.5	36.5	8.3	57.9	7.5	65.8	11.5	3.9
Finland	98.6	0.5	40.3	69.2	71.3	21.6	25.3	5.7
Sweden	85.8	22.8	35.3	72.4	36.5	81.0	34.7	7.0
UK	15.3	47.0	5.6	80.5	5.2	83.6	6.5	23.0

The probability of entry into excessive deficit has been quite low in *Denmark* (27 per cent on average in the 1990s) and has even been decreasing in recent years.

Excessive deficit spells have relatively been short in *Germany* (maximum two years) in the past. But the underlying probability of entering into excessive deficits increased in the 1990s (57 per cent in average) and the probability of exiting has decreased (28 per cent).

Spain and *Portugal* have experienced long excessive deficit spells. The average exit probability decreased considerably (to 9 per cent) in the 1990s.

France was in a sound situation until 1989. Since then, the probability of entering into excessive deficits has increased and the underlying probability of exiting has decreased. Finally, in 1992 the deficit-to-GDP ratio fell under 3 per cent.

Ireland has experienced long excessive deficit episodes in the past. But the probability of entry into such a situation has fallen to only 15 per cent in the 1990s.

Luxembourg is in the best situation. The probability of entering into excessive deficit was 1.5 per cent on average in the 1990s.

The Netherlands has experienced long excessive deficit spells in the past. The exit rate has been quite low since 1987. The probability of entry declined to 49 per cent in 1996, but this positive evolution is quite recent.

Excessive deficit episodes have become longer in *Austria*. The probability of entry has been increasing since 1990 and the exit rate has been declining. The deficit-to-GDP ratio finally fell below 3 per cent in 1993. The last columns in

Table 3.3 show that on average, Austria's probability of entry into excessive deficits has been much higher than its entry probability since 1971.

The situation of public finance in *Finland* radically changed in 1990. The deficit-to-GDP ratio finally fell below 3 per cent in 1992. But the exit probability increased rapidly and Finland left the excessive deficit situation in 1996.

The deficit-to-GDP ratio has been below 3 per cent since 1992 in *Sweden*. The exit rate has been increasing since 1993. This attests to a sound evolution. The last columns in Table 3.3 show that the exit probability was quite large on average (35 per cent) when Sweden was in excessive deficit.

The *United Kingdom* has experienced long excessive deficit spells and the exit probability has been low (6.5 per cent) once the country was in such a situation.

3.4   Conclusion

The emergence and persistence of large public deficits and debt in many industrial countries in the last two decades has generated a widespread concern that discretion in policy-making may lead to excessive deficits. Fiscal discipline has been one of the most debated issues in recent years. However, very little attention has been paid to the dynamics of excessive deficits. This chapter is an attempt to contribute to our understanding of the economic determinants of budgetary dynamics. The following conclusions emerge from the study:

- Government receipts and economic growth play a capital role in the exits, whereas for the entries into excessive deficits the dominant role is played by the primary expenditures. This implies that even if growth and government receipts play a major role in exiting, fiscal policy should then take over and keep a strong control over expenditures to secure a lasting budgetary consolidation.
- In the monetary union the focus should be on the expenditure side in order to prevent any entry into excessive deficits.
- Small but simultaneous changes in the economic situation and government policy may induce important changes in the state of public finances.
- Even if all the member states are now in a non-excessive deficit situation, the evolution of entry and exit probabilities since 1971 shows that some countries (Belgium, Greece, and Italy certainly, but also, though in a smaller extent, many of the other member states) will still be in a fragile position in the near future.

Appendix 3.A.1

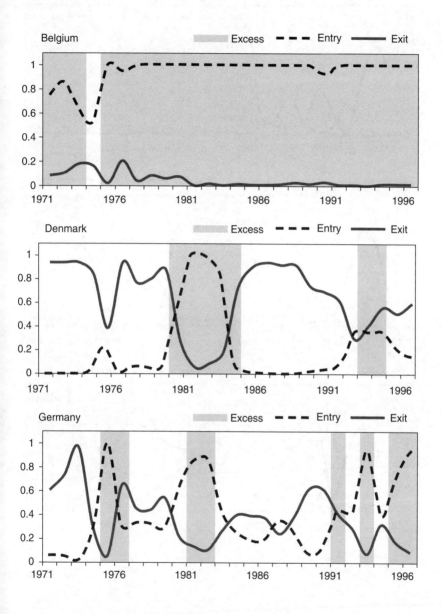

48

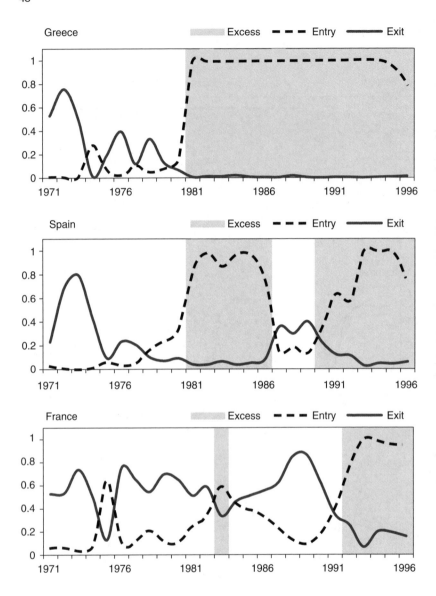

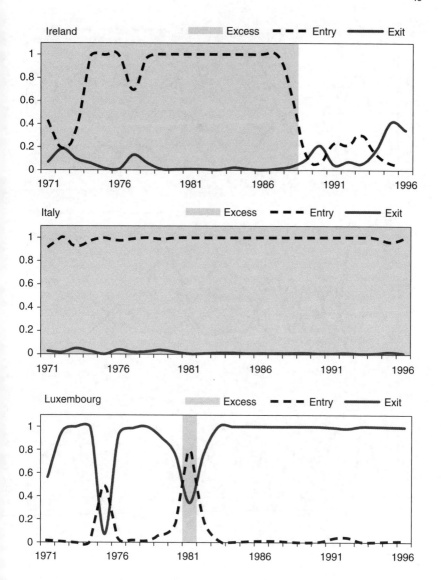

50

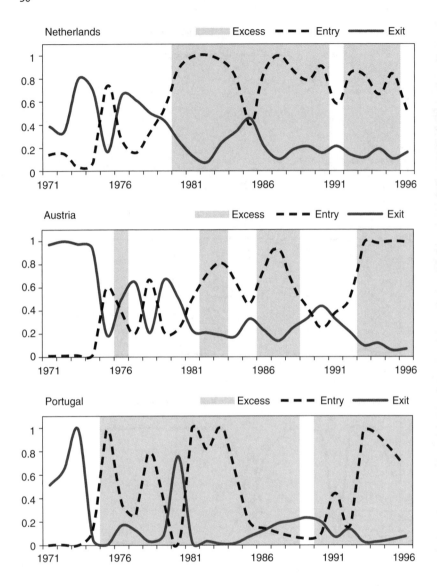

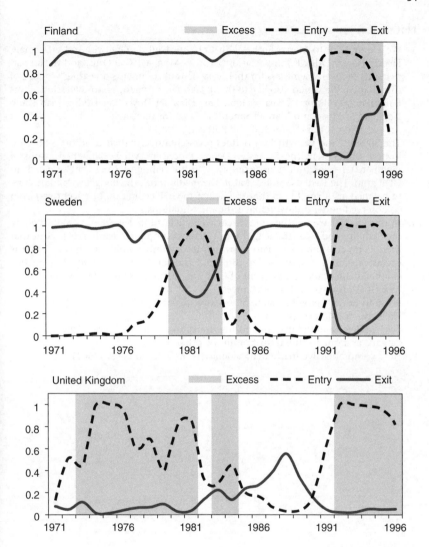

Notes

1. We are grateful to Marco Buti, Merih Celasun, Paul de Grauwe, André Dramais, Freddy Heylen, Alex Koning, Carlos Martinez-Mongay, Ziya Onis, and to the participants of several seminars for their very helpful comments on earlier versions of this chapter. We would also like to thank Jean-Luc Annaert, Tassos Belessiotis, Yves Bouquiaux, Philippe Derveaux, Juan Luis Diaz del Hoyo, Jan Hodes, Joao Paulo Nogueira Martins, and Manuel Sanchis i Marco for their help.
2. An exception is the recent study by Buti *et al.* (1997).
3. The Stability and Growth Pact defines precisely under which conditions and following which steps the Excessive Deficit Procedure will be launched against a member state which does not comply with the ceiling of 3 per cent of deficit to GDP ratio. The Pact also states that in the medium run the budget should be close to balance or in surplus so that the deficit to GDP ceiling of 3 per cent can even be observed under unfavourable economic situations.
4. In this chapter we use the term 'excessive deficit' in its legal sense established by the Stability and Growth Pact, and not in any economic meaning. It is clear that there is no economic standard by which to determine whether a given deficit is excessive or not. Following the threshold laid out by the Stability Pact, in this chapter, deficits above 3 per cent of GDP are classified as being 'excessive'.
5. As well as on wage and price changes.
6. Being in or not being in a state of excessive deficit.
7. Excessive or non-excessive deficit states.
8. Two models are estimated: one for the transition from excessive to non-excessive deficits, and one for the transition in the other direction.
9. For a comprehensive mathematical analysis, we refer to Bayar (2001).

4
Convergence of Fiscal Policies in the Euro Area[1]

Olivier De Bandt[2] and Francesco Paolo Mongelli[3]

4.1 Introduction

In the transition to the European Monetary Union (EMU), a lot of emphasis has been given to monetary convergence and the definition of the common monetary policy. Fiscal policy has also been put under closer scrutiny and a natural question is, therefore, whether the 'euro-area fiscal position' now has a clear empirical content and significance. This chapter aims at determining whether economic, financial and monetary integration on the one hand, and institutional factors on the other, have led to convergence in key fiscal variables across the euro area. The Maastricht convergence criteria have facilitated this process but we investigate here whether the structural forces bringing fiscal positions closer together were a feature of European integration starting already in the 1970s. The alternative scenario is that the euro zone is still characterized by largely idiosyncratic national fiscal policies.

There are several empirical investigations examining the extent to which Europe is becoming more integrated and whether economic developments are becoming more correlated. Artis and Zhang (1995 and 1997) find evidence that business cycles are becoming more synchronous across Europe. Rose (1999) and Frankel and Rose (1998) find evidence of a deepening in trade intensity across most European countries. Artis and Zhang (1998) find increasing linkage of interest rates within European Monetary System (EMS) countries. Angeloni and Dedola (1999) provide evidence that the monetary policy rules followed by the central banks of the euro area have converged in the run-up to EMU. Bayoumi and Eichengreen (1995), Bayoumi and Eichengreen (1995, 1997), Krugman (1993), OECD (1999a) and several other authors have also contributed empirically to this debate (albeit with a different focus, as their main question is whether Europe is an optimum currency area).

Against this background, there is instead remarkably little systematic investigation concerning convergence of key fiscal variables. The main explanation for this gap, that we intend to close in part, may lie in the fact that any research on budgetary policy is plagued by the fact that fiscal policy is in part exogenous and in part endogenous to the business cycle: by studying fiscal variables, one would also capture the correlation between business cycles across countries. Hence, it is not straightforward to distinguish between results that are due to discretionary actions and results that are due to the behaviour of the economy. We attempt to reduce this problem by using cyclically adjusted variables where possible. The approach adopted here is close in spirit to the various contributions of Artis and Zhang (1995 and 1997), and Frankel and Rose (1998).

Convergence of fiscal policies seems a reasonable hypothesis for different reasons. First, the euro area countries have now committed themselves to comply with the Stability and Growth Pact; second, EU countries have initiated a tax harmonization process; third, the Exchange Rate Mechanism (ERM) of the European Monetary System exercised a 'disciplinary' effect on participating countries.

At the same time one must be cautious when applying these concepts to key fiscal indicators, as euro area governments have historically played different economic and financial roles in the economy. This has in turn required the setting up of very different national fiscal structures. Political economy elements were also among the factors contributing to different budgetary performances (see Buti, Franco and Ongena, 1997 and 1998, and references therein). In addition, the underlying European economies are not yet perfectly integrated. Hence, national fiscal policies of most member countries may not exhibit co-movements because the shocks hitting them may have still been largely idiosyncratic, or euro area countries may have responded differently to common shocks (see Bini-Smaghi and Vori, 1992; Bayoumi and Eichengreen, 1995, 1997; and Bruneau and De Bandt, 1999).

It is useful at this stage to clarify how we define convergence.[4] Given a fiscal variable F_t^i in country i, and F_t^j in country j and following Hall *et al.* (1992 and 1993) and Fuss (1999), the two variables *are converging* if the following two complementary conditions are satisfied:

$$\lim_{t \to \infty} E(F_t^i - F_t^j) = a \quad \text{and} \quad \lim_{t \to \infty} Var(F_t^i - bF_t^j - a) = \sigma^2$$

The first condition requires that the expectation of their difference tends to a constant value a being small in relative terms (not necessarily zero), i.e., the variables need not converge completely to a common value. The second condition is that the variance of their relationship also tends to decline reaching a constant value. We check the latter condition by investigating if the dispersion of these variables declines, or at least does not grow over time. As noticed by Hall, Robertson and Nickens (1993) and Fuss (1999), the second condition is also equivalent to cointegration and aims at detecting common trends across countries on key fiscal indicators. In this chapter, it turns out that fiscal variables, measured as ratio to GDP, are not mean-reverting and are therefore non-stationary for the sample we consider, so that cointegration is tested here by means of Equilibrium Correction Model (ECM) and Johansen cointegration. If $b = 1$, the two variables are said to have converged, or to exhibit co-movements, while the variables are converging if $a > 0$ and $b < 1$, or if $a < 0$ and $b > 1$.[5]

It is necessary to qualify such a statement since the convergence process may not be continuous and countries that are converging in the first part of the sample may have effectively converged by the end of the sample period. In such a case of time-varying trends, cointegration would be rejected for the whole period, but accepted on sub-samples. However, running recursive cointegration tests appears difficult with annual fiscal data, and quarterly fiscal data are not yet available for all countries in the euro area.[6] Hence, our options are somewhat limited, and we can only test whether countries are converging for the whole sample period. On the other hand, we can gain some partial insight by investigating whether the difference between individual countries and the euro area comes close to zero at some point in time.

The chapter is organized as follows. Section 4.2 provides a description of the data and their univariate time series properties. Section 4.3 presents several stylized facts on fiscal policies in the euro area countries using cross-correlation indices on cycles and dispersion indicators on the levels of the variables. These preliminary findings are then completed in the following sections. Section 4.4 presents the results of cointegration tests between fiscal indicators across countries. Section 4.5 concludes.

4.2 Data sources and unit root properties

We focus here on three fiscal variables that present complementary facets of fiscal policy: net lending of the government (NLG), which is a 'summary variable' expressing the balance between all components of the budget, total current revenue (REV), and total current expenditure (EXP). While net lending is the most scrutinized fiscal variable – jointly with public debt that is not discussed here – the other variables are more likely to capture long-lasting fiscal co-movements and eventually gradual convergence of national fiscal policies and structures.[7] All variables are expressed as ratio to GDP, which is a natural normalization in order to correct, at least partly, for real and nominal trends in the series. In the remainder of the chapter we will only refer to NLG, REV, and EXP as the corresponding ratio to GDP. For the cointegration analysis we use the cyclically adjusted NLG, REV and EXP ratios to ensure that we are not capturing only the effect of real economic convergence. These variables are denoted as NLGQ, REVQ and EXPQ. Due to the unit elasticity of revenues to GDP, the behaviour of our REV variable is very close to the one of REVQ. This is not true for government expenditures.[8]

A crucial aspects of this chapter is that the average developments of each variable across the euro area are taken as a benchmark. In particular, PPP-adjusted GDP values in 1995 are used to compute such weighted averages.

We investigate the co-movement and gradual convergence in fiscal policies – or the lack thereof – with respect to the euro area average for the following three groups of countries:

1. *Euro area countries*, a group including Austria, Belgium, Finland, France, Germany, Ireland, Italy, Luxembourg, the Netherlands, Portugal, and Spain.
2. *Non-euro area EU countries*, a group including the United Kingdom, Sweden and Greece (that joined the euro area in 2001).
3. *Other selected OECD countries*, a group including the US, Japan and Canada.

The latter two groups of countries constitute a sort of 'control group'. All in all, 16 countries are considered in this chapter. Luxembourg and Denmark are excluded from the sample because comparable data are not available.

We use here a data set based on OECD annual data from the June 1999 *Economic Outlook* database which provides consistent data for all 16 countries in the sample for the 1970–98 period. European countries were characterized by some convergence in the 1970s, but in the early 1980s, following the second oil shock, they tended to diverge. They have, however, tended to resume converging since the mid- to late 1980s, albeit with significant differences.

Before proceeding we need to briefly discuss the univariate time series properties of the data as this will have a bearing on the specifications and interpretations of all the tests. Two types of tests are performed. The first test is the Augmented Dickey-Fuller (ADF) unit root test, where the null hypothesis is that the series have a unit root (the results of the unit root and stationarity tests are available upon request). This test indicates that most fiscal variables seem to have a unit root, i.e., they are I(1). Further testing indicates no higher order of integration (i.e., there is no evidence that the series are I(2) with only a few isolated exceptions).

We also perform the Kwiatowski, Phillips, Schmidt and Shin (1992) (KPSS) stationarity tests, for which the null hypothesis is that the series are stationary. These tests indicate that, overall, these series seem to be stationary for most countries, a result conflicting with the findings of the ADF tests. In the case of NLG, the government budget balance is an adjustment variable, which, from a theoretical standpoint, is expected to be I(0). However, we tend to stick to the I(1) hypothesis, on the basis of the high level of persistence of the series, implying that governments exhibit sluggishness in their response to a worsening of the budget deficit.

There are diverse explanations for this apparent divergence between ADF and KPSS tests. First, the power of both tests is low due to the small size of the sample consisting of only 29 annual observations per variable. Second, most series are likely to have breaks due to the changes in policies that occurred in the sample period in most countries. All in all, it is commonly perceived that ADF tests are more powerful than KPSS tests: hence, we are more inclined to accept the hypothesis that the series have a unit root over the sample which we are considering.[9]

In summary, the view emerging from the above tests is that for the whole sample period NLG, EXP and REV seem to be non-stationary. However, given the small sample size and the limitations of the tests, we cannot completely exclude that in several countries the variables that we found to be non-stationary actually include a deterministic component. For example, the European process of economic and financial integration might have fostered increasingly higher expenditure (and also revenue) in those countries with fewer public infrastructures, a smaller provision of public goods, and an initially lower standard of living (i.e., a public finance 'catching-up' effect).

4.3   Stylized facts of fiscal policy

Our first approach to fiscal convergence among countries in the euro area is based on simple descriptive tests. We compute first the contemporaneous cross-correlation between fiscal indicators and then indicators of fiscal dispersion.

4.3.1   Indicators of short-term cross-correlation

The contemporaneous cross-correlation tests measure the strength of the linear association between the selected fiscal variables for each of the countries in the sample against the corresponding euro area weighted average (using PPP-adjusted GDP values in 1995). For euro area countries, the country is excluded from the euro area average against which the correlation is computed in order to reduce the bias for the larger economies. For the non-euro area countries, i.e. the two 'control groups' (respectively UK, Sweden and Greece, and the US, Japan, and Canada), correlation is computed between these countries, on the one hand, and the whole euro area, on the other.

Our starting point is to extend to fiscal variables the techniques suggested by Artis and Zhang (1997) in the context of EU business cycles. We compute therefore the correlation across fiscal variables. Because the variables investigated seem to be non-stationary we cannot simply compute the correlation of the basic ratios to GDP as there would be an upward bias in the correlation coefficient. Therefore, we concentrate on fiscal cycles. We calculate therefore the correlation in cyclical differences with respect to trends to gauge the extent to which national fiscal policies were altered with respect to underlying fiscal trends. The latter are calculated as follows. For a given fiscal variable F_{it} in country i (e.g. government current expenditures), the trend is defined as $\tilde{F}_{it}$, after smoothing with the Hodrick-Prescott (HP) filter (using $\lambda = 100$ in this case). To reduce the end-point problem we used forecasts based on the OECD June 1999 *Economic Outlook*. As in Artis and Zhang (1998) the cycle for all variables, except government net lending (NLG), is defined as the ratio to the HP filtered series: $c_{it}=(F_{it}-\tilde{F}_{it})/\tilde{F}_{it}$. For NLG cyclical differences are obtained by subtracting current observations from the trend because the denominator is close to zero.[10]

The results are reported in Table 4.1 (a, b and c). We also distinguish between sub-periods in order to assess some additional elements about the changes in fiscal co-movement over time. We follow Angeloni and Dedola (1999), distinguishing between:

1. the *'pre-ERM'* sub-period from 1970 to 1978;
2. the *'soft-ERM'* sub-period from 1979 to 1985;
3. the *'hard-ERM'* sub-period from 1986 to 1992; and
4. the *'pre-EMU'* sub-period from 1993 to 1998.

Due to the small sample size of our data set, the confidence interval of cross-correlation in such short sub-periods is effectively quite large (see unit standard deviation at the bottom of each table).[11] Hence, these values must be interpreted with a great deal of circumspection and taken as simple indications of changes. In order to reduce the confidence interval we also split the sample period in two longer sub-periods: 1970 to 1985 and 1986 to 1998.

From the table, it appears that the correlation in fiscal developments across the euro area is not always very high but is in most cases positive. Furthermore, it has generally increased steadily over the sample period, and more consistently over the 1993–8 sub-period (but often also 1986–98),

Table 4.1 Contemporaneous correlations in cyclical differences with respect to euro area average, 1970–98[1]

	(a) Correlations of net lending, government (NLG)						
	1970–98	*1970–78*	*1979–85*	*1970–85*	*1986–92*	*1993–98*	*1986–98*
Austria	0.538	0.579	0.310	0.494	−0.146	0.895	0.599
Belgium	0.446	0.132	0.677	0.303	0.699	0.706	0.713
Finland	0.298	−0.266	0.195	−0.185	0.642	0.894	0.762
France	0.749	0.851	0.703	0.759	0.535	0.921	0.794
Germany	0.535	0.835	0.139	0.593	0.392	0.573	0.506
Ireland (1977–98)	0.578	0.000	0.453	0.443	0.724	0.812	0.658
Italy	0.573	0.641	0.481	0.579	0.582	0.874	0.605
Netherlands	0.424	0.619	0.462	0.539	−0.203	0.795	0.248
Portugal	0.570	0.708	0.779	0.558	0.609	0.880	0.785
Spain	0.525	0.007	0.657	0.235	0.316	0.943	0.793
Euro area weighted average	*0.573*	*0.634*	*0.443*	*0.554*	*0.427*	*0.786*	*0.623*
United Kingdom	0.616	0.300	−0.296	0.183	0.841	0.962	0.917
Sweden	0.552	−0.258	0.584	0.039	0.763	0.874	0.863
Greece (1975–98)	0.755	0.000	0.651	0.692	−0.335	0.938	0.237
United States	0.715	0.844	0.409	0.706	0.831	0.933	0.762

Table 4.1   (Continued)

	1970–98	1970–78	1979–85	1970–85	1986–92	1993–98	1986–98
Japan	0.501	0.487	−0.110	0.364	0.345	0.813	0.677
Canada	0.606	0.598	0.088	0.391	0.766	0.957	0.803

(b) Correlations of total current revenues (REV)

	1970–98	*1970–78*	*1979–85*	*1970–85*	*1986–92*	*1993–98*	*1986–98*
Austria	0.247	−0.521	−0.297	−0.253	0.754	0.924	0.832
Belgium	0.433	0.502	0.183	0.463	0.374	−0.770	0.365
Finland	0.134	0.468	0.361	0.122	0.268	0.673	0.300
France	0.247	0.227	0.793	0.463	−0.029	−0.239	−0.020
Germany	−0.047	−0.559	0.473	−0.339	0.587	−0.228	0.277
Ireland (1977–98)	0.626	0.000	0.969	0.961	0.415	0.428	0.431
Italy	0.329	−0.106	0.766	0.209	0.222	0.937	0.539
Netherlands	0.562	−0.092	0.787	0.397	0.557	0.964	0.685
Portugal	0.636	0.873	0.675	0.756	0.695	0.553	0.528
Spain	0.287	0.461	−0.118	0.312	0.401	0.777	0.330
Euro area weighted average	*0.214*	*−0.069*	*0.530*	*0.132*	*0.353*	*0.231*	*0.324*
United Kingdom	0.158	0.162	0.857	0.472	−0.542	−0.781	−0.624
Sweden	−0.112	0.703	−0.128	0.334	−0.759	−0.214	−0.561
Greece	0.444	0.623	0.395	0.495	0.460	−0.895	0.387
United States	−0.271	−0.394	−0.178	−0.201	−0.236	−0.560	−0.389
Japan	−0.376	−0.480	0.195	−0.184	−0.556	−0.383	−0.640
Canada	−0.027	−0.617	0.600	−0.052	0.179	0.469	0.032

(c) Correlations of total current expenditures (EXP)

	1970–98	*1970–78*	*1979–85*	*1970–85*	*1986–92*	*1993–98*	*1986–98*
Austria	0.626	0.728	0.012	0.556	0.455	0.778	0.740
Belgium	0.810	0.702	0.962	0.768	0.893	0.979	0.895
Finland	0.758	0.776	0.499	0.541	0.910	0.870	0.922
France	0.737	0.602	0.784	0.672	0.730	0.652	0.820
Germany	0.497	0.181	0.744	0.270	0.810	0.526	0.795
Ireland (1977–98)	0.697	0.000	0.850	0.696	0.778	0.917	0.679
Italy	0.475	0.061	0.961	0.329	0.473	0.751	0.662
Netherlands	0.786	0.949	0.710	0.842	0.806	0.801	0.738
Portugal	0.607	0.680	0.301	0.558	0.826	0.878	0.820
Spain	0.476	0.026	0.202	0.115	0.883	0.965	0.932
Euro area weighted average	*0.581*	*0.328*	*0.710*	*0.426*	*0.724*	*0.701*	*0.785*
United Kingdom	0.794	0.478	0.867	0.634	0.976	0.852	0.943
Sweden	−0.113	−0.210	−0.599	−0.446	0.342	0.915	0.262
Greece	0.108	0.246	−0.617	−0.236	0.858	0.416	0.692

Table 4.1   (Continued)

United States	0.705	0.656	0.826	0.714	0.912	0.950	0.822
Japan	0.524	0.850	0.785	0.791	0.145	−0.585	0.143
Canada	0.284	−0.369	−0.216	−0.239	0.889	0.967	0.871
Standard Deviation (+/−)	*0.186*	*0.333*	*0.378*	*0.250*	*0.378*	*0.408*	*0.277*

[1] Correlations with respect to euro area weighted averages (PPP adjusted GDP values in 1995). For euro area countries the country is excluded from the average against which the correlation is computed and weights are re-scaled. Comparable data for Denmark and Luxembourg were not available. Cyclical differences are obtained by subtracting current observations from the trend obtained by applying the Hodrick Prescott filter with lambda = 100.

Sources: OECD June 1999 *Economic Outlook* (EO) and authors' calculations.

providing evidence of convergence among euro area countries, especially for NLG – one of the criteria of the Maastricht Treaty – and EXP. Instead, the correlation of several other countries in the control groups exhibit swings across variables (e.g., during 1986–98 both the UK and the US displayed very high positive correlation with the euro area for NLG and EXP, but negative correlation for REV). In addition, the correlation coefficients are of course affected by real convergence in terms of business cycles (in particular for NLG and EXP).

More precisely, concerning government net lending (NLG) the euro area average correlation exhibits a significant and steady decline during 1970–92, before rebounding robustly only in the last sub-period in the run-up to EMU. Correlation for the countries in the other two groups displays a more erratic path but also posts some significant increases in the last sub-periods. Overall, during 1986–98 the correlation in the 'non-euro area' and the 'others' is in most cases higher than for the euro area countries, indicating that fiscal discipline was a worldwide movement.

The correlation across indicators of current expenditure (EXP) is in most cases the highest among the three fiscal variables being considered over the whole sample period. Three developments stand out. The first one is that the correlation among euro area countries is clearly on an upward trend,[12] in particular because Spain becomes more correlated with the euro area during the 1986–98 period. The second development is that the dispersion in correlation between euro area countries is also the most even among the variables considered (i.e., it shows the smallest gap between the highest and the lowest correlation values). The third is that there is a remarkably high correlation of the UK and the US with the euro area average (during the whole sample period), Canada (during 1986 and 1998), and Sweden (in the last sub-period).

Total current revenue (REV) provides a different picture. Three remarks can be made. First, correlation across the euro area rises over time, albeit unevenly, and remaining below the correlation in NLG and EXP. Second, during 1986–98 the correlation coefficients are not significantly different from 0 for the euro area as a whole. In particular, the correlation between France and Germany and other euro area countries turns insignificant in the 1993–8 period, while it is negative for Belgium. Third, during 1986–98 in almost all 'non-euro area' countries the correlation with the euro area weighted average declines and turns negative in most cases (e.g. the UK, which had a significant positive correlation with the euro area during 1970–85, is negatively correlated during 1986–98), or becomes insignificant.

These preliminary findings support the hypothesis that convergence in terms of contemporaneous linear association is developing within the euro area. To understand if also the underlying longer-term evolution of these selected fiscal variables is moving closer together we will turn to the analysis of dispersion as well as the cointegration tests in section 4.

4.3.2 Indicators of fiscal dispersion

The second approach to obtain stylized facts is to compute indicators that are very close to standard deviations and coefficients of variation (i.e. standard deviation normalized by the mean) of each fiscal variable across countries. Fiscal variables are now taken in levels, so that we measure the dispersion of levels across countries with respect to a benchmark, which is taken to be the euro area, for the country in the euro area, as well as for those in the 'control group'. Formally, note F_{it}^j, the value of the fiscal indicator i (i=NLG, EXP, REV) in country j and at date t. Define Z as a given set of countries under study (euro-area, European Union countries outside the euro area, other OECD countries). The average level of the fiscal indicator i in the group Z (which includes $n(Z)$ countries), is computed as

$$m^z(t) = \frac{1}{n(Z)} \sum_{j \in Z} F_{it}^j$$

The *standard deviation to the euro area* is the sum of the squared differences between the value of the indicator in each country and the euro area average and is expressed as

$$m^z(t) = \frac{1}{n(Z)} \sum_{j \in Z} (F_{it}^j - m^{euro}(F_{it}^j))^2$$

The *coefficient of variation to the euro area* is simply $\sigma^z(F_{it})/m^z(F_{it})$. In the case of NLG, we present only the standard deviation since the average is usually close to zero. Notice that we use, at this stage, unweighted sums in order to capture the dispersion across national entities and to avoid giving too much weight to the larger countries. One additional reason for using unweighted averages is that weighted averages for the countries in the control groups would have made very little economic sense: what meaning would the GDP weighted fiscal dispersion for the US, Japan, and Canada have?

In Figure 4.1, we plot the *standard deviation* $\sigma^2(F_{it})$ and the *coefficient of variations to the euro area* for all three groups of countries. All charts clearly illustrate a sharper decline in fiscal dispersion among the euro area countries than in the other two groups.[13]

Standard Deviation with respect to the Euro Area

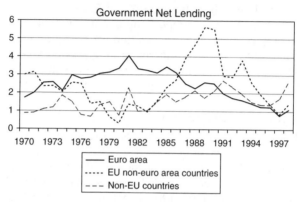

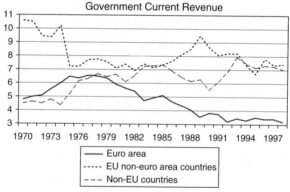

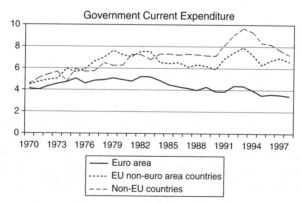

Coefficient of Variation with respect to the Euro Area

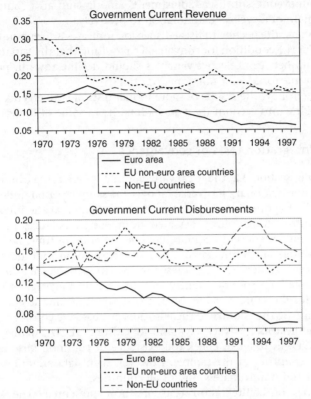

Figure 4.1 Selected indicators of fiscal dispersion 1970–98

Note: Average standard deviation and coefficient of variation (i.e., the standard deviation normalized by the mean) with respect to euro area average for three groups of countries: euro area countries (excluding Luxembourg for which comparable data were not available); EU non-euro area countries (i.e., the UK, Sweden and Greece but excluding Denmark for which comparable data were not available); and some selected non-EU countries (i.e., the US, Japan and Canada). Simple unweighted averages are shown. Euro area averages for euro area countries exclude the specific country for which the indicator of fiscal dispersion is calculated.

Source: OECD June 1999 *Economic Outlook*, and authors' calculations.

Overall, the decline in fiscal dispersion among euro area countries is more distinguishable in the case of current revenue and current expenditure particularly after the onset of the Exchange Rate Mechanism of the EMS (the disciplinary effect argument). In particular, there is a more significant decline in fiscal dispersion across the euro area for current revenue (the coefficient of variation declined from about 0.15 during 1970–4 to 0.065 during 1992–8) than for current expenditure (which in terms of coefficient of variation declined from about 0.13 during 1970–4 to 0.07 during 1992–8). In the case of government net lending, but also of current revenue, the decline in dispersion sets on in the early 1980s but is interrupted in 1985 and 1989–90 by some unevenness in fiscal adjustments among euro area countries and the aftermath of a cyclical deterioration respectively.

In summary, the decline in fiscal dispersion indicates a strong support particularly for the condition for convergence requiring that the variance of the relationship between selected variables should decline toward, possibly, a constant value (or at least not grow over time).

We present now the results of more formal tests of convergence on fiscal trends, taking into account the non-stationarity of some of the variables.

4.4   Cointegration tests of convergence

As we saw in section 4.2, the fiscal variables that we are using can be characterized as non-stationary I(1) variables over the sample period under consideration. The hypothesis we are testing here is whether, at the international level, countries have jointly deviated from budget balance, or have all returned simultaneously to equilibrium over a period of time, i.e., whether fiscal indicators are cointegrated. As for the correlation indicators, we test pairwise cointegration, running these tests on two variables at a time, e.g., a fiscal variable for a specific country and the euro area average of the other countries for the same variable. For the countries outside the euro area we simply compare the country to the euro area average. We consider cyclically adjusted indicators for NLG, EXP and REV (from OECD), namely NLGQ, EXPQ, REVQ, in order to check the existence of common business cycles across the countries in the sample. However, such data are only available since 1974 and unfortunately not for all countries.

Two types of cointegration tests are now presented. They are the Equilibrium Correction Model (ECM) cointegration test – known also as the error correction model – and the Johansen cointegration test.[14] All results in Tables 4.2, 4.3 and 4.4 are run using cyclically adjusted variables. For results on non-adjusted data, see De Bandt and Mongelli (2000).

4.4.1   ECM and Johansen cointegration tests

The *ECM tests*, which we discuss first, are based on a two-step procedure, using the approach proposed by Kremers *et al.* (1992). The results are in columns 1 to 6 of Tables 4.2, 4.3 and 4.4. Let us consider a country j and an indicator i (e.g., NLG). First the long-run equilibrium is estimated on the basis of an unrestricted model in distributed lag form, which is solved numerically. Two specifications are investigated:

$$\alpha_0(L)F_{it}^j = \alpha_1 + \alpha_2(L)F_{it}^{j,\,euro} + \beta\,t + z_{it}^j \quad \text{or} \qquad (4.1a)$$

$$\alpha_0(L)F_{it}^j = \alpha_1 + \alpha_2(L)F_{it}^{j,\,euro} + z_{it}^j \qquad (4.1b)$$

Table 4.2 ECM and Johansen cointegration tests, net lending government cyclically adjusted (NLGQ), 1974–98

| | ECM cointegration test[1] | | | | | | | Johansen cointegration test[2] | | | |
| | Model | Intercept | Trend | Slope | ECM | DW | DF | Hypoth.[3] | L. Trace[4,5] | L-Max[4,5] | |
									r=0	r=0	r=1
Austria**	b	−2.61		0.11	−4.25**	1.54	−4.67	3	27.72*	24.82*	2.90
Belgium		NA	NA	NA	NA	NA	NA		NA	NA	NA
Finland		NA	NA	NA	NA	NA	NA		NA	NA	NA
France	b	16.88		4.04	−2.12	1.95	−0.70	1	15.55	12.03	3.52
Germany	b	−3.43		−0.21	−1.91	2.02	−2.49	1	6.11	4.66	1.45
Ireland	b	22.7		5.27	−0.51	2.23	−0.95		NA	NA	NA
Italy	b	−7.59		1.20	1.17	2.19	1.33	1	9.45	7.64	1.81
Netherlands	b	−11.21		−1.61	−2.42	2.31	−2.04	1	12.35	9.50	2.85
Portugal*	b	0.81		1.43	−3.04*	1.91	−5.58	1	12.34	11.13	1.21
Spain	b	3.8		1.96	−1.35	2.02	−1.71	1	5.75	3.26	2.49
United Kingdom		NA	NA	NA	NA	NA	NA		NA	NA	NA
Sweden*	b	33.16		7.72	−3.62*	2.61	−0.60		NA	NA	NA
Greece	b	−20.86		−2.39	−0.91	1.84	−0.60	1	5.23	4.41	0.82
USA	b	0.81		0.66	−1.18	1.43	−2.04	1	9.19	7.54	1.65
Japan	b	7.53		2.11	−1.00	2.40	−0.07	1	4.31	3.09	1.22

Table 4.2. (Continued)

	ECM cointegration test[1]							Johansen cointegration test[2]		
	Model	Intercept	Trend	Slope	ECM	DW	DF	Hypoth.[3]	L. Trace[4,5]	L-Max[4,5]
Canada	b	−0.07		0.93	−1.26	1.92	−1.97	1	8.43	7.37
								(Hypoth. 1)	20.95	16.14
								(Hypoth. 2)	15.65	14.17
								(Hypoth. 3)	26.72	19.78
										1.06

Critical values (Johansen/10% level, with Cheung and Lai (1993) correction):[6]

[1] Critical values for ECM: model (a) with intercept and trend: 10% −3.50 *; 5% −3.78 *; 1% −4.33 **, and model (b) with intercept only: 10% −3.04 (*); 5% −3.33 *; 1% −3.90 **. In 'ECM' Test, column DF is the value of the Dickey Fuller test on the residuals of the long-run regression.

[2] Johansen cointegration tests between the country specific selected fiscal variables and the Euro Area averages; e.g., the cointegration between NLG for Austria and euro area average NLG excluding A.

[3] Hypothesis 1: Intercept (and no trend) in the cointegrating equation and no intercept in the associated VAR. This is the most restrictive hypothesis. Hypothesis 2: Intercept (and no trend) in the cointegrating equation and in the associated VAR. Hypothesis 3: Intercept and trend in the cointegrating equation, and no trend in the associated VAR. This is the less restrictive among our three hypothesis.

[4] Two lags in level are used for all tests: this is also consistent with the Akaike statistics for most countries.

[5] The series are cointegrated if the number of cointegrating equat. is 1. They are not cointegrated if r = 0, and they are supposedly stationary if r = 2.

[6] Due to the small sample size we use the correction factor of the 'standard' Johansen critical values that is suggested for tests on finite sample sizes by Cheung and Lai (1993): the scaling factor of the standard critical values is SF = no. observ./(no. observ. − no. variables*lags).

Source: OECD and authors' calculations.

Table 4.3 ECM and Johansen cointegration tests, total current revenue cyclically adjusted (REVQ), 1974–98

| | ECM cointegration test[1] | | | | | | | Johansen cointegration test[2] | | | |
| | Model | Intercept | Trend | Slope | ECM | DW | DF | Hypoth.[3] | L. Trace[4,5] | L-Max[4,5] | |
										r = 0	r = 1
Austria**	b	22.44		0.55	−3.65*	1.81	−3.07	1	26.15*	14.07	12.08
Belgium		NA	NA	NA	NA	NA	NA		NA	NA	NA
Finland		NA	NA	NA	NA	NA	NA		NA	NA	NA
France	b	25.03		0.57	−2.83	1.85	−2.80	1	18.27	15.3	2.97
Germany*	b	40.04		0.11	−2.70	2.14	−2.57	2	16.7*	11.68	5.02*
Ireland*	a	−73.69	−1.07	3.01	−3.01	2.29	−1.89	1	19.67	12.83	6.84
Italy	b	−22.96		1.64	−1.05	2.14	−0.97	1	20.14	14.43	5.71
Netherlands**	a	−27.18	−0.99	2.23	−4.47***	1.84	−3.53	1	22.88*	16.58*	6.29
Portugal**	a	−13.39	0.41	0.91	−6.2***	1.96	−3.42	3	36.02*	27.06*	3.96
Spain	a	−22.91	0.17	1.26	−1.49	1.79	−1.50	1	19.58	14.29	5.29
United Kingdom		NA	NA	NA	NA	NA	NA		NA	NA	NA
Sweden		NA	NA	NA	NA	NA	NA		NA	NA	NA
Greece	a	23.06	0.73	−0.11	−1.99	1.97	−1.98	1	15.88	12.21	3.67
USA	b	20.48		0.28	−1.06	1.34	−1.78	1	17.3	14.41	2.89
Japan	b	68.98		−0.79	−2.07	2.33	−4.69	2	16.38*	13.53*	2.84
Canada*	b	5.74		0.81	−1.88	1.76	−1.99	1	22.56*	17.64*	4.92

Note: For notes and explanations, see Table 4.2.

Source: OECD and authors' calculations.

Table 4.4 ECM and Johansen cointegration tests, total current expenditure cyclically adjusted (EXPQ), 1974–98

		ECM cointegration test[1]						Johansen cointegration test[2]			
	Model	Intercept	Trend	Slope	ECM	DW	DF	Hypoth.[3]	L. Trace[4,5]	L-Max[4,5] $r=0$	$r=1$
Austria**	2	10.37		0.79	-3.76*	2.04	-3.55	1	26.54*	18.66*	7.88
Belgium		NA	NA	NA	NA	NA	NA		NA	NA	NA
Finland		NA	NA	NA	NA	NA	NA		NA	NA	NA
France*	2	7.37		0.91	-1.78	1.77	-0.81	1	23.19*	20.53*	2.66
Germany	2	32.84		0.25	-2.68	2.13	-2.26	1	17.89	13.53	4.36
Ireland	2	148.52		-2.46	-2.03	2.09	-2.56		NA	NA	NA
Italy*	2	-21.85		1.51	-1.39	1.98	-1.50	1	21.46*	19.68*	1.78
Netherlands	2	262.69		-5.04	-2.17	1.87	-2.94	1	18.75	11.29	7.46
Portugal**	1	-4.13	0.51	0.66	-4.17*	1.81	-1.85	3	28.64*	18.72	9.92
Spain*	2	18.49		0.46	-1.14	2.17	-3.48	1	21.64*	16.61	5.03
United Kingdom		NA	NA	NA	NA	NA	NA		NA	NA	NA
Sweden		NA	NA	NA	NA	NA	NA		NA	NA	NA
Greece	2	-17.19		1.26	-2.95	1.85	-1.36	1	23.16*	11.73	11.43*
USA	1	1.63	-0.30	0.84	-2.33	2.10	-0.92	1	14.16	11.49	2.67
Japan	2	3.13		0.53	-2.51	2.26	-1.94		NA	NA	NA
Canada	2	-2.93		1.08	-2.01	2.09	-1.39	1	17.90	12.77	5.13

Note: For notes and explanations, see Table 4.2.

Source: OECD and authors' calculations.

depending on whether a deterministic trend is included or not in the regression. Column 1 in the table ('Model') indicates the model that was selected to estimate the long-run equilibrium (eq. 4.1a or 4.1b); the selection procedure is based on the significance of the coefficient on the trend, using a Student t-test on β. F_{it}^j is, as before, a given fiscal indicator in country j, while $F_{it}^{j,\,euro}$ is the corresponding fiscal indicator for the euro area (a weighted average excluding country j).The latter variable is assumed to be *weakly exogenous* for the long-run parameters α, which means that fiscal policy in country i does not affect, in the long run, fiscal policy in the other countries.[15] Note that the $\alpha(L)$'s are polynomials of the lag operator. Applying a third order autoregressive lag model to our annual data,[16] we use the lagged residual $Z_{i,\,t-1}^j$ as equilibrium correction term in the following ECM:

$$\Delta F_{it}^j = \delta_0 + \delta_1\,\Delta F_{it-1}^j + \delta_2\,\Delta F_{it}^{j,euro} + \delta_3\,\Delta F_{it-1}^{j,euro} - \gamma\,z_{it-1}^j + \varepsilon_{it}^j \qquad (4.1c)$$

The ECM test is based on γ, or its *t*-ratio. The country results for the *t*-ratio appear in column 'ECM'. We also provide the value of the DF test on the residual $Z_{i,\,t-1}^j$ (column 'DF'). The 'slope' coefficient corresponds to $\alpha_2(1)/\alpha_0(1)$ in the long-run equation (4.1).

The *Johansen cointegration test*, is based on a bivariate VAR structure on $(F_{it}^j, F_{it}^{j,\,euro})$. Johansen (1995) recommends a sequential testing procedure for which one starts with the strictest specification for the null hypothesis, i.e., hypothesis 1 below (zero cointegration relation), moving to looser specifications with more cointegrating relations, i.e., hypothesis 3. We restrict ourselves here to testing only three competing hypotheses (excluding the hypothesis with quadratic time trends and the most restrictive hypothesis of no intercept either in the cointegrating equation or in the associated VAR). Following Johansen (1995) the hypotheses that we test for are (see column 'Hypothesis'):

- *Hypothesis 1*: Intercept (but no trend) in the cointegrating equation and no intercept in the associated VAR. This is the most restrictive among our three hypotheses. It postulates that the variables have no linear trend and the only deterministic component is the intercept in the cointegrating relation. This is assumption $H^*_1(r)$ in Johansen (1995).
- *Hypothesis 2*: Intercept (but no trend) in the cointegrating equation and trend in the associated VAR. This hypothesis postulates that the variables have linear trends but the cointegration relations have no trends. This is assumption $H_1(r)$ in Johansen (1995).
- *Hypothesis 3*: Intercept and trend in the cointegrating equation, and no trend in the associated VAR. This is the less restrictive among our three hypotheses. It postulates that the cointegration space has a linear trend, which means that we allow for 'trend stationary' variables, and the trend stationarity can either be for a single variable or an equilibrium relation. This is assumption $H^*(r)$ in Johansen (1995).

On the basis of the stationarity tests discussed in section 4.2 we would prefer hypothesis 1 for all three fiscal variables. However, we cannot completely exclude that in several countries these variables may also be affected by a deterministic trend, as the European process of economic and financial integration has fostered increasingly higher expenditure, and revenue, in those countries with fewer public infrastructures, a smaller initial provision of public goods, and generally a lower standard of living. This 'catch-up' effect may not completely emerge from the data but could be better captured, if present, by hypotheses 2 and 3.

In the right-hand part of Tables 4.2, 4.3 and 4.4, we report the trace and the lambda max tests for the first model where the null of no cointegration is rejected at the 10 per cent level. The relevant critical values are based on Osterwald-Lenum (1992) using the small sample correction of the maximum likelihood estimators proposed by Cheung and Lai (1993). Regarding the number of lags, we tried to minimize the bias induced by over-parameterization (Lutkepohl, 1999) by choosing one lag in the model in first difference (hence, two lags in level). Such a choice is found to be optimal on the basis of an Akaike test on an OLS regression of F_{it}^{j} on lags of F_{it}^{euro}, as well as F_{it}^{euro} on lags of F_{it}^{j}. Furthermore, it must be noted that we accept the hypothesis of one cointegration equation either when the L-Trace test rejects the null of rank $= 0$, or when the L-Max test rejects the null of $r = 0$.

4.4.2   Results of the cointegration tests

Tables 4.2, 4.3 and 4.4 for the cyclically adjusted variables provide some evidence in favour of cointegration. In several cases this evidence depends on the type of indicator considered. To simplify the comparisons, in each table the results are summarized in the first column with the name of the country: one star (*) indicates that there is significant evidence of cointegration either from the ECM or from the Johansen test; two stars (**) indicates that both tests converge, thus supporting the existence of cointegration.

In the case of *government net lending* (NLQG), we find limited evidence of cointegration for both the ECM and the Johansen tests. Cointegration is accepted for a few small countries in the euro area such as Austria and Portugal on a cyclically adjusted basis (Table 4.2), and Spain.[17] Surprisingly, Sweden also turned out to be cointegrated with the euro area, although the Swedish budget balance varies more widely (the slope coefficient is equal to 1.77). According to the Johansen test, cointegration is also accepted for the US after introduction of a trend.

All in all, there is no overwhelming evidence of cointegration for NLGQ. There are several possible explanations for this result. One is that the NLGQ is a catch-all term and the countries in the sample have adopted rather different fiscal strategies also in response to exogenous shocks. Another possible explanation is that countries in the sample have started their fiscal adjustment at different points in time. The impact of the changes in the

Italian deficit during the last part of the sample is a case in point. Given the relatively high weight of Italy (20.3 per cent), the significant downward adjustment of the deficit of that country introduces a trend in the euro area average against which the countries are compared. Since most countries did not implement such a drastic and concentrated policy, the hypothesis of cointegration is not supported by the data.

There is more evidence of cointegration in the case of *current government receipts* (REVQ), including Austria, Germany, Ireland, Italy, the Netherlands, and Portugal. As expected, the comparison with non-cyclically adjusted data would not reveal significant differences between the cyclically adjusted current receipt variable (REVQ) and the non-cyclically unadjusted REV, with the exception of the switch between Ireland (cointegrated in cyclically adjusted terms but not in terms of ratio to GDP) and Italy (cointegrated in terms of ratio to GDP but not in cyclically adjusted terms).[18] The distribution of the coefficients in the long-run model is not standard (although the estimator is super-convergent), but they are illustrative of its underlying dynamics.[19] During the period, Austria and Portugal were converging to the euro area: Portugal was converging from below the euro area ('catching-up' process) and Austria from above. Table 4.3 reveals that the intercept for Portugal is negative, while the slope is close to one and the deterministic trend is positive. Germany was also converging from above the euro area average with a positive intercept and a slope coefficient smaller than one (see introduction to this chapter for the explanation of convergence patterns). Italy was converging from below at very high speed with a slope coefficient of 3. On the other hand, the Netherlands is found to be cointegrated with the euro area but with a negative slope coefficient, contradicting convergence. Canada exhibits evidence of international convergence in terms of cyclically adjusted variables, with a positive intercept but a slope coefficient positive but smaller than one, but not for the non-corrected variables.

In the case of *Government expenditure* (EXPQ), Table 4.4 indicates that Austria, France, Italy, Portugal and Spain are found to be cointegrated with their euro area counterpart. Austria, France and Spain were converging from above (with positive intercepts of respectively 10.37, 7.37 and 18.49 percentage point) and slope coefficients below one (i.e., respectively 0.79, 0.91 and 0.46).[20] Italy was converging fast from below and a slope coefficient of 1.51. Portugal is converging in terms of Johansen cointegration. It has a negative intercept, a slope well below one but a positive trend for the ECM test. This country is clearly converging from below in terms of non-cyclically adjusted series (see De Bandt and Mongelli, 2000). Germany is also found to be converging for non-cyclically adjusted current disbursements as percentage of GDP which was above the euro area average from 1970 to 1984, and dipped below the euro average in the second part of the sample period. The existence of a converging trend is accepted for Finland only in terms non-cyclically adjusted series since the intercept is very high and the slope coefficient is

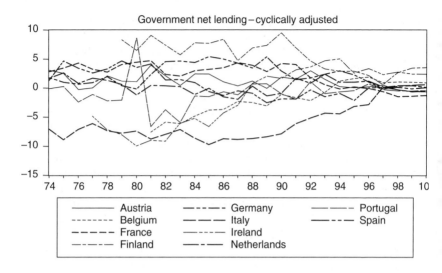

Figure 4.2 NLG: difference with respect to the euro area aggregate excluding the country

negative, but low in absolute values. Actually, EXP in that country experienced sharp movement in the 1990s.

In summary, what do the above cointegration tests tell us? They provide evidence supportive of the convergence conditions in terms of reduction of variance of the difference between the two series. This seems to hold particularly for current revenue and expenditure, and especially for small countries such as Austria and Portugal. The more modest evidence of cointegration for government net lending may be the result of differences in timing and speed in the fiscal adjustment process initiated in the mid- to late 1980s in each country. In addition, failure to detect a stable cointegration relation may be due to shifts in the cointegrating vector as some countries may have finally converged at the end of the sample. In Figure 4.2 we plot, for the cyclically adjusted net government net lending (NLGQ), and for each country j in the euro area, the difference with the euro area counterpart, namely, using our previous definitions, $F_{NLG,t}^{j} - F_{NLG,t}^{j,euro}$. The dispersion between the countries is narrowing until the second half of the 1990s, where it comes close to zero for all countries. However the sample is too short to conclude that the countries have converged as from the mid-1990s. The same figures for REVQ and EXPQ would be less significant.[21]

4.5   Conclusion

This chapter set out to assess whether the euro area is characterized by some convergence in fiscal policies by examining the correlation, dispersion and cointegration of government net lending, total current revenue, and total current expenditure: three variables that are affected by the European process of integration.

The contemporaneous cross-correlation for all three variables is not always very high but is generally positive. Furthermore, it has generally increased steadily over the sample period, and particularly in the latter part. In addition, the dispersion in correlation among euro area countries is also gradually declining over time, above all for government net lending and total current expenditure. We also find convincing evidence that fiscal dispersion has been declining for all three variables at a sustained pace among all countries in the sample, but particularly among euro area countries.

We find some evidence of cointegration across the euro area for total current revenue and also – but less significantly – for total current expenditure. Cointegration on the revenue side is consistent with the process of tax harmonization in several areas most exposed to competition, the gradual synchronization of fiscal policies also in response to more synchronized business cycles, and in the latter part of the sample period with the fulfilment of the Maastricht convergence criteria. The limited cointegration on the expenditure side can be explained, amongst others, with a catch-up process in several low expenditure countries. Less cointegration is found instead for government net lending. This does not necessarily indicate a lack of convergence that is detectable from the raw data and is underpinned by the indicators of fiscal dispersion. The existence of a break in the relationship, with fiscal positions coming very close to each other as from the mid-1990s in connection with the Maastricht process, may be an explanation: while the countries *were converging* before that date, they *have effectively converged* since then. Another explanation is that such a movement results from differences in timing and speed in the fiscal adjustment process in each country. All in all, these findings are significant also because the sample period that we investigate is characterized by many far-reaching economic and institutional changes, and also shifts in the thrust of fiscal policy across each country.

The above tests, jointly interpreted, tend to indicate that although fiscal policy in euro area countries has significantly converged, it remains too early to conclude that fiscal policy in the euro area can be summarized by the (weighted) sum of national fiscal policies. Country-specific components still contribute to a significant share of the variability of the aggregate. Furthermore, additional investigation is needed for the sub-components of these variables that could be more affected by the ongoing economic and financial changes. On the other hand, we have not taken into account different levels in public indebtedness that might reduce the ability (or opportunities) for further fiscal convergence in flow variables in some countries.

In our analysis we checked out the effects of increasing synchronization in business cycles to the extent possible. However, this could not be systematic, in particular because there is, as yet, no consensus regarding the proper way to compute cyclically adjusted indicators and to model jointly the economy and budgetary policy. This is an area in which further research is needed.

Notes

1. This chapter benefited from the comments and suggestions of Mike Artis, Pedro De Lima, Jérôme Henry, Stelios Makrydakis, Hedwig Ongena, Vitor Gaspar and the participants to the workshop on 'Macroeconomic Policy after EMU' held at the European University Institute in Florence on 30 April–1 May 1999. We also wish to thank Beatriz Ruiz Gonzáles for her valuable research assistance. The views expressed in the chapter are the authors' and do not necessarily reflect the views of the European Central Bank nor the Banque de France. We are fully responsible for any error or omission.
2. Banque de France, 41-1376 DEER-SEMEP, 39 Rue Croix de Petits Champs, 75049 Paris Cedex 01, France; email: olivier.debandt@banque-france.fr
3. European Central Bank, DG Economics, Kaiserstrasse 29, D-60311, Frankfurt, Germany; email: francesco.mongelli@ecb.int
4. But other definitions of convergence are possible. For example, the Maastricht Treaty convergence criteria are different from the definition of convergence that we adopt in this chapter. They were cast instead in terms of critical thresholds for the deficit and debt targets – as well as bands for a set of reference financial variables. In this case convergence is achieved when these threshold targets, or bands, are met (or in the case of the debt-ratio have the potential to be met over time). Such definition of convergence has the appeal of being unequivocal, but does not consider the dynamics of convergence.
5. Formally, the series *have converged* and exhibit co-movement – or move in a synchronous manner up to a constant a (following some authors) – if the expectation and the variance of their difference is constant, and not necessarily zero:

$$E(F_t^i - F_t^j) = a \quad \text{and} \quad Var(F_t^i - F_t^j - a) = \sigma^2$$

6. Regarding the availability of quarterly fiscal data, see in particular O. De Bandt and F. Mongelli (2000).
7. Another important variable is government net capital expenditure (CAP), which is the complement to the three other variables, since NLG = REV – EXP – CAP. In order to save space, its evolution is not investigated here, but can be inferred from the three variables discussed in the chapter.
8. Fluctuations in REV, taken as ratio to GDP, express changes in the tax burden, while movements in EXP are affected by its denominator due to the low elasticity of expenditures to GDP. The elasticity of government net lending to GDP is therefore, by construction, intermediate between that of REV and EXP.
9. That is, such variables could meander around without a tendency to return to any long-run level, and their cumulative variance could grow unbounded over time. However, we also know that under normal circumstances fiscal variables do not meander around without boundaries as they are in fact bound by the government budget constraint.
10. In the line of our previous remarks, deviations from trend in REV (i.e. of the ratio of revenues to GDP) express discretionary changes in tax policies. For NLG and EXP, there is a mixture of effects from the business cycle and fiscal policy. In section 4, we concentrate on the trend component, using OECD cyclically adjusted fiscal indicators.

11. These indicative standard deviations are obtained as $SD = 1/\sqrt{n}$ and under the assumption that these variables are normally distributed and not allowing for higher orders of dependence. The true standard deviations are likely to be larger.

12. When the two sub-periods 1970–85 and 1986–98 are compared, this is clear for the cyclical variations, while it is difficult to reject the null hypothesis of constant average coefficient of correlation for the indicators in first difference.

13. We check this result by also plotting the 'usual' indicators of standard deviation and coefficient of variation. In comparison to the indicators presented here, the reference used for the control groups is the mean of the group instead of the euro area average. These charts, that are not shown but are available upon request, confirm that fiscal dispersion declined more significantly across euro area countries.

14. We also ran the Engle Granger cointegration tests with and without a time trend. As the results do not add much to the information from the ECM and the Johansen tests we do not show these additional tests, but they are, however, available on request.

15. In practice, this implies that the equation for $\Delta F_{it}^{j,euro}$ is not necessary for the estimation of the long-run parameters.

16. We chose three lags as a reasonable compromise between a large number of lags and sufficient degree of freedom. The results are robust to the number of lags.

17. In the case of Portugal, such a result may be driven by an unexplained spike in the cyclically adjusted balance for 1980.

18. Owing to the unit elasticity of government receipts to GDP in most countries. See also section 3 for details.

19. A fully modified estimator of Philipps and Loretan (1991) type would be necessary.

20. It it is not possible to use the long-run estimate from the ECM test to assess the form of convergence. In the case of France, such a result obtains, although one can observe a divergence at the end of the sample (stability of the ratio of expenditure to GDP in France and reduction in the euro area).

21. One way to test for such an hypothesis is, following Hall *et al.* (1992) to assess whether the number of cointegration relationships among all countries (and not only two-by-two as we do in the paper) grows over time. Indeed, preliminary results using techniques in Johansen (1995), indicate an increase in the number of cointegration vectors when the 1990s are included in the sample.

5
Fiscal Policy and the Size of Governments

Carlos Martinez-Mongay[1]

5.1 Introduction

Empirical literature on the determinants of the size of the public sector shows that across-country differences in government size can largely be related to differences in a few country and time-specific factors. According to the well-known Wagner's law, the demand for government services is elastic with respect to income, so that the share of total expenditures in the GDP is an increasing function of per capita income (see Ram, 1987). Demographic structures are also determinants of the size of the public sector (see, for instance, Heller and Diamond, 1990; Martinez-Mongay, 2000). Ageing populations raise the demand of certain social services and transfers, such as health care and pensions, thus enlarging the share of their public provision in GDP. In a recent paper, Rodrick (1998) finds and explains a positive association between the degree of exposure to foreign trade and the size of the public sector. The rationale behind this positive correlation is that government expenditures provide insurance in economies exposed to external shocks.

This basic set of three factors (income, demography and international openness) has been successfully used to explain across-country differences in the long-run evolution of government size in a variety of samples, periods and either in isolation or with additional variables.[2] By taking stock of this literature, this chapter analyses the relationship between the stock of the debt and the size of governments, as measured by primary expenditures and taxes. The next section presents a series of stylized facts about the size of the public sector, its differences across OECD countries and its evolution over time. Section 3 looks at the above-mentioned three main determinants of government size and presents some benchmark regressions for alternative indicators of government size. Section 4 analyses the relationship between the stock of public debt and the size of the government. Section 5 presents summary conclusions.

5.2   The size of governments in the OECD, 1960–99

5.2.1   Total expenditures

Following, among others, Persson and Tabellini (1999) we start by defining the size of the public sector as the share of total expenditures[3] of general government in GDP. By taking 5-year averages to offset potential cyclical effects as much as possible, the size of OECD[4] governments in the second part of the 1990s (1995–9) varies from 34 per cent in the US and Japan to 63 per cent in Sweden (Figure 5.1). However, 40 years before, between 1960 and 1964, the minimum share of expenditures in GDP corresponded to Portugal (18 per cent) and the largest to Austria (35 per cent). This suggests that while there has been a general upward trend in the size of governments, the relative position of countries in terms of the share of total expenditures in the GDP has recorded important changes.

Table 5.1 shows the changes observed in the size of OECD governments between 1960 and 1999. Column (a) gives the overall change over the period, i.e. the difference between the 5-year average for 1995–9 and the 5-year average for 1960–4. In the last 40 years, the share of expenditures in GDP increased by more than 10 percentage points of GDP everywhere except in the UK and the US. The change is of 20 percentage points or more in countries such as Denmark, Greece, France, Italy, Austria, Portugal or Finland. Despite the fact that the size of governments in industrial countries has been on a long-run positive path, as indicated by other columns of the table, the

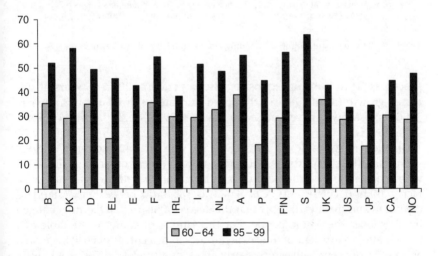

Figure 5.1   The size of governments in the OECD, 1960–99*
* Total expenditure in percentage of GDP, five-year averages over 1960–4 (no data for Spain and Sweden) and 1995–9.

Source: Annual macroeconomic database of DG ECFIN (European Commission) (AMECO).

Table 5.1   Changes in government size, 1960–99*

	95/99–60/64 (a)	65/69–60/64 (b)	70/74–65/69 (c)	75/79–70/74 (d)	80/84–75/79 (e)	85/89–80/84 (f)	90/94–85/89 (g)	95/99–90/94 (h)
B	17	5	4	9	8	−4	−3	−3
DK	29	6	7	5	10	−1	4	−1
D	14	3	3	7	1	−2	1	1
EL	25	3	0	4	7	7	5	−1
E[1]	20	n.a.	n.a.	5	9	5	4	−2
F	19	2	0	6	6	2	1	2
IRL	8	5	6	7	7	−3	−7	−6
I	22	3	2	6	7	4	3	−4
NL	16	5	5	8	7	−2	−2	−6
A	16	3	1	8	3	2	0	0
P	27	1	3	11	10	−3	3	1
FIN	27	4	0	9	2	4	12	−4
S[1]	21	n.a.	n.a.	10	9	−3	6	−4
UK	6	2	2	5	2	−4	1	−3
US	5	1	2	1	2	1	1	−2
JP	17	1	3	7	4	−1	1	2
CA	14	2	5	4	4	1	5	−6
NO	19	5	6	5	0	3	4	−5

B: Belgium; DK: Denmark; D: Germany; EL: Greece; E: Spain; F: France; IRL: Ireland; I: Italy; NL: Netherlands; A: Austria; P: Portugal; FIN: Finland; S: Sweden; UK: United Kingdom; US: United States; JP: Japan; CA: Canada; NO: Norway.
* Government size is total expenditures as a percentage of GDP. Differences between 5-year averages over 1960–99 (1960–4, 1965–9, 1970–4, 1975–9, 1980–4, 1985–9, 1990–4 and 1994–9).
[1]1970–99.
Source: AMECO databank (European Commission, DG ECFIN) and own calculations.

process is far from being explosive. After a period of 20 to 25 years of sustained growth (until 1980–5), the speed of change slowed down in the late 1980s and seems to have reversed in the late 1990s (see the last two columns of Table 5.1).

On the basis of Table 5.1 and Figure 5.1, one can conclude that in every sub-period the size of the public sector widely varies across countries, even within a sample including quite a similar group of nations. As a matter of fact, variation coefficients (calculated as the ratio between the standard deviation and the mean) show that the degree of dispersion has not changed by a lot over the whole period. For the sample of countries in Table 5.1, the variation coefficient of total expenditures in percentage of GDP fluctuated around 21 per cent between the early 1960s and the late 1970s. A relatively weak convergence process has taken place since then, and the variation coefficient declined to 17 per cent in 1995–9. It is worth noting that the convergence process has been stronger within the EU, where the coefficient fell from

20 per cent in the early 1960s to 14 per cent in the late 1990s. The process was particularly strong during the 1980s and, as shown in Chapter 4 (see also Fatás and Mihov, 2001), continued in the second half of the 1990s.[5]

5.2.2 Alternative indicators of government size

The share of total expenditures in GDP is not the only possible way to measure the size of the public sector. Although its use has a self-evident rationale, other government size indicators have been used in the literature. For instance, Rodrick (1998) puts a lot of emphasis on government consumption, mainly for data availability reasons, while Cameron (1978) looks at social transfers and Martinez-Mongay (2000) focuses on taxes. In addition, it could be argued that the total tax burden and total expenditures can be misleading measures of the size of governments. A part of them consists of simple transfers of money, without any effect on income distribution. The problem is that reliable estimates of the so-called tax churning[6] are difficult to obtain, while the consideration of taxes net of transfers is a clear underestimation of the part of the economy actually affected by governments. Indeed, just considering activity (production, value added, employment) of public enterprises would also be misleading, showing a relatively recent and fast declining influence of governments in national economies.

All in all, the more general that government size indicators are, the more accurately they reflect the impact of the public sector in the economy. In this sense, total expenditures would be the most useful indicator for government size. However, given the central goal of this chapter, namely to analyze the long-run relationship between public debt and government size, total expenditures may need to be complemented with other indicators. The main reason for this is that total expenditures include interest payments. These not only depend on past fiscal behaviour affecting the stock of debt, but also of interest rates, which are not under the direct control of fiscal authorities.

As shown in Table 5.2, interest payments account for a significant part of the increase in total expenditures. The share of interest payments in GDP in the late 1990s was twice that recorded in the early 1960s. However, the increase took place before the last decade, where, due to the fall in interest rates and to the reduction of debt levels, the share of interest payments stopped rising or fell across the OECD and, in particular, the EU.

Once interest payments have been deducted from total expenditures, the figures for the share of primary expenditures in GDP in Table 5.2 indicate that the overall conclusion for the long-run evolution and across-country differences in total expenditures still applies to primary expenditures. The bulk of the increase in the share of primary expenditures in GDP took place during the late 1970s and the 1980s, while, during the 1990s, and especially in their second half, primary expenditures grew less than GDP in nominal terms in the majority of countries. Therefore, the generalized fall in the share of total expenditures in GDP during the 1990s shown in Table 5.1 is not only

Table 5.2   Interest payments, primary expenditures and tax revenues in per cent of GDP, 1970–99

	Interest payments			Primary expenditures			Total tax revenues		
	Level 95–99[1]	Change 95–99/ 70–74[2]	Change 95–99/ 90–94[3]	Level 95–99[1]	Change 95–99/ 70–74[2]	Change 95–99/ 90–94[3]	Level 95–99[1]	Change 95–99/ 70–74[2]	Change 95–99/ 90–94[3]
	(a)	(b)	(c)	(d)	(e)	(f)	(g)	(h)	(i)
B	8	4	−3	44	3	0	48	10	2
DK	6	4	−1	52	11	0	51	7	2
D	4	2	1	46	6	1	43	4	2
EL	9	8	−1	37	14	0	37	14	4
E	5	4	0	38	16	−3	35	16	0
F	4	3	0	51	14	1	46	10	2
IRL	4	0	−3	34	−3	−3	34	4	−2
I	9	7	−2	42	9	−2	43	16	1
NL	5	2	−1	43	3	−5	42	4	−2
A	4	3	0	51	10	0	46	8	2
P	5	4	−2	40	19	4	36	16	2
FIN	4	3	1	52	20	−5	47	14	0
S	6	4	1	57	13	−5	52	11	2
UK	4	−1	0	39	2	−3	37	2	1
US	4	2	−1	29	0	−2	28	2	1
JP	4	3	0	31	10	2	27	7	−1
CA	9	5	−1	36	3	−5	37	6	0
NO	2	1	−1	45	7	−4	43	3	1

B: Belgium; DK: Denmark; D: Germany; EL: Greece; E: Spain; F: France; IRL: Ireland; I: Italy; NL: Netherlands; A: Austria; P: Portugal; FIN: Finland; S: Sweden; UK: United Kingdom; US: United States; JP: Japan; CA: Canada; NO: Norway.
[1]5-year averages over 1995–9.
[2]Differences between 5-year averages over 1995–9 and 1970–4.
[3]Differences between 5-year averages over 1995–9 and 1990–4.

Source: AMECO databank (European Commission, DG ECFIN) and own calculations.

due to debt and interest-related factors, but, as long as 5-year averages remove cyclical fluctuations, also to discretionary fiscal retrenchment.

Such a fiscal retrenchment is also evident on the tax side. As expected, in the long run, the share of total tax revenues in GDP follows that of expenditures, so that tax burdens across the OECD rose during the 1970s and the 1980s.[7] Indeed, over shorter periods of time, taxes may behave differently from expenditures. This was the case in the late 1990s. As shown in Table 5.2, as a general rule, taxes increased (decreased) by more (less) than primary expenditures. Moreover, in a number of countries (Spain, Italy, Finland, Sweden, UK, US, Canada or Norway), taxes increased or remained broadly stable while primary expenditures were cut.

5.3   The determinants of government size

Whatever the indicator of government size, Tables 5.1 and 5.2 suggest that despite more or less significant convergence processes, the size of governments depends on country specific factors. This section aims at identifying the factors explaining across-country differences and similarities in government size and, especially, in primary expenditures and tax revenues as shares of GDP.

5.3.1   The demand of government services

According to Wagner's law, the demand of government services is elastic with respect to income. High-income countries should exhibit higher shares of expenditures in GDP than low-income countries. As is well known, a strong convergence process in living standards has taken place during the last 40 years. For the sample as a whole, the variation coefficient of GDP per capita declined from 31 per cent at the beginning of the period to 19 per cent in 1995–9.[8] Yet, as illustrated by Table 5.3 (columns (a) and (b)), there are still large differences across countries in terms of living standards. For instance, in the late 1990s, income per capita in the US was almost three times that of Portugal.

Simple correlation analyses support Wagner's law. The share of expenditures in GDP is an increasing function of GDP per capita. The regression between the 5-year averages of expenditures and income indicates that more than 40 per cent of the variation of government size across countries and over time is related to differences in income per capita.[9] Interestingly, such differences are not of an explosive nature, since a semilogarithmic transformation leads to better econometric results than a linear relationship between expenditures and GDP per capita.[10]

Demography is another factor associated with the long-run evolution of public expenditures. While, *ceteris paribus*, a younger population requires more spending on education, ageing puts pressure on health care and pensions.[11] In most countries, such social services are at least partially provided by the public sector, either directly or through transfers. As shown in column (c) of Table 5.3, dependency ratios were low in most countries in the early 1960s. Leaving aside Japan, where only 6 per cent of the population was aged 65 or over, in most countries the figure was between 9 and 12 per cent. Over the last four decades, the ratio has increased everywhere and a strong convergence process has taken place. In the second half of the 1990s, the lowest record corresponds to Canada (12 per cent) and the highest to Italy and Sweden (17 per cent). Between 1960 and 1999, the variation coefficient in the whole sample declined from 20 to 10 per cent. Simple regression analyses reveal that more than half the variation of the size of governments across countries and over time is associated with differences in demography and, in particular, with the relative importance of people over 65 with respect to the total population.

Table 5.3   Income, dependency and openness, 1960–99[*]

	Income per capita[1]		Dependency[2]		Trade openness[3]	
	Average 1960–64 (a)	Average 99–95 (b)	Average 1960–64 (c)	Average 99–95 (d)	Average 1960–64 (e)	Average 99–95 (f)
B	8	12	12	13	42	53
DK	11	14	11	13	30	30
D	10	13	11	14	17	22
EL	4	8	n.a.	7	14	18
E	5	8	9	10	9	13
F	8	12	12	13	13	17
IRL	5	8	11	11	34	42
I	7	11	10	11	13	18
NL	9	13	9	10	48	50
A	8	11	13	14	24	30
P	4	6	n.a.	15	20	26
FIN	7	11	8	10	21	25
S	10	13	12	14	22	26
UK	9	11	12	11	20	24
US	12	17	9	10	5	7
JP	5	10	6	8	10	11
CA	10	14	8	8	18	22
NO	8	11	11	13	36	38

B: Belgium; DK: Denmark; EL: Greece; E: Spain; F: France; IRL: Ireland; I: Italy; NL: Netherlands; A: Austria; P: Portugal; FIN: Finland; S: Sweden; UK: United Kingdom; US: United States; JP: Japan; CA: Canada; NO: Norway.

[*]The table shows 5-year averages.
[1]GDP per capita in constant purchasing power parities.
[2]The ratio between people of 65 and over and total population.
[3]Average of exports and imports of goods and services in percentage of GDP.

Where the correlation between dependency and expenditures is concerned, the results are very similar if one considers a linear model or a semilogarithmic transformation. The size of the regression coefficient (35.3), compared with the range of the variables in the third and fourth columns of Table 5.3, suggests that the regression is nearly linear. As a matter of fact, the linear regression between expenditures and dependency leads to a R^2 of 54 per cent, which is comparable to that of the semilogarithmic transformation (53 per cent). However, we will follow here Rodrick (1998), rather than Persson and Tabellini (1999), and include the logarithm of dependency. In the end, a semilogarithmic model is flexible enough to encompass a linear form.

Trade openness is another main explanatory factor for across-country differentials in the size of governments. Rodrick (1998) argues that the degree of exposure to international competition increases the need for insurance against external shocks. More open countries will tend to have larger public sectors. Moreover, according to Rodrick, openness not only increases the demand of social protection, as narrowly represented by social transfers, but also public services, which have traditionally been included in the category of public consumption.[12] Overall, larger public sectors would be associated with less income volatility. In line with other works, such as Galí (1994) or Fatás and Mihov (1999), Rodrick concludes that permanent increases in the size of the public sector result in more stable incomes in most countries. Large public sectors would be associated with stronger automatic stabilization cushioning external shocks.

As with income and dependency, trade openness (measured here by the average of exports and imports of goods and services in percentage of GDP) has increased in a majority of countries in the sample over the second half of the twentieth century (see Table 5.3). Yet it is difficult to say that an important convergence process has taken place over the last four decades. As a matter of fact, while the standard deviation of trade openness was 54 per cent of the mean in the early 1960s, the figure was still 50 per cent in the late 1990s.[13] Although in some countries, such as Spain, Ireland, the US or Canada, the process of international integration has been spectacular, in others (Denmark, the Netherlands, Japan, Norway) the changes recorded in the exposure to international competition are marginal. To some extent, openness is related to the size of the country, so that larger countries are less exposed to international competition. While trade openness was below 10 per cent in the US and Japan, the average of exports and imports amounted to almost 50 per cent of GDP in Belgium and the Netherlands.

Simple correlation analyses reveal that, although weaker than in the case of income and dependency, there is a high degree of association between international exposure and government size. More than one-third of the variation of expenditures across countries is due to differences in the degree of exposure to international competition. As in the case of income, there is quite strong evidence that openness should enter the regression in logarithms, since the linear transformation leads to much poorer econometric results. Therefore, across-country differences in expenditures (in per cent of GDP) grow with openness but the growth rate decreases with differences in the level of international integration.

Recent work by Persson and Tabellini (1999, 2000) and Persson (2001) has put emphasis on the relationship between the size and composition of government spending and the political system. This research line predicts systematic effects of electoral rules and political regimes on the share of expenditures in GDP. Overall, it seems that presidential regimes have smaller governments, while majoritarian voting rules lead to smaller welfare states. Such conclusions have been drawn by using large samples of countries over relatively short time periods, which is not our case. Given the relatively high degree of 'political homogeneity' in a significant part of the sample, it does not seem feasible to conduct meaningful analyses of the explanatory power of politics for the size of the public sector.[14]

Before moving to more comprehensive analyses, it could be worth recalling the role played by Baumol's law in the long-run development of nominal expenditures in terms of nominal GDP. Whatever its source and nature, whether triggered by income, demography or international integration, and whether consisting of general services, or social protection or insurance against external shocks, the demand for public services seems to be elastic and grows faster than GDP. Such an apparent behaviour of social services as luxuries could well be partly due to price rather than income effects, which panel regressions are not able to disentangle. As stressed by Buti, Franco and Pench (1999), most public services are subject to the 'Baumol disease of personal services'. Since productivity of personal services grows more slowly than that of tradable goods, the cost of such services grows faster than, let us say, the GDP deflator. *Ceteris paribus*, nominal expenditures would tend to grow faster than nominal GDP. Consequently, across-country differentials in government size could be explained by differentials in the evolution of the relative cost of personal services.

Unfortunately potential price effects cannot be netted out in the context of this chapter. Although it is well known that the relative price of services in terms of the price of manufactures increases over time everywhere, its correlation with size is statistically insignificant. The reason is that such a relative price is an index, thus by changing the base year it is always possible to find a period with large differences in government size across countries but almost the same relative price for services (at around 100) in each country. Therefore, in interpreting the results above, as well as those shown below, one should keep in mind that the relationships explaining across-country differences in government size can also include the effects of differences in the evolution of the price of personal services compared with that of the GDP deflator.

5.3.2 A multivariate analysis

Now we look at the joint explicative power of the three main determinants of government size differentials. Although the emphasis here is on across-country differences in the share of primary expenditures in GDP, relevant empirical evidence will also be presented for total tax revenues and for total expenditures. Column (a) in Table 5.4 shows the regression results for the lagged relationship of primary expenditures (in per cent of GDP) with income, dependency and openness, expressed in logarithms. We use lagged values of the explanatory variables to avoid as much as possible simultaneity biases.[15] All in all, almost two-thirds of the across-country variation in primary expenditures over the period 1960–99 is related to differences in income, demography and exposure to international competition. Leaving aside heteroskedasticity, the potential effects of which have been corrected by using

Table 5.4   Long-run determinants of government size°

	Primary expenditures				Total tax revenues			Total expenditure
	Whole sample[7] (a)	EU sample[8] (b)	1960– 1979[9] (c)	1980– 1999[10] (d)	Whole sample[7] (e)	EU sample[8] (f)	1980– 1999[10] (g)	Whole sample[7] (h)
Intercept	−39.9 (−7.9)*	−33.2 (−3.2)*	−47.9 (−6.6)*	−48.7 (−4.2)*	−39.0 (−8.7)*	−33.7 (−3.8)*	−60.5 (−7.6)*	−49.4 (−9.4)*
PCY[1]	5.4 (2.9)*	12.6 (4.5)*	12.2 (5.4)*	3.7 (1.1)	5.9 (3.9)*	15.0 (7.9)*	6.9 (3.1)*	9.0 (5.3)*
OLD[2]	18.0 (6.6)*	12.0 (2.3)*	14.8 (6.0)*	22.5 (4.9)*	15.8 (7.6)*	8.6 (2.06)*	21.6 (7.6)*	17.8 (6.7)*
TOP[3]	6.8 (6.3)*	4.2 (2.7)*	7.0 (8.0)*	7.2 (4.7)*	6.7 (8.7)*	3.9 (4.2)*	7.6 (7.9)*	8.3 (8.1)*
T[4]	111	83	41	70	111	83	70	116
Adj.R^{2}[5]	0.662	0.559	0.832	0.507	0.737	0.709	0.700	0.728
SBIC[6]	3.362	3.382	2.655	3.646	2.912	2.789	2.928	3.377

° Primary expenditures, total tax revenues and total expenditures are expressed in percentage of GDP (5-year averages; 60–64, 65–69, 70–74, 75–79, 80–84, 85–89, 90–94, 95–99). t-ratios between brackets (based on White's heteroskedastic-consistent standard errors) * significant at 5 per cent.

[1] Per capita income. Logarithm of GDP at constant PPPs per head of population lagged one 5-year period.

[2] Dependency rate. Logarithm of 5-year averages of the ratio (per cent) of people of 65 years and over to total population lagged one 5-year period.

[3] Trade openness. Logarithm of 5-year averages of average of exports and imports of goods and services in percentage of GDP lagged one 5-year period.

[4] Sample size.

[5] Adjusted R^{2}.

[6] Schwarz-Bayes Information Criterion.

[7] All the countries over 1960–99.

[8] EU countries over 1960–99.

[9] All the countries over 1960–79.

[10] All the countries over 1980–99; lagged variables cover the period between 1975 and 1994.

White's heteroskedastic-consistent standard errors, the model does not present evidence of specification errors. Moreover, the results seem to be quite robust with respect to country and time selection.

The most notable feature of the regression only including EU countries (column (b)) is a significant reduction in the explicative power of the model, from 66 per cent in the whole sample to 55 per cent in the EU. This is the result of more similarity in terms of dependency, trade openness and, to a lesser extent, income across the EU than across the whole sample. The degree of similarity has an impact on the estimated coefficients. The regression for the EU presents a larger coefficient of income than for the whole sample, while those of demographic dependency and trade openness are smaller. Yet this does not mean that, let us say, dependency has a lower impact on government size in the EU than in the OECD. It simply means that, being much more similar within the EU, dependency has a lower impact on the differentials in government size across the EU member states. As a matter of fact, the regression for the whole sample tells us that one of the reasons why EU countries have larger public sectors is a higher dependency ratio (see also Table 5.3).

While keeping the overall conclusion unchanged, splitting the whole sample into two periods, before and after 1980 (columns (c) and (d)), suggests that the model had a higher explicative power during the 1960s and the 1970s than after the 1980s. As shown above, economic and demographic convergence processes have increased the degree of similarity across the countries in the sample. As a result, other factors not included in the regression have become as important as income, dependency and trade openness in explaining across-country differences in primary expenditures.

Columns (e), (f) and (g) in Table 5.4 suggest that, over long enough periods of time, across-countries differentials in the tax burden behave much the same as differentials in primary expenditures. Although the adjustment power for the regression in column (e) is slightly higher than in column (a), the coefficients are overall comparable. Unsurprisingly, there are much more similarities with total expenditures (column (h)) for the whole sample. This suggests that taxes and total expenditures tend to evolve in parallel over the long run.[16]

5.4   The size of the public sector and fiscal consolidation

Leaving aside differences between alternative samples and government size indicators, one could conclude that between two-thirds and three-quarters of the variability of government size across countries and over time is explained by differences in income, dependency and openness. On this basis, it would appear that the size of the public sector is largely predetermined and that governments do not have much room for manoeuvre to reduce their size in the long run. Increasing income, dependency and openness would be putting pressure on public expenditures, leading to a steady increase in the size of the public sector.

However, the fact that government size has kept pace with income, dependency and trade does not mean that no other factor can play a role in determining the shares of expenditures and taxes in GDP, but simply that other factors have played no major role over the sample period. Moreover, Table 5.4 seems to indicate that in some cases such other factors have been at least as important as income, dependency and openness. As a matter of fact, governments have plenty of instruments to control their size. For instance, the size of the public sector will vary across countries in function of the generosity of pension schemes. Policies ensuring the long-run sustainability of public finances, such as those consisting of reducing debt levels, increasing employment rates and reforming pension schemes (see European Commission, 2000b) may cause a structural break in the relationship between dependency and expenditures in a country, thereby putting the government size of this country in a descending path.

The residuals of the regression in column (h) of Table 5.4 provide a good illustration of how other factors change the relative size of governments within the sample. Such residuals indicate that at the beginning of the period (until 1975) a majority of EU countries were close to or below the regression 'line'. However, after the first oil-price shock and until the Maastricht era the share of expenditures in GDP grew much faster and more persistently in a majority of EU countries than in the sample as a whole. In the 1990s, especially in their second half, fiscal consolidation resulted in a reversion of previous trends.

Table 5.4 also gives some hints about the role of fiscal policy. Differences in the explicative power of regressions over 1960–79 and 1980–99 for primary expenditures, as well as in their counterparts for total expenditures – not shown here but with comparable results – suggests that a large part of the expansion of the public sector during the 1980s and, in some countries, the early 1990s, has been financed through deficit spending. While the regressions for taxes and expenditures over the whole period 1960–99 seem to be relatively close to each other, in the case of the period 1980–99 the differences between the intercepts in the regressions (g; 60.5) and (d; 48.7) of Table 5.4, indicates that expenditures have been persistently higher than taxes, thus leading to mounting debts and interest payments, which, as shown in section 5.2, account for a non-negligible part of the increase in total expenditures.

Therefore, there seems to be a case for analysing the relationship between alternative indicators of government size and public debt in the long run. The relationship between fiscal policy and public debt has been analysed for the short run. In the US case, Bohn (1998) has shown that there is a strong and positive correlation between the primary surplus in one year and the stock of debt at the end of the previous period. Similar results about the relationship between debt and fiscal variables (surplus, taxes, expenditures) in OECD countries are shown in Chapter 12 by Jacques Mélitz (in the present volume) for annual panel data in first differences.

I have first analysed the relationship between the residuals of the regressions for the whole sample in Table 5.4 (see regressions (a), (e) and (h)) and the stock of debt at three different moments in time: its average level during the same period (DEBTt), its level in the first year of the same period (DEBTt0) and its average level during the previous period (DEBTt-1). Table 5.5 presents the correlation coefficients for the resulting 9 combinations of residuals and debt. Interestingly, the relative position of countries in terms of total expenditures does not seem to be related to the contemporaneous stock of debt.[17] In principle, one would have expected high-debt countries

Table 5.5   Simple correlation coefficients between size residuals and debt stocks

	DEBTt (1)	DEBTt0 (2)	DEBTt-1 (3)
Residuals for total expenditures (4)	−0.00	−0.14	−0.22
Residuals for primary expenditures (5)	−0.33	−0.44	−0.49
Residuals for total taxes (6)	−0.20	−0.22	−0.26

(1) Average stock of debt (per cent of GDP) during the current 5-year period.
(2) Stock of debt (per cent of GDP) in the first year of the current 5-year period.
(3) Average stock of debt (per cent of GDP) during the previous 5-year period.
(4) From the regression in the last column of Table 5.4.
(5) From the regression in the first column of Table 5.4.
(6) From the regression in the fifth column of Table 5.4.

to have more expenditures because they have higher interest burdens. However, it seems that debt differentials affect more the composition of total expenditures than their relative size. Taking into account the correlation for primary expenditures and contemporaneous debt, it seems that higher debt results in lower than expected (given income, dependency and openness) primary expenditures. It appears that primary expenditures have to be smaller to leave some budgetary room to pay for the interest on the debt.[18] However, as shown in the table, higher debt levels would be associated with comparatively lower taxes during the same period.

In less static relationships all the correlation coefficients are negative. The correlation is particularly significant in the case of primary expenditures, where the debt level in the previous period explains more than 20 per cent of the relative position of each country with respect to the regression line. According to Figure 5.2, high-debt countries in one period would tend to exhibit lower residuals the period after. Between the two periods, their primary expenditures would have increased (fallen) by less (more) than for the sample average. This would be indicating that primary expenditures have had a stabilizing response to debt levels. Although the evidence is less strong, taxes seem to have reacted to debt in a destabilizing manner, so that taxes have decreased with lagged debt. However, it is worth noting that the relationship is relatively weak. The absolute value of the correlation coefficient between debt levels and the residuals of the regression for taxes is smaller than for primary expenditures.

Consequently, a complete assessment of the response of fiscal policy to debt needs to compare not only the direction of the change of expenditures and taxes, but also the size of the respective changes. If taxes fall by less than primary expenditures, so that the primary surplus increases,[19] fiscal policy reacts to debt in a stabilizing way. The size of the public sector, as measured by primary expenditures and taxes, is lowered by more (increases by less) than in the sample average. However, if taxes are cut by more than primary expenditures primary deficits will increase. In such a case, and depending on

Carlos Martinez-Mongay 89

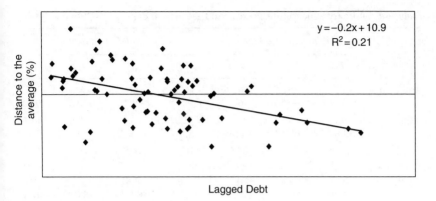

Figure 5.2 Relative position of countries in terms of government size and the stock of debt*
* Regression of the residuals of the regression in the first column of Table 5.4 (primary expenditures) expressed in percentage points of the corresponding fitted values (Y-axis) and the stock of debt lagged one 5-year period in percentage of GDP one period (X-axis).

real growth and real interest rates, the stock of public debt and interest payments could increase. As a result, the size of the public sector, measured by total expenditures, could increase or, depending on the fall in primary expenditures, remain unchanged.

Correlation coefficients in Table 5.5 seem to rule out this latter possibility. Albeit not in a very strong way, the residuals of the regression for total expenditures exhibit a negative relationship with lagged debt. Nevertheless, a more robust answer is given by multivariate analyses.

Table 5.6 presents evidence on the relationship between primary expenditures and taxes, on the one hand, and the stock of debt, on the other. To avoid simultaneity bias we only consider the level of debt at the beginning of the period and that in the previous period. Hence, contemporaneous debt levels are not included in the regressions. Such results should be assessed against the benchmark regression for the period 1980–99 in column (d) of Table 5.4. The reason is that the stock of debt is available in Annual macroeconomic database of DG ECFIN (European Commission) (AMECO) for most countries only since the second half of the 1970s. Therefore, the effective sample period in the regressions including the debt roughly coincides with that covered by the regression over 1980–99.

The first column in Table 5.6 includes income, dependency and openness plus the stock of the debt lagged one period as explanatory variables. The relationship between expenditures and the lagged debt is significant at 5 per cent and negative, while the explicative power of the model jumps from 50 per cent in column (d) of Table 5.4 to almost 75 per cent in the first column of Table 5.6. It appears that high debt ratios lead to relatively lower

Table 5.6   Primary expenditures, taxes and the stock of debt, 1970–99°

	Primary expenditures			Total tax revenues			
	(a)	*(b)*	*(c)*	*(d)*	*(e)*	*(f)*	*(g)*
Intercept	−62.7 (−6.9)*	−57.7 (−8.2)*	−62.6 (−6.8)*	−65.6 (−9.7)*	−55.2 (−9.1)*	−55.0 (−9.3)*	−65.0 (9.7)*
PCY[1]	9.2 (3.6)*	8.7 (4.0)*	9.2 (3.6)*	11.3 (5.5)*	10.2 (5.6)*	10.3 (5.9)*	11.5 (5.7)*
OLD[2]	20.9 (5.2)*	20.7 (5.5)*	21.0 (5.2)*	18.3 (5.3)*	16.8 (5.3)*	18.9 (6.0)*	18.7 (5.9)*
TOP[3]	10.7 (9.9)*	9.4 (7.9)*	10.7 (9.5)*	9.6 (9.7)*	8.6 (8.6)*	8.3 (8.8)*	9.4 (10.0)*
DEB0[4]		−0.11 (−6.0)*			−0.07 (−4.2)*	−0.16 (−3.7)*	
DEB02[5]			0.000 (0.31)			0.001 (2.3)*	0.001 (2.1)*
DEBI[6]	−0.14 (−7.0)*		−0.16 (−3.1)*	−0.08 (−4.3)*			−0.15 (−3.9)*
T[7]	73	86	73	73	86	86	73
Adj.R2[8]	0.740	0.744	0.737	0.789	0.785	0.793	0.798
SBIC[9]	3.209	3.225	3.266	2.813	2.861	2.861	2.817

° Total expenditures and total tax revenues are expressed in percentage of GDP (5-year averages; 60–64, 65–69, 70–74, 75–79, 80–84, 85–89, 90–94, 95–99). t-ratios between brackets (based on White's heteroskedastic-consistent standard errors; * significant at 5 per cent.

[1] Per capita income lagged one 5-year period (in logs, see notes in Table 5.4) Trade openness lagged one 5-year period (in logs, see notes in Table 5.4).
[2] Dependency lagged one 5-year period (in logs, see notes in Table 5.4).
[3] Trade openness lagged one 5-year period (in logs, see notes in Table 5.4).
[4] Debt stock at the beginning of the 5-year period in percentage of GDP.
[5] The square of [4].
[6] Debt stock lagged one period. 5-year averages of the debt to GDP ratio (in per cent).
[7] Sample size.
[8] Adjusted R^2.
[9] Schwarz-Bayes Information Criterion.

levels of primary expenditures in the medium to long term (given income, dependency and openness). Regression (b) suggests that the 'reaction' of primary expenditures to debt levels could be quicker. However, the Schwartz-Bayes Information Criterion (SBIC) indicates that this regression does not represent a clear improvement with respect to regression (a). The third column seems to suggest that the relationship is not quadratic. The best regression for primary expenditures would include income, dependency, openness and the stock of debt, all lagged one 5-year period (column (a)). The coefficient for the stock of debt points to an average fall in primary expenditures of 0.15 percentage points of GDP for every additional increase of 1 percentage point of GDP in the stock of debt.

The results for taxes are presented in columns (d) to (g) of Table 5.6. Regression (d) would suggest that, although taxes respond to debt in a destabilizing way, they do not fall with debt more than primary expenditures. Taxes would fall by 0.08 percentage points of GDP, which is almost half the change in primary expenditures. As a result, the primary surplus increases with debt. Therefore fiscal consolidation seems to lead to a reduction of the size of the public sector (compared to the sample average), as measured by primary expenditures and taxes without increasing primary surpluses. It is worth noting that this conclusion also holds if we consider the stock of debt at the beginning of the period instead of its first lag (see columns (b) and (e) in Table 5.6).

However, on the basis of the explicative power and also, practically, the SBIC, it would seem that the regression for taxes could include the square of the stock of debt at the beginning of the period, as well as the debt of the period before. The former variable enters with a positive sign, suggesting that the relationship between debt and taxes in the short to medium term is positive and non-linear. This would be in line with the non-linear fiscal rule estimated by Bohn (1998), so that the increase in the primary surplus depends positively on the level of the debt at the beginning of the period. In the same line, by using probit models, von Hagen *et al.* (2001, p. 14) conclude that large debt–GDP ratios raise the likelihood of fiscal consolidations beginning.

Comparing regression (g) and (a) the overall response of fiscal policy to debt seems to go in a stabilizing direction also in this case. For very high levels of debt (above 75 per cent of GDP) the response of taxes to debt is stabilizing. The response of taxes is destabilizing for lower levels of debt, but the overall response of fiscal policy (taking into account the change in primary expenditures) is stabilizing.

Testing these results against a sample selection is not an easy task since the period of time for which debt stocks are available in AMECO is relatively short (basically 1980–99 for lagged models) and only for EU countries, the US and Japan. However, just to provide some rough indication about the robustness of the results above, the econometric exercises in Table 5.6 have been replicated for a sample only including the EU countries over 1990–9. In particular, in the case of primary expenditures, lower (relative) government sizes are associated with relatively high levels of debt in the previous period. The coefficient of lagged debt is, in this case, significant at 5 per cent and equal to −0.12, which is statistically comparable to −0.14 in Table 5.6. In the case of taxes, the estimates are also comparable to those in Table 5.6, but their statistical significance is lower.

These results should be taken with much care, since the degree of collinearity between dependency and the intercept is very high in the 1990s.

A very low degree of variability of dependency within the EU leads to an insignificant coefficient of the latter variable, although it exhibits the right sign and size.

5.5   Conclusion

This chapter has presented empirical evidence about the factors explaining across-country differences in the size of governments. There is a strong and positive association of total and primary expenditures in percentage of GDP with income, demographic dependency and trade openness. A similar relationship has been obtained for government size as measured by the share of total tax revenues in GDP. All in all, across-country differentials in the size of governments are related to differences in living standards, dependency and openness.

It has been shown that the size of the public sector is also strongly related to differences in debt levels. Contemporaneous debt is related to differences in the composition of expenditures. Given two identical countries in terms of income, dependency and openness, the country with the highest debt level will tend to have a lower share of primary expenditures in GDP. In addition, high debt levels in the past are associated with lower primary expenditures in the medium to long run. A similar relationship is found for taxes. Moreover, this chapter has presented evidence that the response of taxes to lagged debt levels is smaller in absolute value than that of expenditures. Therefore, it could be concluded that, in the long run, governments respond to high debt levels by reducing their sizes, as measured by primary expenditures and taxes. The overall fiscal policy reaction is debt-stabilizing. Primary surpluses increase, so that the reduction in government size is not financed through an increase in primary deficits.

Notes

1. I am grateful to Paul de Boer, Anne Brunila, Marco Buti, Harry Huizinga and J. von Hagen Jacques Mélitz for helpful comments and suggestions on an earlier version of this work, but all errors and omissions remain my own responsibility. The views expressed in this chapter are mine and should not be attributed to the European Commission.
2. For instance, Persson and Tabellini (1999 and 2000) and Persson (2001) have considered the interplay with political factors.
3. Therefore, these size indicators not only include primary current expenditures, but also interest payments and public investment.
4. We use a representative sample of 18 OECD countries: the EU member states, excluding Luxembourg, Norway, the US, Canada and Japan.
5. Chapter 4 by Francesco Mongelli and Olivier de Bandt, in the present volume, presents an exhaustive analysis on this issue.
6. Tax churning refers to the phenomenon according to which the same households both receive government payments and pay taxes, so that the tax-transfer system

does not make any significant redistribution. The amount of churning indicates to what extent tax and transfers can be restructured without affecting redistribution or the actual level of solidarity and social protection (see OECD, 1998).

7. It is worth noting that, during the 1970s and the 1990s, in a number of countries, especially in the EU, taxes increased less than total expenditures (compare Tables 5.1 and 5.2), which resulted in persistent deficits and mounting debt levels.

8. The figures for the sample including only EU countries are 30 per cent for 1960–4 and 17 per cent for 1995–9.

9. This a simple regression pooling the observations of the 18 countries (the 15 EU member states, excluding Luxembourg, the US Japan, Canada and Norway) over the 8 sub-periods in which the period 1960–99 has been split (1960–4, 1965–9, 1970–4, 1975–9, 1980–4, 1985–9, 1990–4 and 1994–9).

10. Adjustment power in the linear relationship is 33 per cent.

11. For instance, by using a more limited but comparable sample, Martinez-Mongay (2000) obtains quite robust and positive correlation between dependency indicators and social transfers, expenditures (current and total) and tax burdens.

12. This is the general rule, which would apply to a large sample of countries. However, in the case of developed countries with advanced social programmes in place, Rodrick (1998) has shown that it is spending on social security and welfare that is strongly correlated with exposure to external risk.

13. Although dispersion is lower, no convergence process is apparent either in the EU. The variation coefficient decreased from 49 per cent and 46 per cent between 1960 and 1999.

14. Note that, for instance, a dummy for non-democratic regimes would be highly correlated with low income in Greece, Portugal and Spain during the 1960s and part of the 1970s.

15. In any case, it is worth noting that the regression including contemporaneous values of dependency and openness and the income level at the beginning of the corresponding 5-year period is almost identical to the first column of Table 5.4.

16. See Martinez-Mongay and Fernandez-Bayón (2001) for recent empirical evidence.

17. Rodrick (1998) also finds a low significance (only at 10 per cent) for the contemporaneous stock of debt.

18. This indicates that public debt crowds out primary spending. As suggested by Persson and Tabellini (1990), running large deficits today might force future governments to cut spending, thus preventing them from running high levels of primary spending on things that the current government might not like. Crude data for some EU countries in the 1990s suggest that the adjustment could have fallen on public investment. Although of an evident interest, a formal testing of this possibility is out of the scope of this chapter.

19. With respect to the sample average, of course.

6
Budgetary Institutions for Sustainable Public Finances[1]

Jürgen von Hagen, Andrew Hughes Hallett and Rolf Strauch

6.1 Introduction

A growing body of empirical and theoretical literature suggests that the institutions governing the budget process are important determinants of a country's fiscal performance (von Hagen 1992; von Hagen and Harden, 1994a; see the contributions in Poterba and von Hagen, 1999; Strauch and von Hagen, 1999; also Buti and Sapir, 1998). Budgeting institutions encompass the formal and informal rules governing the drafting of the budget law, its passage through the legislature, and its implementation. These rules distribute strategic influence among the participants in the budget process and regulate the flow of information. In doing so, they have important effects of the outcomes of budgeting processes.

6.2 Budgeting institutions for sustainable public finances

The starting point of the institutional approach to public budgeting is to recognize the externality resulting from the fact that government spending is commonly targeted at specific groups in society while being financed from a general tax fund to which all tax-payers contribute. The resulting incongruence between those who pay for and those who benefit from individual public policies implies that individuals bidding for the funding of such policies tend to recognize their full benefit but only a part of their social cost, as the costs are spread out more widely over the entire society. In such situations, common to all modern democracies, policy-makers engage in excessive spending, since the constituencies they represent and who benefit from the public policy programmes they bid for do not bear the full costs of these programmes. Putting the argument into a dynamic context, one can show that the externality problem results in excessive deficits and debts (Velasco, 1999).[2]

6.2.1 Fragmentation of the budget process

In the American form of the argument, politicians representing individual electoral districts use the federal budget process to direct money taken out of the national general tax fund to public policy projects benefiting their electoral districts. The difference between the spatial incidence of the costs and benefits of these projects creates a tendency to overestimate the net marginal benefit from spending. As a result, federal government spending grows too large. Applying this paradigm to a European political context, where politicians often represent countrywide groups in society rather than regions or electoral districts, requires a translation of the geographical dimension into one of different constituencies in society. Still, politicians representing different groups in society spend money taken out of a general tax fund on programmes aimed at different groups in society.[3]

The core of the argument, then, is that public budgeting involves a coordination failure among the relevant decision-makers. The argument suggests that the tendency to spend more and to run large deficits increases with the number of representatives of individual spending interests that are allowed to make autonomous spending decisions, i.e., the more *fragmented* the budget process is. Since the most important representatives of individual spending interests in European governments are the individual spending ministers, an implication of this proposition is that government spending and deficits grow with the number of spending departments and ministers in a country's government. Kontopoulos and Perotti (1999) confirm this proposition empirically for OECD countries.

6.2.2 Institutional solutions: delegation and contracts

Interpreting the problem of excessive spending and deficits as a coordination failure leads one to look at institutional rules improving the coordination of individual actions for solutions. Political economy emphasizes the importance of decision-making rules that promote a comprehensive view of the externality problem, i.e., one that takes the full benefits and costs of all public policy projects into account. The solution to fragmentation of the budget process is thus *centralization* of the budget process, the creation of institutions forcing the participants in the budget process to recognize the true marginal costs and benefits of the projects financed from the general tax fund, and thus to internalize the budgeting externality. There are two basic institutional approaches to achieve centralization (Hallerberg and von Hagen, 1998): the *delegation approach* and the *contract approach*. Both can be found among the budget processes in Europe (von Hagen, 1992). The former emphasizes hierarchical relationships, the latter horizontal relationships among the relevant decision-makers. Under the delegation approach, the budget process vests one decision-maker with significant strategic powers over the other participants. This is usually the finance minister who is thought to be less bound by special interests than ministers heading spending departments. Internalizing the relevant externalities, the finance minister will promote more efficient decisions.

The delegation approach builds on the following key characteristics:

- A finance minister vested with strong agenda-setting power relative to the remaining members of the executive; typically, this involves the right to make binding proposals for the broad budgetary categories and superior information.
- A finance minister vested with strong monitoring capacity in the implementation of the budget and the power to correct deviations from the budget plan, e.g., through cash limits and the requirement of disbursement approvals from the finance department.
- A strong position of the executive relative to the legislature in the parliamentary phase of the budget process; this involves strict limitations on the scope of parliamentary amendments to the executive's budget proposal and a limited role of the upper house of parliament in the process where applicable.

Under a contract approach, the participants start the budget process by negotiating and agreeing on a set of key budgetary parameters, usually spending targets for the individual spending departments. Here, it is the process of negotiation that makes the participants realize the externalities created by the general tax fund.[4] The following features of the process characterize the contract approach:

- A strong emphasis on budgetary targets negotiated among all members of the executive at the beginning of the annual budget cycle. These targets are regarded as binding for all spending departments often and backed up by a multi-annual fiscal programme as part of the coalition contract among the ruling parties.
- A finance minister vested with strong monitoring capacities in the implementation of the budget; yet few agenda-setting powers.
- A weak position of the executive relative to the parliament exemplified by weak or no limits on parliamentary amendments to the budget proposal, and strong monitoring capacities of parliamentary committees overseeing the activities of individual departments of the executive.

To evaluate the importance of centralization of the budget process for budget deficits and debts, von Hagen and Harden (1994b, 1996), following von Hagen (1992), construct an *index of centralization* capturing the most important features of the budget process in European governments. A high value on the index, which ranges from zero to 16, indicates the prevalence of strong elements of centralization in a country's budget process.

Figure 6.1 shows this index together with the average deficit and debt ratios of the EU countries over the 1980s and early 1990s. The upper chart clearly shows that countries with a low degree of centralization have larger deficits than countries with a high degree of centralization. The lower chart shows that the same conclusion can be reached regarding the level of public debt. Strengthening institutions that reduce fragmentation of budget decisions and promote a comprehensive view of the costs and benefits of government activities reduces the government deficit.[5]

More detailed empirical studies for the EU member states (Hallerberg and von Hagen, 1999), for Latin American countries (Stein *et al.*, 1999), for Asian countries (Lao-Araya, 1997), and for state governments in the US (Strauch, 1998) all confirm that centralization of the budget process reduces the deficit bias of fiscal policy. As this literature shows, this result is true in very different cultural and political settings. In addition, Hallerberg and von Hagen (1999) and von Hagen and Harden (1994b) show that countries ranking high on the index of centralization conducted more effective counter-cyclical stabilization

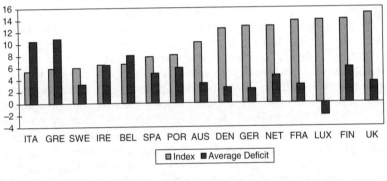

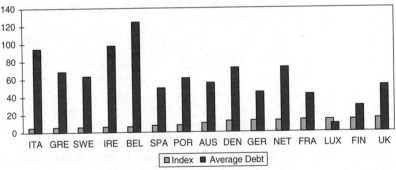

Figure 6.1 Budget processes, deficits and debt

Note: Deficit and debt averages are based on the period 1981–95.

Sources: OECD *Economic Outlook* (1997), European Commission (1996) and von Hagen and Harden (1996).

policies. Thus, the fear that less deficit-prone budget processes become overly rigid and prevent effective stabilization is not empirically warranted.

This body of research, then, provides important background to the provision of the Maastricht Treaty (Article 3 of the Protocol on the EDP) that the governments of the member states ought to implement institutions that enable them to fulfil their obligation to maintain sustainable public finances.

6.3 Institutional reform and institutional choice

The potential of institutions to improve sustainability raises the question, which is the appropriate approach to solving the externality problem of the budget process for a given country? Hallerberg and von Hagen (1998, 1999) show that the two approaches are suited for different types of governments. Delegation is the proper approach for single-party governments, while contracting is better suited for multi-party coalition governments. In a nutshell, it is difficult for a coalition government to work under a strong finance minister, since the latter necessarily comes from one of the coalition parties. Vesting him with special authorities raises concerns among the other parties about a fair treatment of their spending interests in the budget process. At the same time, a commitment to fiscal targets is harder to keep for a single-party government, since there is no effective threat against reneging on the targets. In contrast, the threat to break up the coalition is a very effective one for enforcing negotiated budget targets in multi-party governments. Enforcement of the budget targets under the delegation approach ultimately relies on the ability of the head of the executive to remove incalcitrant spending ministers from office. This power may exist in single-party governments, where the hierarchy in cabinet conforms to the hierarchy of party power structures. But it does not usually exist in coalition governments, where the individual parties in the coalition each have the right to choose the individuals filling the positions assigned to them in the coalition agreement.

The important factor in this context is the national electoral system. Since electoral systems of proportional representation are most likely to produce coalition governments, the contract approach is the more adequate one for states with such systems. In contrast, plurality electoral systems typically produce one-party governments, which makes the delegation approach more adequate for states with such systems. Among the EU states, the suggested pattern of institutional choice is strongly confirmed. As shown in Table 6.1, states with proportional representation (PR) systems chose a contract approach to the budget process to achieve a higher degree of centralization, while states with plurality systems chose a delegation approach as a solution.[6]

Obviously, if the same institutional model does not fit all countries, institutional choice is a difficult and important matter, in which a country's political, economic, and cultural characteristics all come to play. The implication, however, is not to put aside the importance of institutional reforms as an element

Table 6.1 Electoral systems and institutional choice

Electoral system	Institutional choice		
Proportional representation (PR)	Contract	Delegation	Fragmentation
A, B, DK, SF, IRL, L, NL, P, E, S	A, B, DK, SF, IRL, L, NL, P, S*, E*		I, E*, S*
Countries with plurality systems or with PR and restrictive minimum vote requirements			
D, F, GRE, UK		D, F, UK	GRE

*Sweden and Spain introduced measures moving towards a contract model in the 1990s.
Source: von Hagen (1997).

of regaining sustainability of public finances. Instead, it is important to recognize that institutional reform must take into account the peculiarities of the national political systems.

6.3.1 Developments of national budget processes in the 1990s

The 1990s saw important changes in the budget processes of several EU countries, though not all of them in the proper direction to strengthen fiscal discipline. Already in the 1980s Irish governments were taking steps to improve its budget process (De Haan *et al*, 1999; von Hagen, 1998). One element in this was the introduction of specific medium-term fiscal targets. The coalition agreement of December 1994 made explicit reference to these targets and the commitment of the new government to lead Ireland into the monetary union. Starting in 1996, the Irish government introduced explicit multi-annual budgeting, whereby the consequences of budgeting decisions for the next two years have to be taken into account.

The budget process now starts with an annual 'Estimates Circular' that calls upon the spending departments to make expenditure demands complying with these targets. The role of the finance minister then is to negotiate adjustments of the individual demands to assure consistency with the overall targets. Starting in 1996, the implementation phase of the budget was improved by introducing cash-limited programmes: i.e., payments under entitlement programmes are now conditional upon the availability of sufficient funds.

Sweden also undertook drastic measures to improve its budget process in the early 1990s. The reform came as part of broader effort to overhaul the Swedish system of government. As in Ireland, the move was towards centralization under a contract approach (Molander, 1999). The reform of the budget process was cast in a budget and financial management act, giving it some visibility. The annual budget cycle was set on a calendar basis and now starts with a medium-term forecast of the economy and government revenues.

An important element of the new process is a two-day conference of all members of the executive early in the budget process, during which key parameters of the next year's budget are fixed. This includes an expenditure ceiling and the outline of the budget. The results of this conference are published in the 'Economic Spring Bill' giving them stronger commitment power. The reform abolished open-ended appropriations and replaced them with 'flexible' appropriations. Flexible appropriations allow spending departments to carry unused funds over to the following year, and to borrow from next year's appropriations. The parliamentary phase of the Swedish budget process now starts with a vote on the expenditure ceiling and other basic parameters of the budget, which locks these in for the rest of the parliamentary debate. Amendments to the budget proposal at later stages must be offsetting in the sense that a proposal for increasing public spending on a specific programme must include a proposal for cutting expenditures elsewhere.

The implementation phase of the budget was strengthened by improving the finance ministry's monitoring abilities of the flow of funds during the year. All appropriations are monitored on a monthly basis, so that over-runs can be detected in time.

Austria changed its budget process significantly in 1996 in order to improve the chances of achieving the consolidation necessary for meeting the fiscal criteria of the Maastricht Treaty. The new budget process relates to two years, giving the government the opportunity to plan consolidation measures with a longer time horizon. The reform also gave aggregate budgetary targets greater importance for guiding the decisions during the budget process. These targets are negotiated among the members of the cabinet at the beginning of the budget process.

Belgium is another case of improving the budget process under a contract approach and in the context of a broader reform of the national government. Here, important steps were taken while turning Belgium into a federal state (Stienlet, 1999; see also Hallerberg, 2000, and De Haan *et al.*, 1999). Regarding the budget process, a key element in this was the strengthening of the High Council of Finances (HCF).

The HCF had existed since 1936, but traditionally it had played a minor role only as an advisory body to the ministry of finance. Currently, the HCF has 30 members including representatives of the regions, the central government, the central bank, and outside experts. Most important in our context is the HCF's section on fiscal policy, which has 10 members, one from the ministry of finance, six from the regions and three top officials from the central bank. This section can recommend at its own initiative to the Minister of Finance that the borrowing of any level of government ought to be reduced. The section also sets fiscal targets for each level of government.

In June 1992, the Belgian parliament gave the HCF the role of monitoring the compliance of all parts of government with Belgium's Convergence

Programme. The HCF subsequently decided how much each level of government had to contribute to the desired reduction in the debt-to-GDP ratio and the deficit. When the regions failed to comply with their deficit targets in the incipient recession of 1992, the HCF was asked to write a report every March on all levels of government stating whether or not they had reached their fiscal targets in the previous year. If not, the report was expected to cause the offender to revise the current budget in a way that reduced his deficit in the current year. The HCF also required all levels of government to use the same accounting rules.

Thus, the HCF is an interesting example for institutional innovation. The council became the enforcing agent of a fiscal contract that involved not only the national government but the regional governments and the governments of the communities as well. The enforcement worked, because no party to the contract wanted to be accused of being responsible for the country's exclusion from the first wave of entry into the monetary union.

Important reforms of the budget process also occurred in Italy, and, again, they came in the context of reforming fiscal relations between the national and sub-national governments. Italian public finances had been plagued with a notorious lack of fiscal discipline at the local and regional level since the late 1970s (Bordignon, 2000). Following the reforms of local government in Italy during the 1970s, local governments were not allowed to borrow in their own responsibility, but had every incentive to waste public monies. Local governments regularly overspent their budgets and then turned to the national government demanding additional funds. Faced with the threat of a breakdown of local public services, such as health and education, the national government saw no alternative to satisfying these demands. Once the practice had been established, large budget deficits at the local level covered ex post by the national government became the norm.

Starting in 1992, Italian local public finances underwent a far-ranging reform (Bordignon, 2000). The main tenet of the reforms was to re-establish fiscal responsibility at the local level. For this purpose, local governments were assigned own tax revenues, reducing the high degree of vertical imbalance of the public finance system. The central government's responsibility in health services was reduced to financing nationally uniform standards, while the regions were made responsible for covering the cost of any services beyond that standard. In 1995, conditional and unconditional grants from the national government to regions were largely abolished; regions obtained a larger share of tax collections in return. A system of horizontal redistribution of tax revenues among local governments was introduced to reduce inequalities among the regions. Meanwhile, the national government reduced the level of managerial intervention at the local level, thus strengthening the responsibility and accountability of local administrations. Local election procedures were changed, too, to increase the accountability of local politicians to their constituencies.

Adding to the problems of weak fiscal discipline at the local level, the Italian budget process was also weak at the national level (von Hagen, 1992). Significantly, the budget process involved three different ministries, and the executive's position as an agenda setter to the legislature was very weak. An important change in this context occurred, when Italy changed its electoral law abolishing a pure system of proportional representation. Since the 1994 elections, three-quarters of the seats in the Senate and one-quarter of the seats in the Chamber of Deputies are determined according to plurality votes. The intended shift towards a more bipolar party system, however, occurred only in the 1996 elections. Under the Prodi government, new legislation was passed that moved the budget process in the direction of centralization under the delegation approach. The former budget ministry was incorporated in the Treasury, which now has a leading role in the budget process. The Treasury was also given the authority to block expenditures, thus reducing the power of the spending ministries during the implementation phase of the budget. Finally, the budget was reorganized, recognizing 'functional targets' and 'base units' (Hallerberg, 2000; De Haan *et al.*, 1999). The streamlined budget makes it harder for committees and legislators to introduce additional spending into the executive budget proposal.

In Spain, reforms were introduced during the 1990s that moved the budget process towards the contract approach of centralization. The convergence criteria were written into coalition agreements, giving them additional political commitment power. Targets for the annual budget deficit are derived from macroeconomic forecasts and proposed by the finance minister to the cabinet, which takes a decision on these targets. The finance minister's role in the budget preparation became more important, as this minister checks the consistency of the spending ministries' bids with the numerical spending targets set by the cabinet. Any remaining conflicts are solved in cabinet negotiations.

While the five cases considered so far all moved into the direction of improving the budget process, the German government under Chancellor Kohl and finance minister Waigel headed in the opposite direction. The years following German unification saw a gradual worsening of the German budget process, as the government failed to develop a consistent strategy for dealing with the economic problems of unification.[7]

German budgetary institutions were traditionally among the strongest in the EU (von Hagen, 1992). Important aspects of this were the comprehensiveness of the budget law, the strong position of the finance minister relative to other members of the cabinet, and the strict adherence to the budget law in the implementation. A significant aspect of German unification is that the federal government sought and found ways to undermine and circumvent the traditional institutions. This is indicated, first, by the mushrooming of off-budget funds and entities immediately after unification. Thus, while the federal government's debt rose by a mere 3 per cent of GDP from 1989 to 1997, the combined debt of off-budget entities amounted to 12 per cent of GDP in 1997, half the size of federal government debt. These funds were not subject to the usual scrutiny of legislative control. A second indication is the increased use of tax expenditures to subsidize the East German economy. While they lead to reduced revenues, these tax expenditures do not appear as expenses in the budget law. A third indication is the loss of influence of the Finance Ministry over the financial decisions in the unification process. A task force in the Chancellor's office took most important decisions concerning the reconstruction of the East German Länder, with little or no influence of the Finance Ministry. Another indication is the emergence of a variety of informal decision-making forums such as 'round tables' in which representatives of the political parties, social groups and the Chancellor's office made agreements with financial implications that were later presented as unchangeable. A final indication is the increased use of supplementary budgets after 1990. German governments resorted to supplementary budgets only four times between 1952 and 1980; but the Kohl government presented seven supplementary budgets between 1990 and 1997.

Thus, Germany's budget process deteriorated significantly in the wake of unification, becoming much more fragmented than before. Clearly, this reflects the political weakness of a government that had faced few chances for re-election in 1989, and seized unification as an opportunity to stay in power (von Hagen and Strauch, 1999). After 1990, the weakness of the budgetary process reflects the lack of political will to deal with the financial consequences of unification in a consistent matter. Germany's difficulties in meeting the fiscal criteria of the Maastricht process are thus explained, in part at least, by the weakening of her budgetary institutions.

In conclusion, we have four cases of significant improvement of the budget process and one case of deterioration during the 1990s. Ireland, Belgium, Sweden, and Italy all used the opportunity of the Maastricht process to implement better institutions at the national level. In Germany, the ailing of the Kohl government, the difficulties created by the way this government had handled German unification, and, perhaps also, the lack of enthusiasm for monetary union in the German public – which would have made maintaining a higher degree of fiscal discipline for the sake of the Maastricht criteria politically easier – caused a considerable slippage in the quality of its budget process. Judging from earlier experience, one should expect that the consolidations achieved by the first group will be more persistent than that achieved by Germany in the late 1990s.

6.3.2 The Excessive Deficit Procedure, Convergence Programmes, and the Stability and Growth Pact

In the 1990s, the Excessive Deficit Procedure (EDP) together with the Convergence Programmes (CPs) in preparation for EMU constituted an important institutional change of the budget process for all EU member states. The emphasis on multi-annual targets and the regular review procedure required by the Treaty bear resemblance to a budget process under the contract approach. The main difference with a conventional contract-based budget process is that the EDP relies on the European Council and the Commission to enforce the fiscal targets. Thus, enforcement is the role of an agent external to domestic politics. Before the start of EMU, the ultimate penalty for violating the fiscal targets was the denial of membership in the monetary union. After the start of Stage III of EMU, the EDP as strengthened by the Stability and Growth Pact (SGP) continues this *external enforcement* version of the contract approach, with financial fines as the ultimate penalty for violating the targets.

A proper working of these procedures in the 1990s would, of course, have implied a gradual reduction of the debt ratios of the EU countries. In fact, the opposite happened: the EU's average debt ratio was 60 per cent in 1992; it climbed to 73 per cent in 1996. Importantly, this increase was entirely driven by the debt expansions in five states: Germany (44 per cent to 61 per cent), France (40 per cent to 56 per cent), Spain (48 per cent to 70 per cent), Italy (109 per cent to 124 per cent), and the UK (42 per cent to 55 per cent). In contrast, the debt ratios of the other states were stabilized or fell after 1992.[8] The institutional change introduced with the CPs and the EDP apparently worked very effectively for some states, but failed for others.

Above, we argued that the contract approach is not adequate for countries with single-party governments or coalition governments where, as in Germany, there is a large and a small partner and the latter has no feasible political option for an alternative coalition partner. As the EDP-cum-CPs resembles the contract approach, it is appropriate to ask whether the predictions made in Table 6.1 concerning the institutional choice between the delegation and the contract approach tell us something about the successes and failures of these attempts to promote fiscal discipline at the EU level.

Table 6.2 provides an answer. In this table, we report the weighted average increase in the debt-to-GDP ratios for the delegation states, the contract states, and the states with fragmented budget processes identified in Table 6.1. As indicated in Table 6.2, both the delegation states and the states with fragmented budget processes saw large increases in their debt ratios between 1992 and 1996; 15 per cent in the case of the delegation states, 16.5 per cent in the case of states with fragmented budget processes. In contrast, the contract states saw an average increase in their debt ratios of only 2.9 per cent in the same time period. Between 1996 and 1999, the delegation states reduced their debt ratios by an average of 0.2 per cent, the states with low centralization by an average of 7.1 per cent, while the contract states achieved an average reduction of 8 per cent. Clearly, the improvement in fiscal discipline was much greater among the states for which the contract approach is the adequate one. This is prima facie evidence for the proposition that the EDP combined with the CP worked better in states where the budget process

Table 6.2   Budgeting institutions and government debt in the 1990s: change in debt ratio (per cent)

	All EU countries	Delegation states	Contract states	Others
1992–6	13.2	15.0	2.9	16.5
1996–9	−3.5	−0.2	−8.0*	−7.1
	All EU countries	Large states	Small states	Others
1992–6	13.2	15.5	4.0	3.8
1996–9	−3.5	−2.0	−10.2	−9.3

Note: *We treat Sweden and Spain as contract states after 1996.

operates under a contract approach. For Stage III of EMU, this suggests that the Stability Programmes and the SGP will work more effectively in states where the domestic budget process is characterized by a significant degree of centralization under the contract approach. In contrast, the evidence suggests that the combination of Stability Programmes and the SGP will be less effective in assuring fiscal discipline in delegation states or states with rather fragmented budget processes.

An institutional arrangement relying on enforcement by an external agent such as the European Commission presupposes that the external political agent enforcing the fiscal targets carries large weight in the internal political process. A country's size is probably a first indicator of the importance of an external enforcement body: small countries typically pay more attention to international organizations than large countries do; and the more they do so, the more they receive transfers from these organizations (Katzenstein, 1984). This would suggest that the EDP combined with CPs worked more effectively in the small states of the EU than in the large states. To assess this proposition, Table 6.2 reports the changes in the debt-to-GDP ratios for states whose GDP in 1996 was at least 8 per cent of EU GDP (large states), and those whose GDP was less than 2 per cent of EU GDP (small states). The table shows that the average debt ratio of the small states increased much less than that of the large states in the period from 1992 to 1996. Between 1996 and 1999, the small states achieved a much larger reduction in their debt ratios than the large states. States whose GDP is between 2 and 8 per cent of EU GDP behaved much like small states during this period. In sum, the evidence indicates that the fiscal framework of Stage III of EMU will work more effectively in the small European states than in the large states. Note, however, that there is some overlap in the groups of delegation states and large states, while all small states except Greece are contract states. Thus, it is impossible to separate the two arguments clearly.

For further insights into the role of the EDP and the CPs in achieving the Maastricht criteria, we conducted a survey among leading economics journalists in the eleven states of the monetary union. All journalists except those from Germany and Luxembourg responded that the Maastricht criteria were important (Finland) or very important (all others) for economic policy during the 1990s. All journalists except those from Luxembourg and Germany thought that they had an impact of economic policy decisions during this period. Journalists from Belgium, the Netherlands, Italy, Spain and Portugal thought that the fiscal consolidations of the 1990s would not have happened without these criteria. Journalists from Austria, Finland, and Ireland thought that the consolidations of the 1990s would 'perhaps' have happened without these criteria. In contrast, journalists from France and Luxembourg responded that the fiscal consolidations of the 1990s would 'very likely' have happened even without the Maastricht criteria. Finally, journalists from France, Italy, Portugal, and Austria thought that the importance of the criteria for domestic policies derived from the external political pressures they put on the domestic governments. In contrast, journalists from the Netherlands and Finland saw the effectiveness of these criteria resulting from the role of the targets as guidelines for domestic economic policy. That is, they were helpful by providing a medium-term framework for fiscal policy. Journalists from Belgium, Ireland, Spain, and Luxembourg thought that the importance of the criteria came from both their role as guidelines of domestic economic policies and from creating external political pressures.

By pointing to the role of targets guiding decisions over time and the enforcement of these targets by an external agent, these answers confirm that the EDP and the CPs were regarded as a special version of the contract approach to centralizing the budget process. The answers also confirm that this approach was perceived as less effective in large countries and in delegation states (Germany, France).

6.3.3 Internal stability pacts

An important question arising in this context is, to what extent national governments can effectively commit their countries to compliance with the obligations of the EDP and the SGP. In countries where the national government controls all or most of the public finances, the answer to this question depends largely on its budget process. But in countries where sub-national governments control a large part of the public finances, the answer is more difficult. Several countries have tried to implement 'Internal Stability Pacts' between the central and sub-national governments to solve this problem. Apart from the three countries discussed in more detail below, these include Germany and Italy. So far, an agreement on this issue has not been reached between the federal and the state governments in Germany. In Italy, a rule has been introduced making sub-national governments responsible for a part of the central government deficit (Bordignon, 2000), but the effectiveness of this rule has not been tested yet.

Austria

In light of the need to achieve a considerable improvement of the budget balance in a short period of time, the Austrian government tried early on to coordinate fiscal policy with other levels of governments in the federal system. A first agreement was reached on 5 May 1995. The 'Übereinkommen des Bundes, der Länder und der Gemeinden zur Vermeidung öffentlicher Defizite' did not pin down specific deficit levels for the different layers of government, but it pointed out the willingness to consolidate the budget balance, primarily through expenditure reductions. Moreover, a 'Maastricht working group' was established, which should monitor the fiscal performance, clarify the statistical concept of the 'Maastricht deficit' for the Austrian context and make proposals for organizational changes and the improvement of the information system (CP May 1996; Hüttner, 1999).

A further step was achieved during the negotiations for the federal transfer system (*Finanzausgleichsverhandlungen*) when governments agreed on the maximum deficit which could be incurred by each level of government in 1997. Under this arrangement, the federal government was 'accrued' a deficit of 2.7 per cent of GDP and the lower levels of 0.3 per cent of GDP. This distribution reflected the actual situation of public finances at the time. Due to the definition of the Maastricht deficit, sub-national levels of government actually often had a considerable surplus (CP, May 1996; Hüttner, 1996).[9]

Subsequently, this arrangement was replaced by the Austrian Stability Pact ('Vereinbarung zwischen dem Bund, den Ländern und den Gemeinden betreffend die Konsolidierung der Haushaltsführung von Bund, Ländern und Gemeinden'), approved by the parliament in December 1998. The Stability Pact, first, distributed the deficit permissible to lower levels of government among the different entities. The distribution at the Länder level is largely guided by the share of the population living in the Land. In addition, it established different coordination committees: first, a national coordination committee comprising representatives of the federal government, the Länder governments and representations of municipalities; and second, eight coordination committees at the Länder level. The national committee has the task to support or carry forward the coordination of fiscal policy, specifically regarding the renegotiation of deficit shares, establishing guidelines for the medium-term orientation of public finances, monitoring of public finances and elaboration of information standards allowing the mutual surveillance of resource flows. The Länder coordination committees have the equivalent mission for the lower level of government. In addition, it specified the procedure if an excessive deficit should result in a sanction for the country. In principle, the contribution of the federal government and each Land to the sanction payments in the case of an excessive deficit, is proportional to their share of the excessive deficit itself; e.g. the federal government has to cover three-quarters of the sanction payments if it is responsible for three-quarters of the deficit above the 3 per cent limit. Local governments in one Land share collectively the responsibility for the deficit, and their contribution to sanction payments is deducted from their share of joint revenues (*Ertragsanteil*). Länder and local governments are allowed to assign part of their permissible deficit to other entities. No formal procedure has been established if an entity does not comply with its deficit limit and no sanctions according to the Maastricht Treaty are imposed. The deficit shares specified by the internal Stability Pact are in force until the system of intergovernmental transfers is renegotiated and changed which usually happens every four years.

Belgium

Given the task of fiscal adjustments, the federal government was considering a binding agreement with the regions on the fiscal performance from the very beginning of the Maastricht process (see CP June 1996). Actually, a first agreement of cooperation between the federal and regional levels of government was passed in July 1994. Since local government finances are subject to the decisions and restrictions imposed by higher levels of government, this level was not to be included in the accord. Subsequently, other intergovernmental treaties followed in July 1996, for the period 1996 to 1999, and November 1999, for the period 1999 to 2002 (see CP Dec. 1998 and Dec. 1999; Stienlet, 1994). The agreements established permissible deficit levels for Entity I, i.e. the federal government and the social security system, and Entity II, i.e. the regions and local governments.[10] The figures set forth therein are generally based on the recommendations of the High Council of Finance which was also in charge of monitoring and reporting on the convergence process.

The High Council of Finance has existed since 1936, but it was revived and strengthened in the context of the decentralization of the Belgian government system enacted in 1989. The Special Finance Act of 1989 set forth the devolution of public finances over the period 1989–99. Since the regions immediately had unrestricted fiscal authority, but the revenue base was devolved only gradually, there existed the fear that the public deficits could get out of control. Therefore, the High Council of Finance was modified so as to supervise and guide the transition process. Its composition and maintaining role in the context of the Maastricht convergence process are described in detail in Section 6.3.1.

The cooperation agreement between the central and regional governments does not include formal sanctioning procedures, and nor is the High Council endowed with direct sanctioning instruments when it detects a deviation from the permissible deficits. However, the Special Financing Act of 1989 authorizes the federal government to restrict the borrowing capacity of the regions for a period of up to two years, following the advice of the High Council of Finance and after the regions involved have been consulted. In its recommendation, the High Council should consider three macroeconomic criteria: the preservation of the Belgian economic and monetary union, the maintenance of external and internal monetary equilibrium, and the prevention of a structural deterioration of the country's public finances (Stienlet, 1994).[11] Until now, this mechanism has never been invoked.

Spain

Similar to the Belgian case, the Spanish government system underwent a process of significant decentralization in the 1990s.[12] Spanish regions are subject to general financing restraints defined in the law on regional financing or the general regulations applying to the public sector. The following are the most prominent restraints. First, short-term credit transactions of less than a year should only be used to cover transitory treasury requirements. Second, debt financing should only be used for investment expenditures, and the total annual amount of repayments and interests should not exceed one-quarter of the regional current revenue. Third, the central government has to authorize credit transactions or issuance of government debt. Fourth, regions should coordinate with each other and the central government their debt policy in the Fiscal and Financial Policy Council.[13] As a consequence of these regulations, the regions are obliged to submit an annual debt schedule to the government. Once agreed on by both parties, this entails automatic authorization by the central government of all the operations contained therein. However, the government adopted a less formal mechanism of restraining the indebtedness of sub-national governments.

As from 1992, following the release of the March 1992 CP for Spain, the so-called Budget Consolidation Scenarios were signed by the central government and each region, based on bilateral negotiations. These agreements specified the maximum deficit and debt permitted for each region. The Economics and Convergence Programmes (ECP) were revised in March 1995, following the revision of the CP in July 1994. They were again modified in 1998 with the approval of the first Stability Programme. The deficit and debt levels specified in the agreements are unknown to the public and no transparent sanctioning mechanism exists.

6.4 Conclusions

In this chapter, we have reviewed the importance of budgetary institutions for achieving and maintaining sustainable public finances. Several member states improved their institutional framework for public budgeting in the 1990s, moving to processes that provide better solutions to the coordination problem of budgeting. This should enable them to maintain a higher degree of fiscal discipline in the future. Germany, in contrast, experienced a worsening of her institutional framework.

The introduction of the Excessive Deficit Procedure and the Stability and Growth Pact represents an important institutional change for EMU. Both, however, follow a contract approach to centralizing the budget process. While this is the proper approach for most EMU member states, it is not the adequate one for Germany and France (and the UK and Greece). Furthermore, the enforcement power of the EDP together with the SGP will likely be weaker in the future, as the threat of missing EMU membership disappears. One can already observe that the deficit reductions achieved in 1999 were mainly due to the revival of economic growth rather than continued efforts to cut spending. In the absence of a strong external enforcement mechanism, it will be even more important to anchor the fiscal targets that countries present in their Stability Programmes in their national budgetary processes. At the same time, however, the possibility to enforce deficit targets in coalition agreements will be reduced in the future, as the goal of joining the monetary union was a shared commitment of all coalition partners and this goal has now been reached. Stated somewhat differently, the critical decisions regarding the existence of excessive deficits and the need to take corrective actions in individual member states are taken by ECOFIN. Now that the commitment to joining EMU is no longer relevant, it is not entirely clear to what extent finance ministers representing coalition governments in that body will be able to commit their coalition partners to delivering the necessary actions.

These considerations point to several conclusions. First, to ensure the continued effectiveness of the institutional apparatus created by the EDP and the SGP, steps could be taken to link the procedures under the EDP and the SGP more closely to the national budgetary procedures. One such step would be to set both processes on the same calendar, i.e., Stability Programmes should be prepared together with the national budgets. If governments present the Stability Programme to the EU at the same time that they present the budget draft to parliament, the debate at the European level could raise their agenda-setting power in the legislature and increase the likelihood of passing budgets consistent with the Stability Programmes. Improving the linkage between the national budget process and the Stability Programmes would also imply that the multi-annual commitments the governments make at the European level play a greater role in shaping decisions about the annual budget at the national level. This would increase the effectiveness of the Stability Programmes for ensuring sustainable public finances.

Second, the scope of the Stability Programmes should be broadened to include targets for government spending and revenues, as deficits have little commitment value in times of budget surpluses or balance. Where fiscal adjustments become necessary to reduce emerging deficits, the Stability Programmes should explain the quality of the adjustments chosen by the governments, and the Commission and the European Council should make the quality of the adjustments an explicit criterion of their evaluations. This could be combined with requiring countries to present multi-annual programmes for critical issues, such as retirement benefits. The European Commission could then take the opportunity to evaluate the quality of a country's long-term planning and forecasting framework and assess the consistency of current policies with long-term requirements. As a minimum, this would contribute to the public debate about the long-run exigencies of sustainable public finances. Of course, this would require making such assessments public. While one might object to this as too much interference of the Commission in the internal affairs of the member states, the Union has a right to consider the consistency of member states' fiscal policies with long-run sustainability, if it takes the latter seriously.

Third, there is still ample scope for improving the national budget processes of the EMU member states, particularly with regard to improving their ability to cope with unforeseen spending and revenue developments. While the institutional framework at the EU level has so far focused on the governments' intentions to reduce deficits and keep them low, more attention could be paid in the future to rules and mechanisms for dealing with expenditure and revenue shocks.

The role internal stability pacts can play in this context is much harder to assess, as it depends very clearly on constitutional principles, which are special to each country. Where sub-national governments are financially dominated by and heavily dependent on the central government, such pacts may be easy to conclude; but ultimately, they may also be of small relevance, as the central government is the main player in public finances, anyway. Where sub-national governments are more independent, as in Germany, the key constitutional issue is the extent to which sub-national governments can be forced to bear the financial consequences of obligations from an agreement made between the central government and other states. In such a setting, an internal stability pact, if concluded at all, may turn out to be ineffective, leaving the central government with the obligation to take all actions necessary to meet the criteria of the SGP and the EDP. In view of the constitutional differences among the EU member states, it is hard to come to any general assessment in this regard.

Notes

1. This chapter was originally part of our report on 'Fiscal Consolidations in EMU', *European Commission Economic Paper*, 148, March 2001. The report was written while Rolf Strauch was working at the Deutsche Bundesbank. The opinion expressed are those of the authors and do not necessarily reflect views of those institutions to which they are affiliated.
2. Recently a complementary strand of literature has emerged which provides an alternative account for different public spending behaviour across countries based on the principal–agent relationships and incentives for collusion inherent in the electoral system (see Persson and Tabellini 2000, 2001 and the literature quoted therein).
3. Italy's experience with growing welfare payments is a prime example for this mechanism. In the past 30 years, Italian politicians used the disability pension system quite openly to buy voter support. See *New York Times*, 19 September, 1997.

4. See von Hagen and Harden (1996) for a formal discussion of the two approaches.
5. Statistical tests confirm this visual impression. The rank correlation between the degree of centralization of a country's budget process as measured by the index and its average deficit over the period considered is significant and negative ($\rho = -0.69$). Similarly, the rank correlation between the degree of centralization of the budget process and the debt ratio is significant and negative ($\rho = -0.60$). While these statistics are based on long-run averages, Hallerberg and von Hagen (1999) show that the index of centralization has a negative and significant coefficient in panel regressions explaining the annual deficits in the 15 EU member states over the 1980s and 1990s.
6. The odd case in this table is Germany. To understand this case, it is important to realize that Germany's PR system is augmented by a minimum vote requirement: parties winning less than 5 per cent of the votes do not obtain any seat in parliament. As a result of this, post-war German governments have typically been two-party coalitions, one large and one small party (the Liberal Democrats). In this situation, neither coalition partner could threaten effectively to break up the coalition, since neither one would easily find an alternative partner for a new coalition. The ineffectiveness of the threat implies that the contracting approach does not work, making Germany a delegation state instead.
7. See Strauch and von Hagen (1999) and Sturm (1998) for details.
8. Austria's and Finland's debt ratios increased after 1992, but these countries had not yet entered the European Union at the time.
9. Forecasts indicated that sub-national governments would have an overall deficit of ATS 6.4 billion (Hüttner, 1999:97).
10. The agreement of 1996 actually did not establish a deficit limit for the federal government, due to time restrictions (Stienlet, 1994: 228).
11. In addition, some procedural restrictions exist: incurring foreign currency debt or debt from abroad in Belgian Francs is subjected to the approval of the federal Minister of Finance. Similarly, the conditions and timing of debt issuance on domestic capital markets has to be approved by the Minister of Finance. The Minister of Finance has also to be notified of the issuance of other types of debt.
12. The following is based on Gordo and Hernández de Cos (2000) if not indicated otherwise.
13. The Council, composed of the Minister of Economy, Finance and of General Government as well as regional Ministers of Finance, was set up in 1980 to act as a consultative and discussion body for tasks relating to the coordination of the regions' financial activities (Gordo and Hernández de Cos, 2000).

Part II

Fiscal Policy for Stabilization and Growth

7
How to Allow the Automatic Stabilizers to Operate Fully? A Policy-Maker's Guide for EMU Countries

Philippe Mills and Alain Quinet[1]

7.1 Introduction

The Stability and Growth Pact (SGP) allows for and supports symmetric use of the automatic stabilizers: member countries should achieve a budgetary position 'close to balance or in surplus' over the medium term in order to allow the automatic stabilizers to operate fully over the business cycle. Such type of behaviour implies a substantial change compared with past experience. Empirical evidence indicates that European fiscal policies have tended to behave pro-cyclically (Buti, Franco and Ongena, 1997). This has been particularly true during good times, where 'growth dividends' have only been partially used to 'reload the fiscal gun'. This tendency of European fiscal policies to turn pro-cyclical during upswings may be explained, among other things, by the failure to recognize the temporary nature of the fiscal improvements and the difficulties to stand up to pressures for tax cuts when the tax burden is already very high.

There is no simple solution that would overcome this pro-cyclical bias and bring more discipline to fiscal policy-making. Performing a cyclical adjustment in real time is complex, as policy-makers only have a limited knowledge of the shocks and the structural changes affecting the economy. Moreover, the SGP does not provide any 'reward for virtue' during good times and there is no process to sanction deviations from the 'close to balance or in surplus' either. Hence, targeting a stable cyclically-adjusted balance – 'close to balance or in surplus' – can be considered as a guideline rather than a binding rule. Securing the symmetric operation of automatic stabilizers requires an elaborated analytical and institutional framework at the national level to secure the implementation of the SGP.

This chapter does not pretend to provide a comprehensive view of the budgetary institutions and rules that may be appropriate to maintain fiscal sustainability (see, for example, Poterba and Von Hagen, 1999; and Chapter 6 of the present volume). Rather, the objective is to shed light on the usefulness of a medium-term framework including a formal spending rule and mechanisms to secure cyclical surpluses. The second section discusses to what extent a stable cyclically-adjusted position – 'close to balance or in surplus' – can be seen as a relevant benchmark to allow the automatic stabilizers to operate fully. In a third section, we draw the lessons from the difficulty to adjust for the cycle: a spending rule seems more transparent, and easier to monitor than a cyclically-adjusted balance while allowing the automatic stabilizers to operate fully on the revenue side. As several member states have already done, spending rules could usefully be incorporated in stability programmes to secure compliance with the requirements of the SGP and to enhance nominal surpluses during good times. The fourth section concludes.

7.2   Cyclically-adjusted fiscal targets and automatic stabilizers: a critical evaluation

It is well known that the cyclically-adjusted balance suffers from important methodological limitations (for a comprehensive assessment, see Mackenzie, 1989; Blanchard, 1992; Chouraqui *et al.* 1992), especially as a guide for the behaviour of fiscal authorities. In particular, in the EMU framework, targeting a stable cyclically-adjusted position – close to balance or in surplus – over the business cycle, with the idea of allowing automatic stabilizers to operate fully, entails two kinds of risk: automatic stabilizers are not always beneficial for the economy and the methodologies used to adjust for the cycle are complex and are generally unable to correct for the entire impact of the business cycle on the budget balance. These two aspects are discussed hereafter.

7.2.1   Defining automatic stabilizers

If public spending were stable as a share of potential GDP, variations in the budget balance would simply reflect the influence of the business cycle. However, the spending-to-potential GDP ratio is subject to discretionary policy changes and supply shocks. There has been a significant amount of structural change since the beginning of the 1990s in Europe that is still ongoing. These structural changes stem from developments such as German unification, the introduction of the Single Market and Economic and Monetary Union. In the coming years, the diffusion of information and communication technologies, tax reforms and ageing should significantly affect potential GDP. In this context, there is a need to disentangle the cyclical and non-cyclical components of the budget balance to identify the working of automatic stabilizers.

The cyclical and cyclically-adjusted balance-to-GDP ratios are usually derived from the nominal balance by a two-step procedure: an estimate of the output gap, followed by an estimation of the sensitivity of tax and spending items to GDP. The output gap reflects the deviation of actual GDP from a trend or potential GDP as a share of GDP. Once the influence of the output gap has been removed, the cyclically-adjusted or so-called structural component is calculated as a residual. It provides an idea of the budget balance that would prevail under 'normal conditions'. The distinction between discretionary changes and automatic stabilizers is not clear-cut, as some cycle-related fiscal developments – e.g. employment policies – lie somewhere between the passive response of the budget balance and discretionary policy changes. With this difficulty in mind, a stable cyclically-adjusted balance should normally indicate that the stance of fiscal policy has remained unchanged and that variations in the budget balance reflect the impact of cyclical variations in economic activity. More specifically:

- the level of the cyclically-adjusted balance provides an idea of the room to manoeuvre to allow the operation of automatic stabilizers within the 3 per cent of GDP ceiling enshrined in the Treaty of Maastricht and the SGP;
- changes in the cyclically-adjusted balance indicate to what extent fiscal developments depart from the simple working of automatic stabilizers.

However, labelling the sensitivity of public deficits to GDP swings as 'automatic stabilizers' is ambiguous as the stabilization properties of the budget depend on the nature of the underlying economic disturbances. In the face of a fall in aggregate demand, fiscal stabilizers unambiguously act as a shock absorber (Christiano, 1984). The conclusions are different, however, if the economy is affected by a supply shock (Artis and Buti, 2000a; Blanchard, 2000; European Commission, 2000a; and Chapter 12 in this volume). A temporary negative supply shock leaves unchanged long-term potential GDP.[2] Therefore, a fall in economic activity may lead to a deterioration in the output gap and automatic stabilizers may work, but at the cost of higher inflation. A long-lasting negative supply shock leads to a fall in potential GDP relative to aggregate demand. The cyclically-adjusted balance deteriorates, as public expenditures are rigid or indexed on higher prices while potential GDP is falling. In this context, any deterioration in the cyclical balance delays the adjustment towards the new equilibrium level of potential output. More generally, any attempt to prevent demand from falling in line with potential GDP, via a deterioration in the public deficit, can become counterproductive.[3]

In practice, the various shocks that affect the economy can shift both demand and supply. As it is very difficult to disentangle *ex ante* supply and demand shifts on the one hand, and temporary and permanent supply shocks, on the other, there is a high risk of treating changes in the budget position that have structural roots as if they were the result of automatic stabilizers. For example, an estimate of the output gap and the cyclically-adjusted balance

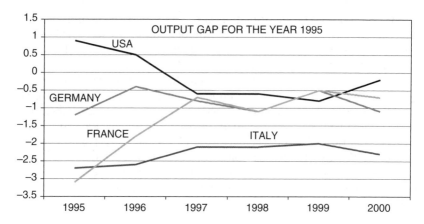

Figure 7.1   Output gap for the year 1995
Source: OECD *Outlooks* (December 1995, 1996, 1997, 1998, 1999, 2000).

for the year 1995 made at the time is likely to be less reliable than one made
five years later, given all the information that has become available in the
intervening period. The revisions are particularly spectacular in the case of
the US economy that experienced a structural break in productivity trend in
the mid-1990s. While the US economy was perceived as suffering from
excess demand in 1995, supply was estimated to outstrip demand two years
later (Figure 7.1). The reverse is true for France: while the French economy
was perceived as suffering from a lack of demand in 1995, more recent estimates point to an output gap close to zero at that time.[4]

7.2.2   Assessing the size of automatic stabilizers

Approaches to disentangle cyclical and 'structural' components of public
deficits mainly differ with respect to the method used to identify the position
of the economy in the business cycle. By contrast, the marginal sensitivity of
the budget balance to GDP is very close from one estimation to another
(Giorno *et al.* 1995; Hagemann, 1999; Roeger and Ongena, 1999). It is therefore generally considered that the main source of uncertainty surrounding the
cyclical adjustment concerns the evaluation of the Nairu (non-accelerating
inflation rate of employment) and the output gap. However, when one is concerned with the symmetric operation of automatic stabilizers over the business
cycle, i.e. with changes in cyclical budget balances, tax elasticities matter, as
they are subject to significant short-term variations.

All technical approaches to adjust for the business cycle tend to suffer from
a pro-cyclical bias: they exhibit a positive correlation between the estimated
cyclically-adjusted balance and the cycle. This arises for two reasons: the
estimate of the output gap is generally based on a procyclical assessment of

potential GDP; the tax elasticities vary during the business cycle while the cyclically-adjusted budget balance is evaluated on the basis of an average long-term elasticity – generally close to unity.

Two ways to identify the business cycle exist. A mechanical approach uses smoothing devices (such as Hodrick-Prescott filters) to establish a trend level of output, with the output gap representing the difference between actual and trend output. A production function approach provides an assessment of the level of GDP consistent with stable wage or price inflation. Various methods give widely different estimates of the output gap. However, all tend to entail a positive correlation between potential output and output gap. Potential GDP based on a production function is pro-cyclical as it captures the cyclical behaviour of the capital stock.[5] In this context, the investment cycle may result in an overstating of the long-term potential GDP growth and the cyclically-adjusted balance. The reverse is true during downturns, but fiscal policy must, as a priority, address the problem of 'bad policies in good times'. While the SGP sets a limit of 3 per cent of GDP on the deterioration of the deficit during downturns, it does not include any concrete 'stick or carrot' during upswings.

The correlation between the output gap and the growth rate of the economy is more pronounced with the Hodrick-Prescott (HP) filter. The symmetric property of the HP filter, which requires that output gaps sum to zero over the sample, tends to limit the absolute size of the output gap at the end of the period. The HP filter tends to overstate the strength of demand during upswings for an acceleration in potential GDP.[6] Conversely, if the end of the sample is characterized by a recession, the estimated trend will be lower.

The estimated elasticity of budget items reflects, at best, the average cyclical responsiveness of these items over the sample period. Most methods (Van den Noord, 2000) aim at finding average long-run value for the elasticity that largely offsets cyclical fluctuations. Elasticities, derived from econometric equations, exhibit a proportional relation between tax basis and tax revenues. However, evidence suggests that actual year-on-year sensitivity may differ substantially from this average responsiveness, as tax revenues fall more rapidly than GDP during a downturn and increase more rapidly during an upswing. This is highlighted for example in the French case by the variations affecting the apparent tax elasticity for state budget taxes. The ratio of the growth rate of tax revenues – assuming unchanged legislation – vis-à-vis GDP growth fluctuates significantly over time. For an average tax elasticity of 0.9 the standard deviation stands at 0.6. Variations are less pronounced at the general government level. For an average elasticity of 1, the standard deviation stands at 0.3 (see Figure 7.2). For the year 1993, where GDP fell by 0.9 per cent, the tax elasticity amplified the effects of the downturn on the public balance, which deteriorated by 1.7 percentage point of GDP to reach 7.3 per cent of GDP.

The sensitivity of tax proceeds to changes in the tax base varies over time as direct taxes react in a non-linear way and are collected with lags.

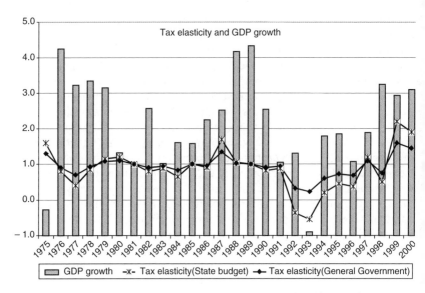

Figure 7.2　Tax elasticity and GDP growth, 1975–2000

Source:　Commission Economique de la Nation (2000) for the State budget. Calculations of the authors for the general government assuming a unitary tax elasticity for the other subsectors of the economy.

Non-linearities may be due to variations in the number of profitable firms and to the progressiveness of the personal income tax regime. Besides, failure to take account of the collection lags may give a misleading picture of the fiscal stance around turning points.

The size of the bias implied by a time-varying tax elasticity is given by the impact of the difference between the effective and the average tax elasticity used to perform the calculation. An improvement in the cyclically-adjusted balance, estimated on the basis of average tax elasticity, may be artificial if the rise in the tax burden is not due to new measures but to a transitory high elasticity. Conversely, a stable cyclically-adjusted balance may mask deterioration in the underlying position of the public finances if some of the cyclical receipts (i.e. receipts corresponding to a tax elasticity above 1) are used to lower taxes or increase spending.

7.2.3　Policy implications

The relevance of cyclical adjustment as a guide to monitor the symmetric operation of automatic stabilizers over the business cycle depends on the ability of the methodology to provide reliable estimates in the more recent period. While it is well known that estimates of the *level* of the cyclically-adjusted balance are uncertain, we have highlighted that measures of the *changes* may be biased as well, given the difficulty to identify supply and demand shocks in real time and the volatility of the aggregate tax elasticity over the business cycle. During an upswing, the net effect may be to overestimate the improvement in the cyclically-adjusted balance. Short-term potential GDP increases in line with the investment boom, while the tax elasticity rises above its long-term average used to perform the cyclical adjustment.

To avoid the risk of overestimating the strength of the fiscal position during upswings, one possible approach is to base the fiscal strategy on a set of cautious macroeconomic assumptions. Such assumptions may generate initial benefits, but as time passes, spending departments and households are likely to anticipate higher than expected revenues and adjust their actions and demands in favour of higher expenditures or tax cuts. Moreover, windfalls may intensify pressures in favour of discretionary measures and so this approach could not guarantee that automatic stabilizers operate in a symmetric way. A more comprehensive response to the difficulties raised by cyclical adjustments is to pay more attention to the interaction between the budget and supply side developments, on the one hand, and between tax elasticities and the cycle, on the other:

• Awareness of supply-side developments implies relying on both statistical and economic approaches to evaluate the output gap. These evaluations require production functions and an analysis of the determinants of the NAIRU.

• Variations in the cyclically-adjusted balance, calculated as a residual once the incidence of the output gap has been removed, should be cross-checked by an evaluation where policy-driven changes are subject to direct estimations.

If the elasticity of public spending vis-à-vis GDP is equal to 0 and the average long-term tax elasticity equal to 1, the cyclically-adjusted balance (bs) can simply be written: $bs \cong g - t(1 - og)$ where g represents the public spending to GDP ratio, t the tax-to-GDP ratio, og the output gap and tog represents the cyclical component of the public balance. One can immediately see that any variation in the tax-to-GDP ratio modifies the cyclically-adjusted balance. However, this variation may be either due to discretionary changes or cyclical fluctuations. A fiscal impulse indicator (Δf), by contrast, based on new tax measures (ε_t) and the relative growth rate of public spending vis-à-vis potential GDP growth ($\Delta G/G_{-1} - \Delta Y_p/Y_{p-1}$) avoids such a pitfall. Formally it can be written as $\Delta f = \varepsilon_t + (\Delta G/G_{-1} - \Delta Y_p/Y_{p-1})g$.

7.3 Anchoring the working of automatic stabilizers: the case for spending rules

In this section, we draw some lessons from these conceptual and technical difficulties to adjust the budget balance for the cycle. Even if a stable cyclically-adjusted balance is a relevant benchmark to allow the automatic stabilizers to operate freely, for practical reasons, a spending rule seems more operationally targeted and easier to monitor. Moreover, a well-designed spending rule can help in avoiding pro-cyclical fiscal policy during economic upswings and enhance the transparency of fiscal policy.

7.3.1   The case for fiscal rules

The case for fiscal rules has strengthened over recent decades, as economic agents have become increasingly forward-looking and aware of the consequences of public debt developments on their welfare. The first objective of fiscal rules is to enhance the transparency and the credibility of fiscal policy. European governments have several fiscal policy objectives, including fiscal consolidation, a lower tax burden, pension reform and macroeconomic stabilization. In this context, there is a need to clarify how these options are inserted in a well-articulated fiscal strategy. A formal rule provides a clear benchmark against which the performance of fiscal policy can be judged: any deviation from the rule has to be explained in public. The second objective of fiscal rules is to enlarge political support in favour of the fiscal strategy. The fiscal strategy needs political and institutional support from social partners and local authorities, which are partly responsible for general government outcomes. A rule could therefore be the vehicle of an 'internal stability pact' to enhance accountability vis-à-vis national and European criteria for all public authorities.

In Europe, two specific arguments can be advanced for adopting broad-based rules at the national level:

- Even if the SGP requires corrective measures to be taken when a 'significant divergence' from budget targets is identified (see European Commission, 2000a), the SGP does not foresee formal sanctions in the event of deviations from the 'close to balance or in surplus' target.
- Fiscal coordination within the Euro zone needs to be strengthened. The SGP has been designed to limit the negative externalities stemming from excessive national deficits. Nevertheless, a more active coordination is necessary in Europe. The adoption of rules by EMU member states could enhance both the predictability and the consistency of the national policy reaction functions to shocks and business cycle fluctuations (Jacquet and Pisani-Ferry, 2000).

The debate on fiscal rules focuses traditionally on a critical trade-off between commitment and the need to retain policy flexibility. In practice, few rules have a track record of satisfactory compliance and pass the test of a severe recession. Balanced budget rules, or more generally nominal deficit targets, may be useful as temporary, strategic initiatives to aid the process of fiscal consolidation when the initial position of the public finances is weak (Kopits and Symansky, 1998). However, a balanced budget rule is at odds with the operation of automatic stabilizers and appears unsustainable in the event of a recession. More generally, rules that lack transparency and are not supported by an institutional framework cannot effectively secure fiscal discipline.

Drawing the lessons from past failures, four main desired properties of the rules can be identified:

- the rule should be intended for application on a permanent basis;
- the rule should be state-contingent, so as to give the authorities sufficient flexibility to react to unforeseen shocks. More specifically, the rule should help fiscal policy-makers to cope with windfalls or shortfalls;
- the rule should be both simple and well defined, in order to be transparent and credible. Application of contingent rules without an explicit mandate to maintain transparency is likely to lead to circumvention and creative accounting;
- the rule should be accompanied by some enforcement mechanisms, including availability of contingency measures during the budget execution, provisions for escape clauses and consequences of non-compliance.

7.3.2 Anchoring the fiscal strategy on spending rules

A majority of European countries such as the Netherlands, Belgium, Denmark, France, Finland Sweden and the United Kingdom have turned more or less explicitly on spending rules since the beginning of the 1990s. The credibility of the anchor is enhanced by the fact that a multi-annual budgeting framework forming part of the budgetary process supports it. In several countries, notably France and Finland, the expenditure growth guidelines are incorporated in the stability programmes. In Sweden and Finland formal expenditure ceilings are approved by parliaments. In countries where such rules figure up front in the fiscal strategy the steep upward trend in expenditure in the early 1990s has been broken and reversed, although other factors have also played a role (Table 7.1).

Somewhat surprisingly, spending rules have not received much attention in the economic literature, although it is widely recognized that

Table 7.1 Public expenditure and GDP (growth rate in percentage points, constant prices)

	1980–94		1995–99	
	Public spending	*GDP*	*Public spending*	*GDP*
France	3.1	1.9	1.6	2.3
Netherlands	1.7	2.1	0.9	3.5
Sweden	2.4	1.4	−0.4	2.4
European Union	3.2	2.2	1.1	2.2

Source: OECD.

expenditure-based fiscal retrenchments are more successful that tax-based consolidations (Alesina and Perotti, 1997; Zaghini, 1999; and Chapter 2 of this volume). Over the long run, a permanent spending rule seems to dominate other rules for the following reasons:

- The rule makes governments accountable for what they can control directly and greatly enhances the transparency of fiscal policy by showing a medium-term commitment to an intermediate target.
- The rule allows the automatic stabilizers to operate fully on the revenue side. It contributes to macroeconomic stabilization while minimizing distortions – the traditional tax smoothing argument. It can even enhance the intertemporal consistency of tax reforms by ensuring that tax cuts are sustainable (see below).
- The cap on the growth rate of expenditures could be set at different growth rates with reference to potential growth estimates, depending on the initial position of the public finances and the tax burden level. If the public balance does not meet the requirements of the SGP, i.e. is not balanced over the cycle, expenditure growth has to be kept below potential GDP growth. The same rule should be applied when governments want to permanently lower the tax burden while still complying with the requirements of the SGP. Public spending should increase in line with potential GDP when the public balance is in line with the SGP and when the tax burden is considered as the right one.

A spending rule is in essence close to a cyclically-adjusted balance target. Both aim at maintaining fiscal prudence while allowing the automatic stabilizers to work fully. The comparative advantages of spending rules are overwhelmingly practical. A stable cyclically-adjusted balance should be considered as a guideline rather than a rule as there is no simple solution to the conceptual and methodological difficulties surrounding the cyclical adjustment. A spending anchor, by contrast, is easy to define and monitor, hence minimizing the risks of pro-cyclicity in the short run. It is important to note that a spending rule and a cyclically-adjusted balance target are mutually compatible over the medium run: the cap on the growth rate of expenditures can be set to achieve a given cyclically-adjusted fiscal target over the medium run. Setting a spending rule in relation to long-run potential GDP largely overcomes the problems raised by cyclical adjustment, as long as the growth rate of potential GDP is based on a prudent assessment (i.e. as long as the investment cycle is not included in the evaluation of long-run potential GDP).

The implementation of a spending rule within the framework of the SGP raises several issues: (i) should the rule be set in nominal or in real terms? (ii) should the rule cover all spending items? (iii) does a spending rule complicate the relations between central governments and sub-national authorities?

(i) Whether the spending norm should be expressed in nominal (as in the UK strategy) or in real terms (as in the Dutch or French strategy) mainly depends on the time horizon. Over a short-term horizon, nominal rules may help fiscal stabilization. If public expenditures are set in nominal terms a positive demand shock or a negative supply shock automatically leads to a downward shift in public spending in real terms. This fall tends to stabilize both the output gap and the position of the public finances. By contrast, a rule set in real terms may be destabilizing. The differences between nominal and real spending rules should not be overemphasized in the case of demand shocks, as modern economies exhibit strong price inertia in response to demand shocks. In the case of an imported inflationary shock (e.g. an oil price hike), by contrast, whether the rule is set in nominal or in real terms makes a difference. A nominal target seems preferable as automatic stabilizers are not desirable in the event of supply shocks, but it requires a high degree of flexibility in real spending, notably wages and entitlements.

Over a medium-term horizon, targeting the evolution of public spending in real terms makes more sense. The distinction between nominal and real spending rules seems *a priori* less relevant, as the norm is always implicitly based on an underlying assessment of trend inflation. The relevant issue is how to deal with surprises or forecast errors. If inflation forecasts are efficient (i.e. entail no systematic bias), the distinction is irrelevant, especially when the multi-year programme permits overspending in one year if offset in the following years. If the inflation rate differs on average from the forecasts, the nominal rule may be difficult to sustain. A nominal spending rule may be stabilizing if the inflation rate differs from the initial path because of a long-lasting demand shock. However, if the inflation rate differs from the initial path because of a forecast error, a nominal spending rule clearly destabilizes the underlying position of the public finances.

(ii) *The coverage of the rule.* The need for transparency and flexibility argues strongly in favour of one general norm. However, a total spending norm may lead to pro-cyclical behaviour on the spending side, as a fall in interest rates may be accommodated with an increase in primary spending. However, in a world where the average cost of public debt is above the potential growth rate of the economy, an interest rate hike may lead to an increase in the public debt over the business cycle, if a primary spending rule were to be followed. As long as the main goal of the spending rule is to make sure that objectives regarding the debt and the tax burden are mutually compatible, interest payments should remain in the control aggregate. The distinction between investment and current spending seems to be of greater relevance. This 'golden rule', enshrined in the UK Code for Fiscal Stability, ensures that spending restraint is achieved on a strategic basis and does not entail a bias against capital spending. The golden rule, however, introduces difficulties of its own, mainly because it is often hard to draw a meaningful distinction between current and capital expenditures and because of its unclear implications for

Table 7.2   Real public expenditure trends according to the degree of fiscal federalism

	Central public spending (as a share of central and local spending in 1973)	Central public spending (as a share of central and local spending in 1990)	Real total spending 1973–90 (yearly growth rate)
Spain	84%	67%	5.2%
France	76%	74%	3.3%
United Kingdom	68%	75%	1.7%

Source: Commission calculations.

intergenerational equity (for a severe refutation, see Buiter, 1998; for a more favourable approach, see Kell, 2001).

(iii) Implementing a spending rule in a decentralized system requires an 'internal stability pact'. Historically, fiscal rules have been enacted to restrain sub-national or local government deficits – with the stabilization function generally carried out at the national or federal level. Restraining local deficits prevents externalities from fiscal misbehaviour in one jurisdiction being transmitted, through higher interest rates, to other subnational jurisdictions and to the national government. Under current legislation, local authorities generally face balanced budget rules: such rules create an incentive to offset by discretionary measures the operation of automatic stabilizers. As long as any significant decision-making responsibility for expenditures is devolved to local levels of government, the incentives could well be for them to spend excessively in good times, therefore undermining the credibility of the rule.

Switching to a spending rule may require a change in the incentives faced by local authorities or to reach a broad-based agreement among public authorities enshrined in an 'internal stability pact'. Two necessary conditions for an internal domestic pact are the effectiveness of the information system and the public nature of the arrangement. Monitoring *ex ante* and *ex post* compliance to the spending rule requires timely fiscal aggregates at the sub-national level. The rules and the procedure should be made public: the implied increase in transparency and accountability would provide in turn an incentive for all public authorities to give more weight to the longer-term consequences of their decisions.

7.3.3   Dealing with windfalls

A spending rule is a necessary but not a sufficient condition to secure the symmetric use of automatic stabilizers. A spending rule may indeed have some asymmetric effect. While allowing the automatic stabilizers to operate fully during downturns, the rule does not guarantee that windfalls – 'growth dividends' and revenues overshoots – during upswings are used to 'reload the fiscal gun'. Two directions can be envisaged to secure 'growth dividends' or better-than-expected tax revenues: the establishment of a reserve fund; the Dutch-type strategy of contingent rule making.

The establishment of reserve funds in several European countries (France, Ireland, ...) as well as in the United States, Canada and New Zealand, aims at smoothing the impact of an ageing population on public finances. On top of smoothing the demographic transition, reserve funds have been set up to secure windfall revenues such as exhaustible oil resources. This has been one of the reasons for the establishment of a State Petroleum Fund in 1990 in Norway. This kind of strategy is of special interest in some countries within EMU, in two different contexts. First, a reserve fund could help in securing nominal surpluses during upswings. Although there is no difference between paying money into the reserve fund and reducing government debt, one can note that the allocation of resources to a reserve fund is less controversial than a further reduction of indebtedness. Second, if social security funds are distinct from the central government and largely under the control of the social partners, as is the case in several European countries, there is a strong tendency for the state budget, in charge of macroeconomic stabilization, to exhibit a more persistent deficit than the social security funds (Table 7.3). A general government account that is 'close to balance or in surplus' will normally imply a surplus of social security funds during upswings. A reserve fund devoted to the pre-funding of pension schemes could help in preserving such a surplus.

Another way of dealing with deviations from the projected revenue developments has been put in the medium-term framework of Dutch fiscal policy since 1998. The Dutch strategy is explicitly based on cautious macroeconomic assumptions. The cautious assumptions imply that the probability of windfalls is greater than the probability of shortfalls. Under the 1999–2002 arrangement, part of the expected revenue overruns to a pre-established baseline path is translated into higher or lower tax cuts in a next budget. Twenty-five per cent of the revenue windfalls are to be used for a reduction of the tax burden and the rest for deficit reduction if the public deficit is greater than 0.75 per cent of GDP. Otherwise, the windfall is to be shared equally between reducing the tax burden and reducing the deficit. This kind a strategy to a certain extent weakens the automatic stabilizers, but at the same time limits the risk of fiscal slippage during good times.

Table 7.3 Public deficits in the euro area (as a share of GDP)

	1993	1994	1995	1996	1997	1998	1999
General government balance	−5.7	−5.2	−5.1	−4.4	−2.6	−2.1	−1.2
Central government balance	−5.2	−4.6	−4.2	−3.8	−2.4	−2.1	−1.5

Source: IMF *World Economic Outlook* (WEO), May 2000.

7.4   Conclusion

The traditional approach to the operation of automatic stabilizers is based on a rather simplistic view; i.e. that GDP fluctuates along a smooth growth path, the public balance responds in a linear way to these fluctuations, and the automatic response of the budget in turn contributes to close the output gap. In practice, European economies are undergoing substantial structural changes and supply shocks. They face substantial fluctuations in short-term potential GDP growth and tax elasticities, which undermine the relevance of traditional cyclical adjustment. Given the difficulty to evaluate a meaningful cyclically-adjusted balance *ex ante*, the operation of automatic stabilizers should be monitored using a wider set of indicators. We have argued, in particular, that a fiscal impulse indicator, directly calculated on the basis of identified discretionary measures, could usefully complement traditional cyclical adjustment.

However, the symmetric operation of automatic stabilizers cannot simply be based on indicators or guidelines, however sophisticated they may be. We have argued that the requirements of the SGP could be more easily met if formal spending rules were incorporated in stability programmes. The basic argument in favour of a spending anchor is that a policy of targeting expenditures preserves microeconomic efficiency while allowing tax revenues to act as automatic stabilizers. The rule is easy to define and to monitor in real time. A medium-term framework based on a spending rule should specify an explicit medium-term target for the budget balance or the stock of debt. It should also include complementary 'contingent rules' to secure nominal surpluses during upswings.

Notes

1. The authors would like to thank Anna Brunila, Robert Hagemann, Bertrand Martinot and the editors for helpful comments. Any remaining errors or omissions are the responsibility of the authors. The views expressed in this chapter belong only to the authors and should not be attributed to the European Commission.
2. At least if the economy is growing along a smooth trend path from which it is disturbed by cyclical fluctuations – an assumption of trend stationarity. Alternatively, the output process could be thought of as a non-stationary process in which all shocks have permanent effects.
3. It may be the case that the progressivity of the tax system can contribute to stabilizing the supply side. In the face of a negative supply shock, lower effective marginal tax rates could encourage greater labour supply. Nevertheless, the stabilization effect is not expected to be strong in the short run, given plausible values of the elasticity of labour supply.
4. Indeed, significant revisions also affect the cyclically-adjusted balances.
5. Assuming a Cobb–Douglas production function, GDP growth depends (y) on total factor productivity gains (λ) and increases in the volumes of capital and labour inputs (k and l respectively):

$$y = \lambda + ak + (1 - a)l$$

where a is the elasticity of output with respect to capital, which equals the capital share in equilibrium.

In the long run, the capital/output ratio and the structural unemployment rate are constant. Potential GDP growth only depends on labour efficiency gains and increases in the labour force: $y = \lambda/(1-a) + l$.

Potential GDP growth can therefore be broken down into long-term and short-run components.

$$y = \frac{\lambda}{(1-a)} + l + \frac{a}{(1-a)}(k-y)$$

The short run (last term of the equation) captures the cyclical fluctuations of the capital-to-GDP ratio. During upswings, the accumulation of capital raises potential GDP above its 'Solovian path'. With a usually close to 0.3, half of the cyclical variations in the capital/output ratio are reflected in potential GDP.

6. Trend GDP calculated with a linear trend is by construction not subject to this criticism. However, a linear trend captures past variations in the structural unemployment rate or in the participation rate, which do not affect GDP growth in the long run.

8
Automatic Stabilizers in the 1990s and Beyond

Paul van den Noord[1]

8.1 Introduction

Many components of government budgets are affected by the macroeconomic situation in ways that operate to smooth the business cycle, i.e. they act as 'automatic stabilizers'. For example, in a recession fewer taxes are collected, which operates to support private incomes and damps the adverse movements in aggregate demand. Conversely, during a boom more taxes are collected, counteracting the expansion in aggregate demand. This stabilizing property is evidently stronger if the tax system is more progressive. Another automatic fiscal stabilizer is the unemployment insurance system: in a downswing the growing payment of unemployment benefits supports demand, and vice versa in an upswing. The flipside is that the fiscal position may display sharp fluctuations, unless discretionary fiscal policy is used to offset the working of the automatic stabilizers.

Although by damping the business cycle automatic fiscal stabilizers may help to reduce the long-lasting economic damage associated with large under-utilized resources, they also entail risks for the economy. One relates to the importance of allowing stabilizers to operate symmetrically over the business cycle. If governments allow automatic fiscal stabilizers to work fully in a downswing but fail to resist the temptation to spend cyclical revenue increases during an upswing, the stabilizers may lead to a bias toward weak underlying (or 'structural') budget positions. The result may be rises in public indebtedness during periods of cyclical weakness that are not subsequently reversed when activity recovers. This, in turn, could lead to higher interest rates as well as requiring higher taxes (or spending reductions) to finance debt servicing. Unstable 'debt dynamics' working to increase debt–GDP ratios over time, due to real interest rates that exceed economic growth rates, may aggravate this problem. A second risk arises from the fact that automatic fiscal stabilizers respond to structural changes in the economic situation as well as to cyclical developments. Consequently, if the economy's growth potential declines, and this is not appreciated by the government in a timely fashion, the operation of automatic fiscal stabilizers is likely to under-mine public finance positions that might otherwise have been sound. Finally, automatic fiscal stabilization results from the operation of tax and benefit systems that primarily serve other objectives such as income security and redistribution. These systems may delay necessary adjustment in the wake of a recession, thus contributing to poor economic performance.

Against this backdrop it is useful to: (i) gauge the impact of automatic sta-bilizers on fiscal positions of OECD countries; (ii) examine the extent to which automatic stabilizers, in combination with discretionary fiscal policy, have contributed to smooth the business cycle; and (iii) assess the longer-term impact of automatic fiscal stabilizers on economic performance. The sections below address each of these issues.

8.2   The impact of the business cycle on fiscal positions

The counter-cyclical demand impulse stemming from automatic fiscal sta-bilizers depends on the sensitivity of government net lending, as a share of GDP, to cyclical variations in output, and the size of those variations. Measurement is largely an unsettled issue. Widely different methods are being employed by both national governments and various international institutions (see Box 8.1). Each method has specific strengths and weak-nesses, but whatever method is employed, the user needs to be aware of a problem of 'simultaneity': the business cycle changes the fiscal position, which in turn affects economic activity. The OECD Secretariat's approach involves three steps:[2]

1. Potential output is estimated on the basis of country-specific Cobb–Douglas production functions, which have been estimated for a sample period covering the past three decades. Accordingly, potential output is deter-mined by the size of the capital stock and potential employment. The lat-ter is computed as the difference between the trend labour force and structural unemployment, or the NAWRU (non-accelerating wage rate of unemployment). The cyclical component of GDP, or output gap, is the difference between actual and potential GDP.
2. Elasticities of various forms of taxation and expenditure with respect to output are calculated to estimate the sensitivity of these items to the cycle. On the revenue side, all tax receipts are adjusted for the cycle, with taxes being grouped into four types (indirect, business, social security and personal income tax). On the expenditure side, estimates of the auto-matic stabilizers are limited to the impact of the cycle on benefits paid to the unemployed.
3. The output gap and the elasticities are used to derive the impact on tax and expenditure arising from the economy's operation above or below potential. This is taken to measure the cyclical component of each item.

Box 8.1   Gauging fiscal automatic stabilizers – different approaches

Different approaches have been developed over time to disentangle cyclical and structural components of government expenditure, (tax) revenues and balances. Most approaches start off from the observation that economic activity influences tax bases (wage bill, profits, consumption, etc.) and unemployment, which, in turn determine tax proceeds and public expenditure. The approaches differ with respect to the method employed to identify the cycle in economic activity and the way to determine the sensitivity of budget items to the cycle. The official methods also differ from one country to another.

Generally speaking, two ways to identify the cycle in economic activity co-exist. A *mechanical* approach uses smoothing devices (such as Hodrick-Prescott filters) to establish a trend level of output; the cyclical component (output gap) is the difference between actual and trend output. In some cases the de-trending of output series is dropped altogether, with the smoothing device applied directly to the tax base and unemployment series. The mechanical approach is relatively simple, transparent and requires little judgmental intervention. A major drawback is the 'end point bias': the difference between actual and trend series tends to become small for recent observations, meaning that economic slack or overheating may escape the observer. This drawback has motivated the development of an alternative approach measuring *potential* rather than trend output, based on a production function. This method, which has been adopted by the OECD Secretariat, is somewhat more complex since it requires judgements on the rate of technological change, its bias (labour or capital augmenting) and, importantly, the rate of structural unemployment. However, it is less susceptible to the end-point problem for recent observations.

Methods to determine the sensitivity of budget items to the cycle can be grouped into three categories:

- A first approach is to run regressions on the observed tax proceeds and public expenditure, with as explanatory variables, discretionary changes in tax or benefit parameters, a trend and a cyclical term (the latter two may be based on trend or potential output measures). From these equations elasticities are derived that measure the impact of a (cyclical) change in output on tax revenues or expenditure (see for an example, Bismut, 1995). The accuracy of this approach strongly depends on the reliability of the policy variables that are included in the regressions. If these fail to cover the whole ground of relevant policy measures, some of the policy-induced effects on the budget may end up in the estimated elasticities, which could therefore be misleading. This approach will only be fruitful if detailed information on

Box 8.1 (continued)

relevant policy changes is available for a long range of years and kept up to date. The collection of such information is time-consuming and this approach is therefore less suited for users that need to cover a large number of countries.

- A second group of methods derive tax and expenditure elasticities from a macroeconometric model, with standard-shock simulations calibrated to show the impact of a 1 per cent (cyclical) increase in output on budget variables. This approach has the advantage that it allows differentiating between various kind of demand shocks (consumption, exports, etc.). On the other hand, it does not resolve the data collection problem alluded to above, because, in order to give accurate results for this purpose, the tax and expenditure equations in the model need to be estimated according to the above procedure.

- A third approach, which has been adopted by the OECD Secretariat (see the appendix to this chapter), proceeds in three steps. First, the elasticities of the relevant tax bases and unemployment with respect to (cyclical) economic activity, i.e. the output gap, are estimated through regression analysis. Next, the elasticities of tax proceeds or expenditure with respect to the relevant bases are extracted from the tax code or simply set to unity in cases where proportionality may be assumed. These two sets of elasticities are subsequently combined into reduced-form elasticities that link the cyclical components of taxes and expenditure to the output gap. While this method aims to strike a balance between accuracy and resource cost, it does not allow a further breakdown of the structural fiscal balance into discretionary and induced components.

In addition, the OECD Secretariat has experimented with a complementary approach, using a structural VAR model to capture the effects on fiscal balances of specific economic shocks in the past in EU countries (Dalsgaard and De Serres, 1999). A main advantage relative to the above approaches is that estimates of output gaps are not required, but the results with this model are not directly comparable to those derived from other approaches. This is the case because the elasticities that are derived from the VAR model include not only the impact of automatic stabilizers, but also that of discretionary fiscal policy to the extent that it reacts in a systematic fashion to economic disturbances.

Combining these estimates gives the full cyclical component of the budget balance and allows the simultaneous calculation of the cyclically-adjusted budget balance, i.e. the general government net borrowing or lending that would take place if the economy were operating at potential.

The cyclical sensitivity of the fiscal position can be captured by a 'semi-elasticity' indicating by how much the fiscal position will change if actual and potential output diverge. This gives rise to a rule of thumb that an output gap amounting to 1 per cent of potential GDP will boost the budget balance by around 0.5 per cent of GDP. This is an average for the OECD area; its impact is larger in, for example, the Nordic countries (around 0.7 per cent of GDP) and smaller in the United States and Japan (less than 0.3 per cent of GDP). It should be noted that these semi-elasticities vary over time as the weights of the various cyclically-sensitive budget items change.

The most important factor determining the cyclical sensitivity of the fiscal position is the *size of the general government sector*. For the most part, the larger the share of government expenditure in domestic output, the greater is the sensitivity of the fiscal position to fluctuations in economic activity (Figure 8.1). The *tax structure* also has a significant impact on the size of automatic stabilizers: the higher the taxation of cyclically sensitive tax bases, the more the tax will vary with the business cycle and hence the greater will be the cyclical sensitivity of the fiscal position. The *progressivity* of taxes, the generosity of unemployment benefits and the cyclical sensitivity of various tax bases and unemployment, finally, are other significant factors in determining the cyclical sensitivity of the fiscal position.

For a number of reasons the estimated semi-elasticities shown in Figure 8.1 are surrounded by significant margins of uncertainty. First, they are based on a combination of time-series regression and information extracted from national tax codes. Accordingly, the estimated cyclical sensitivity of budget

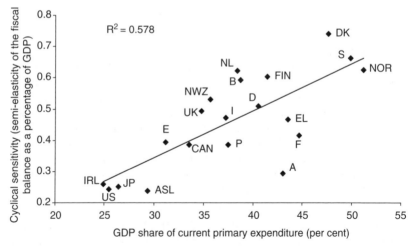

Figure 8.1　Cyclical sensitivity of the fiscal position and government size

Source:　van den Noord (2000), updated on the basis of *OECD Economic Outlook*, 68, Paris, December 2000.

items may be expected to reflect, at best, the 'average' cyclical responsiveness of these items over a sample period. Actual year-to-year behaviour may be more erratic as specific tax bases may react atypically over the cycle. Second, the cyclical behaviour of tax yields may be changing over time due to reforms of tax systems. Reform initiatives since the mid-1980s have generally been geared to flattening personal tax rate structures, which should have worked to reduce the automatic stabilizing properties of tax systems. Third, the response of tax bases to changes in activity may depend on the nature of the economic shock(s) that produced the boom or recession. For example, supply shocks that are associated with improvements in technology and changes in labour supply may coincide with demand shocks that stem from the international trade cycle or movements in household sentiment. In practice it is not always easy to disentangle structural and cyclical influences on output and budgets.

Based on the observed variations in economic activity, the cyclical component of government net lending is estimated to have peaked in the late-1980s boom at 0.4, 0.3 and 1 per cent of GDP in the United States, Japan and the euro area, respectively (Table 8.1). Conversely, the early-1990s recession prompted the cyclical component of these economies' fiscal balances to turn negative, and hence stimulatory, to −0.7, −0.5 and −1.3 per cent, respectively, of GDP. Not surprisingly, economies where activity has been volatile and government sectors are large, display the largest cyclical fluctuations in budget balances. Finland and Sweden are the most striking examples in this regard, although at least part of the volatility registered in these countries reflects a series of one-off, rather than cyclical, shocks. In the second half of the 1990s the cyclical development among OECD countries was diverging. This is reflected also in the cyclical component of the fiscal balance, which in 2000 amounted to a cyclical surplus of 0.6 per cent of GDP in the United States, while Japan and the euro area still displayed deficits (−0.8 and −0.2 per cent). Strikingly, however, within the euro area several smaller countries stand out by substantial cyclical surpluses in 2000.

Once estimates for the cyclical components of budget balances are available, it is possible to compute the discretionary component of these balances and hence the degree to which discretionary policy has either reinforced or overruled the automatic fiscal stabilizers. To this end the cyclical components are subtracted from the total fiscal balance and from this difference the net interest receipts of governments is subtracted, to obtain the primary structural balance. The change in this balance, as a percentage of potential GDP, is interpreted as the net impulse stemming from discretionary fiscal policy. The policy stance is restrictive if this balance increases and stimulatory if the balance declines. Table 8.2 reports the behaviour of discretionary fiscal policy and the impact of automatic stabilizers on budget balances over the past decade. It suggests that in the early-1990s recession eight out of twenty countries partly offset the working of automatic fiscal stabilizers through a tight stance of fiscal policy (Germany, Belgium, Greece,

Table 8.1 Cyclical component of general government financial balances (surplus (+) or deficit (−) as a per cent of GDP)

	Cyclical peak				Subsequent trough				Current situation			
			Fiscal balance				Fiscal balance				Fiscal balance	
	Year	Output gap	Total	Cyclical	Year	Output gap	Total	Cyclical	Year	Output gap	Total[1]	Cyclical
OECD[2]	1989	1.4	−1.9	0.7	1993	−2.1	−4.8	−0.6	2000	0.5	0.5	0.2
of which												
United States	1989	1.6	−3.2	0.4	1991	−2.5	−5.0	−0.7	2000	2.5	2.3	0.6
Japan	1991	2.8	2.9	0.3	1995	−2.3	−3.6	−0.5	2000	−3.2	−6.0	−0.8
Euro area[3]	1990	2.0	−4.5	1.0	1993	−2.6	−5.6	−1.3	2000	−0.3	0.3	−0.2
of which												
Germany	1990	2.4	−2.0	1.1	1993	−1.9	−3.1	−1.0	2000	−0.7	1.4	−0.4
France	1990	1.3	−2.1	0.5	1993	−2.4	−6.0	−1.0	2000	0.3	−1.4	0.1
Italy	1989	1.6	−9.8	0.8	1993	−2.8	−9.4	−1.5	2000	−1.6	−0.1	−0.8
Austria	1991	3.0	−3.0	0.9	1995	−0.8	−5.1	−0.2	2000	0.3	−1.6	0.1
Belgium	1990	3.1	−6.7	2.0	1993	−2.5	−7.3	−1.7	2000	−0.6	−0.1	−0.4
Finland	1989	4.7	6.0	2.6	1993	−11.3	−7.3	−8.8	2000	0.1	4.0	0.1
Ireland	1990	3.0	−2.8	1.1	1994	−5.5	−2.0	−2.1	2000	5.5	5.6	1.4
Netherlands	1990	2.1	−5.7	1.6	1993	−1.1	−3.6	−0.9	2000	1.6	1.6	1.0
Portugal	1990	3.4	−4.0	1.2	1994	−1.8	−4.8	−0.7	2000	0.1	−1.5	0.0
Spain	1990	2.3	−4.1	1.0	1996	−6.3	−4.9	−2.6	2000	−0.4	−0.3	−0.1

Other countries

United Kingdom	1988	4.9	0.6	2.5	1992	−4.0	−6.5	−2.3	2000	0.8	2.7	0.4
Canada	1988	4.0	−4.3	1.7	1992	−5.0	−9.2	−2.6	2000	0.9	2.5	0.3
Australia	1989	0.9	0.0	0.2	1991	−4.7	−3.8	−1.3	2000	1.4	0.9	0.3
Denmark	1986	3.0	3.3	2.3	1993	−5.5	−2.9	−4.4	2000	0.3	2.7	0.2
Greece	1989	2.9	−14.4	1.3	1994	−2.7	−10.0	−1.3	2000	−0.8	−1.0	−0.4
New Zealand	1986	2.3	−6.5	1.4	1992	−5.4	−3.3	−3.1	2000	0.0	0.5	0.0
Norway[4]	1986	2.5	2.6	1.4	1989	−4.3	−2.0	−2.6	2000	1.0	−0.8	0.6
Sweden	1989	4.5	5.2	3.0	1993	−5.3	−10.8	−4.2	2000	1.0	3.4	0.7

[1] In several countries the fiscal position is biased upward due to one-off revenues from the sale of UMTS-licences, notably in Germany (2.5 per cent of GDP), the United Kingdom (2.4 per cent), Italy (1.2 per cent) and the Netherlands (0.7 per cent).

[2] Excluding Czech Republic, Hungary, Iceland, Korea, Mexico, Poland, Switzerland, and Turkey.

[3] Excluding Luxembourg.

[4] Excluding crude oil and natural gas extraction.

Table 8.2   Automatic fiscal stabilizers and the stance of discretionary fiscal policy (as a percentage of (potential) GDP)

	Change in[1]					
	Actual fiscal balance		Cyclical component		Structural primary balance	
	Late-1980s peak to early 1990s trough	Early-1990s trough to 2000	Late-1980s peak to early 1990s trough	Early-1990s trough to 2000	Late-1980s peak to early 1990s trough	Early-1990s trough to 2000
OECD[2]	−2.9	5.2	−1.3	0.8	−1.3	3.4
of which						
United States	−1.8	7.3	−1.2	1.3	−0.4	5.0
Japan	−6.5	−2.3	−0.9	−0.3	−5.6	−1.2
Euro area[3]	−1.1	5.9	−2.3	1.2	1.8	2.5
of which						
Germany	−1.1	4.5	−2.0	0.6	1.5	1.7
France	−3.9	4.6	−1.5	1.1	−1.9	3.4
Italy	0.4	9.3	−2.3	0.7	5.5	2.1
Austria	−2.1	3.5	−1.1	0.3	−0.9	3.1
Belgium	−0.6	7.3	−3.6	1.3	1.8	1.9
Finland	−13.3	11.3	−11.4	8.8	−0.9	4.0
Ireland	0.8	7.5	−3.2	3.5	2.1	1.8
Netherlands	2.1	5.2	−2.4	1.9	4.8	1.6
Portugal	−0.7	3.2	−1.8	0.7	−0.7	0.4
Spain	−0.8	4.7	−3.6	2.5	4.2	0.9
Other countries						
United Kingdom	−7.1	9.3	−4.8	2.7	−3.2	6.8
Canada	−4.8	11.6	−4.3	2.9	−0.1	8.0
Australia	−3.7	4.7	−1.5	1.6	−3.0	1.9
Denmark	−6.2	5.6	−6.7	4.6	−1.4	−0.3
Greece	4.4	9.0	−2.5	0.9	12.0	3.5
New Zealand	3.3	3.7	−4.5	3.1	6.0	−2.1
Norway[4]	−4.7	1.2	−4.0	3.2	−1.1	−1.8
Sweden	−17.1	15.4	−7.2	4.9	−9.5	11.3

[1] The cyclical component and the structural primary surplus do not add up to the actual fiscal balance; the residual consists of the net interest receipts and the one-off revenues from the sale of UMTS-licences.
[2] Excluding Czech Republic, Hungary, Iceland, Korea, Mexico, Poland, Switzerland, and Turkey.
[3] Excluding Luxembourg.
[4] Excluding crude oil and natural gas extraction.

Source: van den Noord (2000), updated on the basis of *OECD Economic Outlook,* 68, Paris, December 2000.

Ireland, Italy, the Netherlands, New Zealand and Spain), whereas it has been expansive elsewhere. With the exceptions of Denmark, Japan, New Zealand and Norway, all countries reverted to or maintained a tight stance of discretionary fiscal policy during the remainder of the decade.

8.3 The short-run effectiveness of automatic fiscal stabilizers

A change in cyclically sensitive government spending (unemployment benefits) or taxes affects spending in the economy mainly through its impact on disposable income, and hence household consumption. Meanwhile the impact of automatic fiscal stabilizers may be reinforced by other mechanisms that operate to smooth the business cycle. For example, the behaviour of imports is sensitive to short-term fluctuations in aggregate demand and therefore help to stabilize variations in economic activity. Similarly, 'permanent income' theories of consumption behaviour suggest that consumer spending responds only slowly to income fluctuations, which would tend to make private saving behaviour stabilizing, while cyclical variations in labour productivity prevent sharp swings in the demand for labour and thus help to stabilize unemployment. Reactions in financial markets and of monetary conditions to cyclical developments should also reinforce the fiscal stabilization mechanisms.[3] The role of monetary policy is central in this regard, although this depends crucially on the exchange rate regime in place. Where exchange rate arrangements permit, monetary policy adjustments designed to ensure price stability should operate to stabilize activity by generating pro-cyclical interest rate developments and at least working to encourage procyclical exchange rate behaviour in a way that provides incentives for further adjustment in international trade flows. Under a fixed exchange rate regime, on the other hand, monetary policy is not available to play such a role, and in some circumstances (e.g. several countries participating in or shadowing the ERM in the early 1990s) may even be destabilizing.

The OECD's INTERLINK model captures the basic macroeconomic relationships that operate, and simulations have been carried out with this model to assess the degree to which budgets have damped cyclical fluctuations over the 1990s. In a first simulation, fiscal stabilizers have been 'switched off' by setting tax and spending flows to their structural levels, from which it is possible to derive the reduction in cyclical volatility in economic activity achieved by the automatic fiscal stabilizers. In a second simulation, in turn, discretionary fiscal policy is switched off, hence assuming that the structural primary budget balance (and the underlying structural tax and expenditure ratios to GDP) remained unchanged during the 1990s. This should give an impression of what the shape of the business cycle had been, had fiscal policy relied solely but fully on the working of automatic fiscal stabilizers. In both simulations, monetary policy is assumed to have responded to economic developments in much the same way as it has usually behaved historically, i.e. leaning against the business cycle to some extent. In practical terms this has been approximated by a 'Taylor rule', which implies that interest rates are raised if either inflation or the output gap rise above their baseline levels, in all countries except for those (other than Germany) that participated in the ERM throughout the 1990s until the start of monetary union and whose fluctuation band was left unchanged during the turbulence of the early and mid-1990s (i.e. France, Austria, Belgium, Denmark, the Netherlands and Spain). For the latter group of countries, nominal interest rates were kept constant. Nominal exchange rates were held fixed and the simulations run on a country-by-country basis, which means that international linkages were switched off. The results are reported in Table 8.3.

The first simulation suggests that over the 1990s the automatic fiscal stabilizers have worked to damp the cyclical fluctuations in economic activity

Table 8.3   The simulated impact of fiscal policy on the cyclical volatility of GDP (root mean square of output gap, 1991–9)[1]

| | Actual[2] | Increase (+) or decrease (−) attributable to | | Memorandum item: increase (+) or decrease (−) of debt ratio to GDP due to discretionary policy |
		Automatic stabilizers	Discretionary policy	
Finland	5.7	−7.8	−2.9	17.4
Ireland	3.6	−0.4	−0.7	−9.3
Sweden	2.9	−1.0	−1.1	26.1
New Zealand	2.8	−0.9	−0.4	..
Canada	2.7	−0.7	0.8	−105.8
Japan	2.6	−0.4	−2.3	74.4
Italy	2.3	−0.7	1.7	−67.8
Spain	1.9	−0.4	−1.1	−16.3
Belgium	1.8	−0.5	0.7	−10.4
France	1.8	−0.3	0.1	16.3
Greece	1.8	−0.3	−2.6	−43.2
Australia	1.7	−0.3	−1.7	30.3
United Kingdom	1.6	−0.7	−0.4	22.5
United States	1.6	−0.3	−2.4	−13.8
Germany	1.4	−0.8	−0.3	−10.1
Austria	1.3	−0.1	−1.4	−17.1
Netherlands	1.1	−0.4	−1.5	−23.3
Average of above	2.3	−0.9	−0.9	−8.1

[1] The formula for the root mean square of the output gap reads:

$$\sqrt{\frac{1}{9} \sum_{t=1991}^{1999} gap_t^2}$$

where:
$gap_t = (y - y^*)/y^*$; $y = GDP$ and $y^* = $ potential GDP.
For technical reasons, results for Denmark, Norway and Portugal are not available.
[2] Countries are ranked according to cyclical variability of the output gap.

Source: van den Noord (2000).

by almost a third on average compared with the counterfactual without automatic fiscal stabilizers at work. However, there is considerable cross-country
variation, in part reflecting the relative openness of economies and differences in monetary policy responsiveness. In particular, Finland provides a
clear example where automatic fiscal stabilizers are essential: without them,
output volatility in the 1990s would have been twice as high. The ranking of
countries with regard to the stabilizing impact of automatic fiscal stabilizers
in Table 8.3 is broadly in line with other studies, but some studies report
somewhat higher levels of stabilization for the European countries; see, for
example, Buti and Sapir (1998).

There are important qualifications to these results. First, in countries where
fiscal positions threatened to become unsustainable, even if this was due to
cyclical weakness, business and financial market confidence deteriorated.
Therefore risk premia in real long-term interest rates rose (Orr *et al.*, 1995),
which had a negative influence on economic activity. When this occurs, the
negative effect on private spending operates to diminish or even to reverse
the supportive effects of automatic fiscal stabilizers. Such confidence effects
are not incorporated in INTERLINK and, therefore, not reflected in the results
reported in Table 8.3. When financial markets respond to rising budget
deficits this way, there is little alternative to correcting the fiscal position even
if this means overriding the automatic stabilizers. Several cases have been
reported where such policy responses helped to reverse increases in long-term
interest rates and contributed to a brisk recovery, notably in Finland,
Denmark, Ireland and Sweden (see Giavazzi and Pagano, 1990b and 1995a).

Second, the model simulations may also understate the extent of 'non-
Keynesian' responses to fiscal automatic stimulus, by which is meant an
increase in household saving rates in reaction to deteriorating fiscal balances.
If this occurs, the demand impetus stemming from the fiscal automatic
stabilizers may be smaller than expected or even negative. Such 'perverse' savings reactions are all the more likely if public debt is already high, since the
private sector may fear tax increases further down the road to offset a debt
explosion (Sutherland, 1997). In Europe, for instance, the intense public
debates prior to the ratification of the Maastricht Treaty have made the public well aware of fiscal issues, and may thus have prompted such forward-
looking saving behaviour (Martinot, 1999). This could happen again if, for
example, the public deficit approaches the 3 per cent of GDP benchmark in
a future recession. Unfortunately, while forward-looking saving behaviour
invalidates the impact of fiscal automatic stabilizers on economic activity, the
adverse impact on government borrowing remains.

The simulations described above treat discretionary fiscal policy adjustments as if they were not influenced either by the operation of automatic
stabilizers or by the situation in the economy. However, the overall degree
of fiscal stabilization reflects both the operation of the stabilizers themselves
and their influence on, and interaction with, discretionary policies. Thus, if

automatic stabilizers are overridden by discretionary adjustments, their impact will be neutralized. On the other hand, if they are reinforced by discretionary adjustments, the overall fiscal impulse will be stronger. In fact, Table 8.2 suggests that in the early-1990s recession many countries reinforced the automatic fiscal stabilizers through an easy stance of fiscal policy (United States, Japan, France, United Kingdom, Canada, Australia, Austria, Denmark, Finland, Norway, Portugal and Sweden). In the second scenario simulated with INTERLINK the fiscal stance is assumed to have been neutral for the 1990s (see Table 8.3). It suggests that the use of discretionary fiscal policy on average slashed the fluctuations in economic activity by almost one-third – similar to the estimated automatic stabilization effect, but with much greater cross-country variation.

Not surprisingly, the simulations suggest that in countries in the European Union the tight stance of discretionary fiscal policy in fact contributed to delay the recovery from the 1993 recession. However, there was no other option in many EU countries given the poor state of public finances at the time of the Maastricht Treaty and beyond. Had fiscal automatic stabilizers been allowed to work without any discretionary adjustments in the euro area, the simulations suggest that 1999 budget deficits would on average be six times as high as their actual levels. This would undoubtedly have boosted long-term interest rates, perhaps significantly, and would have extended the episode of exchange rate turbulence that marked the early and mid-1990s. Obviously this would have made the establishment of monetary union extremely difficult. Nevertheless, several European countries that eased fiscal policy during the recession and tightened later (France, the United Kingdom and Sweden) had some success in terms of stabilizing the economy this way, but at the cost of fiscal positions that were still weaker in 1999 and substantially higher debt ratios.

Among the non-European Union countries, the United States managed to use fiscal policy to stabilize the cycle and obtained this result while achieving a better debt position than it otherwise would have realized. Discretionary fiscal policy thus acted as a powerful complement to automatic fiscal stabilization; it contributed to both a virtuous circle of sustainable economic growth and steadily improving public finances. In Japan the variability of economic activity has also been significantly limited as a result of discretionary fiscal policy. However, since both automatic and discretionary components of fiscal policy have been mostly stimulatory over the decade they caused a dramatic deterioration of the public debt-to-GDP ratio.

8.4   The impact of automatic fiscal stabilizers on longer-term performance

There are a number of ways in which fiscal stabilizers may impinge on longer-term economic performance. On the positive side, achievement of longer-term objectives of sustainable economic growth, full employment and price stability, requires short-run macroeconomic stabilization policy to ensure the maintenance of an appropriate level of aggregate demand. Recurrent large under-utilization of resources can have damaging longer-term effects if it leads to under-investment in, and failure to maintain, physical and, more importantly, human capital. While periods of overheating may have some similar, offsetting effects in a favourable direction, it is likely that sharp fluctuations around the trend on balance have negative implications for the economy's longer-term potential.

Moreover, the theoretical literature strongly suggests that it is less costly to keep tax rates stable over the cycle, and hence allow automatic fiscal stabilizers to operate, than to adjust tax rates from one year to another. Such a policy may, in any event, prove to be ineffective if activity keeps moving as attempts are made to stabilize the fiscal position. Similar arguments will apply to adjusting spending parameters such as unemployment benefit rates. Automatic stabilization can also be justified on the ground that the government faces fewer liquidity constraints and a lower risk premium than the private sector and therefore is likely to be more efficient at consumption smoothing through cyclical downturns than households are.

There is also a negative side, or at least there are risks, involved in using automatic fiscal stabilizers. First, unless care is taken to ensure that automatic stabilizers operate symmetrically over the business cycle, the result may be permanently higher government indebtedness and associated servicing cost. Most importantly, this involves ensuring that the stabilizers are allowed to work in booms as well as during slowdowns so that they do not bias structural budget positions toward deficits. The risk of unsustainable debt accumulation is heightened by adverse debt dynamics that may emerge when real interest rates exceed growth rates. As a result, debt expands at a faster rate than GDP, hence the debt-to-GDP ratio rises unless there is a sufficiently large primary surplus.[4] The long-run damage to economic growth that results from sustaining high public debt levels in the wake of a recession without subsequently reducing them may be substantial, because taxes, and the distortions they create, as well as real long-term interest rates would have to be higher.

Adverse debt dynamics were indeed very prominent in most OECD countries during the 1990s, especially in countries that had high debt levels from the outset such as Italy, Canada and Belgium.[5] Such poor starting positions stemmed from the earlier failure to use fiscal automatic stabilizers symmetrically during previous business cycles – i.e. the tendency to let automatic stabilizers work fully in a recession while overriding them by discretionary fiscal expansion in upswings (Leibfritz *et al.*, 1994). Most countries have succeeded in offsetting any adverse debt dynamics in the 1990 by strong fiscal consolidation – with the notable exception of Japan where massive fiscal easing contributed to the ballooning of public debt. In the future, governments should guard against the asymmetric use of automatic fiscal stabilizers, although this obviously does not preclude all discretionary action, particularly for structural reasons. If, for example, the tax burden is heavy and found to exert a negative impact on economic growth, governments may aim to cut taxes even during an economic upswing. However, such tax cuts need to be matched with simultaneous reductions in expenditure in order not to weaken the fiscal position.

Second, there is a risk of governments treating changes in budget positions that have structural roots as if they were the result of automatic stabilizers, or vice versa. This is to misjudge the underlying fiscal situation and may lead to inappropriate policies. Of central importance in judging the underlying, structural, budget position is a sound assessment of structural change, particularly as it affects the level of potential output. Once evidence suggests that changes affecting the level or the growth rate of potential output have occurred, fiscal policies should be reviewed and, where necessary, adjusted. Otherwise, fiscal policy may be set on an unsustainable course and there is a risk of provoking adverse private-sector reactions once financial markets and consumers realize this. Improving the analytical tools available to governments to gauge the economy's potential and the structural fiscal position thus appears to be important for future policy-making.

Finally, but very importantly, automatic fiscal stabilization is often created by mechanisms that allow people and businesses affected by changing economic circumstances to delay their adjustment to change. Such mechanisms include the functioning of social security systems, labour market institutions and many parts of tax systems whose effects on incentives have been analysed in detail in the various OECD *Jobs Strategy* publications – see, for example, OECD (1999b). These systems therefore need to be designed to ensure that the incentives to which they give rise are consistent with flexible labour and product markets that heighten the economy's ability to adapt well to change. This need not diminish and may even strengthen the automatic fiscal stabilizers. For example, shortening benefit duration strengthens work incentives without affecting the short-run automatic stabilization properties of the unemployment insurance system. To take another example, introducing in-work benefits at the lower end of the pay scale, while providing work incentives, raises tax progressivity at the same time (Bassanini *et al.*, 1999). In any event, when a future economic shock requires a major reallocation of resources, the role of automatic fiscal stabilizers should at best be one of temporarily easing the pain, to allow time for the necessary adjustments to take place – not to postpone these adjustments indefinitely.

8.5 Summing up

We have assessed to what extent government budgets were affected by the macroeconomic situation and operated to smooth the business cycle in

OECD countries during the 1990s. It could be demonstrated that automatic fiscal stabilizers by themselves have generally reduced cyclical volatility in the wake of the recession in the early 1990s. However, a need to consolidate budgets prompted several countries, notably in Europe, to take discretionary action to reduce, or even more than offset, the working of automatic stabilizers. This may have slowed down the economic recovery, but the alternative of fully relying on automatic stabilizers, and perhaps allowing fiscal deficits to run out of hand as a result, would clearly have been very risky in view of the deplorable debt situation at the time.

Once fiscal consolidation is achieved, a return to letting the automatic fiscal stabilizers play out freely may be envisaged. It could raise long-term economic performance by preventing sharp economic fluctuations and avoiding frequent changes in spending or tax rates. However, the risks inherent to this policy choice must be minimized. In particular, discretionary fiscal policy responses should be symmetric over the cycle in order to avoid a deficit bias, the assessment of structural or potential economic growth needs to be prudent and the mechanisms that generate automatic stabilization should be consistent with the requirements of efficient markets.

Appendix 8.A.1: cyclical adjustment of budget balances

The cyclically-adjusted budget balance is derived by (re-)calculating the items on the government appropriation account which would be obtained if output (GDP) were at its potential level. Thus:

$$b^* = (\textstyle\sum_i(T_i^*) - G^* + X)/Y^*$$

where:

b^* = structural component of budget balance (ratio to potential output)
G^* = structural government expenditures (excluding capital and interest spending)
T_i^* = structural component for the ith category of tax
X = non-tax revenues – capital and interest spending
Y^* = level of potential output

and:

$$T_i^*/T_i = (Y^*/Y)^{\alpha i}$$
$$G^*/G = (Y^*/Y)^{\beta}$$

where:

T_i = actual tax revenues for the ith category of tax
G = actual government expenditures (excluding capital and interest spending)
Y = level of actual output
α_i = elasticity of ith tax category with respect to output
β = elasticity of current primary government expenditures with respect to output (composite of the elasticity of unemployment-related expenditure with respect to output and the share of unemployment-related expenditure in total current primary expenditure)

For the purpose of accurately assessing the extent of automatic stabilization, four different categories of taxes are distinguished, each portraying different degrees of built-in elasticity (see Table 8.A.1):

- Corporate tax, which on average represents 3.5 per cent of GDP in the countries covered, exhibits the highest sensitivity to output changes. This characteristic reflects that corporate profits, which form the bulk of the tax base, fluctuate sharply over the cycle, thus transmitting similar fluctuations to the yield of the corporate tax, while statutory tax rates are assumed to be constant. Accordingly, the average output elasticity of corporate income tax is estimated at around 1.25, with somewhat higher values (around 2) found for the United States, Japan, France, Austria and Denmark and lower ones (less than 1) for Germany, Italy, the United Kingdom, Belgium, Finland, Greece, New Zealand and Sweden.
- As concerns personal income tax, whose share in GDP amounts to some 12.5 per cent on average in the countries that are covered, rate progression and exemptions make for a sharper variation in revenue compared to its tax base. Indeed, as income rises, a larger share of personal income falls above the exemption limit and taxable income slides up the rate brackets. On the other hand, personal income varies less sharply than does real GDP, due to a muted short-run responsiveness of employment and wages – and hence personal earnings – to variations in economic activity. With these factors broadly offsetting each other, the average GDP elasticity of personal income tax is close to 1 on average. Note, however, that some countries (the United Kingdom, Finland, Greece and Sweden) show significantly higher values, whereas others (Japan) have substantially lower ones.
- Social security tax, which on average yields 12 per cent of GDP, varies less sharply than its tax base due to the existence of statutory contribution ceilings, which are defined either per individual or per household. Therefore, as income rises, a larger share of income falls above the contribution ceiling(s) and the average effective tax rate tends to drop. With, in addition, personal income portraying less volatility than GDP, the cross-country average GDP elasticity of social security tax amounts to just over 0.75, with values above 1 found in the United Kingdom and Greece, and values less than 0.5 in Japan.
- Indirect tax, which is the largest tax category among the countries covered (14 per cent of GDP), is mostly proportional to its main tax base – private consumption – even if some countries employ higher rates for certain income-elastic (luxury) goods. Accordingly, the GDP elasticity of the tax revenue of indirect taxes amounts to almost 1 on average; however, Norway and Denmark well exceed that average whereas Japan, Australia, Austria and Ireland are significantly below it.
- The built-in elasticity of government expenditure, finally, which reflects cyclical variations in unemployment-related spending only, is relatively minor given the small share of such spending in the total. For most countries elasticities in the 0 to −0.25 range have been adopted, albeit Denmark and the Netherlands portray significantly stronger expenditure flexibility.

The methodology for estimating these elasticities is explained in Van den Noord (2000). It involves three steps. In a first step, the elasticities of the relevant tax bases and unemployment with respect to the output gap are estimated through regression analysis. In the second step the elasticities of personal income tax and social security contributions are extracted from the tax code for different earnings brackets and subsequently weighted together on the basis of each bracket's share in aggregate earnings. Meanwhile the tax elasticities of indirect and corporate tax with respect to their main

Table 8.A.1 Tax and expenditure elasticities

	Tax				Current expenditure	Total balance[1]
	Corporate	Personal	Indirect	Social security		
United States	1.8	0.6	0.9	0.6	−0.1	0.25
Japan	2.1	0.4	0.5	0.3	−0.1	0.26
Germany	0.8	1.3	1.0	1.0	−0.1	0.51
France	1.8	0.6	0.7	0.5	−0.2	0.46
Italy	1.4	0.8	1.3	0.6	−0.1	0.48
United Kingdom	0.6	1.4	1.1	1.2	−0.2	0.50
Canada	1.0	1.2	0.7	0.9	−0.2	0.41
Australia	1.6	0.6	0.4	0.6	−0.2	0.28
Austria	1.9	0.7	0.5	0.5	0.0	0.31
Belgium	0.9	1.3	0.9	1.0	−0.3	0.67
Denmark	1.6	0.7	1.6	0.7	−0.5	0.85
Finland	0.7	1.3	0.9	1.1	−0.4	0.63
Greece	0.9	2.2	0.8	1.1	0.0	0.42
Ireland	1.2	1.0	0.5	0.8	−0.3	0.32
Netherlands	1.1	1.4	0.7	0.8	−0.7	0.76
New Zealand	0.9	1.2	1.2	1.1	−0.3	0.57
Norway (mainland)	1.3	0.9	1.6	0.8	−0.1	0.46
Portugal	1.2	1.2	0.6	0.9	−0.1	0.38
Spain	1.1	1.1	1.2	0.8	−0.1	0.40
Sweden	0.9	1.2	0.9	1.0	−0.3	0.79
Average	1.24	1.05	0.89	0.82	−0.21	0.49
Standard deviation	0.43	0.40	0.35	0.22	0.17	0.18

[1] Semi-elasticity (change in budget balance as a per cent of GDP for a 1 percentage-point change in the output gap). Based on weights for 1999.

Source: van den Noord (2000) and *OECD Economic Outlook, Sources and Methods*.

tax bases, private consumption and the operating surplus, are set to unity, and the elasticity of current primary expenditure with respect to unemployment-related expenditure is approximated by the share of unemployment-related in current primary expenditure. In the third and final step these two sets of elasticities are combined into the set of reduced-form elasticities reported in Table 8.A.1.

Notes

1. Economics Department, Organization of Economic Cooperation and Development (OECD), Paris. This chapter is a revised and updated version of an earlier paper by the same author: see Van den Noord (2000). He is writing in a personal capacity and therefore the chapter does not necessarily reflect the view of the Organization or its Member countries.
2. See, for further detail, Giorno *et al.* (1995), Van den Noord (2000) and *OECD Economic Outlook, Sources and Methods*, http://www.oecd.org/eco/out/source.htm

3. For example, estimates for the United States suggest that stabilization through financial markets' reactions offset as much as 60 per cent of the cyclical variations in output. See Asdrubali *et al.* (1996).

4. Permanent effects can arise for either of two further reasons: downswings and upswings can differ in terms of their intensity; or they can differ in terms of their duration. A second order effect can also arise as a consequence of interest rate variations over the cycle.

5. In contrast, in Greece, also a high-debt country, debt dynamics have worked favourably due to high inflation, but (foreign-currency denominated) debt nevertheless soared as the exchange rate depreciated.

9
Fiscal Policy in EMU: The Stabilization Aspect

Hans Wijkander and Werner Roeger[1]

9.1 Introduction

Within EMU, monetary and exchange rate policies are no longer available at a national level, and as a result, fiscal policy has gained in importance as a means to mitigate efficiency and equity problems that follow economic downturns.[2] The purpose of this chapter is to discuss the need to achieve stabilization through budgetary policies and to highlight the degree of stabilization a country can obtain for given weakening of its budget.

Since a few years back, before the creation of EMU, the member states in the European Union have vigorously consolidated their budgets through increased revenue and lower expenditure. The primary goal was to meet the Maastricht criteria of less than 3 per cent of GDP budget deficit and less than 60 per cent of GDP government debt. The consolidation process has continued after the creation of EMU but now with the aim of achieving, on average, close to balanced budgets within a few years. This implies that further reforms of expenditure and tax systems will take place.

Traditionally, efficiency and equity constitute the main dimensions for evaluation of tax reforms. However, in the new environment of EMU, the stabilizing property of the 'fiscal package' is a dimension that deserves additional attention. That holds in particular for how the stabilizing effect can be increased. Obvious ways to achieve more stabilization through the budget than previously would be to expand the public share of the economy or to rearrange the budget so that taxes and expenditures become more progressive with regard to variations in incomes (OECD, 1993). However, a larger public sector or increased progressivity of some items in the budgets such as labour income tax and some transfers to households are undesired for efficiency reasons. Indeed increased progressivity would undo recent tax reforms. Achieving more stabilization through reduced taxes and increased spending may in addition lead to a potential conflict with the Stability and Growth Pact. A close to balanced budget gives considerable leeway for increased expenditures and lower taxes in downturns (automatic or discretionary), but in some countries where budget balances are highly sensitive to variations in economic activity and general economic activity experiences large decreases, there may still be a risk of running into conflict with the Stability and Growth Pact (compare Andersen, 1997, and Bayoumi and Eichengreen, 1995).

In the light of the increased importance of fiscal policy and the problems with increasing the size of the public sector and the progressivity of taxes and expenditures, there is a case to explore if there are budget items that may contribute significantly to stabilization without creating the disincentive effects of labour income taxation and certain transfers to households. The constraint imposed by the Stability and Growth Pact makes it interesting to explore whether or not there are ways to increase the stabilizing capability of government budgets for given weakening of budgets. If that can be achieved, the risks of running into conflict with the Stability and Growth Pact may be reduced without sacrificing the efficiency and equity gains from increased stability.[3]

Essentially the framework of the discussion in the chapter is Keynesian and the conclusions are also in many cases well known within that framework. The choice of approach lets the analysis open to criticism of the Keynesian framework but the chosen framework seems to be a manageable way to capture important features of the functioning of the economies.

The chapter is organized as follows. Section 2 briefly assesses the potential welfare gains of stabilization policy. Section 3 deals with sensitivities of budgets to variations in GDP and business-cycle swings in EU member states. The section establishes that if the pattern of business-cycle swings has not changed significantly recently or if EMU in itself will lead to such changes, there seems be a need for stabilization through fiscal policy. Section 4 deals with the efficiency of stabilizers. For convenience reasons and in order to highlight the main message we compare only two countries, France and Germany. We indicate that there may be quite substantial differences among countries in regard to efficiency of stabilization of their budgets and that there may be large differences among different policy parameters. The study is carried out within the QUEST-model (a DG ECFIN macro model). We also conclude that the stabilizing efficiency of different budget items is similar between the two countries. At the aggregate level of these simulations, tax on labour income and transfers to households seem not to be efficient for stabilization purposes. Concluding comments are in section 5.

9.2   Potential welfare gains from stabilization policy

This section briefly explores the cost of business-cycles swings of consumption by using standard microeconomic theory. The reason why variation in consumption may be regarded as costly is that marginal utility of consumption is usually assumed to be decreasing, which is implied by concavity of the utility function. Suppose utility is given by

$$U = \int_0^\infty \sum_i \pi_i u(C_{it}) e^{-rt} dt \tag{9.1}$$

Consider now the following simple calculation on the temporal utility function (where we drop the time index).

$$u(\overline{C} - K) = \sum_i \pi_i u(C_i) \tag{9.2}$$

It can be shown that

$$K \approx -\frac{u''}{2u'} \operatorname{var}(C) \text{ or } \frac{K}{\overline{C}} \approx -\frac{u'' \overline{C} \operatorname{var}(C)}{2u' \ (\overline{C})^2} \tag{9.3}$$

where $\dfrac{\operatorname{var}(C)}{(\overline{C})^2} = \operatorname{var}(consumption\,gap)$

As a benchmark case it seems reasonable to take the relative risk aversion, $-u''\overline{C}/u'$, as 2 (see, e.g., Friend and Blume, 1975). This implies that the relative cost of risk equals the relative variance of C or the consumption gap. It follows that a 1 per cent reduction of the relative variance corresponds to a 1 per cent increase in the certainty equivalent of C. Hence, from Table 9.1 we can conclude that the relative cost of risk among the member countries varies between 0.9 per cent to 9.3 per cent of C.

In the following we do not use consumption variation in the analysis since GDP variations are generally used in the context of stabilization policy. A comparison between Tables 9.1 and 9.2 shows that the ranking of countries by consumption volatility coincides to a large degree with the ranking according to size of output gap, which should also be expected on theoretical grounds.

Table 9.1 Variance of consumption gaps for the European Union member states, 1960–96

B	DK	D	EL	E	F	IRL	I	L	NL	A	P	FIN	S	UK
2.3	3.2	3.0	4.2	7.4	0.9	5.5	2.6	3.9	2.8	1.4	9.3	7.9	2.3	3.6

Source: European Commission.

Table 9.2 Standard deviation of output gaps for the European Union member states, 1960–96

B	DK	D	EL	E	F	IRL	I	L	NL	A	P	FIN	S	UK
1.7	1.8	2.0	2.1	2.5	1.4	2.1	1.7	3.1	1.6	1.7	2.8	3.6	1.9	2.2

Source: Buti and Sapir (1998), p. 129.

9.3   Sensitivities of budgets and business-cycle swings

Studies within the European Commission indicate that the patterns of business-cycle swings differ between the member countries. Table 9.2 shows the standard deviations of GDP (or equivalently, output gaps) in the member countries for the period 1960 to 1995.[4]

The most volatile economy among the member states is the Finnish (standard deviation 3.6 per cent of GDP). The decline of the Finnish economy in 1991 contributed significantly to this high volatility; without it the volatility would have been 2.5 per cent of GDP, which is still high, but not the highest. The reason for the relatively high volatility of the Finnish economy probably is the weight of the relatively volatile forest industry. It is probably the case that more diversified economies are, *ceteris paribus*, less volatile. The least volatile economy is the French (standard deviation 1.4 percentage of GDP). Note also that the volatility of the German economy is almost 50 per cent larger than the French (standard deviation 2.0). It is tempting to attribute that difference to different policy stances where France, at least up to the mid-1980s, has put more short-term emphasis on employment than Germany, while inflation, since the mid-1970s, has played a larger role in Germany.

Table 9.3. shows calculated elasticities of budget balances, that is, the percentage change in budget balances resulting from a one per cent increase in GDP, for the EU member countries in 1995.

The highest sensitivity is found in Sweden and the lowest in Greece. Two factors that affect the sensitivities are the size of the public sector and the sensitivity of taxes and expenditures to GDP swings. The Swedish economy is high, while the Greek is low, on both these accounts. The sizes of public sectors in Austria and the Netherlands are roughly the same but the

Table 9.3 Marginal elasticities of budget balances to GDP for the European Union member states, 1995

B	DK	D	EL	E	F	IRL	I	L	NL	A	P	FIN	S	UK
0.6	0.7	0.5	0.4	0.6	0.5	0.5	0.5	0.6	0.8	0.5	0.5	0.6	0.9	0.6

Source: Buti, Franco and Ongena (1997), p. 8.

sensitivities of their budgets to swings in GDP differ significantly. The explanation for this lies in the structures of their budgets and the variation of unemployment over the business cycle. The French and the German budgets are about equally sensitive to changes in GDP.

Table 9.4 shows the volatility of the cyclical components of budget balances. The volatilities vary between 0.7 in Greece and Italy to 2.2 in Finland. The reason for the relatively large volatility of the Finnish budget balance is most likely to be found in the relatively volatile output and the sensitivity of the budget. It seems as if Finland to a rather large extent has used the budget to mitigate output variations. Note also that the cyclical component of the German budget balance is somewhat higher than that of the French – 1.0 as compared to 0.8. Hence, the German budget has experienced somewhat larger swings than the French budget and the German output has been more volatile than the French has. If the shocks to the economies have not been significantly different the implication probably is that France to a larger extent than Germany has relied on output stabilizing monetary and exchange rate policies. This is probably relevant, at least, for the period up to the early 1980s. The well-known anti-inflationary stance of the German monetary policy since the mid-1970s lends additional support for such a conclusion.

Table 9.5 shows the number of years with negative output gaps of 2 per cent or more over the period 1960 to 1996, that is 37 years. As can be seen from the table, such a situation has occurred on average every sixth year during the period in question. In some countries they have been somewhat more frequent, and in France they have been significantly less frequent.[5] The total number of instances for the EU 15 countries is 93 but the number of instances where the aggregate EU 15 economy experienced such episodes

Table 9.4 Volatility of cyclical component in budget balances for European Union member states, 1961–96

B	DK	D	EL	E	F	IRL	I	L	NL	A	P	FIN	S	UK
1.0	1.2	1.0	0.7	1.5	0.8	1.2	0.7	1.7	1.3	0.8	1.1	2.2	1.8	1.4

Source: Buti, Franco and Ongena (1997), p. 8.

Table 9.5 Number of years with negative output gaps of 2 per cent or more, 1960 to 1996 (37 years)

B	DK	D	EL	E	F	IRL	I	L	NL	A	P	FIN	S	UK	EU	EU15
6	7	6	6	7	2	8	6	8	6	6	5	8	6	6	93	2

Source: European Commission.

was only two! This implies that the covariation between output gaps has not been large, with the implication that counter-cyclical monetary policy probably would have been used only sparsely if the same pattern had occurred in an EMU context. Whether or not the pattern will be the same in EMU or if it will be significantly different is an open question. Increased integration among EU countries may have made their output swings more synchronized with the implication that a common counter-cyclical monetary policy is more appropriate. However, pre-EMU data on output swings may underestimate the effects of asymmetric shocks since monetary and exchange rate policies may, at least in some instances of potentially significant downturns, have been effective in counteracting the shocks. Finally, since EMU represents a significant stability-oriented institutional change, the risk of politically or labour-market-induced asymmetric shocks may decrease. The conclusion therefore is that it is unclear whether or not the new regime will increase or reduce the need for stability-oriented fiscal policy but it cannot be excluded that fiscal policy may be significantly more important in an EMU context than in a pre-EMU context.

9.4   Efficiency of stabilizers

Studies within the European Commission and elsewhere (Buti and Sapir, 1998; Italianer and Vanheukelen, 1993; OECD, 1993) indicate that automatic stabilizers partly absorb macroeconomic shocks. However, the estimated degree of stabilization varies among the studies. Italianer and Vanheukelen (1993) report that between 20 and 50 per cent of a demand shock would be absorbed by automatic stabilizers. OECD (1993) reports that around 25 per cent of a shock would be absorbed. The main factors determining the stabilizing effects of fiscal policy are, according to the OECD (1993), the size of the public sector relative to GDP, the progressivity of the tax system, the sensitivity of specific tax bases such as labour income and the degree of openness.

The European Commission services have carried out a detailed study of differences in the stabilizing impact of automatic stabilizers among the EU 15 countries. The study is carried out as estimations in the QUEST-model. The experiment is an exogenous 1 per cent increase in private consumption. The stabilizing impacts of the budgets are measured as the differences in outputs when the working of the automatic stabilizers are blocked and when they are allowed to fully operate. Hence the method controls for different sensitivities of the underlying economies. An interesting result obtained is that the stabilizing effect of the German budget is about 30 per cent larger than that of the French budget. However, a drawback of the studies in an EMU and Stability and Growth Pact context is that the stabilizing effects are not related to changes in the budget deficit. In a situation where there is a constraint on the budget deficit a measure that captures this aspect might be useful.

In an attempt to shed additional light over whether or not there are differences among countries in regard to efficiency of stabilization and to explain the causes of such differences, we have made a study of France and Germany. The reason for choosing these two countries is that they are quite similar in many ways. The sizes of public sectors are roughly the same, they are about equally open economies and the sensitivities of their budget balance to changes in GDP are about the same. Hence, by comparing France and Germany we approximately control for the size of the public sector and the overall progressivity of the budgets.

The philosophy of the study is as follows. Government budgets include many items that respond to changes in general economic activity. Examples are tax receipts from personal income taxation, corporate income taxation and VAT, and expenditure increases on unemployment benefits. How such budgetary items react to changes in general economic activity depends on the legislative framework rules as well as more or less temporary changes in the systems. Some budgetary items react differently in different countries, with the result that the budgets may achieve different degrees of stabilization. Knowledge about such differences may potentially serve as important inputs in tax reforms and may be exploited to increase the stabilizing properties of the government budget.

However, as has been discussed above, the effect of a change in a particular budget item may affect budget balances differently in different countries. In order to control for such differences we measure the differences in stabilizing efficiency as the stabilization achieved divided by the change in budget balance. We refer to that measure as stabilizing efficiency. Although the index is myopic and does not include effects on economic efficiency and equity, it serves the purpose of highlighting that different budget items are differently efficient with regard to stabilization, which is the limited purpose of the analysis. The index only reflects short-run stabilization. Future effects, for example, due to irreversibility of policies, are not included in the index. A full-blown evaluation of policy options is, of course, a completely different matter and would be significantly more demanding.

The method used implies that we do not classify policies in terms of automatic stabilizers and discretionary policies. Instead we rely on actual behaviour and we calculate the contemporaneous one-year correlation between output gaps and the total changes in the policy parameters, that is, both the automatic stabilizers and the discretionary changes. These estimates of policy responses are used in the simulations of the economies' responses to shocks. Such a method, of course, implies that we do not directly enter into the interesting debate about to what extent time lags on fiscal policy prevents it from being fully efficient. On the other hand, our policy experiments have a flavour of realism since they are based on estimated behaviour of government budgets and there should be little doubt as to whether the suggested budgetary adjustments are feasible. It should also be mentioned that the policy responses refer to situations which the countries have actually experienced.

We made the study in the following way. First, for each country, government reactions in various dimensions were estimated. These dimensions were changes in the effective corporate and labour tax rates[6] as well as changes in transfers to households, government purchases and salaries to government employees as a share of GDP. Second these 'reaction parameters' were used in the QUEST-model to calculate the change in GDP and budget deficit resulting from a positive shock to demand when the different budget items responded in accordance with the estimated parameters. Third, the resulting changes in GDP and budget deficit from a demand shock were calculated but with the budget items locked at their pre-shock levels. This result serves as a benchmark. Four, an index to measure stabilizing efficiency was constructed. The two equilibria were compared with regard to changes in GDP and budget balance. The index was calculated according to the following formula:

$$\text{Stabilizing efficiency} = \frac{\Delta GDP - \Delta GDP_{NS}}{\Delta GD - \Delta GD_{NS}}$$

where ΔGDP and ΔGD are the changes in output and deficit when stabilizers worked. ΔGDP_{NS} and ΔGD_{NS} are the changes in output and deficit when policy parameters were unchanged.

The estimated reactions are shown in Table 9.6.[7] The data is presented in graphs in Appendix 9.A.1 so as to visualize the relation between policy parameters and output swings. In both countries a positive output gap has triggered (i) an increase of the effective corporate tax rate – in France with 0.20 percentage points and in Germany with 0.37 percentage points; (ii) a lower effective tax rate on labour by 0.10 percentage points and a decrease in transfers to households 0.43 percentage points in France. Both these variables were unaffected in Germany for the whole period considered, but there was a change in correlation between output and transfers to households in the beginning of the 1980s. (iii) Government purchases decreased as a share of GDP in France, 0.05 percentage points, and increased by 0.07 percentage points in Germany. (iv) Government wages decreased as shares of GDP; with 0.20 percentage points in France and with 0.06 percentage points in Germany. On the whole, the impression is that the French budget responds in a more counter-cyclical fashion than the German budget with the exception of the effective corporate income tax rate.

Table 9.7 shows the responses to a shock to demand of 1 per cent of GDP. The difference in stabilizing efficiency between the German and the French budgets is about 50 per cent. The major reasons are that the French budget has responded considerably more strongly with increased transfers to households

Table 9.6 Estimated government reactions to output gaps in France and Germany

	France	Germany
Corporate tax rate percentage points	0.20	0.37*
Labour tax rate percentage points	−0.10	0
Transfers to households as share of GDP	−0.43*	0
Government purchases as share of GDP	−0.05*	0.07*
Government salaries as share of GDP	−0.20*	−0.06*

*Significant at 5% level. The regressions are for the period 1974–91, 95 depending on data availability.
Source: European Commission.

Table 9.7 Response to a negative demand shock

Estimated stabilization	France	Germany
ΔGDP	−0.87	−0.96
Government deficit (ΔGD)	0.70	0.37
No-stabilization GDP (ΔGDP$_{NS}$)	−1.05	−1.06
No-stabilization government deficit (ΔGD$_{NS}$)	−0.06	0.09
Efficiency	*0.24*	*0.36*

Source: European Commission.

and more strongly on labour taxes than the German budget. Temporarily increased transfers or lowered labour taxes have only small effects on demand due to consumption smoothing. On the other hand, the French budget has also reacted more strongly with regard to government salaries, which go directly into the calculation of GDP and in addition give rise to a secondary effect through increased demand. That reaction tends to increase the efficiency of the French budget. The German budget reacted more strongly on government purchases, which are subject to leakages, and on corporate taxes. Together, it turns out that the German budget achieves more stabilization in relation to weakening of the budget than the French. The main reason probably is that the strong reaction of the highly efficient government salaries in France is counteracted by the less efficient transfers to households and lower labour taxes.

In a final experiment we calculated the stabilizing efficiency of different policy parameters. We proceeded in the following way. We changed each policy parameter in isolation in such a way that the deficit to GDP ratio increased by approximately 0.2 percentage points. The purpose of changing policy parameters so that a similar effect on deficit to GDP ratio is obtained is to achieve comparability. The effects on GDP and government deficit were compared to the no-stabilization benchmark. The results are presented in Table 9.8. The formula for calculating the stabilizing efficiency of a particular budget item is as follows:

$$\text{Stabilizing efficiency of item } i = \frac{\Delta GDP_i - \Delta GDP_{NS}}{\Delta GD_i - \Delta GD_{NS}}$$

The most striking result is in our view the similar efficiency of policy instruments between the countries. It is also noteworthy that the efficiency

Table 9.8   Efficiency of individual budget items

	France	Germany
No-stabilization		
Δ GDP	−1.05	−1.06
Δ Deficit	−0.06	0.09
Labour tax rate		
Δ GDP	−1.05	−1.06
Δ Deficit	0.18	0.30
Efficiency	0	0
Corporate tax rate		
Δ GDP	−1.00	−1.01
Δ Deficit	0.14	0.29
Efficiency	0.25	0.25
Transfer as percentage of GDP		
Δ GDP	−1.02	−1.02
Δ Deficit	0.14	0.32
Efficiency	0.15	0.17
Government purchases as percentage of GDP		
Δ GDP	−0.95	−0.96
Δ Deficit	0.17	0.30
Efficiency	0.43	0.48
Government employment as percentage of GDP		
Δ GDP	−0.66	−0.68
Δ Deficit	0.17	0.28
Efficiency	1.70	2.00
VAT rate		
Δ GDP	−0.93	−0.92
Δ Deficit	0.16	0.29
Efficiency	0.55	0.70

Source: European Commission.

of the effective labour tax rate is very low in both countries. The reasons are the large part of non-progressive social security contributions in labour tax, slow adjustment of employment and consumption smoothing.[8] Transfers to households and the corporate tax rate are also not very efficient policy instruments. On the other hand, government employment is in comparison very efficient in both countries; somewhat more in Germany than in France. The VAT rate and government purchases are also relatively efficient. A potential conclusion is that decreased effective tax rates on labour in downturns, for example through increased progressivity of labour income tax schedules, and increased transfers to households which may be expected to further distort economic incentives and are undesirable for that reason, seem not to be very efficient from a stabilization point of view. This tends to mitigate the policy conflict between stabilization and economic efficiency. However, should changes in labour taxes and transfers to households for one or another reason, such as their weights in the budgets, be judged necessary, a more disaggregated analysis would be required to shed light over the more efficient ways to use these instruments. It seems likely that the largest stabilizing effects would come from tax reductions and transfer increases to households that cannot smooth out income variations to the extent they would like, that is, households that are credit constrained. In particular such a policy might be efficient if it can be designed so as to not to lead to significant wage increases or to create large disincentives to work. However, the problems in identifying households that have a high propensity to consume and to design tax reductions and transfer increases that do not have significant negative side effects may be considerable.

The policies that are highly efficient from a stabilizing point of view such as government employment are problematic for a number of reasons. Expanding government employment in recession periods and decreasing it in upturns may be difficult for political reasons since such a policy may require layoffs in the upturn periods. Such layoffs may involve political costs if labour demand is not strong enough to quickly re-employ the fired workers. The implication is that the layoffs may never take place and the policy may tend to increase the size of the public sector. Another problem with the policy that may arise if the policy is used extensively is that it may be increasingly difficult to find well-motivated projects. That may reduce the economic efficiency of the policy. However, governments are regularly engaged in various types of projects that require workers on a temporary basis, such as building projects, and it seems not to be impossible to change the timing of such projects so as to improve stabilization. Likewise, the timing of government purchases can be changed in order to improve stabilization and the government can also change the timing pattern of employing workers due to normal worker turnover.

The VAT rate seems to be rather efficient from a stabilizing point of view. The reason probably is that consumers may take the opportunity to increase their purchases in times of low rates at the expense of purchases at other times. Hence, the effects would be to change the consumption pattern over time (in the model experiment, increased consumer purchases partially offset the initial demand shock). Such a change in the consumption pattern over the business cycle would also tend to change the time profile of government revenue; smaller increases in upturns and smaller decreases in downturns. This would probably be a desirable change. However, the political process for changing the VAT rates may involve considerable time lags when it comes to changes in the rates and to their restoration at original levels. It may also be administratively problematic to change VAT rates on short notice. If such lags are significant (the situation may differ from country to country because the political systems and situations differ) the VAT rates may not be an efficient means to achieve stabilization since they may actually work in a destabilizing way. Moreover, harmonization policies within the EU may constrain the options for using the VAT rates for stabilizing purposes.

To summarize: the government budget will automatically dampen the effects of shocks both through changes in the level of government net borrowing and through the adjustments of different budget items. Some budget items contribute more than others to stabilization in relation to their effects on the balance of the budget. Increased automatic stabilization can be achieved through changes in magnitude of responses of highly efficient budget items or through smaller responses on inefficient budget items (with unaffected budget balance). On top of the automatic stabilizers, discretionary policy may further strengthen the stabilizing effects but such policies may have significant negative side effects that limit their usefulness. The implication is that discretionary policy can be useful, but in comparison to the automatic stabilizers, the contribution will probably be little.

9.5   Concluding comments

The issue dealt with in this chapter is probably politically relevant in an EMU context where the participating countries have (i) lost access to monetary and exchange-rate policies at a national level, (ii) are constrained with regard to budget deficits, and (iii) do not want to increase the progressivity of tax and expenditure systems for efficiency reasons but may still experience economic downturns that are costly in terms of equity and economic efficiency. In such a perspective stability is an issue to be considered in relation to tax and expenditure policies. This chapter represents a first attempt to explore the options fiscal policy offers.

Appendix 9.A.1

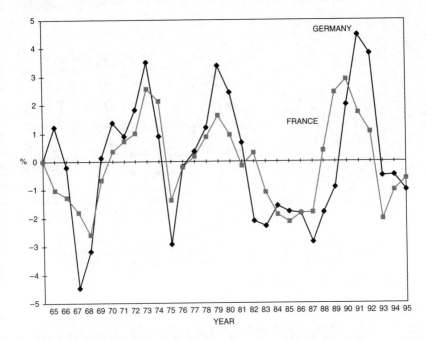

Figure 1. Output gap

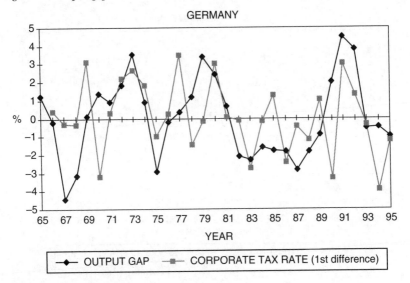

Figure 2a. Output gap vs. corporate tax rate

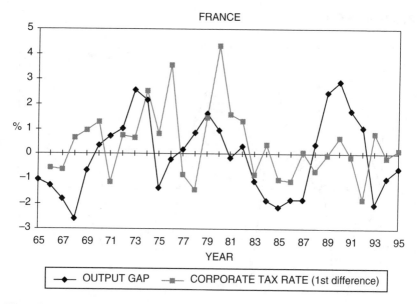

Figure 2b. Output gap vs. corporate tax rate

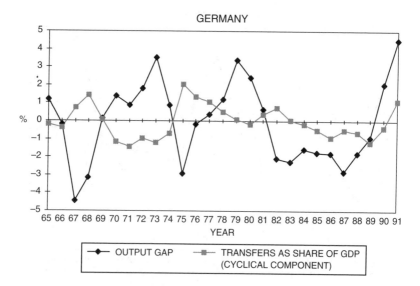

Figure 3a. Output gap vs. transfers

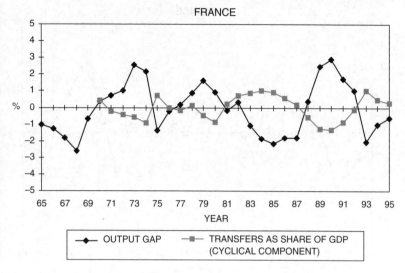

Figure 3b. Output gap vs. transfers

Figure 4a. Output gap vs. government purchases

164

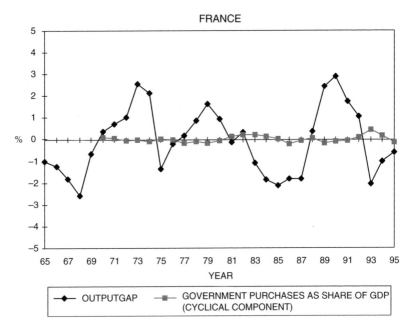

Figure 4b. Output gap vs. government purchases

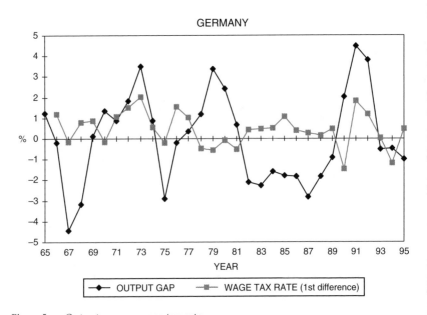

Figure 5a. Output gap vs. wage tax rate

165

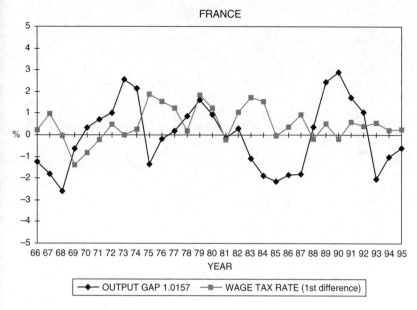

Figure 5b. Output gap vs. wage tax rate

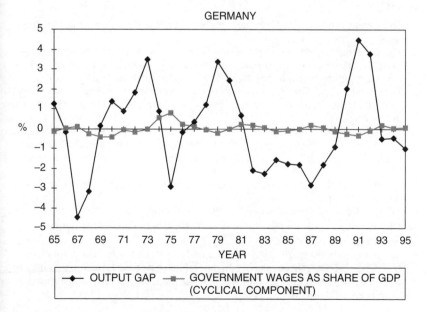

Figure 6a. Output gap vs. government wages

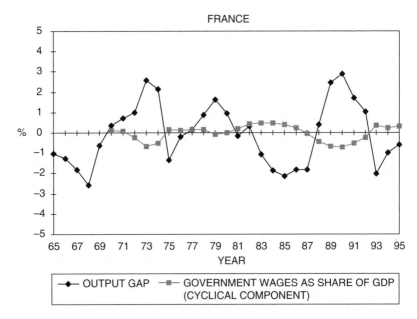

Figure 6b.   Output gap vs. government wages

Notes

1. The views expressed in this chapter are those of the authors and are not attributable to the European Commission.
2. The countries within the 'D-mark zone' had already before the creation of EMU quite limited possibilities to pursue monetary and exchange rate policies under normal circumstances but they had some room for manoeuvering.
3. The Stability and Growth Pact imposes an asymmetric constraint on budget balances. Hence, it has consequences for the level of budget balance that is needed in upswings.
4. Standard deviation measures the average difference between actual GDP and the calculated trend value. Hence, a large standard deviation indicates that the amplitudes of swings in GDP are large. Output gaps are calculated with Hodrick-Prescott filter.
5. The reason may very well be output-stability oriented monetary and exchange rate policies in France.
6. Tax on labour income and social security contributions.
7. The regression equation was $x_i = \alpha_{i0} + \alpha_{i1} YGAP$, where $YGAP$ is the output gap in percentage of GDP.
8. In the simulations progressivity of labour taxes plays no role since GDP changes exactly cancel out GDP changes in the no stabilization case. However, that may be a strongly model-specific and a more general result is that progressivity matters. Compare OECD (1993).

10
Gauging Ricardian Equivalence
Anne Brunila[1]

10.1 Introduction

The last decade or so in Europe is characterized by a vigorous fiscal consolidation as EU countries geared their fiscal policies to fulfil the convergence criteria[2] set out in the Maastricht Treaty and to qualify for the third stage of the Economic and Monetary Union by 1998. During the run-up to EMU a large number of EU countries had to reduce budget deficits and public debt levels to a significant degree. The low growth environment of the mid-1990s made fiscal consolidation based on substantial expenditure cuts and/or tax increases politically difficult as tight fiscal policies were seen detrimental to economic growth and employment in Europe. Moreover, the desirability of the additional discipline imposed on fiscal policy by the Stability and Growth Pact has been questioned on the ground that in EMU fiscal policy is the only policy tool left for stabilization purposes.[3] With this in view it has been argued that governments' room for manoeuvre should not be restricted but rather given greater flexibility to parry asymmetric shocks.

The quest for the impact of fiscal policy on the economy and its efficiency as a tool for economic stabilization has experienced a clear renaissance among policy-makers and economists after the creation of EMU and the new fiscal policy framework. Clear-cut answers to these issues are however hard to find as economic theory as well as empirical evidence result in sharp controversies. Most of the debate centres around two opposite views: the Keynesian or conventional and the Ricardian view.[4] The former, held by most economists and policy-makers, claims that government deficits can be used to stimulate economic activity at least in the short term, because the private sector perceives government debt as net wealth. Hence, a debt financed tax cut or increase in government spending boosts private consumption and aggregate demand. The short-term expansionary effects are however offset to a great extent by negative long-term effects caused by a declining savings ratio, rising interest rates and lower investment.

The Ricardian view, on the other hand, holds that tax cuts financed by budget deficits have no impact on economic activity, not even in the short run, because the private sector accurately anticipates the future tax liability implied by government borrowing. Hence, a lowering of taxes today will merely induce consumers to increase saving in order to avoid sharp decline in their future disposable income and consumption due to higher taxes. Hence, in anticipation of a future tax hike that will be needed to repay the new debt, consumers will save the entire tax cut, leaving consumption, national saving and aggregate demand unchanged. The Ricardian equivalence proposition leads thus to quite drastic policy implications: since a debt financed tax cut has no effect on aggregate demand, attempts to stabilize economic fluctuations via budget deficits are futile.[5]

As regards the effects of government consumption on economic activity, the conventional approach holds that changes in government consumption have no direct effect on private consumption since consumers' current disposable income remains unaltered. However, they will have one-to-one effect on aggregate demand. Ricardian equivalence, on the other hand, suggests that government consumption has a negative but less than one-to-one impact on private consumption and aggregate demand, since government consumption expenditure, whether financed by taxes or debt, implies absorption of real resources by the government sector.

The equivalence hypothesis holds literally only under fairly strong assumptions.[6] Of these assumptions, perhaps the most heavily criticized in the literature are the infinite planning horizon of the consumers and perfect capital markets. If consumers are short-sighted or anticipate that part of the debt will be passed on to future generations, the hypothesis will not hold. In the limit, in which consumers anticipate that the entire government debt will be passed to future generations, the effects of fiscal policy are the same in both the conventional and Ricardian frameworks.

Capital market imperfections in turn may restrict consumers' borrowing possibilities at times when current incomes are small relative to expected lifetime wealth. In this case consumption will be determined by current disposable income rather than by expectations as to future income, taxes and government transfers (i.e. permanent income). As a result of binding credit constraints, the impact of taxation and income transfers on aggregate demand may tend to be more Keynesian than Ricardian.

As such, there is little reason to believe that Ricardian equivalence holds exactly in the real world. This is not however the key issue. For the evaluation of the effects of fiscal policy the important question is whether there are significant departures from it. From this perspective, the equivalence proposition can be used as a benchmark, the validity of which can be empirically tested.

Since Barro's seminal paper (1974) on the debt neutrality, there has emerged a considerable amount of empirical research on its validity as an appropriate description of reality. The overwhelming body of empirical evidence on

Ricardian equivalence concerns the US. The findings are however to a large extent controversial and cannot be applied to other countries as such. Lack of studies applying the same approach, the same empirical methodology and comparable data for a larger set of countries is clearly a shortcoming.

The aim of this chapter is to fill some of the gaps in existing research by providing empirical results on the effects of government deficits and debt on private consumption in ten EU countries over the period from the early 1960s to the mid-1990s. Ricardian equivalence is used as a starting point or benchmark against which the nature and magnitude of departures of the economy from the idealized model is investigated. The first departure examined is the finiteness of the planning horizon of consumers. The shorter the consumers' planning horizon, the larger the positive effects of government debt financing on private consumption, because new government bond issues are perceived largely as an increase in consumers' net wealth. In the opposite case, when the planning horizon approaches close to infinity, Ricardian equivalence holds and government deficit financing has no effect on private consumption.

To account for other possible departures from the Ricardian benchmark, the assumption of perfect capital markets is relaxed next by allowing consumption to depend not only on permanent income but also on current disposable income due to credit constraints. If consumption proves to be sensitive to fluctuations in current income, the underlying permanent income hypothesis is not valid and the Ricardian equivalence hypothesis fails.

The basic framework is based on the discrete-time counterpart of Blanchard's (1985) overlapping generations model which allows for the derivation of an estimable aggregate consumption function that is expressed in terms of fundamental behavioural parameters. The model is augmented to incorporate government consumption as a direct conveyer of utility to consumers, as suggested by Aschauer (1985). By generalizing the basic set-up to incorporate liquidity constrained consumers in line with Hall (1978) and Campbell and Mankiw (1989), a weak form of Ricardian equivalence is introduced.

The rest of the chapter is organized as follows. In section 10.2, the empirical consumption function is derived from a formal intertemporal maximization framework with finite horizons and government consumption. Section 10.3 discusses the estimation issues and the data and reports the results. Section 10.4 tests the weak form of Ricardian equivalence by incorporating credit constrained consumers in the estimation equation. Concluding remarks are drawn in section 10.5.

10.2 A permanent income model with finite horizons

In order to trace the effect of fiscal policy on private consumption, a widely used framework of a stochastic intertemporal utility maximization of rational consumers subject to the lifetime budget constraint is used. Ricardian equivalence and the conventional hypothesis on the impact of fiscal policy are nested in the same framework by assuming uncertain lifetime and finite planning horizon for consumers in line with Blanchard (1985). Finite planning horizon introduces a wedge between the real rate of return on government bonds and the rate at which consumers discount their uncertain future labour income, thereby causing Ricardian equivalence to fail. Ricardian equivalence holds only in the special case of infinite planning horizon under which the discount rates on government bonds and labour income coincide.

Consumer behaviour is characterized by the permanent income/life cycle hypothesis, which states that consumers base their current consumption decisions on their expectations on their lifetime wealth (permanent income) rather than on current income. In each period, each consumer is assumed to face a known probability of survival, γ, which is independent of age. Probability of surviving from period t through period $t + j$ is thus γ^j and the expected life of each consumer, or the length of consumers' planning horizon, is $1/(1 - \gamma)$.

Consumers are assumed to have unrestricted access to capital markets at which they may accumulate or decumulate assets at the same constant real rate of return r as the government. A zero-profit condition in these markets together with the simple population structure[7] and lifetime uncertainty implies an effective, risk-adjusted interest factor of $(1+r)/\gamma$ for individual consumers.

Assuming that consumers maximize expected life-time utility under quadratic utility function and exogenous uncertainty,[8] it can be shown (see Brunila, 1997) that the aggregate per capita private consumption, c_t^p, depends on the expected value of the future stream of disposable income (after-tax income including government transfer payments), $E_t H_t$,[9] expected value of aggregate per capita government consumption, $E_t G_t$,[10] current government consumption, g_t, and initial financial assets (or debt incurred), including government bonds, a_{t-1}. Because of the lifetime uncertainty (finite planning horizon) future disposable income is discounted by risk-adjusted interest factor, $(1+r)/\gamma$. The term in brackets in equation (10.1) represents thus total expected wealth, $E_t W_t$:

$$c_t^p = \beta_0 + \beta_1[E_t H_t + \theta E_t G_t + (1+r)a_{t-1}] - \theta g_t \qquad (10.1)$$

with

$$\beta_0 = \frac{\gamma(\delta - r)c^*}{(1-r)(1+r-\gamma)} \quad \text{and} \quad \beta_1 = 1 - \frac{\gamma(1+\delta)}{(1+r)^2}$$

The parameter β_1, which is the constant marginal propensity to consume out of total expected wealth, is a function of the survival probability, γ, the constant positive rate of subjective time preference, δ, and the real interest rate, r. The constant term β_0 is determined by the above mentioned parameters and the bliss level of consumption, c^*.

The effect of government consumption on private consumption is captured by allowing individuals to derive utility not only from private consumption but also from government consumption. If total effective real per capita consumption is defined as a linear combination of private consumption and a portion θ of government consumption, then one unit of government consumption yields the same utility as θ units of contemporaneous private consumption. The term $\theta E_t G_t$ in the definition of wealth implies that with $E_t G_t$ unchanged, an increase in government consumption today implies some direct crowding out (in) of contemporaneous private consumption, if $\theta > 0$ (<0).

In the framework of the permanent income model, rational forward-looking consumers should take into account the future implications of current financing decisions of the government in making their consumption decisions. This implies that they will hold government bonds only if they are certain that the government will raise sufficient tax revenue to cover both expenditures and debt repayment in the future. The important implication of this is that consumers with rational expectations take into account the sustainability of government finances in their optimizing problem. For government intertemporal budget constraint to hold, expansionary policies today, whether in the form of expenditure increases or tax reductions, must be offset by expenditure cuts or tax increases in the future.

Imposing the no-Ponzi-game solvency constraint[11] for the government sector, which rules out the possibility to roll over government debt continuously, gives the following intertemporal budget constraint for the government:

$$E_t T_t = E_t G_t + E_t T R_t + (1+r)b_{t-1} \qquad (10.2)$$

The government budget constraint equates the present value of expected tax receipts, $E_t T_t$, to the initial government debt, b_{t-1}, plus the present values of expected government consumption, $E_t G_t$, and transfer payments, $E_t TR_t$. From this intertemporal constraint, it follows that for a given path of government consumption a deficit financed cut in current taxes leads to higher future taxes having the same expected value as the tax cut.

By substituting the expression for taxes in equation (10.2) into the private consumption function (10.1), and eliminating the financial wealth, a_{t-1}, from the equation yields the following consolidated model for private consumption, c_t^{P}.[12]

$$c_t^P = -r\,\beta_0 + (1+r)(1-\beta_1)c_{t-1}^P + \beta_1(1-\gamma)E_t Y_t$$

$$+\beta_1(1-\gamma)(\theta-1)E_t G_t - \theta\,g_t + (1+r)(1-\beta_1)\theta\,g_{t-1}$$

$$-\beta_1(1+r)(1-\gamma)b_{t-1} + \beta_1\gamma\,(e_{Yt}+\theta\,e_{Gt}) + u_t \qquad (10.3)$$

where error terms

$$e_{Yt} = (E_t - E_{t-1}) \sum_{j=0}^{\infty} \left(\frac{\gamma}{1+r} \right)^j y_{t+j}$$

and

$$e_{Gt} = (E_t - E_{t-1}) \sum_{j=0}^{\infty} \left(\frac{\gamma}{1+r} \right)^j g_{t+j}$$

reflect the revisions of expectations about the sequence of labour income y_{t+j} and government consumption g_{t+j} that consumers make as new information about future labour income and government consumption becomes available. Hence, the unexpected change in private consumption from $t-1$ to t is related to the changes in the expected lifetime wealth (i.e. permanent income) generated by unexpected changes (or innovations) in labour income and government consumption. The additional error term u_t is added to represent stochastic, or transitory, component of consumption, defined as zero-mean shocks to the utility function and measurement errors in consumption.

Equation (10.3) states that private consumption is determined by the total expected wealth, which depends on the expected present values of future labour income ($E_t Y_t$) plus government consumption and the initial value of the government debt commitment, as well as lagged private consumption and current and lagged government consumption. The parameters γ and θ play a crucial role in determining whether the effects of fiscal policy are Ricardian or Keynesian.

With γ equal to unity, forward-looking rational consumers have infinite horizon and consider today's deficit financing as tomorrow's tax liabilities. Hence, deficits have no wealth effect and no effect on current consumption. Consumers base their consumption decisions on lifetime (permanent) income, which depends on the present value of government consumption but not on the timing of tax collections. With γ equal to unity private consumption is affected only by a distributed lag on government consumption, reflecting dynamic effects of substitution between government consumption and private consumption at a point in time, as well as unexpected changes in labour income and government consumption and not by the form of finance. Moreover, an infinite planning horizon implies that the propensity to consume out of total expected wealth, β_1, should be close to $r/(1+r)$.

The parameter γ less than unity implies that, due to a shorter planning horizon, consumers will regard their holdings of government bonds as net wealth. When this is the case, a current tax cut financed by issuing new government debt will increase expected human wealth and private consumption, because consumers do not completely internalize the future burden of the government debt associated with a current tax cut. The positive effect derived from an intertemporal reallocation of taxes is due to the different discount rates: if $0 < \gamma < 1$, consumers discount taxes at a rate $\gamma/(1+r)$ whereas the future interest income on government bonds is discounted at the rate $1/(1+r)$.[13] The future tax increase is thus given a smaller weight by finite-horizon consumers than the weight attached by them to the current tax cut, which implies that private saving does not rise by enough to fully offset the increase in the budget deficit, which causes government deficit financing to be non-neutral. In the case of extreme myopia ($\gamma = 0$), consumers treat government bonds fully as a net wealth.

A positive value for θ implies that government consumption and private consumption are substitutes, whereas a negative θ would suggest complementarity. With θ equal to zero government consumption has no effect on private consumption. Hence, with the expected present value of government consumption, $E_t G_t$, unchanged, substitutability (complementarity) implies that private consumption declines (increases) with increases in government consumption in accordance with the parameter θ. The greater the utility substitution (complementarity) at the margin between private consumption and government consumption, the larger the negative (positive) response of private consumption to an increase in government consumption. However, as long as $0 < \theta < 1$, aggregate demand will rise by a fraction $(1-\theta)$ of an increase in government consumption. If government consumption is a perfect substitute for private consumption ($\theta = 1$), then there would be complete crowding out of private consumption.

Finally, when $\gamma < 1$ and $\theta \neq 0$, expected human wealth, government consumption and government debt affect current consumption over and beyond the impact of lagged consumption.

10.3   Estimation issues and empirical results

To obtain a reduced form consumption function, unobservable future paths of labour income y_{t+j} and government consumption g_{t+j} are eliminated from the estimation equation using the method proposed by Hayashi (1982), where stochastic difference equations implied by the rational expectations assumption are utilized. Difference equations expressing changes in expected values of labour income and government consumption from period $t-1$ to period t are given by

$$E_t Y_t - \frac{1+r}{\gamma} E_{t-1} Y_{t-1} = -\frac{1+r}{\gamma} y_{t-1} + e_{Yt}$$

$$E_t G_t - \frac{1+r}{\gamma} E_{t-1} G_{t-1} = -\frac{1+r}{\gamma} g_{t-1} + e_{Gt'} \tag{10.4}$$

where e_{Yt} and e_{Gt} denote the expectational revisions of consumers from period $t-1$ to period t. These surprise terms are, by construction, orthogonal to the information set available in $t-1$, I_{t-1}, and thus serially uncorrelated. They may, however, be correlated with variables dated period t and contemporaneously correlated with each other.

Using equations (10.4) to form $c_t^P - [(1+r)/\gamma]c_{t-1}^P$, the unobservable variables can be removed from equation (10.3). Rearranging gives the following expression for c_t^P in terms of observable variables:

$$c_t^P = \beta_0 + \left[(1+r)(1-\beta_1) + \frac{1+r}{\gamma} \right] c_{t-1}^P - (1-\beta_1)\frac{(1+r)^2}{\gamma} c_{t-2}^P$$

$$-\beta_1(1-\gamma)\frac{1+r}{\gamma} y_{t-1} - \theta g_t + \theta \left(1 - \beta_1 \left(\frac{\gamma-1}{\theta}+1 \right) + \gamma \right) \frac{1+r}{\gamma} g_{t-1}$$

$$-\theta(1-\beta_1)\frac{(1+r)^2}{\gamma} g_{t-2} - \beta_1(1-\gamma)(1+r)b_{t-1}$$

$$+\beta_1(1-\gamma)\frac{(1+r)^2}{\gamma} b_{t-2} + V_t \qquad (10.5)$$

where

$$\beta_0' = \frac{r(\delta-r)}{(1+r)}\bar{c} \quad \text{and} \quad \beta_1 = 1 - \frac{\gamma(1+\delta)}{(1+r)^2}$$

and the error term V_t has the following structure:

$$V_t = \beta_1(e_{Yt} + \theta e_{Gt}) - \beta_1(1+r)(e_{Yt-1} + \theta e_{Gt-1}) + u_t - \frac{1+r}{\gamma} u_{t-1}$$

Since the error terms u_t, e_{Yt} and e_{Gt} may be correlated, the error structure has an unrestricted variance-covariance matrix. This means that one cannot disentangle the response of private consumption to innovations in labour income or in government consumption.

The error structure of equation (10.5) involves a number of problems, which risk resulting in inconsistent parameter estimates. To avoid misspecification requires the use of instrumental variables estimator, where at least twice-lagged variables are chosen as instruments, which by definition are orthogonal to e_{Yt} and e_{Gt}. Twice-lagged instruments imply that the error term in equation (10.5) has a first-order moving average structure (MA(1)). To obtain asymptotically efficient estimates without imposing either conditional homoscedasticity or independence over time on the disturbances of the model, Hansen's (1982) Generalised Method of Moments (GMM) estimator is used.[14] The reported standard errors are thus heteroscedasticity and

Table 10.1 Countries in the sample, estimation period and data on public finances

Country	Estimation period	Government debt/GDP	Government debt/income taxes	Government consumption/ GDP
Austria	1963–1994	0.40	1.89	0.16
Belgium	1964–1994	0.93	3.80	0.15
Finland	1963–1994	0.21	0.92	0.17
France	1964–1993	0.35	1.64	0.17
Germany	1963–1993	0.31	1.23	0.18
Greece	1964–1994	0.43	3.22	0.16
Italy	1964–1994	0.64	3.37	0.15
Netherlands	1964–1994	0.61	2.29	0.15
Sweden	1964–1994	0.46	1.56	0.24
UK	1963–1994	0.74	4.78	0.20

Note: Government debt includes general government gross debt, taxes denote household income taxes and government consumption includes general government consumption.

autocorrelation consistent. The model adequacy and the validity of orthogonality conditions implied by the rational expectations hypothesis is tested by Hansen's (1982) over-identifying restrictions test (J-test) while theory-generated restrictions on parameter estimates are tested using the Wald-test.

The annual time series data are from the OECD National Accounts and the sample consists of ten EU countries listed in Table 10.1. The criterion for including a country was the availability of at least thirty observations for the actual estimation period given that some observations are lost due to the use of lagged instruments. A detailed description of the data is given in appendix 10.A.1.

Private consumption, c_t^p, is measured by per capita total private consumption expenditures at constant prices, labour income, y_t, is measured by per capita non-property income. Government consumption, g_t, is measured by general government per capita final consumption expenditures at constant prices, and government debt, b_t, by the book value of general government gross debt deflated by the consumer price index. The real interest rate was fixed at 3 per cent in the estimations. It conforms closely to the observed average international long-term real interest rate over the estimation period.[15]

10.3.1 Empirical results

The estimates of the parameters β_1, γ and θ for each country are given in Table 10.2. The unrestricted version of the consumption equation is estimated first and the theoretical restrictions on γ and θ are tested using the Wald-test. The high probability values of the J-test (shown in parentheses in Table 10.2) indicate that the unrestricted form of the model performs satisfactorily: tests of the over-identifying restrictions do not reject the model for

Table 10.2   GMM estimation of equation (10.5) for selected EU countries

	Unrestricted estimates				Wald-test		
	β_1	γ	θ	J-test	$\gamma = 1$	$\theta = 0$	$\gamma = 1$ $\theta = 0$
Austria	.331	1.048*	−1.671	2.368	0.025	2.841	2.909
	(.418)	(.308)	(.991)	(0.937)	(0.875)	(0.092)	(0.233)
Belgium	.523*	.964*	−.952	4.860	0.967	1.518	1.715
	(.184)	(.037)	(.772)	(0.677)	(0.325)	(0.218)	(0.424)
Finland[1]	.639*	1.033*	2.723*	7.106	0.282	6.489	9.726
	(.059)	(.062)	(1.069)	(0.626)	(0.595)	(0.011)	(0.008)
France	.255	1.030*	−4.937*	7.641	0.014	—	12.473
	(.363)	(.249)	(1.549)	(0.571)	(0.904)		(0.002)
Germany	.470*	.841*	−2.002*	5.711	13.238	5.401	21.226
	(.178)	(.043)	(.861)	(0.456)	(0.000)	(0.020)	(0.000)
Greece	.779*	1.070*	−3.306*	5.486	4.008	75.419	78.152
	(.212)	(.035)	(.381)	(0.359)	(0.050)	(0.000)	(0.000)
Italy	.560*	.988*	1.451	7.255	0.065	0.628	1.284
	(.146)	(.046)	(1.830)	(0.403)	(0.799)	(0.428)	(0.526)
Netherlands	.428	1.015*	−2.695*	6.725	0.021	15.747	20.568
	(.263)	(.105)	(.679)	(0.567)	(0.885)	(0.000)	(0.000)
Sweden[2]	.161	.899*	4.938*	1.544	0.018	4.080	7.209
	(.122)	(.155)	(1.533)	(0.992)	(0.893)	(0.043)	(0.027)
UK	.264	1.107*	−.593	6.892	0.066	0.709	1.359
	(.368)	(.415)	(.704)	(0.331)	(0.797)	(0.400)	(0.507)

Notes: Heteroscedasticity and autocorrelation-consistent standard errors are in parentheses. The J-test is a test of the validity of over-identifying restrictions with its significance level in parentheses. The Wald-test is for the validity of the imposed restrictions with its significance level in parentheses. The asterisk (*) denotes the statistical significance at least at the 5 per cent level. The instruments include the constant, the second and third lag of private consumption, government consumption, before-tax labour income, government debt and household income taxes.

[1] Wald-test for restrictions $\theta = 1$ is 2.598 (0.107) and $\gamma = 1$ and $\theta = 1$ is 3.342 (0.188).
[2] Wald-test for the joint restriction $\gamma = 1$ and $\theta = 1$ is 4.112 (0.128).

any of the countries in the sample. More specifically, the estimates of γ turn out to be statistically significant and of the expected sign and magnitude for all countries, whereas the estimate of θ is not as precise.[16] The main anomaly pertains to the results of β_1, the propensity to consume out of wealth, since it is almost invariably too high given the overall parameter structure.

As suggested by the theoretical framework, the effects of government financing decisions on private consumption depend crucially on the estimated parameter value of γ, i.e. on the length of average horizon for private consumption and saving decisions, $1/(1-\gamma)$. Estimated parameter values for γ less than unity results in a shorter planning horizon for the private sector and hence in fiscal policy non-neutrality. As shown in Table 10.2 the unrestricted estimate of γ proves to be close to unity for all other countries except for Germany and the UK. The hypothesis of an infinite planning horizon (i.e. $\gamma = 1$), and thus Ricardian debt neutrality, can however be rejected only for Germany. The results thus seem to give some support to the Ricardian debt neutrality hypothesis and infinite planning horizon as a valid approximation of consumer behaviour in nine out of ten EU countries in the sample. This suggests that consumers in these countries are sufficiently Ricardian in behaviour to increase their saving one-to-one with increases in government deficit financing.

The parameter estimates of θ tend to vary more across countries than those of γ and show relatively high values. The unrestricted estimate of θ turns out to be negative and statistically significant for France, Germany, Greece and the Netherlands. As expected, the restriction $\theta=0$ is rejected at the 5 per cent significance level for these countries. For Finland and Sweden, the estimates of θ are positive and statistically significant.[17] Hence, instead of being complements, as for the countries above, government consumption and private consumption are found to be substitutes in Finland and Sweden, implying that increases in government consumption crowd out private consumption.

For Finland and Sweden the restriction $\theta=0$ is rejected at the 5 per cent significance level, while the restriction $\theta=1$, implying complete crowding out of private consumption, cannot be rejected by the Wald-test at conventional levels of significance for either country. This result indicates that in Finland and Sweden changes in government consumption do not affect aggregate demand.

For Austria, Belgium, Italy and the UK, the estimated value of θ proves to be statistically insignificant and the restriction $\theta=0$ cannot be rejected by the Wald-test for these countries, suggesting that government consumption and private consumption tend to be unrelated.

Finally, the joint hypothesis of an infinite horizon and no substitutability or complementarity between the government consumption and private consumption (i.e. $\gamma=1$ and $\theta=0$) cannot be rejected at the 5 per cent level for Austria, Belgium, Italy and the UK, whereas it is strongly rejected for Finland, France, Germany, Greece, the Netherlands and Sweden. For completeness, the joint restriction, $\gamma=1$ and $\theta=1$, is tested for Finland and Sweden. According to the Wald-test, the joint restriction cannot be rejected for either country, indicating complete fiscal policy neutrality. In other words, this result suggests that it is useless to try to stabilize economic fluctuations by timing of taxes or changing government consumption in these two countries.

The unrestricted estimate of β_1, the propensity to consume out of wealth, turns out to be excessively high given an infinite planning horizon or even a planning horizon of approximately six years in the case of Germany. The value of β_1 around .5 implies a planning horizon of only two years at most, suggesting that the evidence in favour of the Ricardian equivalence hypothesis should be interpreted with caution. Measurement errors in consumption and labour income could explain this puzzling result. Also the elimination of non-human wealth from the estimation equation, which was done because of the lack of data, might bias the estimates of β_1 upwards.[18]

10.4   Weak form of Ricardian equivalence: the significance of credit constraints

The model outlined above assumes that all consumers can freely substitute consumption today for consumption tomorrow at the given interest rate. In reality, all consumers are not able to borrow against their future income stream due to credit constraints[19] and capital market imperfections. Credit constraints, by preventing the consumer from realizing his desired (optimal) consumption plan, can thus cause private consumption to track current income far more than predicted by the intertemporal optimization framework, even if consumers were rational and forward-looking.

To test whether the underlying permanent income model and optimizing behaviour is supported by the data and whether there are significant deviations from the underlying permanent income model due to excess sensitivity, a simple framework incorporating the credit constrained consumers in the forward-looking permanent income consumption model is derived. This is done by assuming two types of consumers along the lines proposed by Hall (1978). In this approach, excess sensitivity of consumption to predictable changes in income is accounted for by a constant fraction of the population behaving as Keynesian rule-of-thumb consumers. Thus aggregate per capita consumption is assumed to be a weighted average with constant weights λ,[20] denoting the fraction of disposable income going to rule-of-thumb consumers, and $1-\lambda$, denoting the fraction going to finite-horizon permanent-income consumers.[21] Since rule-of-thumb consumers are assumed to follow a simple Keynesian consumption function, their budget constraint implies that the best they can do is to consume all their disposable income. Consumption of the rule-of-thumb consumers is thus $c_t^K = \lambda h_t$.

Nesting the consumption of the two types of consumers gives aggregate per capita consumption, c_t, as a linear function of the consumption of the forward-looking permanent-income consumers, c_t^P (equation 10.3) and the rule-of-thumb consumers, c_t^K:

$$
\begin{aligned}
c_t = &-r\,\beta_0 + (1+r)(1-\beta_1)\,c_{t-1} + \beta_1(1-\gamma)(1-\lambda)\,E_t Y_t \\
&+ \beta_1(1-\gamma)(\theta-1)(1-\lambda)E_t G_t + \lambda h_t - \lambda(1+r)(1-\beta_1)h_{t-1} \\
&- \theta(1-\lambda)g_t + (1+r)(1-\beta_1)\theta(1-\lambda)g_{t-1} \\
&- \beta_1(1+r)(1-\gamma)(1-\lambda)b_{t-1} + \beta_1(1-\lambda)(e_{Yt}+\theta\,e_{Gt}) + u_t
\end{aligned} \tag{10.6}
$$

The corresponding empirical reduced-form per capita consumption function in terms of observable variables is then:[22]

$$c_t = \beta_0' + \left[(1+r)(1-\beta_1) + \frac{1+r}{\gamma} \right] c_{t-1} - \frac{(1+r)^2}{\gamma} (1-\beta_1)c_{t-2} + \lambda h_t$$

$$- \lambda \left[(1+r)(1-\beta_1) + \frac{1+r}{\gamma} \right] h_{t-1} + \lambda \frac{(1+r)^2}{\gamma} (1-\beta_1)h_{t-2}$$

$$- \beta_1(1-\gamma)(1-\lambda)\frac{1+r}{\gamma} y_{t-1} - \theta(1-\lambda) g_t$$

$$+ \theta \frac{1+r}{\gamma} \left[1+\gamma - \frac{\beta_1(\theta+\gamma-1)}{\theta} \right] g_{t-1}$$

$$- \theta \frac{(1+r)^2}{\gamma}(1-\beta_1)(1-\lambda)g_{t-2}$$

$$- \beta_1(1+r)(1-\gamma)(1-\lambda)\left(b_{t-1} - \frac{1+r}{\gamma}b_{t-2} \right) + V_t \qquad (10.7)$$

The error term V_t has the following first-order moving average structure:

$$V_t = \beta_1(1-\lambda)(e_{Yt} + \theta\, e_{Gt}) - \beta_1(1-\lambda)(1+r)(e_{Yt-1} + \theta\, e_{Gt-1})$$

$$+ (1-\lambda)u_t - (1-\lambda)\frac{1+r}{\gamma}\, u_{t-1}$$

Direct estimation of λ has the advantage of providing a measure of the economic importance of deviations from the permanent income model and Ricardian equivalence in a tractable manner. Critical assumptions from the point of view of debt neutrality are whether the planning horizon of forward-looking consumers is infinite, i.e. γ close to unity, and whether the fraction of rule-of-thumb consumers, λ, is zero. In this case one could claim that forward-looking optimizing behaviour and Ricardian equivalence are approximately true even if the estimate of λ were statistically significant, since most income would go to infinite-horizon permanent-income consumers. Conversely, if the estimate of λ is large and statistically significant, then one can conclude that the evidence is against the permanent income hypothesis and Ricardian equivalence even if the fraction $1-\lambda$ of consumers are rational and have infinite horizons. Hence, under excess sensitivity, the obvious consequence is that government budget deficits have real effects because private consumption is not invariant to changes in the timing of taxes and transfers, giving a scope for fiscal stabilization.

Estimation results based on the constant λ-model are reported in Table 10.3. The obvious conclusion when comparing these results to the permanent income model (Table 10.2) is that the unrestricted parameter estimates

Table 10.3   GMM estimation of equation (10.8) for selected EU countries

	Unrestricted estimates					Wald-test		
	β_1	γ	θ	λ	*J-test*	$\gamma=1$	$\theta=0$	$\gamma=0$ $\lambda=0$
Austria	.890*	1.032*	−1.505	.510*	2.598	0.049	6.777	7.079
	(.181)	(.143)	(1.405)	(.196)	(0.627)	(0.825)	(0.009)	(0.029)
Belgium	.941*	1.021*	.103	.679*	4.881	0.223	28.887	29.428
	(.126)	(.045)	(.071)	(.126)	(0.559)	(0.637)	(0.000)	(0.000)
Finland	.690*	.966*	3.212	−.016	0.522	0.184	1.373	1.481
	(.084)	(.079)	(1.817)	(.014)	(0.971)	(0.668)	(0.241)	(0.477)
France	.568	1.027*	-.084	.416*	4.409	0.200	35.055	45.573
	(.379)	(.061)	(.077)	(.070)	(0.492)	(0.655)	(0.000)	(0.000)
Germany	.528*	1.106*	.004	.764*	2.098	0.249	34.236	89.079
	(.225)	(.213)	(.020)	(.130)	(0.910)	(0.618)	(0.000)	(0.000)
Greece	.549*	1.123*	.032	.537*	5.335	3.342	83.443	99.936
	(.157)	(.067)	(.040)	(.059)	(0.502)	(0.067)	(0.000)	(0.000)
Italy	.194	1.073	.043	.554*	10.109	0.012	14.974	15.530
	(.667)	(.666)	(.040)	(.143)	(0.120)	(0.912)	(0.000)	(0.000)
Netherlands	.536*	1.065*	−1.709*	.069	4.311	0.622	2.757	2.887
	(.140)	(.082)	(.566)	(.042)	(0.505)	(0.430)	(0.097)	(0.236)
Sweden	.102	.961*	4.155	−.001	0.452	0.011	0.017	0.027
	(.361)	(.375)	(2.239)	(.011)	(0.994)	(0.917)	(0.896)	(0.986)
UK	−.579	.740*	.010	.542*	5.226	2.007	16.227	16.677
	(.601)	(.183)	(.052)	(.135)	(0.515)	(0.156)	(0.000)	(0.000)

Notes: Heteroscedasticity and autocorrelation-consistent standard errors are in parentheses. The J-test is a test of the validity of over-identifying restrictions with its significance level in parentheses. The Wald-test is for the validity of the imposed restrictions with its significance level in parentheses. The asterisk (*) denotes the statistical significance at least at the 5 per cent level. The instruments include a constant, the second and third lag of private consumption, government consumption, before-tax labour income, disposable income, government debt.

of γ are roughly of the same order of magnitude and statistically significant in both specifications. As regards the estimated value of γ, only minor deviations can be detected. In general, the value of γ tends to increase slightly, the notable exception being Germany, where the value of γ increases markedly, and the UK, where the value of γ decreases considerably, when the current income consumers are accounted for. The qualitative results change however only in the case of Germany so that in the constant λ-model the hypothesis of an infinite planning horizon cannot be rejected.

Estimates of λ in Table 10.3 indicate that there are marked differences across countries in the effect of current income on private consumption. The rule-of-thumb consumers' share of disposable income obtains relatively large values and is significantly different from zero in seven countries, i.e. in Austria, Belgium, France, Germany, Greece, Italy and the UK, suggesting the importance of taking into account the effect of current income on consumption.

The estimate of λ in these countries varies between .42 and .76, so that the estimated effect of current income on private consumption is lowest in France and highest in Germany. As expected, the hypothesis that current income and permanent income are equal ($\lambda = 0$) is strongly rejected by the Wald-test in each of these countries, as is the joint restriction, $\gamma = 1$ and $\lambda = 0$.

For Finland and Sweden, the estimate of λ has the wrong sign, but the values are small and statistically not different from zero.[23] The estimate of λ is statistically insignificant also for the Netherlands. The hypothesis of no excess sensitivity (restriction $\lambda = 0$) cannot be rejected for any of these three countries. Finally, the joint restriction, $\gamma = 1$ and $\lambda = 0$, cannot be rejected for these countries, suggesting that consumer behaviour exhibits Ricardian rather than Keynesian properties. However, as before, the results are dubious since the estimated values of β_1 are all too high to conform the estimated values of γ in Finland and the Netherlands.

This pattern of results is largely consistent with previous findings[24] even though the data, econometric methods and sample periods are different. Specifically, the effect of current income on consumption has been found to be insignificant in the Netherlands and Sweden and relatively strong in France, Greece, Italy and the UK. These results support the arguments put forward by Hayashi (1982) and Evans (1988, 1993) that the expectation of a future binding credit constraint with a zero borrowing limit is equivalent to a shortening of the consumer's planning horizon.

The results concerning the estimates of θ are qualitatively much the same as before. However, the statistical significance of θ drops in most cases, the only exception being the Netherlands. Not surprisingly, the restriction $\theta = 0$, reflecting the independence of private consumption and government consumption, cannot be rejected for any other country in the sample.[25] The imprecise estimates of θ might, at least partially, be due to the problems related to the proper measurement of government consumption. Since it is usually measured by wages and salaries of public sector employees, it is likely to be highly correlated with current disposable income, thus causing the estimate of θ to become statistically insignificant when current income is included in the model.

All in all, the inclusion of the excess sensitivity hypothesis in the forward-looking consumption model alters considerably the conclusions drawn on the basis of permanent income model on the effects of fiscal policy on private consumption and on Ricardian equivalence as a valid approximation of reality. The results obtained from the model incorporating credit constrained, rule-of-thumb consumers suggest that fiscal policy has been non-neutral in the majority of EU countries in the sample during the estimation period. Furthermore, deviations from Ricardian debt neutrality seem to arise from excess sensitivity of consumption to current income rather than from the shorter planning horizon for consumers. This indicates that the impact of credit constraints on the extent to which government debt shifts tax burden to future generations is quantitatively possibly more important than the impact of finite horizons or myopia.

10.5   Concluding remarks

Empirical evidence on Ricardian debt neutrality proved to be highly sensitive to the model specification. In accordance with the earlier literature on Ricardian equivalence, results based on the permanent income model tend to give strong support to the forward-looking behaviour of consumers and thus to Ricardian equivalence. If taken literally, this would mean that consumers in most EU countries take into account all future implications of current fiscal policy when making their consumption decisions, thus rendering any effort to stabilize short-term economic fluctuations futile.

The results however change markedly as financial market imperfections prohibiting consumers to smooth consumption over transitory fluctuations in income are taken into account. The findings based on a model nesting the forward-looking permanent income consumers and credit constrained rule-of-thumb consumers suggest that aggregate consumption responds not only to changes in expected lifetime wealth but also to changes in current disposable income and hence to changes in government taxes and income transfers. Nevertheless, it should be noted that according to the results, the possibilities of using fiscal policy as a counter-cyclical tool seem to be almost without exception significantly weaker than in the pure Keynesian case.

An important implication of these results is that empirical tests on Ricardian equivalence using the permanent income framework are likely to suffer from misspecification problems which cast doubt on the validity of the found support for Ricardian equivalence.

From the standpoint of economic policy the findings imply that, contrary to Ricardian implication, policy-makers should indeed pay attention to budget deficits in assessing economic stability. The results thus give justification for the kind of fiscal discipline required by the Stability and Growth Pact. If the equivalence hypothesis were true, constraints on budget deficits would be unnecessary because the budget deficit has no effect on real economy or on interest rates. However, in the world as it appears according to the findings, fiscal policy discipline envisaged by the Stability and Growth Pact is needed to restrict the temptation to run overly expansionary fiscal policies in the monetary union, that would lead to higher interest rates and lower potential for long-term growth.

Finally, it is possible that Ricardian effects will strengthen in the future so that debt-financed fiscal stimulation could lead to less-than-expected expansion and larger government deficits. This view gains support from the fact that public discussions in recent years concerning government deficits and debt, as well as expenditure cuts and tax hikes effected in order to reduce them, have increased the awareness of the private sector in European countries of how past fiscal measures affect present and future fiscal policy decisions. Moreover, the liberalization of financial markets has reduced credit constraints, which – at least in principle – should weaken the dependency of private consumption on current disposable income.

Appendix 10. A.1: the data

The data are from OECD National Accounts, Vol. II, covering the period 1960–94 for Austria, Greece and the UK, the period 1961–94 for Belgium, Italy, the Netherlands and Sweden, the period 1960–95 for Finland, the period 1960–93 for Germany, and the period 1961–93 for France. The data for Germany refer to West Germany until 1991 and the united Germany thereafter. All variables are in per capita terms and deflated by the implicit price deflator of which the base year is 1990.

Private consumption c_t: private final consumption expenditure.

Pre-tax (non-property) income y_t: the sum of household sector wages, salaries, employers' social security contributions and other non-property income (i.e. operating surplus of private unincorporated businesses and withdrawals from quasi-corporate enterprises).

Taxes t_t: household income taxes and other direct taxes, employees' social security contributions and fees, fines and penalties.

Government consumption g_t: general government final consumption expenditure.

Government debt b_t: data are end-of-year observations of outstanding general government debt at book value. The series is extrapolated by using the data of general government net lending for the years 1961–3 for Italy and the years 1960–9 for Austria and the UK, and by using the data on central government debt from IMF International Financial Statistics for the years 1961–9 for Belgium, the Netherlands and Sweden, and the years 1961–76 for France.

Price deflator: the ratio of final private consumption expenditures at current prices to the value of these expenditures at the base-year prices.

Population: end-of-year total population.

Notes

1. European Commission, DG ECFIN. The views expressed in this chapter are those of the author and are not attributable to the European Commission. I am grateful to Marco Buti and Carlos Martinez-Mongay for helpful comments and suggestions. All errors and omissions remain the author's responsibility.
2. According to the Maastricht Treaty member states have to avoid excessive deficits defined in terms of a reference value of 3 per cent of GDP and in terms of public debt reference value of 60 per cent of GDP.
3. Recent reviews on the academic debate on the desirability of the SGP; see Beetsma (2001) and Canzoneri and Diba (2001).
4. A recent survey on the literature concerning the diverging views on the macroeconomic effects of government debt is given by Elmendorf and Mankiw (1998).
5. As pointed out e.g. in Brunila (1997) and Elmendorf and Mankiw (1998) Ricardian equivalence does not render all fiscal policy irrelevant. If the government cuts taxes today and households expect this tax cut to be met with future cuts in government expenditure, then households' permanent income does rise, which stimulates consumption and reduces national saving. But it is the expected cut in the government expenditure, rather than the tax cut, that stimulates consumption.

The reduction in expected future government expenditure would alter permanent income and consumption because they imply lower taxes at some time,
even if current taxes are unchanged.

6. For a detailed discussion about the assumptions required for Ricardian equivalence to hold, see Bernheim (1987), Leiderman and Blejer (1988), Seater (1993).

7. The population is normalized such that the initial size of each generation is one.
   As a fraction γ of consumers in each generation survives each period, there are γ^k
   members of the consumers of age k in each period. The size of the population is
   therefore constant and given by

$$\sum_{d=0}^{\infty} \gamma^k = \frac{1}{1-\gamma}$$

8. Although the quadratic formulation has some serious shortcomings (see Zeldes,
   1989), it is widely used because it delivers a linear Euler equation which can easily
   be combined with the linear budget constraint to derive a closed-form solution to
   the consumption problem.

9.

$$E_t H_t = \sum_{j=0}^{\infty} \left(\frac{\gamma}{1+r}\right)^2 E_t(y_{t+j} + t \, r_{t+j} - t_{t+j})$$

where y_t denotes labour income, tr_t government transfer payments and t_t taxes.

10. $$E_t G_t = \sum_{j=0}^{\infty} \left(\frac{\gamma}{1+r}\right)^j E_t g_{t+j}$$

11. To prevent the government from infinite debt-financing and ever-increasing debt
    burden (Ponzi-game), the expected growth of the government debt must be less
    than the real interest rate.

12. This is done in view of the empirical implementation, as internationally compa-
    rable and reliable data on consumers' financial assets were not readily available.

13. The difference between the two reflects, in essence, transfers from generations
    not currently alive to those who are, and these transfers do not add to aggregate
    wealth.

14. In order for the GMM estimator to be asymptotically justifiable, all variables
    should be stationary. In case of non-stationarity, inference and estimation may
    proceed in the standard way, if the regressors are cointegrated and the uncondi-
    tional mean of their first differences is non-zero. It is shown in Brunila (1997)
    that these conditions are fulfilled for equation (10.5).

15. The variability of the real interest rate has, however, been quite substantial dur-
    ing the sample period. It should also be noted that the real interest rate was very
    low and even negative in several countries in the sample in the 1970s.

16. The robustness of the estimation results with respect to the interest rate assump-
    tion and estimation period was checked using the data as a panel. In these esti-
    mations a real interest rate of 5 per cent was used instead of 3 per cent and a
    subperiod starting in 1970. The estimate of γ proved to be robust with respect to
    both changes whereas the estimate of θ was to some extent sensitive to the inter-
    est rate applied as well as to the estimation period. Specifically, the absolute value
    and statistical significance of θ increased in both cases, making the complemen-
    tarity of government consumption and private consumption stronger in both
    cases (see Brunila, 1997).

17. Of recent studies, Karras (1994) and Evans and Karras (1996) found that private consumption and government consumption are complements in Finland, while for Sweden Karras reports them to be unrelated and Evans and Karras to be substitutes.

18. Some evidence of this is presented in Himarios (1995).

19. Under potentially binding credit constraints, the underlying Euler equation does not hold since some consumers who would like to borrow at the given interest rate but are prevented from doing so consume relatively less in period t and relatively more in period $t + 1$ than in the absence of credit constraints.

20. As λ essentially measures the excess sensitivity of consumption to current disposable income, it can be used as a test of misspecification of the original model.

21. The assumption that the proportion of credit constrained consumers is constant over time can be critized as one could expect that the importance of credit constraints has diminished over time in line with the deregulation of financial markers. Brunila (1997) did not however find support for this hypothesis, while Sefton and In't Veld (1999) found that financial deregulation in some countries has resulted in a significant reduction in the share of income received by credit constrained consumers.

22. Derivation of the function; see Brunila (1997).

23. The similar result was also found by Evans and Karras (1996).

24. See Jappelli and Pagano (1989), Campbell and Mankiw (1991), Evans and Karras (1996), Auerbach and Feenberg (2000).

25. The statistical significance of θ also proved to be sensitive to the inclusion of current income in the estimation equation in Evans and Karras (1996). They found, as here, that when the current income is omitted from the estimation equation, the values of θ tended to be statistically significant and negative, while the inclusion of current income in the model tended to erode the statistical significance of the parameter θ.

11
Impact of Large Public Debt on Growth in the EU: A Discussion of Potential Channels[1]

Nigel Chalk and Vito Tanzi

11.1 Introduction

Public debt did not always attract much attention on the part of economists or policy-makers. While at times in the past it had been the centre of attention, at other times and especially in the second half of the twentieth century, it has been largely ignored. One of the first public figures to call attention to public debt in the past two decades was Jacques de Larosiére, then Managing Director of the IMF. In a speech delivered at the 1984 Congress of the International Institute of Public Finance, in Innsbruck, Austria, he called attention to the fast growth in public debt and predicted that difficulties would arise if that trend were not reversed. That speech attracted a lot of attention especially in the press. However, until very recently, public debt as a share of gross domestic product continued to grow for many industrial countries and reached very high levels in some of them.

In this chapter, we focus on the potential impact that a large public debt could have on growth in the EU. In section 2, we discuss six channels through which a high public debt could have a negative impact on growth. Some of these channels are more easily testable than others. In section 3 we attempt to submit at least some of these channels to empirical tests. Unfortunately, data availability limits the extent of this empirical testing. In section 4 we draw some conclusions.

11.2 Theoretical section

Writing almost three centuries ago David Hume stated his strong dislike for public borrowing. Some of his statements are worth citing:

> It is very tempting to a minister to employ such an expedient, as enables him to make a great figure during his administration, without overburdening the people with taxes, or exciting any immediate clamors against

himself. The practice, therefore, of contracting debt will almost infallibly be abused in every government. [Therefore] ... the consequence ... must indeed, be one of ... two events; either the nation must destroy public credit, or public credit will destroy the nation. (Hume, 1955)

Hume's conclusion may be seen as too extreme because many countries which have relied on public debt have not been destroyed by it, but many have argued that countries have been harmed by a reliance on debt financing. In this section we will identify several potential channels through which a high and growing public debt might negatively affect economic growth. In the next section we shall subject some of the identified hypotheses to empirical tests. Some of these potential channels are more hypothetical than others and have not been discussed in the relevant literature. And some may be difficult to test empirically.

11.2.1 First channel

In the absence of default risk by the government, and especially in the absence of inflation, public debt gives individuals and enterprises the option of channelling their savings or profits toward income-generating, risk-free assets. Also, the transaction costs in buying government securities are generally very low and the denominations of the securities are often small enough to allow many potential investors to participate in debt issues. Thus individuals and institutions such as pension funds, but also enterprises, can convert their liquid balances into assets that over the relevant maturity guarantee a fixed, nominal rate of return. The existence of small denominations and risk-free investments may make individuals' investment decisions more risk-averse than they would be in the absence of such instruments. It is thus conceivable that more risky and, presumably, more productive investment options may be at least partially avoided by those with surplus balances thus raising the cost of venture capital for investors. For this reason the growth of public debt may have some negative impact on economic growth.

If the size of the public debt is large enough to affect the real rate of interest on that debt, and especially if the default risk on government securities remains low, while the share of debt to GDP rises, the diversion of private saving and eventually of private wealth toward public debt could become particularly pronounced thus increasing the difficulty that the private sector will have in raising needed resources. There is evidence from some countries that when real interest rates become high, public debt often becomes the most profitable investment for both individuals and enterprises, especially if the high real interest rate on debt acts to slow the growth of the economy;[2] thus real investment into private capital accumulation falls and the investment that does take place tends to prefer safer channels.[3] In these circumstances growth is likely to suffer, especially if the government uses the borrowed funds for economically unproductive purposes. This will be especially true if, contrary to the Ricardian hypothesis, the country's saving rate falls while public debt rises, or if individuals, in anticipation of high taxes or increased risk, begin to take their capital out of the country.

11.2.2   Second channel

Governments that face large public debts and high and growing interest payments can react in three different ways or more often in a combination of these ways.

First, governments may *let the overall deficit grow*. Given particular values of the real growth rate, *g*, of the real interest rate, *r*, and of the primary deficit, *d*, this could lead to increases in the debt-to-GDP ratio and put in motion an unsustainable debt dynamic. Thus, the option of letting the fiscal deficit grow is generally costly and limited in scope since it will eventually have to be reversed. It is an option that was partly followed by many industrial countries over the past three decades. The longer a country relies on this option, the more costly it will become especially if, as discussed above, the increasing debt leads to increases in real interest rates and/or to lower growth rates. In time this course of action could lead to a financial crisis as, for example, it did in Brazil in 1998.

Growing fiscal deficits may well generate negative expectations about the future and, thus, through their effect on the decisions of economic agents, have a negative impact on economic growth. For example, capital flight may accompany growing fiscal deficits. For papers that have tested the direct impact of fiscal deficits on growth using cross-country data see Martin and Fardmanesh (1990); Levine and Renelt (1992); and Easterly and Rebelo (1993). There are also some studies that have found a correlation between fiscal deficits and real interest rates, although stronger relationships have been found between public debts and interest rates.

Second, governments may *reduce the fiscal deficit by cutting public spending*. Politically this alternative is never easy because the affected groups will oppose the spending cuts. Given the tyranny of past commitments and the existence of hard-to-change legal obligations, the spending that can more easily be cut is discretionary spending which, in some cases, is a relatively small proportion of total spending. For example, in the short run the cutting of pension payments is difficult and reducing the cost of servicing the public debt is not possible. Often, it is also difficult to reduce expenditure on health and education which to a large extent goes for wages and salaries; employees cannot be easily dismissed and sustained reductions in real wages are difficult. Because of political considerations, as for example, the voting power of retirees, spending on the aged, which *economically speaking* is unproductive, is rarely touched. Thus, often the easiest expenditures to reduce are the ones with the least powerful constituencies, namely public investment and operation and maintenance expenditure.

Under the normal assumption that spending for public investment and for operation and maintenance contributes more to growth than spending on transfers and pensions, maintaining the latter at the expense of the former is likely to have a negative impact on growth. Similarly, reducing spending on the accumulation of human capital (such as education and health) to offset growing interest payments is also likely to have a deleterious effect on growth. Operation and maintenance expenditure is particularly affected in times of fiscal stringency. Reduction in this expenditure leads to a deterioration of a country's infrastructure thus often imposing costs on the private sector and requiring more public investment in future years.

Third, the government may react to a growing interest burden by *increasing taxes*. There is now a large but predominantly theoretical literature that argues that high taxes can have a negative impact on important macroeconomic variables such as saving, investment, employment and growth. The literature is too extensive to be reviewed here. The empirical literature on the same topic is more limited and somewhat less assertive in its conclusions. We would like to mention a few papers which have reached strong results. Daveri and Tabellini (1997) shows there is a large impact of payroll taxes on employment; by reducing employment, higher payroll taxes would then presumably affect growth (see also Phelps, 1994). For a review of the literature on the impact of payroll taxes on employment, see OECD (1995), Leibfritz *et al.* (1997), and Zee (1997). Tanzi and Zee (2001), using OECD data, has shown that over the past 25 years tax increases, and especially increases in direct taxes, have been associated with statistically significant declines in the saving rates of households. If increases in debt/GDP ratios lead to increases in spending to service the debt which, in turn, lead to sustained increases in taxes (especially direct taxes) and lower household savings, then the net result of these changes would likely be a fall in private investment and in the growth rate.

In connection with the increase in taxes, it may be worthwhile to make a distinction between increases that are seen as temporary and those that are seen as permanent. The increases in tax rates that accompany an increase in the share of public debt into GDP can be expected to be lasting in time rather than just temporary. Thus, individuals and enterprises will have all the time needed to make adjustments in their economic activities and decisions to take account of the higher taxes. This implies that the welfare costs and, more generally, the costs in terms of forgone growth are likely to be higher than when the tax increases are assumed to be temporary. In this latter case, economic agents are less likely to make significant changes in their behaviour. Incidentally, the theoretical literature has focused too much on the question of retiring the public debt and not enough on the simpler and more realistic question of servicing a large and possibly growing public debt. The costs associated with servicing a large public debt may be more difficult to assess but they are likely to be substantial; furthermore, they are likely to grow with the increase in the size of the debt. Faced with what they perceive to be permanent tax increases, individuals and enterprises can be expected to take actions aimed at avoiding or even evading the high tax rates. These actions may involve capital flight, investing abroad, migrating, and engaging in underground economic activities and in tax evasion, in addition to all the domestic actions aimed at legally reducing the burden of taxation. The cumulative impact of these effects is likely to be a reduction in the rate of growth of a country.

In a globalized world, some of these results may have to be qualified to recognize that capital movements across countries are important so that the fiscal deficit of one country can be financed by the savings of another country. Therefore, the results may only be detected from the aggregation for groups of countries. However, capital is less likely to flow to countries where taxes are going up. Furthermore, financing fiscal deficits through foreign borrowing introduces other kinds of problems because the servicing of foreign debt introduces difficulties and rigidities, which are absent when debt is largely domestic, and subjects the borrowing countries to the vagaries of changes in exchange rates and interest rates.

To attempt to put more structure on the relationship between fiscal aggregates and growth that will ultimately be examined in the empirical section of this chapter, we take a simple overlapping generations model with debt, physical capital and fiscal policy and try to describe the effect of debt, public investment, and taxation on a country's growth rate that encompasses the effects outlined in both channels 1 and 2. The model is similar to that used by Barro (1990) and Mendoza *et al.* (1997). The model assumes that the stock of public capital (such as infrastructure) directly effects the productivity of the privately employed inputs of labour and physical capital. The intuition is that the more roads and bridges a country builds, the more productive its private producers are likely to be. The production technology is assumed to have constant returns to scale with respect to augmentable resources (i.e. the stocks of public and private capital) but increasing returns to scale overall. Such an assumption allows for the possibility of endogenous growth and permits fiscal policy to effect long-term growth.[4] The model is constructed as follows:

Aggregate technology

Let the aggregate production function be given by

$$Y_t = K_{G,t}^{1-\alpha} K_t^\alpha L_t^\beta \tag{11.1}$$

where Y_t is aggregate production, $K_{G,t}$ is the stock of public capital assets such as infrastructure, K_t is the aggregate stock of private capital, and L_t is the aggregate supply of labour. Assume also, for simplicity, that $\alpha + \beta = 1$. This is akin to the so-called 'Ak' models that are typical in the endogenous growth literature (see Barro and Sala-i-Martin, 1992, or Jones and Manuelli, 1997, for a survey).

Household behaviour

Households are described by the optimization problem of consumers who live for two periods, receive income when young, and save for their old age. The consumer problem is summarized by the optimization:

$$\max \ \ln c_t + \beta \ln c_{t+1}$$

$$\text{s.t. } c_t + z_t = w_t(1-t) \tag{11.2}$$

$$c_{t+1} = R_t z_t(1-t)$$

where c_t is individual consumption, z_t is individual savings, w_t is the worker's earnings when young, R_t and is the rate of return from investing. The gross income from returns on savings and on wage income are taxed at the income tax rate of t. One unit of labour is supplied inelastically by each of the L_t workers in the population. The individual optimization problem results in the individual savings equation:

$$z_t = \frac{\beta}{1+\beta} \ w_t(1-t) = s w_t(1-t) \tag{11.3}$$

The public sector

The simplified government budget identity, assuming a no-arbitrage condition that equalizes the returns on government debt and private capital, is given by

$$B_{t+1} = R_t B_t + G_t - (t w_t L_t + t R_t K_t + t R_t B_t)) \tag{11.4}$$

where end-period government indebtedness is given by the sum of debt at the beginning of the period B_t, interest expenditures, total spending on government capital G_t, less the proceeds of taxation of labour income $t w_t L_t$ and investment income $t R_t (K_t + B_t)$. Assuming, for simplicity, that public capital depreciates at a rate δ_G, the stock of public capital evolves according to

$$K_{G,t+1} = (1 - \delta_G) K_{G,t} + G_t \tag{11.5}$$

The firm problem

Firms have to choose the inputs of capital and labour to maximize profits given by the following objective function:

$$\max_{\{K_t, L_t\}} K_{G,t}^{1-\alpha} K_t^\alpha L_t^\beta - w_t L_t - r_t K_t \tag{11.6}$$

where private capital depreciation is assumed to be zero for simplicity. Profit maximization by the firms implies

$$R_t = 1 + \alpha \, \frac{Y_t}{K_t} \tag{11.7}$$

$$w_t = \beta \, \frac{Y_t}{L_t} \tag{11.8}$$

Capital market clearing

Capital market clearing implies all private sector asset holdings must be invested either into public debt or into private investment:

$$z_t L_t = s(1-t)\beta Y_t = B_{t+1} + K_{t+1} \tag{11.9}$$

Rewriting

$$K_{t+1} = s(1-t)\beta Y_t - B_{t+1} \tag{11.10}$$

The determinants of growth

The endogenous growth rate of the economy is given by

$$\frac{Y_{t+1}}{Y_t} = \left(\frac{K_{G,t+1}}{Y_t}\right)^{1-\alpha} \left(\frac{K_{t+1}}{Y_t}\right)^{\alpha} L_{t+1}^{\beta} \tag{11.11}$$

Normalizing $L_t = 1$ (here we have abstracted from exogenous population growth) and substituting (11.5) and (11.10) into (11.11) we arrive at an expression for the growth rate of the economy:

$$\frac{Y_{t+1}}{Y_t} = \left[\frac{(1-\delta_G)K_{G,t} + G_t}{Y_t}\right]^{1-\alpha} \left[s(1-t)\beta - \frac{B_{t+1}}{Y_t}\right]^{\alpha} \tag{11.12}$$

The resulting specification shows, as was discussed above, that the growth rate depends:

- negatively on the size of the government debt (since higher debt inevitably diverts savings away from productive private capital formation); this partially captures the effect of high government debt diverting savings from productive activity as outlined in channel 1.
- negatively on the average rate of direct taxes (since higher direct taxes reduce savings[5]); this is the effect of higher taxes outlined in channel 2.
- positively on the level of government capital spending (higher capital spending has a positive direct effect on growth through the endogenous growth channel of public infrastructure); this is the public spending effect outlined also in channel 2.

- positively on the accumulated stock of public capital (since the higher the level of capital, the more endogenous growth one gets in a model with constant-returns to augmentable resources); again this is alluded to in channel 2.

11.2.3 Third channel

Some years ago Benjamin Friedman advanced the hypothesis that there may be an absolute limit to the ratio of total debt (public plus private) into GDP that an economy could bear (see Friedman, 1981). He tested this hypothesis for the United States and showed that, in fact, for the 1953–80 period, there seemed to be such a constancy in that ratio. However, by the late 1980s the share of total debt to GDP had risen well over the previous historical average, leading him to worry about this phenomenon. At that time, the main cause for the growth in total debt was the fiscal deficit. It is not clear whether the more recent increase in this ratio is a temporary aberration or whether the Friedman's hypothesis applies to other countries.

If Friedman's hypothesis is still valid and if it applies more generally than in the United States,[6] it would imply that the growth in public debt would involve a direct crowding out in the level of the private debt in order to maintain the overall debt/GDP constancy. If we assume, realistically, that private debt promotes growth more than public debt, because it is likely to fund more productive investment, we may have another channel through which the growth of public debt reduces economic growth. The faster growth by the US economy in the 1990s may in part be attributed to the fact that private debt has been replacing public debt. The slow growth of the Japanese economy in the 1990s may be due to the fact that the reverse is happening in Japan. However, testing this effect empirically requires a large amount of information that is not available for the cross-section of EU countries considered here. While this channel could, potentially, be evaluated empirically, the availability of data constrains us in this particular study.

11.2.4 Fourth channel

Countries that have faced major increases in public debt and in the cost of servicing that debt, such as Belgium, Ireland, and Italy, have at times attempted to reduce that cost by reducing the interest rates paid to the holders of government securities (see Tanzi and King, 1995; and Norregaard, 1997). They have accomplished this by giving special tax concessions to debt holders, for example by subjecting the interest income to low final withholding taxes; thus reducing interest payments but at the same time reducing tax receipts. This policy often results in a distortion of the financial market as well as of the tax system. In Italy, for example, over the years, the tax system became significantly distorted by the issuance of non-taxed or low-taxed public debt instruments. These instruments became a favoured investment channel for those wanting to avoid or even evade taxes. This distortion led to a major fragmentation of the financial market. It has been reported that at one time in Italy there were as many as 30 different tax rates on financial assets (see Cangiano, 1993). The bearer nature of some government securities (the BOTs) made them favoured instruments for tax evaders, leading some to state that the public debt was being serviced by tax evasion. These effects are likely to affect economic growth through the distortion in the financial market and through distortions in the tax system which affect the allocation of capital among investment instruments. Although difficult to assess directly, in the next section of this chapter we shall attempt to provide some indirect evidence on the importance of differential tax treatment of public debt in the EU member states.

11.2.5   Fifth channel

In the process of reducing the cost of servicing the debt in some cases – including Italy in the 1980s – governments have forced banks, public enterprises, and social security administrations (pension funds) to buy government bonds. This policy of financial repression reduces the cost of servicing the debt to the government by creating quasi-fiscal activities (i.e. implicit taxes on lenders) and implicitly it increases the cost of borrowing for the private sector because less credit is available to it and because the banks have to make up for the implicit costs of buying government securities. Fiscal transparency is reduced and major distortions are introduced in the financial market. It was estimated that in Italy, in the early 1980s, the government was saving several percentage points of GDP in interest cost through this channel. Other countries have also reduced their interest costs through this channel (see Tanzi, 1998). Obviously, the forced diversion of credit to the public sector must have negative implications for financial markets and for growth in general. The lack of transparency that it creates is also likely to reduce the quality of economic policy and to increase the probability that mistakes will be made by policy-makers. By the very nature of quasi-fiscal activities described above, it is not possible to obtain explicit statistics on the size of these activities in order to assess the relevance of this channel empirically. As a result, section 11.3 of this chapter will not look into the possible relevance of this channel.

11.2.6   Sixth channel

A large and growing public debt will often have an impact on monetary policy, especially, but not only, when Central Banks are not independent. It is likely that at various points the Ministry of Finance will put pressure on the central bank to pursue a more expansionary credit policy in order to reduce interest rates and the cost of servicing the public debt. Conflicts between the Ministry of Finance and the Central Bank on this issue have been frequent in many countries. Of course, when monetary expansion is not anticipated, or when inflationary expectations are slow to adjust, this policy may reduce the cost of servicing the public debt. However, the advantage is generally short-lived because inflationary expectations soon adjust to the monetary expansions and nominal interest rates adjust to the higher inflationary expansions.

Given the normal shape of the yield curve, governments can also save on interest costs by shortening the maturity structure of their debt. *Ceteris paribus*, an inverse relation between the size of the public debt and the average maturity of the debt can be expected. As the ratio of public debt to GDP increases, the maturity of the debt is likely to become shorter. But a short maturity brings with it some costs. The short maturity makes debt management more difficult because of the frequent need to replace maturing securities with new debt. In 1981, 60 per cent of Italian public debt had a maturity of less than one year while the average maturity of the stock was only one-and-a-half years (see Alesina, Prati and Tabellini, 1990). This situation creates constraints for monetary policy and inevitably reduces the degrees of freedom of the monetary authorities. It also increases the exposure of the countries to the vagaries of international interest rates or of the domestic inflation rate. Furthermore, when the maturity of public debt instruments becomes very short, the public securities become closer substitute for money. They may reduce the need to hold money and both reduce seignorage and complicate the conduct of monetary policy. While in the past this effect may have been important in EU countries, it is difficult to examine the hypothesis directly. We will provide some information on the current maturity structure of debt in the EU, which suggests maturities have actually been increasing in recent years. Also note that, with the advent of the EMU, looking forward, this channel is unlikely to be important in the EMU member states.

In the next section we attempt to provide some empirical backing to some of the hypotheses outlined above, notably channels 1 and 2, with some additional empirical information on channels 4 and 6. Unfortunately, due to data limitations, we shall not be able to investigate whether there is backing to all of the channels we have described.

11.3   An empirical assessment of some of the channels through which public debt may affect economic growth

Assessing the relative importance of the channels described in the theoretical section of the chapter, through which a high and growing public debt may affect economic growth, is ultimately an empirical question. In order to provide some insight into these various channels we look at information on the 11 countries of EMU and the UK.[7] An annual data base that covers these 12 countries is constructed using information from the IMF's *Government Financial Statistics* and the *World Economic Outlook* from 1970 to 1998.

In the discussion that follows we are cautioned by the many empirical problems other authors have had in establishing a relation between debt, fiscal variables, and growth as typified by the extensive literature in the area. Levine and Renelt (1992) demonstrate this quite powerfully by showing the empirical links between growth and public spending or taxes are, at best, fragile to the inclusion of different explanatory variables into the regression. Also a number of other studies have found quite mixed results. Agell *et al.* (1997) provide a useful survey of the literature and concludes there is a very uncertain impact of fiscal policy on growth. Barro (1991), Kormendi and Meguire (1985), and Landau (1986) have found negative effects of total public spending on growth, while Landau (1986) finds government investment has an insignificant effect on growth. Sala-i-Martin (1997) finds no significant effect of any measures of public spending on growth, while Aschauer (1989) finds public investment has a positive growth impact. King and Rebelo (1990) find a negative effect of income tax on growth, while Engen and Skinner (1992) find both public spending and taxes have a negative effect on economic growth. Finally, Mendoza *et al.* (1997) show that tax rates are generally not significant in explaining growth although direct taxes do appear to have a negative effect on private investment. As the brief summary above shows, it is difficult to find strong and robust relations between fiscal variables and economic growth and so any empirical correlations shown in the following section should be interpreted with caution.

11.3.1   A summary of the data

Table 11.1 provides a broad summary of the data for the EU sample countries as a whole. It is clear that the past two decades have witnessed a dramatic worsening of the fiscal position of this group of countries. Their public debt as a share of output increased from 38 per cent of GDP in 1980 to almost 70 per cent of GDP by end-1998 (although since 1996 gross debt has been declining as a ratio of output). In line with the increase in public indebtedness, budgetary interest payments have risen 1.5 per cent of GDP between 1980 and 1998. The primary deficit increased in the early 1980s but, as a response to the growing debt burden, policy measures were put in place in the mid-1980s or later to stem the increasing debt burden. These measures were further reinvigorated in the latter part of the 1990s resulting in an improvement in the primary surplus to over 2.5 per cent of GDP in 1998. The overall fiscal balance deteriorated during the first half of the 1980s, but began improving in the latter part of the decade, before relapsing in the early 1990s as interest rates rose, increasing the cost of servicing public debt. The latter part of the decade, however, saw a strong trend towards more fiscal discipline, in large part due to Maastricht conditions; this trend has pushed the overall deficit for the EU countries to below 2 per cent of GDP. The improved fiscal position was facilitated by an increase in tax revenues from 31 per cent of output in 1980 to 35 per cent of output in 1997 and by a partial decline in capital spending particularly in the latter part of the 1990s. In addition, the decline in inflation and nominal interest rates has also helped to reduce

Table 11.1 Summary of key aggregates for the EU

	1970s average	1980	1980s average	1990	1990s average	1998
Gross debt	...	37.8	49.0	54.7	64.3	69.7
Net debt	...	...	41.2	40.4	52.5	59.9
Overall balance	...	−3.5	−4.1	−3.7	−4.1	−1.7
Primary balance	...	−0.5	0.1	0.9	0.8	2.6
Total expenditure	...	45.9	48.2	47.9	49.7	47.4
Current expenditure	...	40.5	41.7	40.6	42.8	42.4[1]
Capital expenditure	2.6	2.4	2.3	2.7	2.2	1.2[1]
Interest payments	...	3.0	4.2	4.6	5.0	4.4
Tax revenue	29.2	31.4	32.9	33.4	34.3	35.0[1]
Direct taxes	8.6	9.3	9.9	10.6	10.3	10.7[1]
Indirect taxes	8.7	9.0	9.4	9.7	9.8	9.9[1]
Private savings	21.7	21.7	21.6	21.9	21.4	20.1
Private investment	23.9	23.3	21.2	22.2	19.7	18.7
Growth rate (unweighted)	3.8	3.6	2.8	3.5	2.7	3.8
Real long-term bond yield	0.2	1.0	4.1	5.9	5.1	3.2
Real short-term deposit rate	−1.4	0.8	2.9	5.5	4.4	2.6

[1] Latest data available are for 1997.

Source: *World Economic Outlook* (2000) and *Government Finance Statistics* (1999).

the fiscal outlays during this period. The fall in nominal interest rates, due to lower inflationary expectations, also contributed to this improvement. Current non-interest expenditures during the 1990s, however, were not brought under control and, indeed, on average, have risen during the past two decades.

At the same time as public debt was growing in the EU countries, the long-run growth rates were on a downward path, falling from an average of 3.8 per cent in the 1970s to an average of 2.7 per cent in the 1980s before bottoming out at 0.5 per cent in 1993. The late 1990s however, have seen a rebound in growth in the EU countries with an average growth rate of 3.5 per cent despite the strong fiscal retrenchment during this same period. The increase in the government debt burden had also coincided with an upward pressure on real interest rates. However, interest rates have reversed their course in the late 1990s. Private savings have been remarkably unchanged during this whole period although, since 1995, there has been some evidence of a downward trend in private savings at the same time as public sector savings have been on the rise.

11.3.2 First and second channel

As part of a preliminary assessment of the empirical significance of these two channels we begin by presenting some broad statistics from the panel dataset. Looking at the first channel described above, if an alternative low-risk, low transaction cost investment instrument is able to impact the level of savings that are devoted to productive capital accumulation then this effect should be reflected in a positive correlation between the size of the outstanding debt and the level of real interest rates. If savings are diverted into public securities rather than private capital formation then a higher real rate of interest will be required in order to clear capital markets. However, if the world is Ricardian then no such correlation will exist. Of course, this correlation could be driven by a reverse causation whereby higher interest rates increase debt servicing costs, raise the deficit, and increase overall indebtedness. However, regressing lagged debt on interest rates yields similar results as those presented here, suggesting changes in the path of debt precede changes in interest rates.

The evidence for a correlation between public debt and interest rates is mixed in the EU sample. For Finland, Ireland, Italy, Netherlands and Spain there appears to be a consistent empirical relationship, with higher debt driving up domestic real interest rates. However, for Germany, Luxembourg, Portugal and the UK the relationship does not appear to be present in the data over any sample period. Table 11.2 summarizes the correlations and their significance for the countries in our sample. If one looks at the EU panel *as a group*, there appears to be a more consistent, stable relationship between the level of public debt and the real interest rate. In particular, across the entire cross-section, a pooled random effects regression of interest rates on debt suggests that a 10 per cent of GDP increase in the average EU debt–GDP ratio will lead to an increase in real interest rates by 0.6 percentage points (see Table 11.2). The size of the effect, while still highly significant, is however smaller for the 1980–98 subsample. In addition, the

Table 11.2   Correlations between real interest rates and gross debt in the EU

Country	1970–98		1980–98	
	Correlation	*t-statistic*	*Correlation*	*t-statistic*
Austria	0.06	5.61	0.03	1.50
Belgium	0.02	1.93	0.01	0.87
Finland	0.15	4.92	−0.01	0.34
France	0.10	2.66	0.08	2.84
Germany	0.02	1.30	0.04	1.09
Ireland	0.13	3.96	0.13	3.39
Italy	0.14	5.99	0.08	2.39
Luxembourg	−0.16	0.88	−0.16	0.88
Netherlands	0.11	5.45	0.04	2.62
Portugal	0.08	0.55	0.08	0.54
Spain	0.16	4.56	0.06	1.92
UK	−0.13	3.23	0.04	0.84
EU11 + UK	0.06	7.83	0.01	4.40

significance of the relation is robust to different functional specifications and inclusion of lagged variables and autoregressive terms.[8] The existence of an impact of debt on interest rates at the regional level but with less evidence of an effect at the individual country level, seems to suggest that there is a common capital market in the EU, and that it is changes in the debt in the region as a whole that are of more relevance for interest rates than the path of the debt for individual states.

For the EU as a whole, higher debt appears to have been associated with an increase in real interest rates in the past. Has this been reflected also in a decline in private capital accumulation? Despite an upturn in the late 1980s, the data shows that private investment has been on a steady downward trend for the past three decades at the same time as public debt was rising. From Table 11.1 it can be seen that investment has fallen from 23 per cent of output in 1980 to under 19 per cent in 1998 and there is a strong, negative, statistical correlation between private investment and the size of the public debt (see Table 11.3). Having said this, and as shown by Mendoza *et al.* (1997) for the impact of direct taxes, these negative effects on investment do not necessarily translate into a negative impact on growth; a more complete examination of the direct link between debt and growth is provided below.

Table 11.3 shows that, while private investment may be effected by public debt, there is less evidence of an inverse relation between debt and private savings (indeed changes in private savings seem somewhat autonomous for the EU countries over the period sampled).

Overall, there seems to be empirical support for the first channel highlighted in section 11.2 through which higher public debt can affect growth. For the EU as a whole, contrary to the Ricardian proposition, higher debt does appear to put upward pressure on real interest rates while at the same time it is negatively correlated with private investment. Both these empirical regularities suggest that higher debt in the EU does crowd out private capital formation and could potentially have a corresponding deleterious effect on growth (assuming public spending is in general less productive than private investment).

Turning now to the second channel described above, involving the impact of higher government debt on the fiscal aggregates. Is it the case that, for the

Table 11.3 Correlations between savings and investment and gross debt in the EU

	1970–98		1980–98	
	Correlation	*t-statistic*	*Correlation*	*t-statistic*
Private savings	0.01	0.95	0.02	2.46
Private investment	−0.08	12.21	−0.09	9.80

EU countries, the higher debt service burden has led to an increase in direct taxation or a reduction in productive public investment which, in turn, has had a negative impact on growth?

For the EU group as a whole there is a strong negative correlation between the size of government indebtedness and its expenditure on accumulating public capital. Figures 11.1 and 11.2 show this relationship across the cross-section of countries and through time. From Table 11.1 it is clear that since

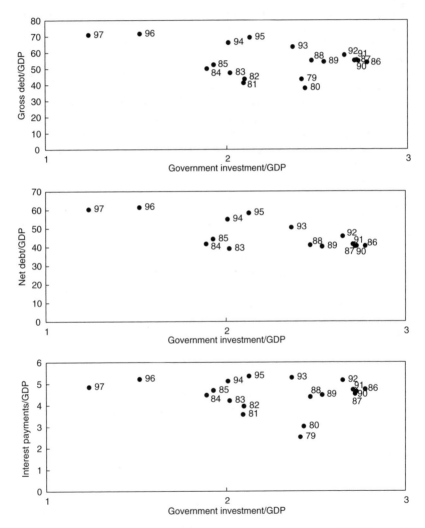

Figure 11.1 Effect of debt on government investment: average for all EMU countries plus the United Kingdom

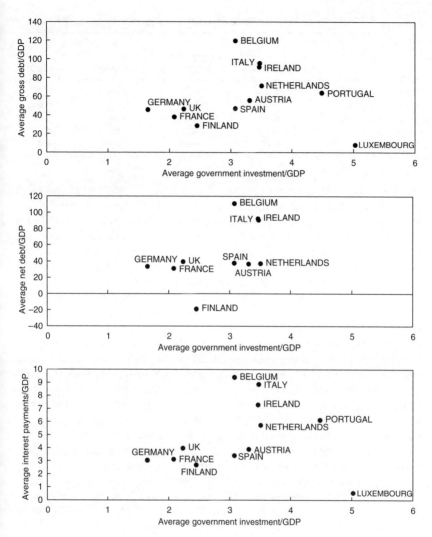

Figure 11.2 Effect of debt on government investment: country average 1980–98

1980 the increase in public debt has corresponded to a contemporaneous reduction in public investment of around 1.25 per cent of GDP. This correlation is captured in a random effects model panel regression,[9] summarized in Table 11.4, which shows that, on average for the time period and the EU countries in the sample, a 10 per cent of GDP rise in the public debt ratio reduces government investment expenditure on average by 0.1 per cent of GDP. For the shortened sample period of 1980–98 the magnitude of this

Table 11.4   Correlations between fiscal aggregates and gross debt in the EU

	1970–98		1980–98	
	Correlation	*t-statistic*	*Correlation*	*t-statistic*
Capital expenditure	−0.01	6.11	−0.03	7.47
Current expenditure	0.14	11.71	0.09	6.67
Total tax revenues	0.11	15.48	0.08	9.25
Direct taxes	0.04	9.22	0.02	4.12
Indirect taxes	0.02	6.18	0.02	5.27

effect is larger with a 10 per cent of GDP increase in debt being associated with a reduction in public investment of over 0.25 per cent of GDP. We should note that, ideally, we would like to see if higher debt is associated with lower spending on *productive* public services (which include capital spending but also outlays on human capital accumulation such as health and education). Therefore, the results using capital spending should be cautioned by the fact this may be a poor measure of productive public spending.[10]

Table 11.1 shows that from 1980 to 1997 the substantial increase in public debt was accompanied by a significant rise in tax revenues of 3.6 per cent of GDP (including a 1.5 per cent of GDP rise in direct taxes and 0.9 per cent of GDP increase in indirect taxes). Figure 11.3 shows a strong relation through time between the level of public indebtedness and the share of output being taken in taxes. There is, however, a less clear relationship between the average size of the debt and level of taxes across countries (see Figure 11.4). Despite this, the correlation between debt and taxes in a random effects panel regression is strong, with the empirical results suggesting that an increase in debt by 10 per cent of GDP will, on average, increase taxes by around 1 per cent of GDP (a similar empirical magnitude as the rough calculation derived from the changes in debt and taxes shown in Table 11.1). While the higher public debt appears associated with an increase in the average effective tax rates for both indirect and direct taxes, the increase appears more pronounced for direct taxes with a 10 per cent of GDP rise in public debt increasing direct taxes 0.4 per cent of GDP while only leading to a 0.2 per cent of GDP increase in indirect taxes (see Table 11.4).

To summarize, the empirical evidence suggests that higher public debt reduces the amount of private savings which are diverted toward productive private capital accumulation and results in higher real interest rates. In addition, higher debt in the EU is typically accompanied by higher taxes, particularly direct taxes, and lower government investment. Do these relationships then translate into a significant impact of government debt on the aggregate growth rate of the economy?

To answer this question we look at whether, within the countries of the EU, there is any empirical support for the simple model of debt, public

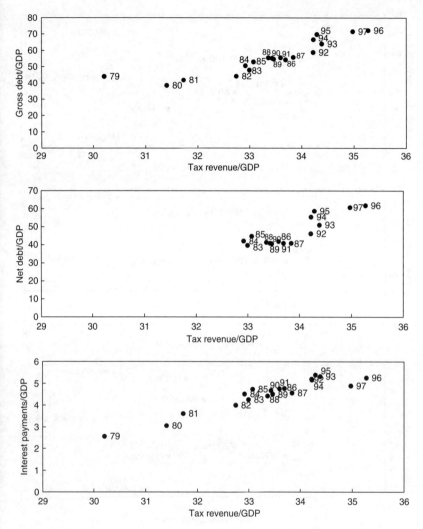

Figure 11.3 Effect of debt on tax revenues: average for the EMU countries plus the United Kingdom

spending, and growth we outlined in section 11.2 and estimate a linearized version of the equation:

$$\frac{Y_{t+1}}{Y_t} = \left[\frac{(1-\delta_G)K_{G,t}+G_t}{Y_t} \right]^{1-\alpha} \left[s(1-t)\beta - \frac{B_{t+1}}{Y_t} \right]^{\alpha}$$

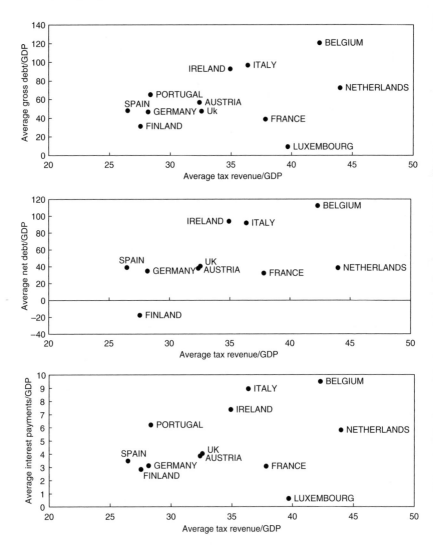

Figure 11.4   Effect of debt on tax revenues: country average 1980–98

Certainly the partial bivariate correlations between growth and debt, public investment, and direct taxes are encouraging (Table 11.5). There does appear to be a negative correlation between direct taxes and growth and also between debt and growth. At the same time public investment is positively related to economic growth.

We constructed a panel regression using Seemingly Unrelated Regression (SUR), fixed effects, and random effects models that includes government capital spending as a ratio of output, the debt–GDP ratio, and the level of direct taxes as determinants for growth. What is lacking, however, is a consistent data series for the level of public capital formation to include into the growth regression. This is unfortunate, since the model above would suggest such information is likely to be an important predictor of a country's growth performance. The results of the regression are given in Table 11.6.

The evidence is clearly mixed. The SUR model gives broadly the right empirical signs to the variables, but restricting the constants for each country to be identical results in a very poor fit and the parameter restrictions are

Table 11.5 Correlations between fiscal aggregates and economic growth in the EU

	1970–98	
	Correlation	t-statistic
Public debt	−0.02	3.01
Public investment	0.25	1.70
Direct taxes	−0.08	1.69

Table 11.6 Growth regressions for EU countries

	Sample period	Debt	Public investment	Direct taxes	R-squared
SUR	1970–98	−0.01	0.34	−0.07	0.02
		(0.95)	(3.41)	(2.02)	
	1980–98	−0.02	0.30	−0.06	0.00
		(5.42)	(4.16)	(2.00)	
Fixed effects	1970–98	−0.03	−0.43	−0.22	0.19
		(4.29)	(2.95)	(3.43)	
	1980–98	−0.04	−0.13	−0.12	0.16
		(5.00)	(1.20)	(1.92)	
Fixed effects	1970–98	−0.02		−0.27	0.17
		(3.79)		(5.27)	
	1980–98	−0.02		−0.21	0.17
		(4.00)		(4.13)	
Random effects	1970–98	−0.01	0.10	−0.03	0.09
		(1.88)	(0.57)	(0.55)	
	1980–98	−0.01	0.04	0.07	0.13
		(1.15)	(0.20)	(1.17)	
Random effects	1970–98	−0.01		−0.08	0.13
		(1.92)		(1.42)	
	1980–98	−0.01		0.05	0.16
		(0.81)		(0.75)	

t-statistics are included in parentheses adjusted for heteroscedasticity.

consequently rejected by statistical tests. Allowing for country-specific fixed effects improves the fit but results in public investment being a poor explanatory variable for aggregate growth performance. This contrasts with findings by Aschauer (1989) and Easterly and Rebelo (1993) that public investment is a factor for growth. It could be, as de la Fuente (1997) suggests, that for the industrialized countries typified in our sample of EU states, there are little or no growth effects from public capital formation since such countries have reached a position of diminishing returns to public infrastructure investment.

Dropping public investment from the equation is not rejected using parameter restrictions, and the resulting, more parsimonious formulation suggests that both higher debt and direct taxes (which in some part result from the higher levels of debt service) have a deleterious impact on long-run growth. In particular a 10 per cent of GDP increase in the debt *or* a 1 per cent of GDP increase in direct taxes will each reduce growth by around 0.25 percentage points. One interpretation of the lack of a significant effect for public investment could be that, as we have mentioned above, the capital/current expenditure distinction does not capture well the difference between 'productive' and 'non-productive' public spending. For example, one could argue that current spending on health or education is productive and would contribute to economic growth. However, constructing estimates of productive expenditures was constrained by the availability of disaggregated fiscal data for the sample countries. Alternatively, it could be, as Levine and Renelt (1992) suggest, that the empirical link between public spending and growth is, in fact, rather fragile.

For comparison, and to illustrate the fragility of the growth regressions, Table 11.6 also presents the results from an alternative random effects model of the growth equation, which results in a worse fit and seems to suggest that none of the variables have a clear role as a determinant of economic growth. However, the non-correlation amongst the individual effects and the error term is rejected by a Hausman test suggesting that, statistically, the random effects formulation is not appropriate for this panel and the results from the fixed effects estimation should be the preferred formulation.

11.3.3 Fourth channel

It was certainly the case that in the EU during the 1970s many countries with high debts also had a concomitant set of distortions in the tax system with multiple statutory tax concessions for the interest income from public debt. This clearly must have led to some distortion in the allocation of resources (away from the fully taxed private capital and towards lower taxed but unproductive sovereign liabilities). However, it is less clear that this is an important factor in the present-day EU.

As Table 11.7 shows, only Spain has a differential tax treatment for government debt relative to other forms of debt instruments.[11] Even then, the

Table 11.7 Taxation of interest income in the EU

	Withholding tax on govt. debt	Withholding tax on non-govt. debt	Marginal PIT rates	Tax regime[1]	Comments
Austria	25	25	10–50	W	
Belgium	15	15	25–55	P/W	
Finland	28	28	0–38	W	Deposits in Finnish bank accounts exempt from withholding.
France	0	0	10.5–54	P/W	Taxpayer may opt for a final flat rate of 15% on interest.
Germany	31.65	31.65	0–53	P	
Ireland	24	24	24–46	P and W	Withholding tax on bank deposits is final.
Italy	12.5	12.5 or 27	19–46	W	27% withholding applies to current accounts and certain bonds.
Luxembourg	0	0	0–46	P	
Netherlands	0	0	6.2–60	P	
Portugal	20	20		P/W	
Spain	0	25	20–56	P	Treasury notes are exempt from withholding but subject to PIT.
UK	20	20	20–40	P	

[1] P indicates the interest is subject to progressive PIT rates and withholding is creditable; W indicates withholding tax is final and the interest is not subject to PIT; P/W indicates residents can choose between final withholding or taxation at progressive PIT rates.

Source: International Bureau of Fiscal Documentation, 1999.

lack of a withholding tax on public debt is only a minor distortion since all interest income is subject to the personal income tax with withholding taxes paid being creditable against assessed PIT. It should be noted, however, that although the statutory tax legislation does not provide for a blanket tax preference for government debt in many of the EU countries, there are specific government debt issues that are deemed exempt from income tax. However, the recourse to making a specific issue exempt is a carry-over from the past (i.e. applies to longer-term maturities that were issued some time ago but are still in circulation) rather than an ongoing policy. On the whole, then, the impact of debt on growth through distortions to the tax system and the allocation of capital is likely to be an unimportant channel by which debt affects growth in the EU.

11.3.4   Sixth channel

The evidence that the substitutability between money and government debt increases as a country's debt stock rises, is mixed. As Table 11.8 and Figure 11.5 show, it is true that the high debt countries of the EU, particularly Belgium and Italy, do tend to have a larger proportion of their debt in short-term instruments that are close substitutes for money. However, Spain and to some extent France also have a debt maturity structure that is very biased towards short-term instruments despite having a debt stock that is around the average for the EU. However, the maturity structure in the EU has, even within the past decade, become much more homogenous with even the outlying countries such as Italy and Belgium lengthening their maturities considerably and reducing the recourse to short-term instruments (see Alesina, Prati and Tabellini, 1990, for a discussion of Italy). Also it should be noted that the data concerning the precise structure of public debt is sparse. The only internationally comparable data that was available was that produced by Eurostat which is available only from 1991. However, summary information on the average maturity of the stock of public debt or a breakdown of the maturity of debt by currency denomination is not available (clearly, in looking at the maturity of debt and its substitutability for money

Table 11.8   Maturity of EU debt (in percent of outstanding liabilities)

	1998				1992			
	Bills	Short term loans	Bonds	Medium & long term loans	Bills	Short term loans	Bonds	Medium & long term loans
Austria	0.1	0.0	75.1	24.8	1.8	0.6	61.3	36.4
Belgium	13.8	1.2	75.3	9.7	18.1	6.3	65.5	10.1
Finland	4.8	0.0	85.1	10.1	8.0	0.1	75.5	16.5
France	7.6	1.4	75.7	15.3	28.4	5.4	42.7	23.5
Germany	1.1	1.7	54.5	42.7	3.1	1.3	49.1	46.5
Ireland	5.0	2.9	62.8	29.4	4.0	7.3	64.6	24.1
Italy	12.0	0.4	82.0	5.6	25.8	6.6	61.4	6.2
Luxembourg	0.0	1.7	58.2	40.2	0.0	5.0	29.3	65.7
Netherlands	3.1	1.7	71.2	24.0	0.1	1.6	57.0	41.3
Portugal	4.1	0.7	88.1	7.1	17.5	1.4	75.1	5.9
Spain	18.4	0.0	66.8	14.8	37.9	0.0	35.4	26.7
United Kingdom	1.4	4.8	91.4	2.4	4.1	6.4	85.9	3.5

Source: Eurostat.

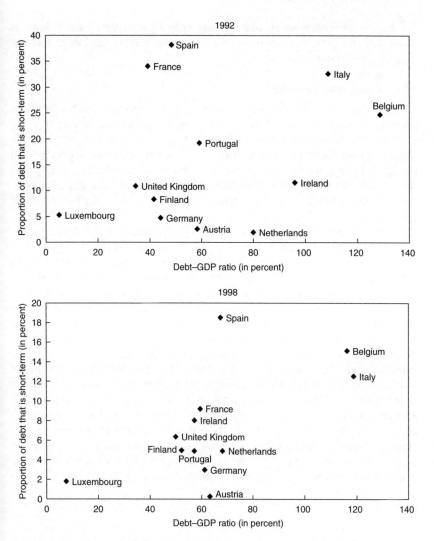

Figure 11.5 Effect of debt on maturity structure in 1992 and 1998

Source: Eurostat.

one would want to focus on the maturity structure of debt denominated in the *domestic* currency). Finally, it is likely that with the constraints imposed by the ERM, the advent of EMU and the devolution of monetary autonomy to the ECB, the impact of higher debt by any individual country on monetary policy – and thus the impact of debt on growth through this channel – is likely to be a less important consideration that before. However, this is not to say that an EU-wide increase in debt will have a neutral impact on the conduct of monetary policy and consequently on economic growth but it is likely such an occurrence is now, to a large extent, restrained by the stability and growth pact.

11.4   Concluding remarks

In this chapter we have identified various channels through which a large and growing public debt could have negative effects on growth. Some of these channels were known; some much less so. We have also attempted to provide some empirical backing for these theoretically identified channels. As is often the case in this kind of work, we have run into various data limitations that have made our attempt less conclusive than we would have liked. As with other studies of this type, the empirical results are also sensitive to model specification.

A growing public debt appears to lead to higher direct taxes, lower public investment and, ultimately, a lower growth rate. In addition, higher debt does seem to crowd out private capital formation and raise interest rates. On the other hand, in the EU context, high debt seems not to be associated with more distortionary tax systems or with increased distortion to monetary policy. It is inevitable though, even when correlations between debt and growth are found, there will be doubts as to whether these correlations are capturing a causal relation or something more spurious. However, it must be remembered that even a relatively small change in the growth rate of a country, if compounded over many years, can make a substantial difference in its income level. Given the evidence for the EU, its possible lower debt will have non-negligible effects on growth rates, and the welfare impact over time of lowering public debt could be large. In the most recent years, the ratio of public debt into GDP has started to decline in the countries of the European Union; we believe this has the potential to bring substantial benefits in terms of output growth. Hopefully this trend will continue and accelerate, thus removing an obstacle to the growth potential of the EU countries.

Notes

1. Revised version of the chapter presented at the seminar on Public Debt and Fiscal Policy in EMU at the European Commission, September 17, 1999, Brussels. The authors would like to thank Helen Blyth and Amina Elmi for research assistance and Marco Cangiano, Martin Kaufman, and Carlos Martinez-Mongay for valuable comments; all errors remain our own.
2. In extreme cases not only net saving but also depreciation funds may be invested in government securities.
3. Hume had already recognized this possibility. In his words, 'The greater part of the public stock being always in the hands of idle people, who live on their revenue, our fund, in that view, give great encouragement to an useless and unactive life' (1955, p. 96). The fact that a significant share of public debt is owned either by retirees or by pension funds who tend to be more risk averse may strengthen this possibility.

4. In a standard neoclassical growth model a strong neutrality result obtains, since growth is determined exogenously by population growth or exogenous technological development and so is unaffected by fiscal policy developments by assumption.

5. In a model of more general preferences the tax on interest income would lead to an income and substitution effect on savings and the effect of taxation could be ambiguous. In the model above, the choice of logarithmic preferences implies that income and substitution effects exactly cancel and savings are independent of the rate of taxation on capital income.

6. In an unpublished paper he showed that Canada, Germany, Japan, and the United Kingdom also exhibited similar broad constancy between total debt and GDP. See Friedman (1982).

7. In the text below we shall loosely use the term 'EU countries' to signify this group of the EMU 11 and the UK.

8. A formal Granger causality test for the EU as a whole is inconclusive for the 1970–98 period but shows that debt 'Granger-causes' interest rates in the 1980–98 sub-sample but not vice versa.

9. A fixed effects model or SUR formulation produces similar results to the random effects model presented here.

10. See Easterly and Rebelo (1993), Barro and Sala-i-Martin (1995), or Glomm and Ravikumar (1997) for a survey.

11. See Norregaard (1997) for a discussion of the tax treatment of government bonds.

Part III

Monetary and Fiscal Policy Interactions in EMU

12
Debt, Deficits and the Behaviour of Monetary and Fiscal Authorities

Jacques Mélitz[1]

12.1 Introduction

The fiscal criteria of the Maastricht Treaty and the recent Pact for Stability raise many questions about the behaviour of fiscal authorities: How do fiscal authorities respond to government debt? How do they respond to the business cycle? Other significant questions concern policy interactions with the monetary authorities: How does loose fiscal policy impinge on monetary policy? How does tight monetary policy affect fiscal policy? The recent advent of EMU adds a new dimension to these questions: How will fiscal policy change under the new regime? As regards this last question, the issue of 'automatic stabilization' assumes particular significance. In principle, EMU could substantially alter discretionary fiscal behaviour. But the very term 'automatic' implies that the automatic stabilizers will be unaffected. Consequently, if the automatic stabilizers are really strong, as is often supposed, the members of EMU might be expected to benefit from sizeable smoothing from these stabilizers alone, and the degree of change in discretionary policy is less important. Current thinking in the European Commission runs along these lines. This study deals exclusively with such questions. The work uses pooled data for the largest possible number of OECD countries, 19 in all. These include every member of the European Union (EU) except Luxembourg. The five other countries in the sample are the US, Canada, Japan, Australia and Japan. Separate work was done on the 14 EU members. Three basic conclusions emerge. First, the fiscal authorities respond in a stabilizing manner to debt–output ratios. As levels of public indebtedness rise relative to output, ratios of taxes to output go up and ratios of government spending to output fall. These results hold up for the EU countries by themselves as well as for all 19 in the sample.

Second, monetary and fiscal policy move in opposite directions. Looser fiscal policy promotes tighter monetary policy, and tighter monetary policy encourages more expansionary fiscal policy. The contractionary response of monetary policy to an easing of fiscal policy is clearer in the sample of all

19 countries than for the 14 EU members alone, and this contractionary response can be questioned altogether if Germany is removed from the EU sample. However, there is no support for the pessimistic view that monetary policy accommodates loose fiscal policy. The tightening of fiscal policy in response to easier monetary policy, in turn, results entirely from spending behaviour. Taxes do not contribute at all. This next conclusion is also extremely robust. It holds for the EU countries alone, with or without Germany.

Third, and most challenging of all, the results imply a weak stabilizing response of deficit spending to the cycle. Taxes move in a stabilizing manner in response to news about output (with Student t's of the order of 10). However, government expenditures react currently as well (with equally high Student t's) but in a destabilizing direction. Net stabilization therefore only occurs because of a larger reaction of taxes than expenditures. A year after output news, more stabilization follows, this time coming from expenditures, but the extra stabilization is moderate. All of these results are extremely robust and hold for the EU14 as well as for all 19 countries.

After presenting the test outcomes, I will argue that the estimated responses to the cycle should be seen as entirely automatic and independent of decision-making. If this is so, we can expect much less automatic stabilization from fiscal policy under EMU than has been assumed.

One matter of vocabulary should be cleared up at the start. 'Stabilizing fiscal policy' will refer here strictly to the direction of change of the government budget balance in response to the cycle. Specifically, any rise in tax receipts or fall in government spending in response to expansion will be said to be stabilizing. The term 'automatic stabilizers' will be understood the same way. Ordinarily, 'stabilizing fiscal policy' and 'automatic stabilization' carry the wider connotation of a stabilizing effect on the economy. But unless otherwise specified, this added connotation is not intended here. The reason for this narrow usage of the term is that the automatic stabilizers, as treated here, need not have stabilizing effects. Indeed we have known for a long time that Ricardian neutrality may prevent the automatic stabilizers from having any influence at all on the economy. However, the grounds for caution are more extensive. Already in 1984 Christiano had assembled a host of reasons for destabilizing effects of 'automatic stabilizers' on the economy, some of them holding in a strict Keynesian context (based on the dynamics and foresight), others in a real-business-cycle one (for example, because of labour/leisure choices). The theory of real business cycles is particularly ambivalent about the automatic stabilizers' impact on output and consumption (see Baxter and King, 1993), and the empirical validity of the predictions of the theory about fiscal policy is now a subject of active research (Galí, 1994; and Fatás and Mihov, 1998). I will try to skirt these issues entirely. However, I will not succeed entirely, mainly because of the question of simultaneity bias. Still, in the absence of any word to the contrary, all of my references to 'stabilizing' fiscal policy should be understood strictly in the previous narrow sense. The point is that the stabilizing or destabilizing repercussions of official behaviour on the economy depends on other evidence, which I do not really study below.

The order of the discussion will be as follows: the hypotheses (section 12.2), the main tests and results (12.3), further tests (12.4), comparison with other studies (12.5), the concept of automatic stabilization (12.6) and the conclusion (12.7).

12.2 Hypotheses

Since the interactions between fiscal and monetary authorities are a central concern of the study, the reaction functions of the fiscal and the monetary authorities will be estimated simultaneously. Monetary policy can be examined on the basis of monthly series, but fiscal policy cannot. At best, quarterly series must serve for fiscal policy. But even quarterly series are problematic: those regarding tax receipts are highly seasonal, and the ones for government expenditures are subject to accident and manipulation. In addition, reliance on quarterly series would limit the international range of the study. For all these reasons, I will stick to annual observations in dealing with fiscal policy. This will then restrict me to annual observations regarding monetary policy as well. As a result, even 40 observations per variable for any country will be many.[2] Consequently, I will use pooled data for the largest possible number of countries, all 19 mentioned above.

It is now conventional to use the intervention rate of the monetary authorities on the money market, R_m, as a measure of monetary policy. The appropriate measure of this rate obviously differs by country, and in deciding on a series, it was often necessary to compromise between the desire for continuous data and the one for the best possible index of the marginal cost of central bank funds. My chosen measures of R_m follow in appendix 12.A1. The basic measure of fiscal policy in the study will be the primary surplus (the surplus exclusive of interest payments), S_p, divided by potential output, Y^*. There are two reasons for using the primary rather than the total surplus. First, the interest on the debt could create a spurious relationship between monetary and fiscal policy. Second, the intertemporal budget constraint of the fiscal authorities relates to the primary surplus. The reason for dividing the primary surplus by some measure of output is to make sure that the dependent variable in the fiscal policy equation takes the form of a ratio, as do all of the other variables in the equations (so that the coefficients are easier to interpret). The choice of dividing by potential output instead of current output comes because the dependent variable of the fiscal policy equation should reflect official behaviour. The authorities obviously have more control over the ratio of the primary surplus to potential output than they do over the ratio of this surplus to current output.

I will also examine government tax receipts and expenditures separately, as is done with increasing frequency. More specifically, the study will divide up S_p/Y^* between government consumption plus transfer payments, $(G_c+TR)/Y^*$, and tax receipts minus public investment spending, $(T-G_i)/Y^*$. The choice of this particular division privileges the distinction between government net saving and 'exhaustive' government expenditures. In making this division, I was influenced by Alesina and Perotti (1995b), who argued that taxes and public investment were easier to adjust than government consumption at times of consolidations. According to them, governments tended to rely heavily on rises in taxes and reductions in investment during episodes of major retrenchment, and were prone to increase their consumption and transfer payments during episodes of major fiscal-policy expansion. At a later point I will extend the analysis and try to distinguish the behaviour of G_c/Y^* and TR/Y^*. But at no stage will I study government investment separately.

The hypotheses suppose that monetary and fiscal policies depend partly on initial information, partly on fresh developments, whether anticipated or not. In the case of monetary policy, I assume the relevant initial information to regard the nominal long-term interest rate R_{lt}, the relation of output to potential output, Y/Y^*, and the weight of the public sector in the economy, as measured either by the ratio of taxes to output, T/Y, or else by the ratio of debt to output, D/Y, or both. The long-term interest rate is used to reflect official concern with inflation. A general failure of the authorities to respond to rises in R_{lt} by increasing R_m would be inflationary. The relevant new developments within the period regard output, inflation, and desired portfolio shifts in and out of money. In the case of fiscal policy, the pertinent initial conditions concern Y/Y^*, inflation π, and the burden of the public debt, as measured either by D/Y or by the interest on the debt relative to output. Movements in the burden of the debt in the recent past (lagged values of $\Delta D/Y$) could also be relevant. The current or new developments pertain to output and inflation. Because of possible interactions between monetary and fiscal policy, the study also prominently considers the response of R_m to S_p/Y^* and S_p/Y^* to R_m. The variables D_p, S_p, Y and Y^* are all measured at current rather than constant prices. This choice makes no difference in the case of the ratios S_p/Y^* and Y/Y^*. But since there is good reason to think of the public debt D in current prices and therefore of the debt–output ratio D/Y the same way, I decided to measure all of these variables at current prices.

Measuring the relevant news poses a delicate problem, since all the data could be affected by current policy responses, and for purposes of the investigation, these events should be independent of policy or exogenous. Therefore, I tried to control for monetary- and fiscal-policy effects on the relevant variables. The current developments in output and inflation are then measured as follows:

$$\Delta\left(\frac{Y}{Y^*}\right) = a_0 + [a_1 \Delta(R_m - R_{lr})](L) + \left[a_2 \frac{\Delta(S_p/P)}{(S_p/P)_{-1}}\right](L) + \theta_y$$

$$\Delta\pi = b_0 + [b_1 \Delta(R_m - R_{lr})](L) + \left[b_2 \frac{\Delta(S_p/P)}{(S_p/P)_{-1}}\right](L) + \theta_\pi$$

where the policy instruments are in brackets, the notation (L) signifies both current and lagged values of the bracketed terms, and the residuals, θ_y and θ_π, represent the exogenous element of the current events. In the instances where I treated $T - G_i$ and $G_c + TR$ separately rather than using their sum S_p, corresponding definitions of θ_y and θ_π follow.

The adoption of $R_m - R_{lr}$ instead of R_m, and $(S_p/P)/(S_p/P)_{t-1}$ instead of S_p/Y^*, in the previous equations, needs a word of explanation. While R_m is evidently the basic instrument of monetary policy, there is reason to consider the impact of this policy as depending upon a movement in R_m relative to R_{lt} rather than R_m alone. If R_m as such were present in the equations, then whenever R_{lt} rose for any reason, including anticipated inflation, the resulting impact of the fall of $R_m - R_{lt}$ on inflation and output would be treated as unaffected by monetary policy. But this would be wrong, since by keeping R_m the same, the authorities would be engaging in expansionary monetary policy. On this ground, $R_m - R_{lr}$ seems to be superior to R_m as a measure of monetary policy in the equations.

With respect to fiscal policy, the use of $\Delta(S_p/P)/(S_p/P)_{t-1}$ is motivated by the absence of separate deflators for S_p and Y, thus S_p and Y^*. As a result, whether we measure S_p and Y^* at current prices or constant prices, S_p/Y^* will be the same. Yet it seems right to choose a measure of fiscal policy reflecting a real influence to the utmost. For this reason, I adopted $\Delta(S_p/P)/(S_p/P)_{t-1}$ in preference to $\Delta(S_p/Y^*)$.

The same principles that serve to identify θ_y and θ_π were also applied in identifying the exogenous current changes in the demand for money θ_m. In this next case, the dependent variables in the regressions were either $\Delta(M/P)$ or $\Delta(M/Y)$ (instead of $\Delta(Y/Y^*)$ or $\Delta\pi$) and various measures of M were tried.

I shall now proceed to the tests.

12.3   Data, tests and main results

As mentioned earlier, requisite data for the tests were collected for 19 OECD countries altogether. The annual data begin as early as 1959 for some countries and as late as 1976 for others. They all run through 1995. I chose to carry out the econometric tests in lagged-adjustment form. Quite specifically, I estimated

$$\Delta_t X = f(X_{t-1}, \Delta_{t-1}Y, \theta_t, \Delta_t Z)$$

where $\Delta_t X$ is the current change in the monetary- or fiscal-policy variable, as the case may be, X_{t-1} is its lagged value, $\Delta_{t-1}Y$ the matrix of lagged changes in values of relevant initial conditions (starting with the change from $t-2$ to $t-1$), θ_t the matrix of the current developments, and $\Delta_t Z$ the change in the opposite policy variable from X. Regardless of the use of S_p or $T-G_i$ and G_c+TR separately, $\Delta_t Z$ in the monetary policy equation is always $\Delta_t(S_p/Y^*)$.

The main test methods were two-stage-least-squares (2SLS), and generalized 2SLS or three-stage-least-squares (3SLS). Whenever fiscal policy was split into two parts, the appropriate constraint on S_p/Y^* was applied in the monetary policy equation. Table 12.1 reports the leading results for the full sample period and all 19 countries. First in order of presentation are the results for the two-equation system, concerning strictly ΔR_m and $\Delta(S_p/Y^*)$. Next come those for the three-equation system which decomposes $\Delta(T-G_i)/Y^*$ and $\Delta(G_c+TR)/Y^*$. In the first stage of the estimation, some instruments were added as exogenous variables. These instruments are past inflation rates for recent years (in both consumer and producer prices) and past levels of the dependent variables prior to $t-1$ (X_{t-2}, etc.). The exact beginning dates for the estimates, which differ for individual countries, appear in the note below.[3] Starting the tests in 1973 (instead of 1964) would have given rise to a more synchronous treatment of the different countries. But experiments show that otherwise there would have been little change: if anything, the results would improve. A fully synchronous treatment of all countries would have meant limiting the study period too much.

All the variables mentioned in discussing the hypotheses were tested. But the estimates in the table exclude most of those that proved insignificant in earlier experiments. Thus, the lagged values of the levels of the fiscal variables (either $[(T-G_i)/Y^*]_{-1}$ or $[(G_c+TR)/Y^*]_{-1}$) do not appear. It seems from the tests, therefore, that full adjustment of fiscal policy takes place within one period, or one year. But the same is not true regarding monetary policy, where $(R_m)_{-1}$ in the table is highly significant. The coefficient of $(R_m)_{-1}$ in the relevant equation(s) says that a bit over two-thirds of the adjustment of monetary policy occurs within the current year, while the rest follows later. This difference in speed of the adjustment of fiscal and monetary policy could reflect the fact that the fiscal policy response is essentially automatic – or at least that is my favoured interpretation. Current news about inflation and the demand for money also proved insignificant in earlier tests and are omitted. The only contemporary exogenous events in the table therefore concern output.[4] All the estimates took place with fixed effects for individual countries. The 2SLS estimates differ little from the 3SLS ones, and the only reason for reporting the 2SLS ones is to give some idea of the quality of the fits of the separate equations. The 3SLS estimates offer no such possibility.

Table 12.1 The basic two-equation and three-equation model

Estimation method	Dependent variable	$(R_m)_{-1}$	$\Delta_{-1}R_{lt}$	$\Delta_{-1}\left(\frac{D}{Y}\right)^2$	$\Delta_{-1}\frac{Y}{Y^\star}$	θ_y	$\Delta\frac{S_p}{Y^\star}$	ΔR_m	
2SLS	ΔR_m	-0.31 (8.9)	0.21 (2.5)		0.06 (2)		-0.48 (3.2)		$\overline{R}^2=0.18$ F=5.085***
	$\Delta\frac{S_p}{Y^\star}$			0.07 (4.3)	0.08 (3.5)	0.03 (1.4)		-0.15 (2.2)	$\overline{R}^2=0.10$ F=2.017**
3SLS	ΔR_m	-0.26 (7.6)	0.17 (2.2)		0.08 (2.8)		-0.86 (6.1)		
	$\Delta\frac{S_p}{Y^\star}$			0.04 (3)	0.08 (3.7)	0.03 (1.5)		-0.26 (4.1)	system weighted $R^2=0.21$
2SLS	ΔR_m	-0.32 (9)	0.22 (2.6)		0.06 (2)		-0.42 (2.4)		$\overline{R}^2=0.17$ F=4.98***
	$\Delta\frac{T-G_i}{Y^\star}$			0.03 (2.5)	0.01 (0.6)	0.31 (14.9)		0.06 (1)	$\overline{R}^2=0.35$ F=11.52
	$\Delta\frac{G_c+TR}{Y^\star}$			-0.04 (3.3)	-0.06 (4.2)	0.27 (16.2)		0.15 (3.1)	$\overline{R}^2=0.46$ F=17.53

Table 12.1 (Continued)

Estimation method	Dependent variable	$(R_m)_{-1}$	$\Delta_{-1}R_{lt}$	$\Delta_{-1}\left(\dfrac{D}{Y}\right)^2$	$\Delta_{-1}\dfrac{Y}{Y^\star}$	θ_y	$\Delta\dfrac{S_p}{Y^\star}$	ΔR_m	
	ΔR_m	−0.28 (8.2)	0.22 (2.8)		0.07 (2.6)		−0.69 (4.1)		
3SLS	$\Delta\left(\dfrac{T-G_i}{Y^\star}\right)$			0.03 (2)	0.01 (0.6)	0.31 (15.1)		0.02 (0.3)	system weighted $R^2 = 0.35$
	$\Delta\left(\dfrac{G_c+TR}{Y^\star}\right)$			−0.03 (2.6)	−0.07 (4.3)	0.27 (16.6)		0.19 (4.1)	

Number of observations: 423. *t* value in parentheses.

** Indicates significance at the 5 percentage-point level.

*** Indicates significance at the 1 percentage-point level (higher F values still more significant).

As can be seen, the general fit of the three-equation model is far superior to that of the two-equation one. However, this superiority is almost entirely due to the separate treatment of the impact of news about output on $(T-G_i)/Y^*$ and $(G_c+TR)/Y^*$. The separate responses of $(T-G_i)/Y^*$ and $(G_c+TR)/Y^*$ to θ_y are estimated with an extraordinary degree of precision, whereas the estimate of the response of $\Delta(S_p/Y^*)$ to θ_y in the two-equation system appears with a Student t of only around 1.5. In other respects, the estimates of the two- and three-equation systems are similar. Perhaps the negative interaction between the monetary and fiscal authorities emerges more clearly in the two-equation system. But that is just about the only other difference of note.

The fiscal policy equations generally perform much better than the monetary policy one in the three-equation model. According to the 2SLS estimates (where the R^2's of the separate equations can be viewed individually), the adjusted R^2 for the tax-minus-investment equation is 35 per cent and that for the expenditure one 46 per cent, as opposed to only 17 per cent for the monetary policy equation. Some of the national dummy variables (unshown) also prove to be important in the monetary policy equation (those for Greece, Spain, Portugal and Italy especially). But despite the presence of these dummies, omitted variables evidently explain most of the variance in monetary policy behaviour in the study period. We can only infer that omitted variables – for example, international differences in exchange rate regimes, openness, and wage–price flexibility – play a large role in connection with monetary policy. Similar international differences (if no others) apparently matter less in explaining the variance of fiscal policy, and national distinctions do not matter much either, since the national dummy variables are not important in the fiscal policy equations. Indeed, based on general fit, the degree of international uniformity in government spending behaviour is even surprising.

Let us next examine monetary policy and fiscal policy separately. As regards monetary policy, the sole indication of any response to anticipated inflation concerns the long-term interest rate. The one other initial condition that emerges as significant in the monetary policy equation is the level of economic activity: the authorities respond to the business cycle in a stabilizing manner after a year. Monetary policy also reacts without a lag to fiscal policy as such. Quite interestingly, the monetary authorities tend to tighten when fiscal policy loosens.

In the case of fiscal policy, the tests reveal no reaction to inflation – whether past inflation or current inflationary developments. This is not necessarily cause for surprise, since taxes are largely indexed, and the Olivera–Tanzi effect could cancel any tendency that might otherwise exist for inflation to raise real taxes. In addition, there is no obvious reason why inflation should systematically affect aggregate real government spending. On the other hand, the tests clearly say that fiscal policy responds to government debt in a stabilizing manner, both on the tax and the spending side. Based on the impact of $(D/Y)^2$, the response to debt heightens as the debt–output ratio rises. As a matter of fact, D/Y and the ratio of interest on the debt to output performed just as well as $(D/Y)^2$ in earlier tests, and my use of $(D/Y)^2$ is simply a choice but an acceptable one. Experiments with $(D_{t-1}-D_{t-2})/Y_{t-1}$ also proved to be futile. There is no evidence of any sensitivity of fiscal policy to any mere *deterioration* of the debt.

The influence of monetary policy on fiscal policy is also challenging. Evidently fiscal policy eases when monetary policy tightens. Here again, the action takes place essentially on the spending side.

Most interesting of all are the fiscal policy responses to the business cycle. Based on the estimates, the clearest *stabilizing* response of fiscal policy to the cycle comes with a lag. As seen in the estimate of the three-equation system, this next response also results exclusively from spending: $(G_c+TR)/Y^*$ reacts negatively to $(Y/Y^*)_{t-1}$. On the other hand, the current responses of fiscal policy to the cycle are much weaker than generally supposed. While an adverse shock to output (a negative θ_y) reduces taxes, it reduces government spending as well, and any stabilizing movement results from the stronger reaction of taxes than of spending. This stronger reaction is also marginally significant because of the enormous Student t's on both sides. The same conclusion emerges from the two-equation system, where we find a stabilizing response of the primary *surplus* to θ_y which is significant at the 10–15 per cent confidence level. Given the separate responses of government spending to θ_y and $(Y/Y^*)_{t-1}$, it appears that spending reacts in a destabilizing manner to a recession at first (a negative θ_y) before turning around and responding in a stable fashion a year later. The right interpretation will receive more attention below. But a simple account would be that a certain bureaucratic impulse prevails at the start. When tax receipts falter, government tends to nibble at individual ministerial budgets and transfer programmes, and when tax receipts flow in from everywhere, the government tends to be more lenient in meeting budget requests from the individual ministries and in disbursing transfer payments that are permitted by legislation.

Table 12.2 delves deeper into the choice of θ_y instead of Y/Y^* in the estimates and the results associated with the business cycle. This choice of θ_y is intended strictly to avoid simultaneous-equation bias. According to textbook logic (which can be challenged, as mentioned in the introduction), a rise in $(T-G_i)/Y^*$ should lower Y/Y^* and a rise in $(G_c+TR)/Y^*$ should raise Y/Y^*. If the reasoning is correct, the use of Y/Y^* instead of θ_y would lead the series for $\Delta[(T-G_i)/Y^*]$ to be associated with excessively low values of $\Delta(Y/Y^*)$ and would bias the coefficient of $\Delta(Y/Y^*)$ on the tax side upward, while it should lead the series for $\Delta[(G_c+TR)/Y^*]$ to be associated with excessively high values of $\Delta(Y/Y^*)$ and should bias the coefficient of $\Delta(Y/Y^*)$ on the spending side downward. Alternatively stated, using Y/Y^* instead of θ_y means associating increases (decreases) in primary surpluses with excessively

Table 12.2 The basic three-equation model (revised)

Estimation method	Dependent variable	$(R_m)_{-1}$	$\Delta_{-1}R_{lt}$	$\Delta_{-1}\left(\dfrac{D}{Y}\right)^2$	$\Delta_{-1}\dfrac{Y}{Y^*}$	$\Delta\dfrac{Y}{Y^*}$	$\Delta\dfrac{S_p}{Y^*}$	ΔR_m	
	ΔR_m	-0.28 (8.5)	0.24 (2.9)		0.06 (2)		-0.27 (1.7)		$\overline{R}^2 = 0.16$ F = 6.06***
2SLS	$\Delta\dfrac{T-G_i}{Y^*}$			0.03 (2.3)	0.02 (1.2)	0.34 (20.4)		0.12 (2.2)	$\overline{R}^2 = 0.51$ F = 28.38
	$\Delta\dfrac{G_c+TR}{Y^*}$			-0.04 (3.8)	-0.08 (4.9)	0.21 (12.8)		0.15 (2.8)	$\overline{R}^2 = 0.37$ F = 16.8
	ΔR_m	-0.27 (8.2)	0.24 (3.1)		0.07 (2.3)		-0.39 (2.5)		
3SLS	$\Delta\left(\dfrac{T-G_i}{Y^*}\right)$			0.03 (2.2)	0.02 (1.3)	0.34 (20.5)		0.12 (2.2)	system weighted $R^2 = 0.37$
	$\Delta\left(\dfrac{G_c+TR}{Y^*}\right)$			-0.04 (3.5)	-0.08 (5.1)	0.21 (12.8)		0.19 (3.7)	

Number of observations: 423. *t* value in parentheses.

** Indicates significance at the 5 percentage-point level.

*** Indicates significance at the 1 percentage-point level (higher F values still more significant).

small rises (drops) in output during the expansionary (contractionary) phase of the cycle, and therefore means biasing the estimate of the impact of Y/Y^* upward. Table 12.2 confirms this logic.

The table shows what happens when we estimate the three-equation model with $\Delta(Y/Y^*)$ instead of θ_y. All the lagged influences come out as clearly as before. But the coefficient of $\Delta(Y/Y^*)$ becomes much higher in the tax equation than the spending equation. The textbook reasoning thus applies: an exaggerated level of automatic stabilization appears. Not surprisingly either, the interaction between monetary and fiscal policy becomes more blurry. In principle, failure to correct for reciprocal effects of the policy instruments on economic activity can only make it more difficult to isolate the interaction between the monetary and fiscal policy instruments. This is exactly what happens. The Student t associated with $\Delta(S_p/Y^*)$ in the monetary policy equation in Table 12.2 falls below the level in Table 12.1, while the effects of $\Delta(R_m)$ on taxes and spending now tend to cancel each other out. These last two effects become almost equally important (whereas only the one on spending mattered before) and of the same sign.

12.4   Further tests

In this next section, we will consider a variety of major additional questions, which concern robustness and the distinction between government consumption and transfer payments.

12.4.1   Robustness

Table 12.3 reports the results of the estimates for the 14 member countries of the European Union as such rather than all 19 OECD countries in the sample. These estimates show some improvement in general fits, but also some deterioration pertaining to monetary policy. The response of central banks to fiscal policy becomes murkier and no plain evidence remains of any reaction of monetary policy to the business cycle. Of course, this could simply reflect a tendency of all monetary authorities outside Germany in the EMS to follow the lead of the Deutsche Bundesbank regardless of domestic conditions. In addition, what remains of the earlier, negative response of monetary policy to expansionary fiscal policy could depend entirely on Germany. The second set of estimates in Table 12.3 confirms the last suspicion: the presence of the German central bank in the sample is indeed vital for the conservative response of monetary policy to expansionary fiscal policy. Similarly, as is not shown in the table but can be reported, if we leave out both the US and Germany from the full 19-country sample, the same deterioration occurs in the monetary policy equation: that is, the fiscal policy variable ceases to matter (as does the lagged value of the cycle, Y/Y^*). In effect, therefore, the presence of the Federal Reserve and the Bundesbank in the sample has a lot to do with the conservative stance of monetary policy.

Table 12.3 3SLS tests of robustness

Subject	Dependent variable	$(R_m)_{-1}$	$\Delta_{-1}R_{lt}$	$\Delta_{-1}\left(\frac{D}{Y}\right)^2$	$\Delta_{-1}\frac{Y}{Y^*}$	θ_y	$\Delta\frac{S_p}{Y^*}$	ΔR_m	
	ΔR_m	-0.30 (7.2)	0.22 (2.5)		0.03 (1)		-0.33 (1.9)		
1. The European Union	$\Delta\left(\frac{T-G_i}{Y^*}\right)$			0.03 (1.9)	$\cong 0$	0.31 (13.8)		0.03 (0.4)	system weighted $R^2 = 0.39$
	$\Delta\left(\frac{G_c-TR}{Y^*}\right)$			-0.03 (2.1)	-0.05 (3.2)	0.29 (15.9)		0.22 (4.1)	number of observations = 302
	ΔR_m	-0.31 (7)	0.21 (2.3)		0.02 (0.6)		-0.17 (1)		
2. The European Union without Germany	$\Delta\left(\frac{T-G_i}{Y^*}\right)$			0.03 (2.1)	0.01 (0.4)	0.32 (13.6)		-0.07 (1)	system weighted $R^2 = 0.40$
	$\Delta\left(\frac{G_c-TR}{Y^*}\right)$			-0.03 (2.1)	-0.05 (2.8)	0.29 (15.5)		0.22 (3.7)	number of observations = 271

Table 12.3 (Continued)

Subject	Dependent variable	$(R_m)_{-1}$	$\Delta_{-1}R_{lt}$	$\Delta_{-1}\left(\dfrac{D}{Y}\right)^2$	$\Delta_{-1}\dfrac{Y}{Y^*}$	θ_y	$\Delta\dfrac{S_p}{Y^*}$	ΔR_m	
3. Common influences of time[1]	ΔR_m	−0.38 (10)	0.19 (2.4)		0.05 (1.8)		−0.48 (3.1)		system weighted $R^2 = 0.40$
	$\Delta\left(\dfrac{T-G_i}{Y^*}\right)$			0.04 (2.6)	0.02 (0.8)	0.31 (15.4)		−0.04 (0.7)	
	$\Delta\left(\dfrac{G_c+TR}{Y^*}\right)$			−0.03 (2.8)	−0.06 (4)	0.27 (16.3)		0.08 (1.9)	number of observations = 423
4. Common influences of time: the EU without Germany[2]	ΔR_m	−0.38 (7.4)	0.15 (1.5)		0.01 (0.5)		−0.29 (1.6)		system weighted $R^2 = 0.45$
	$\Delta\left(\dfrac{T-G_i}{Y^*}\right)$			0.03 (2)	0.01 (0.3)	0.32 (13.6)		−0.08 (0.1)	
	$\Delta\left(\dfrac{G_c+TR}{Y^*}\right)$			−0.03 (2.2)	−0.04 (2.5)	0.29 (15.7)		0.13 (2.3)	number of observations = 271

[1] The dummy variables for time are 1963–8, 1969–73, 1974–84, 1985–90, 1991–4. The significant ones (all positive) are as follows (Student *t*'s in parentheses): in the first equation, 1979–84 (3.6) and 1985–90 (1.9); in the second equation, 1963–8 (2.1); in the third equation 1969–73 (2.6) and 1974–8 (3).

[2] The dummy variables for time are 1974–8, 1979–84, 1985–90 and 1991–5 (starting date of estimation period 1973). The significant ones are as follows: (Student *t*'s and signs in parentheses): in the first equation, 1979–84 (3); in the second equation 1985–90 (−2.4) and 1991–5 (−2.6); in the third equation, 1974–8 (2).

Another series of questions about robustness relates to the stability of the reported behaviour during the sample period. Chow-tests clearly lead to a rejection of stability if we break up the study period into two parts around the middle. Another way to proceed is to introduce dummy variables for consecutive time intervals. This other method provides a means of controlling for common changes in policy under the impact of common problems and possible imitative behaviour in policy decisions. The use of the technique does indeed produce an increase in the quality of the fits but, if carried too far – that is, if too many individual dates are included – the interaction between monetary and fiscal policy disappears. Nonetheless, a third set of estimates in Table 12.3 shows that if we introduce indices for six five-year intervals, we clearly get an improvement. This raises the quality of the estimates while the interaction between monetary and fiscal policy stays fairly plain. In this case, the estimate for the EU sample without Germany also provides better results than before for monetary policy. As seen in the fourth and last division of Table 12.3, there is also a negative reaction of monetary to fiscal policy at the 10 per cent confidence level for the EC14 even without Germany.[5]

12.4.2 Decomposition of government consumption and transfer payments

Major interest also centres on the question of the decomposition of government spending behaviour between consumption and transfer payments. Table 12.4 shows what happens when the 2SLS and 3SLS estimates of Table 12.1 are repeated for a four-equation model breaking up fiscal policy into three parts: $(T-G_i)/Y^*$, G_c/Y^* and TR/Y^*. The estimates imply much more uniformity in behaviour for government consumption than transfer payments across countries. The G_c/Y^* equation yields a notably better fit than the one for TR/Y^*. It is also interesting to see that consumption and transfer payments both contribute to the earlier destabilizing response of government spending to current news about output. Furthermore, the separate responses of TR/Y^* and G_c/Y^* to θ_y agree perfectly with the earlier estimate of the sum of the two in Table 12.1. In addition, the lagged stabilizing response of fiscal policy to the cycle can be seen to be essentially the work of transfer payments. This could be interpreted as a delayed response of unemployment compensation, since unemployment is known to move sluggishly over the cycle. That explanation, in turn, would help to see why transfer payments are just as destabilizing as government consumption at first (the stabilizing response of unemployment compensation coming only later, with a lag). Notably too, the opposite reaction of fiscal policy to monetary policy shows up exclusively in transfer payments. But the stabilizing adjustment of spending to debt comes principally from government consumption.

All the same, the four-equation model in Table 12.4 does not perform as well as the three-equation one in Table 12.1. The weighted R^2 for the 3SLS

Table 12.4 The decomposition of government consumption and transfer payments

Estimation method	Dependent variable	$(R_m)_{-1}$	$\Delta_{-1}R_{lt}$	$\Delta_{-1}\left(\frac{D}{Y}\right)^2$	$\Delta_{-1}\frac{Y}{Y^*}$	θ_y	$\Delta\frac{S_p}{Y^*}$	R_m	
	ΔR_m	-0.32 (9.2)	0.22 (2.9)		0.05 (1.7)		-0.27 (1.8)		$\bar{R}^2=0.17$ F=4.9***
	$\Delta\left(\dfrac{T-G_i}{Y^*}\right)$			0.03 (2.1)	0.03 (1.5)	0.32 (14.2)		0.03 (0.5)	$\bar{R}^2=0.33$ F=10.5
2SLS	$\Delta\left(\dfrac{G_c}{Y^*}\right)$			-0.03 (5.3)	-0.01 (1.3)	0.14 (16.5)		0.02 (1)	$\bar{R}^2=0.46$ F=17.5
	$\Delta\dfrac{TR}{Y^*}$			-0.01 (1.8)	-0.04 (3.5)	0.14 (11)		0.07 (2.2)	$\bar{R}^2=0.30$ F=9.3

							system weighted $R^2=0.29$
ΔR_m	−0.30 (8.9)	0.22 (3)		0.06 (2.1)	0.32 (14.4)	−0.42 (2.8)	0.01 (0.1)
$\Delta\left(\dfrac{T-G_i}{Y^*}\right)$			0.03 (1.8)	0.03 (1.6)	0.14 (16.4)		0.03 (1.2)
3SLS $\quad\Delta\dfrac{G_c}{Y^*}$			−0.03 (5.2)	−0.01 (1.3)	0.14 (11)		0.09 (2.7)
$\Delta\dfrac{TR}{Y^*}$			−0.01 (1.5)	−0.04 (3.6)			

Number of observations: 423.

*** indicates significance at the 1 percentage-point level (higher F values still more significant).

estimate covering all 19 countries in the new table is 29 per cent, well below the earlier 35 per cent level. If we look further behind this deterioration, we also find that the cross-equation correlation between the 2SLS residuals of the G_c/Y^* and TR/Y^* equations is almost 50 per cent – much higher than the one between any other pair of equations. Thus, governments do not necessarily draw as clear a line between public consumption and transfer payments in adjusting their spending as the four-equation model says. An alternative explanation would be that statistical flaws are at work. Informed sources agree that the statistical divisions of various governments make some conflicting choices of distinction between public consumption and transfer payments (see the associated reflections in Perotti, 1996b). Still, the four-equation model works well enough to give weight to its strongest results.

12.5   Other studies

To take stock, there are three outstanding results of the study: namely, (i) the stabilizing response of governments to debt; (ii) the opposite interaction between fiscal and monetary policy;[6] and (iii) the moderation of the counter-cyclical reaction of fiscal policy. What evidence have we from other sources about all three results, especially the last one?

We must look for answers in other studies dealing with the same or similar countries. The evidence for countries with much higher inflation rates – say, occasionally above 50 per cent annually – would not be particularly relevant. Gavin and Perotti (1997) confirm this last view in a study of Latin American countries. So does Fry (1998) in research covering a world sample of developing countries. Studies of subaltern governments within countries are also not exactly to the point, since in these cases the tax capacities of the governments are far more limited, and the interactions between the authorities and the central bank are bound to differ. Such other studies may have multiple interests,[7] but they cannot serve either to confirm or negate our findings.

To my knowledge, the only effort to deal with the same set of questions for the same set of countries is Wyplosz (1999). Though limited to EMU members, his study offers pooled estimates of the official reaction functions of monetary and fiscal authorities that are based on annual observations, as mine does. Wyplosz's specification differs from my own in several respects. He proceeds in levels rather than first differences (in conformity with Taylor, 1993, and Clarida, Galí and Gertler, 1998, in treating central bank behaviour). In addition, Wyplosz estimates the reaction functions of the monetary and fiscal authorities separately (though experimenting with 3SLS estimates which contain the opposite policy variable as endogenous). Finally, he incorporates relative unit labour costs as an explanatory variable.

Given Wyplosz's formulation in levels, it is not surprising that he obtains much higher R^2's than I do, nor that he finds the lagged dependent variables notably more significant. But in other respects, our estimates are very close, as he recognizes. The same stabilizing response to debt arises. So does the same interaction between monetary and fiscal policy (though, in his case, with a one-year lag, and in the instance of monetary policy, strictly in the 3SLS estimate that allows for simultaneity). Furthermore, he finds the same mildness of the stabilizing response to the cycle as I do. According to his estimate, an extra percent of output above potential raises the primary budget surplus by 0.18 of the change. In mine, the response is about 0.10 (as is found by adding up the coefficients of $(Y/Y^*)_{t-1}$ and θ_y in the fiscal policy equations of Table 12.1). Unfortunately, Wyplosz does not distinguish between government spending and receipts, so that we can only guess what the outcome would be.

In light of my results and Wyplosz's, the evidence in favour of the strength of the automatic stabilizers may demand reconsideration. If we do re-examine the issue, we find the supporting evidence for the importance of automatic stabilization to hinge largely on preconception. The typical practice in estimating the automatic stabilizers is to limit attention strictly to the responses of taxes and unemployment compensation to the cycle, and to treat other elements of the budget as exogenous and the work of current policy decisions. The most detailed estimates of automatic stabilizers on hand, coming from the OECD, rest exclusively on measures of the respective responses of personal income taxes, corporate income taxes, indirect taxes, social security taxes, and unemployment compensation to the cycle (see Giorno *et al.*, 1995 and the recent update by Van den Noord in Chapter 8 of the present volume).[8] The IMF, proceeds in a similar fashion (see IMF, 1993, pp. 99–103). These kinds of tests usually yield estimates saying that a fall in output below potential causes a rise in government deficits of about half the size of the fall in output.[9] Based on the same assumption of the exogeneity of government expenditures (except for G_i), I get a response of fiscal policy to the cycle of 31 per cent to 37 per cent – not too different from 50 per cent. Thirty-one per cent of the response is due to the coefficient of θ_y in the tax-minus-investment equation, and the rest comes from the assumption that some part of the lagged effect of Y/Y^* on spending can be attributed to unemployment compensation. But there are also a few isolated estimates of the responses of the fiscal authorities to the cycle that do not proceed in the previous way and do look at all parts of the government budget. What do they say? I know of four recent examples: Fiorito (1997), Gavin and Perotti (1997), Virén (1998), and Fatás and Mihov (1999). Arreaza, Sørensen and Yosha (1999) might be considered a fifth, but I have doubts, which I will expose in a footnote below. In none of the first four cases is there any adjustment for simultaneity. For this reason, the estimates can be biased upward, as already explained. In addition, Fatás and Mihov engage strictly in a bivariate analysis in which only fiscal policy and the cycle are present. So does Fiorito (1997). Virén (1998) and Gavin and Perotti (1997) add a third variable: inflation in Virén's case, the percentage change in the terms of trade in Gavin and Perotti's. Still, the paucity of variables in these studies may be another source of differences.

To report on the four studies in turn, Fatás and Mihov estimate the impact of the cycle on the primary deficit (the negative of the primary surplus) over basically the same sample as I use, and they do pooling as well. They come up with an estimate of −0.26 (with a standard error of 0.04). Thus theirs is an intermediate result between the usual one of −0.5, based on strict concern with taxes and unemployment compensation, and mine of −0.1. However, when Fatás and Mihov decompose the responses of some parts of the budget, the outcome deviates markedly from mine. The response of taxes is 0.82 (with a standard error of 0.05), and that of government spending on goods and services ($G_c + G_i$) is 0.03 (with a standard error of 0.006). Their estimated response of $G_c + G_i$ is particularly at odds with my results (though of the same sign).

In Virén's study, the ratio of the observed deficit to output serves as the measure of fiscal policy. Virén uses VARs to estimate the response of this ratio to the cycle for 21 different countries individually: the 19 in my sample plus Switzerland and Iceland. On average for the countries, he finds that a one-standard-deviation change in output lowers the deficit–output ratio by 0.55 of the change (see Table 12.1, columns D1, D2, and D3). Thus, Virén's estimate confirms the usual views.

Gavin and Perotti (1997) centre on Latin America, but also provide a pertinent estimate for 'industrial' countries as a point of comparison. This last estimate, which rests on pooled data for 16 of the 19 countries in my study (all except Canada, Greece and Portugal), says that a one-percentage-point rise in output will raise the total fiscal surplus by 0.37 (with a Student t of about 11) of the rise in output.[10] Thus, their estimate is of the same general order as the OECD's and close to Virén's. When Gavin and Perotti divide up the government surplus into parts, their results also resemble Fatás and Mihov's rather than mine. They come up with a response of 0.93 (with a Student t of 12) to the cycle for taxes and no response of any note for spending.

The final study, by Fiorito, concerning the G7, is the only one to use quarterly instead of annual data. This study is also by far the most disaggregative: it looks at co-movements of real GDP with eight different sub-components of government expenditures and four sub-components of government receipts. In effect, the analysis relates strictly to correlations, and therefore all the inferences about influences hinge on leads and lags, as the author recognizes. The general impression is not favourable to my results. There are too many cases of sub-categories of government expenditures that are negatively correlated with lagged real output. As a general point of contrast, the author finds less uniformity of co-movements between government expenditures and output than between government receipts and output, whereas I obtain a higher quality of fits for government expenditures than for taxes (but, notably, only when I take simultaneity into account: that is, in Table 12.1, not Table 12.2).

On the whole, these last studies give greater support to the usual view of the strength of counter-cyclical fiscal policy than to my findings. But since all of the studies stick – or nearly so – to a unicausal explanation of official behaviour, and all of them fail to correct for simultaneity, I conclude that the issue remains wide open. It is all the more so in the light of the corroborative results of Wyplosz, who is the only author to apply similar methods to the same data.[11]

12.6   Interpretation

Two fundamental issues remain for discussion. How do we interpret the policy record of deficits and debts over recent decades in the light of the estimates in this work? How much *automatic* stabilization is there?

12.6.1   The fiscal policy record

On the first issue, the Services of the European Commission offer a basic point of comparison. In an important study (Buti and Sapir, 1998), these Services analyse the record of fiscal policy in the EU since the 1970s on the usual view of the automatic stabilizers (see also Buti, Franco and Ongena 1997). In addition, the Services consider all movements in primary surpluses which do not come from the automatic stabilizers as discretionary responses to the cycle. Since the authors agree with the OECD estimates of the automatic stabilizers as about one-half the size of any deviation from normal output and they find that the deficits did not grow nearly as much during recessions in the EU as this estimate would imply, they conclude that contractionary fiscal policy prevailed during recessions. In other words, governments kept debt in check at those times. Since deficits persisted during mild phases of expansions and only abated at the peaks, the authors also conclude that fiscal discipline was lacking during the expansionary phases. Finally, since debt–output ratios grew by about 30 per centage points (from 40 per cent to 70 per cent levels) from the early 1970s to the mid-1990s, they conclude that the deterioration of fiscal discipline during expansions was far greater than the strengthening of fiscal discipline during recessions.

My results require a different reading of the same facts. According to my study, fiscal policy responded in a stabilizing manner in all phases of the cycle but only mildly so. In the case of contractions, there is minor disagreement. On either interpretation, fiscal policy was only moderately easy. But under expansion, the divergence is important. Based on my interpretation, fiscal policy was moderately tight. Thus, in my case, the explosion of debt/output ratios in the EU, and the OECD as a whole, must be explained independently of the cycle. It is easy to see what such an alternative explanation might be. Life expectancy lengthened greatly during the period. The retired population became much larger as a percentage of the labour force. The demand for medical care also shot up as wealth increased and the population aged. Consequently, public spending on pensions and medical care progressed rapidly, while taxes did not keep pace. This went on during recessions and expansions alike. For a corroborating analysis, consult Shigehara (1995). Based on the view I propose, note also that these exogenous forces must have been powerful enough to overcome the stabilizing response of governments to the debt–output ratios.

12.6.2   Automatic stabilization

Another basic question is whether the fiscal policy responses to the cycle in my analysis should be regarded as automatic. Could the destabilizing behaviour of government spending be attributed to deliberate policy choices?

There are two reasons for considering the destabilizing spending behaviour as automatic. First, any deliberate attempt to engage in pro-cyclical spending – even if understood merely as an attempt to mitigate the automatic stabilizers – would be difficult to explain. No *systematic* efforts of the sort have ever even been envisaged. It would be strange to think that such efforts nevertheless prevail in the OECD. Second, my estimates of the coefficients of θ_y in the spending equations are extremely significant. They have Student t's as high as those on the tax side. If the destabilizing spending were then a matter of deliberate policy, the international adherence to the policy would be as well defined as the automatic stabilizers themselves, as those are usually understood. This seems unlikely.

On the other hand, it is easy to see why destabilizing spending could be automatic. The literature on bureaucracy and public choice offers an obvious perspective. Like many an ordinary organization, government could simply loosen its purse strings when receipts abound and do the opposite when revenues merely trickle in. Under expansion, the income bonuses of civil servants would grow; public employees would climb more easily up the salary ladder; appropriations would possibly be spent more quickly and readily. There could even be greater largesse in paying out legal entitlements. In one case – public spending on health – there are some separate indications of a pro-cyclical tendency in spending, apart from any discretionary official behaviour. People seem to avail themselves more of health services during booms than during contractions.[12]

A certain analogy with monetary policy may be apt. For decades, economists assumed that central banks controlled base money since they could do so in principle. But when the Volcker administration decided to engage in strict base control in the US in 1979, it was discovered that the effort required major changes in administrative procedures. After a period of experimentation, the Fed opted to return to control of the short-term interest rate and to abandon base control. Since that episode, we generally view the short-term interest rate as the basic instrument of monetary policy, and the monetary base as an intermediate target. Perhaps a similar adaptation is fitting as regards fiscal policy. We now consider the government as directly controlling public spending on goods and services. But what government really controls are appropriations, guidelines, schedules and entitlements, which, in turn, give rise to a value of G_c+TR to which the government is able to react. This account of government spending is indeed the prevailing one in detailed descriptions of the budgetary process. Yet, in theoretical disquisitions, we assume that G_c+TR can be seen as a direct instrument of control. But if bureaucratic impulses really generate strong pro-cyclical movements in G_c+TR, as my study would mean, the assumption is wrong, and we should properly view G_c+TR as an intermediate target.[13]

12.7   Conclusion

In conclusion, it is fitting to give some thought to the possible impact of the advent of EMU on the three major results of the study – the stabilizing fiscal-policy responses to debt, the negative interaction between monetary and fiscal policy, and the weakness of automatic stabilization. Indeed, the first two results might easily be upset by monetary union. As a matter of fact, the official thinking underlying the Maastricht Treaty anticipates a major mutation in public behaviour regarding debt under the new system. The legal architecture of EMU, and the subsequent Stability and Growth Pact, are both designed to avoid an expected weakening of fiscal discipline. Lamfalussy's influential contribution to the Delors report (1989) is important in this respect. According to Lamfalussy, monetary union brings an ability to borrow on a broader capital market than before and an end to earlier worries about interest rate penalties coming from market expectations of exchange rate depreciation in relation to fellow union members. As a result, governments may then be tempted to adopt looser fiscal policy. Thus, the fiscal authorities need to be reined in. Of course, this is a view that can be challenged: it is possible to reason, quite the opposite, that shorn of their previous monetary influence, governments will act more prudently than before once they enter EMU, especially if they start off with an important overhang of debt from earlier times. But even on this last interpretation, a regime-change in behaviour is expected. As regards the second major conclusion of the study – about the interactions between monetary and fiscal authorities – it is almost transparent that EMU may upset behaviour. Consequently, we cannot simply extend the first two major conclusions of the study to EMU, and the implications of those conclusions for the future of the system are difficult to read. On the other hand, the third conclusion, concerning *automatic* stabilization, has a clear meaning for EMU. Almost by assumption, automatic responses of taxes and government expenditures to the cycle will not be affected by EMU. Therefore, based on the view that the automatic stabilizers impinge heavily on the economy (which is not necessarily followed here), the country members of EMU might be expected to get substantial smoothing of real activity from the automatic stabilizers alone, apart from any reinforcement by deliberate fiscal policy. On those premises, one could then follow Buti, Franco and Ongena (1998) and reason that if only the members of EMU manage to get their houses in order and reduce their public deficits well below the 3 per cent ceiling of the Maastrict Treaty and the Stability and Growth Pact, the country members of the system can reap ample benefits of macroeconomic stabilization from automatic fiscal policy alone. But if the automatic stabilizers are as weak as my study says, little smoothing of economic activity will come from this source.[14] In this next case, the implication is different: discretionary fiscal policy remains important under EMU. As a corolary, the coordination of fiscal policies in the EMU may need careful attention too.

Appendix 12.A.1: data

All of the data concerning output, potential output, prices, goverment expenditures and receipts come from the OECD data base. The following table indicates the series for the central bank intervention rate, R_m, and the long-term interest rate, R_{lt}.

Country	Intervention rate: R_m	Long-term interest rate: R_{lt}	Source
Australia	Short-term money market rate	Long-term obligations: secondary market	OECD
Austria	3-month VIBOR	Government bonds	IMF
Belgium	Rate on cash surpluses at the central bank	Government bonds	OECD & IMF
Canada	Weekly tender rate of the central bank	Government bonds	OECD
Denmark	Rate on trade bills charged by banks	Government bonds	OECD
Finland	Daily interbank rate	Rate on bank loans	OECD
France	Money market rate	Public and semi-public bonds	OECD
Germany	3-month FIBOR	Long term obligations: secondary market	OECD
Greece	Central bank intervention rate	Government bonds	IMF
Ireland	Central Bank intervention rate	Government bonds	IMF
Italy	Money market rate	Government bills	OECD
Japan	Daily central bank rate	Government bonds	OECD
Netherlands	Brokers' call rates	Government bonds	OECD
Norway	Central bank intervention rate	Government bonds	IMF

Country	Intervention rate: R_m	Long-term interest rate: R_{lt}	Source
Portugal	Central bank intervention rate	Government bonds	IMF
Spain	Daily interbank rate	Government securities (medium term)	OECD
Sweden	Central bank daily rate	Government bonds	OECD
UK	Money market rate	Government bonds	OECD
US	Federal funds rate	Government bonds	OECD

Many of the money series which served to calculate the money demand shock θ_m came from the IMF, others from the OECD. But since none of those shocks were retained, the details about sources and definitions are omitted.

Notes

1. University of Strathclyde, CREST-INSEE, and CEPR. The author wishes to thank Matthieu Fayolle for excellent research assistance and Marco Buti, Isabelle Braun-Lemaire, Francis Kramarz, Carlos Martinez-Mongay, Heikki Oksanen, and Paul Levine for valuable comments. A longer version of this chapter appeared in Mélitz (2000), which notably contained a sub-section relating to episodes of vigorous fiscal policy.
2. This paucity of data may explain why study of the interactions between monetary and fiscal authorities still remains predominantly a theoretical topic. Much of the empirical work on these official interactions has also rested on simulation analysis. For some interesting recent examples, see van Aarle, Bovenberg and Raith (1995), Agell, Calmfors and Jonsson (1996), and Levine and Brociner (1994).
3. These dates are, namely: Canada and Germany 1964; the US 1965; Australia, Denmark, Greece, France, Italy, the Netherlands, Sweden and the UK 1972; Belgium and Japan 1973; Austria 1975; Norway and Spain 1977; Finland 1978; Ireland 1979; and Portugal 1981.
4. In the estimates giving rise to the series for θ_y, those which gave the best results, and which were consequently retained, proved to be the ones without any lagged values for monetary and fiscal policy.
5. Of course, German behaviour could still underlie the result, since other monetary officials could be following a German lead (i.e., tracking the Deutschmark).
6. This negative interaction should be interpreted as saying that more tightening (easing) of one instrument means less tightening (easing) of the other. Both instruments may still concurrently be tight (or easy, as the case may be).
7. Two prominent examples are Bayoumi and Eichengreen (1995), and Sørensen, Wu and Yosha (1999).
8. See also a particularly detailed test by Cohen and Follette (2000), which, however, only concerns the US.
9. But with significant dispersion between individual countries. See Ribe (1995) and Chapter 8 by Paul Van den Noord in the present volume.
10. Bayoumi and Eichengreen (1995) perform similar tests on 8 OECD countries, each taken individually, but they always treat central and local governments separately (while dropping two of the 8 countries because 'the results were unsatisfactory' (note 19)).

11. On the surface at least, Arreaza, Sørensen and Yosha (1999) also furnish estimates of the response of government budgets to the cycle. In addition, their work seems to agree with mine at first sight, since they clearly report a tendency for government consumption to rise during the expansionary phase of the cycle. But the terms of their discussion raise doubts. According to their interpretation, mere *constancy* of government consumption in the face of a boom is highly stabilizing, since it contributes to saving and the smoothing of consumption. On the other hand, taxes need to grow faster than output during a boom in order to be stabilizing, as otherwise the taxes still encourage current (relative to future) consumption. Thus, upon finding that both taxes and government consumption grow less than output in a boom, the authors conclude that government consumption is stabilizing and taxes are destabilizing. In addition and quite significantly, Arreaza *et al.* adapt their test specifications to their interpretation. For this last reason as well, their test results are difficult to compare with mine and any of those I discuss (all of which relate strictly to the public budget's response to the cycle).

12. In conformity, Decressin (1999) documents a pro-cyclical reshuffling of per capita transfer payments on health services between expanding and contracting regions of Italy. On the other hand, there is also reason to think that pensions and retirement benefits move in a counter-cyclical manner. But even in that case, as long as those counter-cyclical movements took place with a lag, there would be no contradiction. The stabilizing response of TR to the lagged value of Y/Y^* in my tests would then simply need to be seen as coming from pensions as well as unemployment compensation.

13. In a recent study, Blanchard and Perotti (1999) try to identify discretionary fiscal policy in the US by switching from annual to quarterly data. To quote them: 'With enough institutional information about the tax and transfer systems and the timing of tax collections, one can construct estimates of the automatic effects of unexpected activity on fiscal variables, and, by implication, obtain estimates of fiscal shocks.' Further they say: 'The same would not be true if we used annual data: to some degree, fiscal policy can be adjusted in response to unexpected changes in GDP within a year.' However, based on my results, the move to the quarterly frequency may do little. If government expenditures (especially those on goods and services) really respond automatically to the cycle, no amount of institutional detail about taxes and transfers alone (and ignoring other spending) will account adequately for the automatic responses, any more at the quarterly than the annual frequency.

14. The European Commission (2000a), section 5, suggests that the destabilizing responses of government expenditures (exclusive of unemployment compensation) to the cycle in my study may be considered as only 'quasi-automatic'. By inference, the destabilizing responses are more easily modified than the stabilizing ones coming from taxes and unemployment compensation. It is true that the destabilizing behaviour on the spending side could be modified. But the inevitability of the stabilizing behaviour on the tax side can also be questioned. Tax collection can lag. Tax obligations may be imposed on the income of earlier years. Thus, it is not clear there is really anything less automatic – say, less robust and easier to reform – about the destabilizing behaviour on the spending side than the stabilizing behaviour on the tax one.

13
Monetary and Fiscal Policy Interactions Under a Stability Pact[1]
Marco Buti, Werner Roeger and Jan in't Veld

13.1   Introduction

The completion of EMU – based on the precise mission to the ECB to maintain price stability and guidelines for the conduct of national fiscal policies – has prompted a renewed interest on the interplay between monetary and fiscal policies.

The traditional Optimal Currency Areas literature pointed out long ago that, in a monetary union, fiscal policy has to play a more important role in cyclical stabilization given the loss of national monetary independence. This is particularly the case if shocks are not perfectly correlated across frontiers. Fiscal flexibility, together with budgetary discipline and coordination, has come to be seen as a central-pillar fiscal policy in a currency area (European Commission, 1990). The Stability and Growth Pact (SGP) has been the operational response of EU countries to the quest for budgetary discipline in EMU.

Recent theoretical and empirical developments have shed new light on the 'old' issue of the interactions between monetary and fiscal authorities. At the theoretical level, much work has been devoted to the rationale for fiscal constraints in a monetary union.

A formal model of the SGP is provided by Beetsma and Uhlig (1999) (see also Beetsma, 2001). In a two-period model of a monetary union, myopic governments who know that they may be replaced at the beginning of the second period issue more debt than a social planner would do. This would constrain monetary policy in the second period. This effect is magnified in a monetary union because the adverse impact on the common monetary policy is diluted. As a result, the incentive to restrain public debt accumulation is reduced and we end up with an overburdened monetary policy. Hence, a pact limiting public debt accumulation increases welfare in a monetary union.

However, Chari and Kehoe (1998) argue that the desirability of imposing fiscal constraints crucially depends of the ability of the single monetary authority to commit to its future policies. Only to the extent that monetary policy cannot commit, are there gains from imposing budgetary constraints. This conclusion is 'consistent with the view that the framers of the treaty thought that it is extremely difficult to commit monetary policy and therefore wisely included debt constraints as an integral part of the treaty' (Chari and Kehoe, 1998, p. 2).

The degree of commitment by the central bank affects the design of stabilization policies in a monetary union. If the central bank is 'strong', fiscal constraints are damaging because they limit the room for manoeuvre by fiscal authorities in responding to shocks. This result is emphasized by Cooper and Kempf (2000). These authors conclude that only if shocks are highly correlated across countries and the central bank is strongly committed to price stability does a fiscally constrained monetary union dominate the outcome with multiple currencies. Under idiosyncratic shocks, moving to a fiscally constrained monetary union would be welfare-reducing: 'if the set of policy instruments open to fiscal authorities is sufficiently restricted, then monetary union may not increase welfare. Despite having commitment power, the central bank lacks the tools to stabilize in the presence of country specific shocks that are not perfectly correlated' (Cooper and Kempf, 2000, p. 27).

The conclusion that a monetary union with a strong central bank and no limits on fiscal policies is optimal has been questioned. Recent contributions have pointed out that 'strength' or 'weakness' of the central bank is not exogenous to the behaviour of fiscal authorities.

The so-called Fiscal Theory of the Price Level (FTPL) has highlighted that if government solvency is not guaranteed, monetary policy will not be able to control the price level. In order to ensure stability, fiscal policy has to react sufficiently strongly to a rise in the interest rate in the event of inflationary pressures by increasing the primary surplus. In other words, an 'active' monetary policy aiming at keeping inflation in check – as the ECB is mandated to behave – has to go hand in hand with an 'active' fiscal policy.[2] Once the FTPL is applied to the EMU institutional set-up, however, seemingly different conclusions are drawn. While Sims (1999) considers the Maastricht-cum-SGP rules insufficient to rule out FTPL's doom scenario, Canzoneri and Diba (2001) conclude that the SGP appears far too strict from the point of view of guaranteeing fiscal solvency. The latter authors, in particular, call for shifting the attention from nominal to cyclically adjusted budget balances in assessing compliance of EMU members with budgetary prudence so as not to hamper fiscal stabilization.

The ability of budgetary authorities to affect monetary commitment is also explored in a number of recent papers by Dixit and Lambertini (see, Dixit and Lambertini, 2000a,b,c; and Dixit, 2000). In a game theoretic framework, monetary and fiscal authorities minimize a quadratic loss function in inflation and output, but final targets and the weight attributed to them vary (typically the central bank is assumed to be more inflation-conservative). These authors conclude that fiscal discretion 'destroys monetary commitment' and, as such, may justify rules imposed on budgetary behaviour. But imposing rules is not sufficient *per se*: another important conclusion by Dixit and Lambertini is that if final targets differ (e.g. the central bank is an inflation hawk and the fiscal authority aims at pushing output beyond its natural level), a race between monetary and fiscal policy would lead the equilibrium levels of output and inflation far away from the preferred choices. Hence, agreement on the final targets between monetary and fiscal authorities is paramount to lead to a Nash equilibrium which is close to the authorities' preferred choices.

The importance of the difference in objectives of monetary and fiscal authorities is also stressed by Demertzis *et al.* (1999a), and Hughes Hallett and Viegi in Chapter 14 in the present volume who find that if the two authorities pursue their separate goals independently, a conflict arises. From a political economy viewpoint, the authors point out that the establishment of a conservative central bank – strongly biased in favour of price stability – may increase the chances of left-of-centre governments – mainly output-concerned – being elected. This divergence of preferences would heighten the monetary and fiscal conflicts and, by the same token, increase the gains from coordination.

Quite unrelated to this theoretical development, an empirical literature has addressed in recent years the issue of how monetary and fiscal authorities 'actually' behave.

In a seminal paper, Jacques Mélitz uses pooled data for 19 OECD countries, including 14 EU members (except Luxembourg), over the period 1960 until 1995 (Mélitz, 1997, and Chapter 12 in the present volume). He finds that monetary and fiscal policy tend to move in opposite directions. In his definition, the two policies are 'strategic substitutes': looser fiscal policy promotes tighter monetary policy while tighter monetary policy triggers an expansionary fiscal policy. In other words, the 'Sargent and Wallace' scenario of a sustained fiscal boost eventually triggering a monetary relaxation does not find confirmation in the data. As the author points out in Chapter 12, 'This negative interaction should be interpreted as saying that tightening (easing) of one instrument means less tightening (easing) of the other. Both instruments may still concurrently be tight (or easy, as the case may be)' (Chapter 12, note 6).

Evidence of strategic substitutability is also found in Wyplosz (1999): the central bank raises the interest rate when the deficit increases. In other words, '(b)oth (authorities) attempt to keep inflation in check and to conduct counter-cyclical policies, but each does less when the other moves in the same direction' (Wyplosz, 1999, p. 43). The result that fiscal policy tends to relax when monetary conditions become tighter is confirmed by von Hagen *et al.* in Chapter 2 of the present volume, for a panel of 20 OECD countries from 1973 to 1989. These authors, however, find that monetary conditions react positively to a tighter fiscal policy, and that implies that the reaction of monetary policy to fiscal policy has the opposite sign from the reaction of fiscal policy to monetary policy.

To what extent has the EMU project influenced the reaction function of monetary and fiscal authorities? As shown in Chapter 2, von Hagen *et al.* find evidence of a 'Maastricht effect' in the 1990s in the EU: 'on average in the EMU member states, fiscal policy in the 1990s was less reactive to cyclical fluctuations of output and changes in monetary policy than it was in earlier times'. A recent report by the European Commission (2000a) argues that monetary policy has, on average, loosened since the beginning of the 1990s (albeit starting from a very tight position), thereby supporting the budgetary retrenchment by EU countries to meet the Maastricht criteria for joining EMU.[3] Hence, in Mélitz's definition, monetary and fiscal policies have been strategic substitutes in the last decade in most EU countries.[4]

The theoretical literature reviewed above looks at the rationale for budgetary constraints but rarely embodies explicitly EMU and SGP-relevant rules in budgetary behaviour. While a number of studies[5] encompass a cost of 'fiscal policy activism', to our knowledge no paper encompasses the 3 per cent cum 'close-to-balance' rule of the SGP which would ensure budgetary prudence while leaving room for manoeuvre for fiscal stabilization. The empirical literature, while providing interesting insights, lacks theoretical foundations and, as such, is of limited usefulness in understanding the reaction function of monetary and fiscal authorities and, especially, in anticipating the type of interactions which will prevail in EMU. As we argue below, strategic substitutability and complementarity between the two policies – and its interpretation in terms of 'conflict' or 'cooperation' – depend crucially on the typology of shocks hitting the economy and on the objective functions of monetary and fiscal authorities.

Our chapter provides a simple analytical setting for assessing the interactions of monetary and fiscal authorities when the latter are subject to upper limits on the budget deficit. A particular emphasis is put on the design of stabilization policies.

The structure of the chapter is as follows. In section 2 we outline a simple model of monetary and fiscal behaviour capturing some of the main features of the Maastricht institutional framework. The solution of the game between monetary and fiscal authorities under non-cooperation and cooperation is provided in sections 3 and 4, respectively. Section 5 presents some numerical simulations with the Commission Services' QUEST model on the quantitative relevance of the theoretical findings. Section 6 provides a summing up of the main results and discusses some policy implications.

13.2   A simple model of monetary and fiscal policy interactions

The Maastricht Treaty and secondary legislation provide a clear assignment of objectives to monetary and fiscal authorities in EMU.

The primary task of the ECB is to maintain price stability. In order to achieve price stability, the single monetary authority is entrusted with both 'goal' and 'instrument' independence. To the extent that price stability is not jeopardized, the ECB is called upon to support the general economic policies in the Community.

The SGP is the backbone of fiscal policy in EMU. The Pact can be seen as strengthening the procedures introduced by the Maastricht Treaty, at least in relation to the deficit criterion. Its objective is to ensure that fiscal prudence – as embodied in the Treaty fiscal criteria – applies not only in the run-up to the single currency, but becomes a permanent feature of the EMU. It demands that the countries of the European Union (EU) aim for 'medium-term objectives of budgetary positions close to balance or in surplus'. This objective is believed to ensure budgetary discipline whilst preserving sufficient room for manoeuvre for fiscal stabilization without infringing the 3 per cent of GDP deficit ceiling.

The model outlined below aims at capturing in a simplified fashion some of the main features of the Maastricht monetary and fiscal architecture, namely the objectives of price stability and fiscal prudence.

The model encompasses a demand-(IS) equation and a supply-(Phillips curve) equation of standard type determining the value of the output gap, y, and inflation, π:

$$y^D = \phi_1 d - \phi_2(i - \pi^e) + \varepsilon_1 \tag{13.1}$$

$$y^S = \omega(\pi - \pi^e) + \varepsilon_2 \tag{13.2}$$

where d is the budget deficit, i is the nominal interest rate, ε_1 is a demand shock and ε_2 is a supply shock. The superscript 'e' indicates expected variables. The rest of the world is omitted. The coefficient ω in (13.2) can be interpreted as the degree of labour market flexibility: a high ω implies that an inflation surprise, by lowering real wages, entails a strong rise in supply; on the contrary, a low ω implies that real wages are rigid and supply responds little to unexpected inflation.

The budget deficit is defined as follows:

$$d = d_s - \alpha y \tag{13.3}$$

where d_s is the cyclically-adjusted balance and α is the cyclical sensitivity of the budget.[6] The nominal deficit d should not exceed a deficit ceiling: $d \leq \bar{d}$. By replacing (13.3) in (13.1) and solving for y and π, we obtain:

$$y = \frac{1}{1 + \phi_1 \alpha} [\phi_1 d_s - \phi_2(i - \pi^e) + \varepsilon_1] \tag{13.4}$$

$$\pi = \frac{1}{\omega(1 + \phi_1 \alpha)} (\phi_1 d_s - \phi_2 i + \varepsilon_1) - \frac{\varepsilon_2}{\omega} + \left[1 + \frac{\phi_2}{\omega(1 + \phi_1 \alpha)}\right] \pi^e \tag{13.5}$$

The policy rules specify the setting of d_s by fiscal authorities and i by the central bank.

The instrument of fiscal authorities is the cyclically-adjusted budget balance. This formulation implies that when interest rates move there occurs an internal compensation between the interest burden and the primary balance. This specification of the fiscal policy rule simplifies considerably the algebra, but misses a potentially important channel of interaction between monetary and fiscal policy via the effect of monetary decisions on interest payments. This effect is quantitatively limited if the stock of public debt is low and/or its maturity is relatively long. It also implies that, in the jargon of the FTPL, that fiscal policy is 'active', that is it reacts to a change in monetary policy.

Fiscal policy can be in *an unconstrained or a constrained regime*. In the first case, the fiscal authority chooses d_s to minimize the following loss function:

$$L(FP) = (d_s - d'_s)^2 + \theta(y - y')^2 \tag{13.6}$$

Equation (13.6) indicates that the government cares about output and would like to deviate as little as possible from the medium term target d'_s which is consistent with the 'close to balance' rule of the SGP. In other words, fiscal authorities have a preferred output target, but policy activism to achieve it is costly.

A crucial choice concerns the preferred output gap: if the fiscal authority simply aims at stabilizing the business cycle, y' will be equal to zero. A strict interpretation of the SGP provisions (see, e.g. Buti *et al.*, 1998) would imply setting a sufficiently ambitious budgetary target and just let automatic stabilizers work. This implies θ and $y' = 0$. Instead, if the government aims at a level of output higher than the natural level (i.e. an unemployment below the natural rate), y' is positive. This formulation seems to us more consistent with actual preferences and institutional arrangements than models in the Barro–Gordon tradition which attribute to the central bank the willingness to reduce unemployment rate below its natural level via surprise inflation.[7]

If, in the case of particularly severe shocks or too high medium-term target, fiscal policy is constrained, d_s will change so as to satisfy $d = \bar{d}$ for any value of y.

The basic assumption underlying this behaviour is that member countries treat the prospect of infringing the deficit ceiling as one to be strictly avoided. That is, we assume that the cost of risking the triggering of the sanctions procedure of the SGP is regarded by all countries as large. Those costs include not only the formal financial penalties envisaged in the sanctions procedure but also the costs that the market might inflict and the loss of reputation that could be involved. For Eichengreen and Wyplosz (1998), this implies that the 3 per cent limit is going to be viewed as a 'hard' ceiling. The experiences with the implementation of the Pact confirm such indication (see European Commission, 2000a; and Buti and Martinot, 2000). As we do not consider situations where political horse-trading may imply delaying or not the implementing of the sanctions, our analysis can be treated as a 'full credibility' benchmark.

The monetary authority aims at maintaining price stability. It is also assumed that the central bank faces a cost in changing the interest rate. This is consistent with the assumption that, as supported by recent evidence, the central bank smooths out the interest rate.[8] As a consequence, it minimizes the following loss function:

$$L(CB) = \pi^2 + \beta(i - i_o)^2 \tag{13.7}$$

where i_o is the historical interest rate. In equation (13.7), the inflation target has been set to zero.

The lack of an output stabilization term in $L(CB)$ simplifies the algebra but does not change qualitatively the results if we maintain that inflation stabilization has a substantially higher weight than output stabilization in the central bank preferences.

A justification for interest rate smoothing is that, in the case of conflict between inflation and output stabilization, the central bank moves slowly towards the required interest rate level. In this case, the smoothing term in (13.7) can be seen partly as a way to take care of output stabilization by the central bank.[9] It will be shown later that interest rate smoothing is crucial in maintaining a role for fiscal stabilization in the case of demand shocks.

Equation (13.7) attempts to capture an inherently dynamic behaviour such as interest rate smoothing within an a-temporal setting. Our formulation implies that, at each point in time, if the inflation rate is off target, the interest rate is changed to close the gap, but only partly. Hence, following a shock, the interest rate converges gradually towards a value that is consistent with the inflation target. What we are looking at below is a situation in which the adjustment has been completed and the interest rate has reached its equilibrium level. We show that this equilibrium level depends on the preferences of fiscal authorities. What we examine in the next sections is the reaction of monetary and fiscal variables to shocks starting from a position of long-run equilibrium.

Given the demand and supply equations and the behavioural rules of fiscal and monetary authorities, the Nash and the cooperative solution are presented in sections 13.3 and 13.4, respectively.

13.3 Nash equilibrium

13.3.1 Unconstrained fiscal policy

In the unconstrained regime, minimization of (13.6) gives the following expression for d_s:

$$d_s = \frac{(1 + \phi_1 \alpha)[(1 + \phi_1 \alpha)d_s' + \theta \phi_1 y'] + \theta \phi_1 [\phi_2(i - \pi^e) - \varepsilon_1]}{(1 + \phi_1 \alpha)^2 + \theta \phi_1^2} \tag{13.8}$$

The structural budget balance is raised when monetary policy tightens while it reacts negatively to a rise in expected inflation and to positive demand shocks.

Solving the central bank minimization problem gives the following expression of i:

$$i = \frac{i_o \beta \omega^2 (1 + \phi_1 \alpha)^2 + \phi_2 [\phi_1 d_s + \phi_2 \pi^e + \varepsilon_1 - (1 + \phi_1 \alpha)\varepsilon_2]}{\beta \omega^2 (1 + \phi_1 \alpha)^2 + \phi_2^2} \tag{13.9}$$

An expansionary fiscal policy leads to monetary tightening. The interest rate is increased in the event of a positive demand shock and is reduced in the event of a positive supply shock.

The interplay between monetary and fiscal behaviour is illustrated in Figure 13.1 which pictures the reaction functions in the policy instruments space. Both reaction functions are positively sloped. The slope of fiscal authorities' reaction function (FP) is higher than that of monetary authorities (CB).[10]

The Nash equilibrium is determined by the intersection of the two reaction functions.

Since the central bank does not pursue an output objective, it does not face a dilemma between output and inflation. Hence, in equilibrium, it can always meet its inflation target provided that it sets the appropriate interest rate. The equilibrium interest rate, i', is obtained from equation (13.8), under the assumption of no shocks and $\pi^e = \pi = 0$:

$$i' = \frac{\phi_1}{\phi_2} \left(d_s' + \frac{\theta \phi_1 y'}{1 + \phi_1 \alpha} \right) \tag{13.10}$$

where the term in brackets is the level of the budget balance prevailing in equilibrium. In the absence of shocks, the central bank meets the inflation

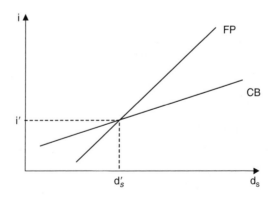

Figure 13.1 FP and CB reaction functions

target while there exists a 'deficit bias' if $y' > 0$. The intuition for this result is similar to that of the classic Barro–Gordon inflation bias for monetary policy: fiscal authorities keep stimulating demand in the attempt to push output beyond its natural level until the cost of further increasing the deficit brings it too far from target. Clearly, a Maastricht-type ceiling reduces the equilibrium budget deficit via a lower structural target d'_s. It is easy to show that if the budget deficit does not enter FP, the system is unstable as the government keeps stimulating the economy (while being always frustrated in equilibrium). From this perspective, the SGP helps in anchoring the system and preventing a 'passive' fiscal policy from bringing about the FTPL insolvency scenario.[11]

The authorities' reaction functions shift in response to shocks. In the case of a negative demand shock (such as a fall in private consumption), FP moves to the right and CB shifts down. The new equilibrium is a lower interest rate while the change in the budget deficit is ambiguous. However, under normal values of the parameters, one may expect a rise in the budget deficit. In the case of a supply shock (such as an oil price rise), monetary and fiscal policies move in the opposite direction: the interest rate goes up to keep inflation under control and, as a response, the budget deficit expands to prop up output. The new equilibrium is characterized by a higher interest rate and a higher budget deficit. Hence, the likelihood of the budget deficit exceeding the target and shifting fiscal policy into the constrained regime is higher under supply shocks.

In order to obtain the expression of the output gap and inflation in the event of demand and supply shocks, we cross-substitute from (13.8) and (13.9) and, after replacing i' from (13.10), we plug the solution for d_s and i in (13.4) and (13.5). Under rational expectations, we obtain:

$$y = \frac{\beta\,\omega^2(1+\phi_1\,\alpha)\varepsilon_1 + \phi_2^2\,\varepsilon_2}{\phi_2^2 + \beta\,\omega^2[(1+\phi_1\,\alpha)^2 + \theta\,\phi_1^2]} \tag{13.11}$$

$$\pi = \frac{\beta\,\omega\left\{(1+\phi_1\alpha)\varepsilon_1 - [(1+\phi_1\alpha)^2 + \theta\,\phi_1^2]\varepsilon_2\right\}}{\phi_2^2 + \beta\,\omega^2[(1+\phi_1\,\alpha)^2 + \theta\,\phi_1^2]} \tag{13.12}$$

Equations (13.11) and (13.12) show the fundamental role played by interest rate smoothing. If, contrary to the assumption above, β is set equal to zero, all demand-side parameters disappear from the solution. This implies that the central bank can offset perfectly any demand shock. The intuition is straight forward: as the output gap and inflation move in the same direction, the central bank faces no dilemma and, via a sufficiently strong response of interest rates, is able to close the output gap and preserve at the same time its inflation target. If β is positive, the central bank faces a cost in changing the interest rate. Hence, demand shocks are not fully smoothed and fiscal stabilization comes back into play. Under $\beta=0$, supply shocks feed through unsmoothed while the inflation target is always met.[12]

The impact of structural parameters and policy preferences on the output gap and inflation are summarized in Table 13.1. The sign of the partial derivatives is as expected. In particular, a high degree of interest rate smoothing – implying a low response of monetary policy to shocks – is destabilizing in the case of demand shocks while it is output-stabilizing and inflation-destabilizing in the case of supply shocks. A high preference for output stabilization by fiscal authorities helps in stabilizing output and inflation in the event of demand shocks, but is inflation-destabilizing in the case of supply shocks.

As shown in Table 13.1, large automatic stabilizers (α) and high effectiveness of fiscal policy (ϕ_1) may not lead to overall higher stabilization in the case of demand shocks. This seemingly counter-intuitive result occurs if monetary policy is very effective. In such a case, the combination of a higher response by the budget deficit and a lower reaction by the interest rate (due to interest rate smoothing) may imply a lower overall degree of stabilization. While theoretically interesting, under normal values of the parameters, higher budgetary stabilizers and a more effective fiscal policy can be expected to lead to higher output stabilization.

The above results help highlight the preference of each authority for the behaviour of the other authority. This can be obtained by replacing the solution for the y, π, d_s and i in the FP and CB loss functions (equations (13.6) and (13.7), respectively) and cross-differentiating for the monetary and fiscal parameters. While the algebra is messy, the conclusions are fairly straightforward.

The central bank would like to see higher fiscal stabilization in the event of demand shocks because that will allow lower deviations of inflation from target for given changes in the interest rate (or, conversely, attain the same degree of inflation stabilization with a smaller variation of the interest rate from its equilibrium level). On the contrary, monetary authorities would prefer lower fiscal stabilization in the event of supply shocks because that will result in lower changes in inflation and interest rates. The preference of

Table 13.1 Influence of policy parameters and preferences on y and π

		ϕ_1	ϕ_2	α	θ	β
ε_1	y	$+/-$	$-$	$+/-$	$-$	$+$
	π	$+/-$	$-$	$+/-$	$-$	$+$
ε_2	y	$-$	$+$	$-$	$-$	$-$
	π	$+$	$-$	$+$	$+$	$+$

Note: A positive (negative) sign indicates that a rise in the variable leads to an amplification (smoothening) of the shock.

Table 13.2 Preference of the fiscal authority for monetary reaction

Shock	Negative	Positive small	Positive large
ε_1	small β, large ϕ_2	large β, small ϕ_2	small β, large ϕ_2
ε_2	large β, small ϕ_2	small β, large ϕ_2	large β, small ϕ_2

fiscal authorities on monetary behaviour depends on the assumptions on the target level of the output gap. If the government pursues 'pure' output stabilization (i.e. $y' = 0$), it would like to see high monetary stabilization in the case of demand shocks (that is high ϕ_2 and low β) and low monetary stabilization in the case of supply shocks. Hence, each authority would like the other to do *more* in the case of demand shocks and *less* in the case of supply shocks.

The conclusions are less straightforward if the government aims at a positive output gap ($y' > 0$). The above results apply in the case of negative shocks and large positive shocks. However, as highlighted in Table 13.2, in the case of positive but small shocks, the government preference for monetary response is different. Let us consider first a positive demand shock bringing the output gap close to y'. In such a case, the government would benefit from a weak response by the central bank (occurring if the preference for interest rate smoothing, β, is large) because this will allow the output gap to remain in the neighbourhood of y'. In the case of a positive small supply shock shifting the output gap towards but still below y', the fiscal authority would like to see a strong monetary response because higher inflation stabilization will imply a further increase in the output gap (thereby bringing y closer to y'). These results are relevant for the discussion of the cases of 'fiscal dominance' and 'monetary dominance' in section 13.4.

13.3.2 Constrained fiscal policy

In the above analysis, we have assumed that the budget balance is sufficiently far from the deficit ceiling so that fiscal policy is unconstrained. However, if, following a severe negative shock, the nominal deficit hits the deficit ceiling, we shift to a fiscally constrained regime.[13] In such a case, the fiscal reaction function simply becomes:

$$d_s = \bar{d} + \alpha y \tag{13.13}$$

This implies that the discretionary part of the budget moves to compensate for the effect of the automatic stabilizers and thus all fiscal stabilization is forsaken. The reaction function of the fiscal authority is negatively sloped and, unlike the unconstrained regime, it shifts to the left in the case of a negative demand shock.

Under a constrained fiscal policy, the solution of y and π is the following:

$$y = \frac{\beta\,\omega^2\varepsilon_1 + \phi_2^2\,\varepsilon_2}{\phi_2^2 + \beta\,\omega^2} \tag{13.14}$$

$$\pi = \frac{\beta\,\omega\,(\varepsilon_1 - \varepsilon_2)}{\phi_2^2 + \beta\,\omega^2} \tag{13.15}$$

Compared to the unconstrained regime, we have lower output and inflation stabilization in the event of demand shocks[14] and lower output stabilization and higher inflation stabilization in the event of supply shocks.

13.4   Cooperative equilibrium

In the cooperative solution the two policy instruments, d_s and i, are chosen so as to minimize the joint loss function of fiscal and monetary authorities:

$$L(FPCB) = \eta\lfloor (d_s - d_s')^2 + \theta\,(y - y')^2 \rfloor + (1 - \eta)\lfloor \pi^2 + \beta\,(i - i')^2 \rfloor \tag{13.16}$$

where $0 \le \eta \le 1$ gives the 'bargaining power' of the two policy authorities: a large (small) η indicates a strong (weak) fiscal authority.

Given the cumbersome algebra, we illustrate the main results under simplifying assumptions on a number of parameters.

An important result is that if fiscal policy pursues 'pure' output stabilization (i.e. $y' = 0$), under no shocks the Nash and the cooperative equilibria are the same (namely $y = \pi = 0$). However, if the government targets a positive output gap ($y' > 0$), the equilibrium solution is characterized by a 'deficit bias' *and* an 'inflation bias'. Under the assumption $\phi_1 = \beta = 0$, the expression of the inflation bias is the following:

$$\pi = \frac{y'\omega\,\eta\,\theta}{\phi_2(1 - \eta)} \tag{13.17}$$

Clearly, the inflation bias is a positive function of the bargaining power of the fiscal authority and the output gap target. The reason is that, via the combined loss function, the central bank encompasses the fiscal policy target of a positive output gap. Therefore, as in the classic Barro–Gordon result, the central bank stimulates the economy until the (temporary) output gains are compensated by the additional costs of a further rise in inflation (and, in the general case, by the cost of shifting the interest rate away from its equilibrium value).

In order to examine some of the mechanisms at work, it is useful to consider two extreme cases of cooperation: 'fiscal dominance' ($\eta = 1$) and 'monetary dominance' ($\eta = 0$).

Under *fiscal dominance*, the government uses both policy instruments to minimize its own loss function. Since deviating from the output target is costly, it will set d_s equal to the deficit target[15] and use i for stabilization purposes.

If the government pursues 'pure' stabilization ($y' = 0$), in equilibrium the output gap is zero but, in the absence of a nominal anchor, the inflation rate is undetermined. If the government pursues a positive output gap ($y' > 0$), it will keep lowering i in the attempt to push output beyond its natural level. Since i cannot be lowered below zero, from equation (13.1) we obtain:

$$\frac{\phi_1}{\phi_2} d_s - \frac{(1+\phi_1\alpha)y'}{\phi_2} + \pi^e + \frac{\varepsilon_1}{\phi_2} = 0 \tag{13.18}$$

Hence, in 'equilibrium', the inflation rate is the following:

$$\pi = -\frac{\phi_1}{\phi_2} d_s' + \frac{(1+\phi_1\alpha)}{\phi_2} y' \tag{13.19}$$

Under *monetary dominance*, the interest rate is kept fixed at its equilibrium level and the budget deficit is used by the central bank to achieve the inflation target. If the central bank sets a sufficiently low fiscal target, fiscal policy will never be constrained. Output and inflation will be stabilized perfectly under demand shocks while supply shocks will show up in an equivalent change in the output gap with no impact on inflation.

Table 13.3 summarizes the main results of the analysis. Inflation and output under monetary dominance are identical to the Nash solution without interest rate smoothing ($\beta = 0$), with the difference that it is the fiscal instrument and not the interest rate that is used to stabilize inflation. In the case of demand shocks, monetary dominance and fiscal dominance provide more macroeconomic stabilization than does Nash. The reason is that, unlike the Nash solution, one policy instrument (i under fiscal dominance and d_s under monetary dominance) can be used freely to offset perfectly the shock.

Table 13.3 Output and inflation stabilization under various regimes

	Monetary dominance	Fiscal dominance ($y' = 0$)	Nash ($\beta > 0$)	Nash ($\beta = 0$)
y	ε_2	0	$\dfrac{\beta\,\omega^2(1+\phi_1\alpha)\varepsilon_1 + \phi_2^2\,\varepsilon_2}{\phi_2^2 + \beta\,\omega^2[(1+\phi_1\alpha)^2 + \theta\,\phi_1^2]}$	ε_2
π	0	$\pi^e - \dfrac{\varepsilon_2}{\omega}$	$\dfrac{\beta\,\omega\{(1+\phi_1\alpha)\varepsilon_1 - [(1+\phi_1\alpha)^2 + \theta\,\phi_1^2]\varepsilon_2\}}{\phi_2^2 + \beta\,\omega^2[(1+\phi_1\alpha)^2 + \theta\,\phi_1^2]}$	0

What conclusions can be drawn on the incentives of monetary and fiscal authorities to cooperate?

Clearly, if the government aims at attaining a positive output gap, there is no incentive for an inflation-conservative central bank – as the ECB is mandated to be – to engage in cooperation because it would have to accept an inflation bias in equilibrium. Notice however that, in general, there is a *trade-off between the inflation and the deficit bias* because the use of the interest rate to stimulate demand would partly take the place of the rise in the deficit. To the extent that under non-cooperation a high deficit bias leads to a unsustainable accumulation of public debt, the central bank would face an unpalatable choice between higher inflation now (to reduce the deficit bias) and (debt monetization and hence) higher inflation in the future.

If the government pursues 'pure' cyclical smoothing, under no shocks, the Nash equilibrium and the cooperative equilibrium both imply $g = 0$ and $\pi = 0$. Hence, the incentives for cooperation depend on welfare gains and losses in response to shocks.

Under demand shocks, as both policies move in the same direction the gains from cooperation are ambiguous. This is illustrated in Figure 13.2 which pictures the policy reactions to a negative demand shock. Both policies are restrictive and the new Nash equilibrium is E'. The Bliss points for the two authorities are indicated by B_{FP} and B_{CB}: ideally, as discussed before, each authority would prefer the whole stabilization be borne by the other authority. The line between the two Bliss points is the contract coordination line. As shown in the graph, E' is very close to such a line, indicating that any gain from coordination for both authorities, even if positive, is necessarily minor and could be even negative if the coordination process involves 'transaction costs'.

In the case of supply shocks, since under Nash the two policy instruments move in opposite directions, there are unambiguous gains from

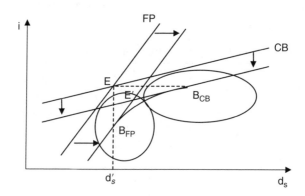

Figure 13.2   Negative demand shock

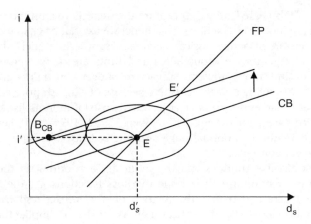

Figure 13.3 Negative supply shock

cooperation. This can be easily understood since, in the non-cooperative solution, part of the change in the interest rate occurs in order to offset the change in the opposite direction in the budget deficit. This additional change in the interest rate, K, is given by:

$$K = -\frac{\phi_1^2 \phi_2 \varepsilon_2}{(1 + \phi_1 \alpha)\left\{\phi_2^2 + \beta \omega^2\left[(1 + \phi_1 \alpha)^2 + \theta \phi_1^2\right]\right\}} \tag{13.20}$$

This result is illustrated in Figure 13.3 which shows the policy reactions to a negative supply shock. Given the policy preferences of the central bank, the latter would like fiscal policy to turn restrictive to keep inflation under control. Conversely, the government would like to see no change in the interest rate so that all the shock will feed through into higher inflation.[16] Instead, under no cooperation, each authority moves in the opposite direction to that hoped for by the other authority. As shown in the graph, the degree of output and inflation stabilization implied by non-cooperation could be achieved at lower values of both policy instruments.[17] Given interest rate smoothing in CB and the deficit target in FP, this implies a welfare gain for both authorities. Cooperation also implies a lower likelihood to shift in the fiscally constrained regime.

The empirical investigation in section 13.5 provides support for these conclusions.

13.5 Illustration of policy interactions with the QUEST model

The present section attempts to provide some quantitative evidence on some of the effects derived in sections 13.3 and 13.4. We use a 2-country version of the DG ECFINs QUEST model to capture the quantitative importance of fiscal–monetary policy interactions. The model we use can be characterized as a modern version of a neoclassical Keynesian synthesis model. This means behavioural equations of households and firms are derived from explicit dynamic optimization problems subject to budget constraints and adjustment costs. Monetary policy is effective because of sluggish price adjustment in the goods market due to price adjustment costs of monopolistically competitive firms (see, for example, Rotemberg, 1982, 1996; and Hairault and Portier, 1993) and the nominal wage response is delayed because of overlapping one-year contracts.[18]

Both the fiscal authorities and the monetary authorities set their policy instruments to minimize their respective loss functions. As the empirical model used here is dynamic, the focus is on the impact responses to the shocks, to stay close to the theoretical analysis above. This implies that the fiscal authorities as well as the monetary authorities face a high rate of time preference, optimize their respective responses over the short run and discount the medium to long-term effects more heavily. Another difference with the theoretical model is that here the policy response of the monetary authorities is not formulated in terms of interest rates but in terms of the money supply. This is inconsequential since both instruments are linked via a stable money demand equation in the model. The instrument for the fiscal authorities is government expenditure g.

The underlying utility function corresponds to the specification in the theoretical section. In particular we assume that fiscal policy does not care about inflation and monetary policy puts zero weight on output stabilization. Also in order to mimic as closely as possible the stabilization motive of both policy-makers we assume a high discount rate. Monetary policy sets the money supply m so as to minimize the following loss function:

$$L(CB_t) = \sum_{i=t}^{\infty} \delta^i \left(\pi_i^2 + \beta \left(i_i - i_{i-1} \right)^2 \right) \tag{13.21}$$

where δ the rate of time preference, π_t is inflation, i_t the nominal interest rate and β the weight given to interest rate smoothing. The fiscal authorities set their instrument, government consumption g, to minimize the following loss function:

$$L(FP_t) = \sum_{i=t}^{\infty} \delta^i \left\{ (Y_i - \overline{Y})^2 + \gamma (d - \overline{d})^2 \right\} \tag{13.22}$$

where $Y - \overline{Y}$ is the output gap, $d - \overline{d}$ the deficit deviation from target, and γ the weight given to the deficit target. Here we deviate from the theoretical model by explicitly specifying a debt rule which guarantees fiscal solvency.

$$\Delta g_t = f_1 \left(b_0 - B_t / Y_t \right) - f_2 \Delta \left(B_t / Y_t \right) \tag{13.23}$$

In order to simplify the optimization problem faced by fiscal policy, the parameters f_1 and f_2 of that rule are not set optimally but only act as a constraint on a government which accepts responsibility for budget sustainability. This is a mild form of the SGP and captures the 'close-to-balance' rule. However, the debt rule as specified in this chapter will not automatically guarantee that fiscal policy will meet the deficit target for all shocks. In cases where the deficit target is violated in the experiments conducted below we will look at an unconstrained as well as a constrained optimization problem.

13.5.1   Non-Cooperation

Given the dynamic complexity as well as non-linearity of the model it is impossible to derive explicit decision rules for monetary and fiscal policy. Here we briefly describe how the reaction functions are derived in this chapter.

Let T_t be a vector of target variables, X_t a vector of instruments, S_t a vector of state variables and ε_t a vector of exogenous shocks, then in a linear approximation, the target variables can be expressed as follows:

$$T_t = a_s S + a_x X_t + a_\varepsilon \varepsilon_t \tag{13.24}$$

In general the instruments, when set optimally, will be related to both the state of the economy and exogenous shocks:

$$X_t = b_s S_t + b_\varepsilon \varepsilon_t \tag{13.25}$$

and the parameters will be complicated functions of both the structural parameters of the model and the preferences of policy-makers. To find the optimal policy response it is easier if X_t can be expressed as a function of the shocks only. Using the fact that for any covariance stationary process there exists a moving average representation, the state variables can be expressed as a moving average of current and past shocks:

$$S_t = c(L)\varepsilon_t \tag{13.26}$$

This can be used to express the instruments as functions of shocks only, as follows:

$$X_t = d(L)\varepsilon_t \tag{13.27}$$

Optimization therefore requires selecting parameters such that the fiscal and monetary objective function is minimized. Computationally this is a complicated problem since the dimension of the parameter set is not known *a priori*. In order to economize on the search we assume that the MA process can be approximated by an ARIMA representation, which in the case of the monetary policy rule only involves lagged money and current shocks. In the case of fiscal expenditure, the response is restricted to current innovations, besides the response implied by the sustainability constraint. Thus the general form of the rules over which we optimize is given by

$$m_t = m_{t-1} + c_2\varepsilon_1 + c_3\varepsilon_2 \tag{13.28}$$

$$g_t = \bar{g} - f_1(b - b_0) - f_2\Delta b + f_3\varepsilon_1 + f_4\varepsilon_2 \tag{13.29}$$

Given the standard money demand equation in the model, this rule can be rewritten in terms of an interest rate rule as follows:

$$\Delta i_t = \frac{1}{\varphi}(\Delta y_t + \Delta\pi_t) - c_2\varepsilon_{1t} - c_3\varepsilon_{2t} \tag{13.28a}$$

where φ denotes the semi-interest elasticity of real balances with respect to nominal interest rates. As can be seen from this expression, the optimal rule comes close to a Taylor rule formulated in first differences and equal weights given to both output growth deviations from trend[19] and inflation. However, according to the optimal rule the central bank takes into account the source of the shock. In the case of a positive/negative demand shock it will increase/lower interest rates more than implied by changes in GDP and inflation, while in the case of a positive/negative supply shock monetary policy will be less/more restrictive than implied by the Taylor rule.

For the demand and supply shocks we assume that the demand shock is a temporary shock to consumption, ex-ante 1 per cent of GDP in the first quarter, which is phased out in following quarters. The supply shock is a persistent technology shock, of similar magnitude to 1 per cent of GDP. Since a persistent technology shock leads to a new long-run level of potential GDP, the question therefore arises whether fiscal policy[20] should target the historic or future potential output. We assume in this analysis that fiscal policy targets the historic level of potential output. Given the high discount rate, the government is mainly interested in short-run stabilization. An immediate move towards the new potential output target would be counter-intuitive, since the short-run perspective of the government would force fiscal policy to adjust output strongly towards the new lower level. This would be inconsistent with the notion that the output gap term in the utility function represents an output smoothing motive for fiscal policy. Finally it must be noted that for less persistent supply shocks the first year response of the model economy would not differ qualitatively from a permanent shock. For the given specifications of the loss functions and for the types of shocks considered here, the following monetary and fiscal reaction functions for the Nash equilibrium are obtained in the unconstrained regime:

$$g_t = \bar{g} - 0.04(b - b_0) - 0.05\Delta b - 0.3\varepsilon_1 - 3.0\varepsilon_2 \tag{13.30}$$

$$m_t = m_{t-1} - 0.000125\varepsilon_1 + 0.025\varepsilon_2 \tag{13.31}$$

Figures 13.4 and 13.5 illustrate the fiscal and monetary reaction functions under negative demand and supply shocks respectively, and Table 13.4 gives the corresponding welfare losses for both authorities under the Nash solution.

The response parameter for a demand shock is negative. In the case of a negative consumption shock, $\varepsilon_1 < 0$, the fiscal authorities respond by raising expenditure to boost output. The monetary authorities respond by offsetting the deflationary impact of this shock and raise the money supply and reduce interest rates, which will also stimulate domestic demand. Thus, under demand shocks, both policies move in the same direction, and if one

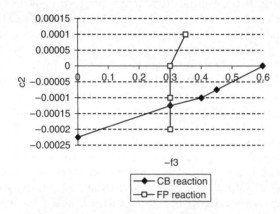

Figure 13.4 Optimal policy response – negative demand shock

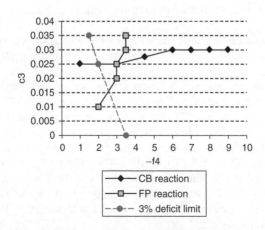

Figure 13.5 Optimal policy response – negative supply shock

Note: Monetary reaction function: $m_t = m_{t-1} + c_2\varepsilon_1 + c_3\varepsilon_2$

Fiscal reaction function: $g_t = \bar{g} - f_1(b - b_0) - f_2\Delta b + f_3\varepsilon_1 + f_4\varepsilon_2$

authority does more, the other has to do less. This is illustrated in Figure 13.4 which depicts the optimal settings of the respective response parameters for the monetary and fiscal authorities under this particular shock. On the vertical axis, the size of the monetary reaction is given, where a smaller negative value represents a smaller monetary expansion or higher interest rates. The horizontal axis gives the absolute value of the fiscal response parameter, and a larger parameter implies a larger increase in government expenditure and a larger deficit. If the response of the fiscal authorities becomes stronger and they raise expenditure by more, the monetary authorities can reduce the size of the monetary loosening. Thus, in Figure 13.4, the CB reaction function is upward-sloping. If the central bank reacts more strongly to the negative demand shock and raises the money supply by more, that will help to prop up output again and the fiscal authorities will have to do less. Thus the FP reaction curve is also upward-sloping. The FP reaction curve is steeper than the CB curve, consistent with the analysis in section 13.3.

In the case of a negative supply shock, $\varepsilon_2 < 0$, monetary and fiscal policies go in opposite directions. The response parameter for a supply shock is positive in the monetary reaction function. Monetary policy contracts to offset the inflationary impact of this negative technology shock and the central bank raises interest rates. The fiscal authorities respond by increasing government expenditure to prop up output (i.e. negative coefficient). The policy responses now move output and inflation in opposite directions. The CB reaction reduces output even further and fiscal policy responds by raising expenditure even more. Hence in Figure 13.5 the FP reaction curve is upward-sloping. If the fiscal authorities react more strongly and increase expenditure, then the monetary authorities will react to the additional inflationary pressure by a further monetary tightening. Thus the CB curve is also upward-sloping.

The Nash solution is then determined by the intersection of the CB and FP reaction curves. The policy parameters and their corresponding welfare losses are given in Table 13.4.

In case of the demand shock, fiscal and monetary authorities are able to stabilize output and inflation. The rise in the deficit remains small and well within the limits of the SGP. However, under the particular supply shock given here, the Nash equilibrium in this optimization game, with this inflation-conservative central bank that stabilizes inflation immediately, implies a large response of the fiscal authorities. The optimal fiscal response in this setting would mean that the deficit would exceed the SGP limit of 3 per cent. The 3 per cent deficit limit under this shock implies the fiscal response parameter could not exceed the range of 2–3.5 as indicated by the dotted line in Figure 13.5.

Thus, the SGP constrained optimum lies far to the left of the Nash solution with a lower fiscal response to the shock and an also slightly lower monetary response. As shown in Table 13.4, the implied output gap in the constrained

Table 13.4 Policy responses under negative supply and demand shocks

	Negative supply shock (1% of GDP)		Negative demand shock (1% of GDP)	
(a) Nash optimal response:				
Fiscal policy parameter	$f_4 = -3.0$		$f_3 = -0.30$	
Monetary policy parameter	$c_3 = 0.025$		$c_2 = -0.000125$	
	FP:	CB:	FP:	CB:
	47.40755	0.06552	0.01081	0.00029
Effect on:				
GDP		-1.40		0
Inflation		0.14		0
Deficit		3.8		0.11
(b) Nash optimal response – constrained fiscal policy:				
Fiscal policy parameter	$f_4 = -2.0$			
Monetary policy parameter	$c_3 = 0.025$			
	FP:	CB:		
	46.19591	0.04868		
Effect on:				
GDP		-1.48		
Inflation		0.10		
Deficit		2.76		

Note: Monetary reaction function: $m_t = m_{t-1} + c_2\varepsilon_1 + c_3\varepsilon_2$
Fiscal reaction function: $g_t = \bar{g} - f_1(b-b_0) - f_2\Delta b + f_3\varepsilon_1 + f_4\varepsilon_2$

case is larger than under the Nash (FP loss exceeds that under the Nash) while inflation is lower (CB loss smaller). In terms of welfare losses, CB gains a lot from the deficit constraint and the CB loss is reduced to a quarter of that under the Nash solution, while the additional loss of FP is relatively small.

13.5.2 Cooperation

Under demand shocks, monetary and fiscal policies move in the same direction, and from the theoretical analysis it is not unambiguously evident whether both parties would gain from cooperation. It was shown above that the fiscal and monetary authorities are able to stabilize output and inflation in this scenario and the respective welfare losses are relatively small. With the deficit entering the FP loss function, a larger fiscal policy response increases the fiscal welfare losses and no improvement relative to the Nash solution can be achieved where both parties would be better off.

In the case of a negative supply shock, as shown in Table 13.5, both parties are unambiguously better off under cooperation. Policies move in opposite directions and part of the monetary tightening occurs in order to offset the effects of the fiscal expansion and vice versa (see eq. 13.20). Thus both

Table 13.5 Example of welfare improving policy coordination under negative supply shock

Fiscal policy parameter	$f_4 = -1.0$	
Monetary policy parameter	$c_3 = 0.02$	
	FP:	CB:
	39.96268	0.04230
Effect on:		
GDP		-1.35
Inflation		0.16
Deficit		1.51

authorities can gain from reacting less. When the fiscal authorities reduce the size of the expansion and the central bank tightens less, both FP and CB are better off. In Figure 13.5, there is a whole region below and to the left of the Nash outcome where both FP and CB gain from coordination. The example given here raises the deficit to 1.5 per cent of GDP. Both CB and FP benefit from coordination, but relative to the unconstrained Nash outcome, the gain for CB is largest, as the fiscal response is reduced by most. It is important to bear in mind that these results of positive gains from coordination hold only under these specific scenarios. It is assumed in this exercise that fiscal authorities do not target an output level beyond the natural level and no inflation bias arises.

13.6 Conclusions

This chapter has looked at the interactions between monetary and fiscal authorities when fiscal policy is constrained by upper limits on the budget deficits, as in EMU.

Conflicts between monetary and fiscal policy arise when the central bank's objective function differs from that of fiscal authorities. This is generally assumed in the literature. In particular, it is assumed that the fiscal authority has less incentive to stabilize inflation, while inflation stabilization is the most important goal of the central bank. Also different degrees of output stabilization as well as different output targets can be consistent with the objectives of both authorities. In this chapter it has been assumed that the central bank adheres to strict inflation control and attaches zero weight to output stabilization; however the central bank also tries to smooth nominal interest rates. The latter element is introduced because, first, there is sufficient empirical evidence in its favour and, second, it restricts the power of monetary policy with respect to neutralizing demand shocks and allows for more interesting policy interactions.

For fiscal policy it is assumed that the government does not care about inflation but only about output stabilization (around a level which can be higher than the natural rate). The SGP introduces an additional constraint on fiscal policy. This constraint is introduced in the model via the objective function which penalizes deficits which deviate from the 'close-to-balance' target of the SGP. The government does not necessarily choose a deficit target that would (for given stabilizers) never violate the Maastricht threshold because it faces a trade-off between the loss of utility in normal times from a deficit that is set lower than required under solvency and the cost of violating the 3 per cent limit by not setting the target low enough in case of large negative shocks.

Because of this trade-off, fiscal policy will – depending on the size of shocks – operate under two different regimes. Under the fiscally unconstrained regime, the government chooses instruments in order to maximize its objective function. Under the fiscally constrained regime, the choice of the fiscal instrument is dictated by the Maastricht deficit limit.

Within this theoretical framework, we analysed how parameters of fiscal and monetary policies and the preferences of the central bank affect the response of output and inflation to shocks.

The main results of the theoretical analysis are summarized hereafter.

Under *non-cooperation*, demand shocks affect output and inflation only insofar as the central bank smoothes the interest rate. The central bank prefers high fiscal stabilization under demand shocks and low fiscal stabilization under supply shocks; conversely, the government would like to see low interest rate smoothing under demand shocks and high smoothing under supply shocks. Given the move of policies in opposite directions, under negative supply shocks there is a higher likelihood to shift into the fiscally constrained regime. If fiscal authorities target a positive output gap, there is a 'deficit bias' in equilibrium. However, under non-cooperation, since the central bank does not aim at pushing output beyond its natural level, there is no 'inflation bias'.

Under *cooperation*, if fiscal authorities pursue a positive output gap, there is in equilibrium an 'inflation bias' and a 'deficit bias', though the latter is lower than under Nash. If the government only pursues 'pure' cyclical stabilization, the gains from cooperation are ambiguous and necessarily small under demand shocks, but there are positive gains from coordination under supply shocks. This implies that, provided that the objective of the government is output stabilization around its natural level, policy coordination may be looked at as an insurance against future shocks.

Our simulations with the QUEST model lend support to these theoretical predictions. It is shown that the Nash solution, under a sufficiently severe negative supply shock, implies a violation of the deficit threshold. The simulations also confirm that there are positive gains from coordinating the policy response to supply shocks.

These results help to shed light on a number of issue which have been raised in the academic and policy debate.

It has been shown that the *substitutability* or *complementarity* between monetary and fiscal policies crucially depends on the type of shocks hitting the economy. In the event of supply shocks, the two policies move in opposite directions: a loosening (tightening) of fiscal policy goes hand in hand with a tightening (loosening) of monetary policy. Hence there is a clear conflict between the two arms of macroeconomic policy. The empirical observation, however, of a policy substitutability does not imply necessarily a conflict. For instance, as mentioned above, a relaxation of monetary policy during periods of budgetary consolidation – as in the EU during the 1990s – may actually imply 'implicit' coordination: by helping to cushion the output losses due to the budgetary retrenchment, the expansionary monetary policy facilitates the task of fiscal authorities.[21] Under demand shocks, both policies move in the same direction, but if one does more, the other one does less. In this case, there exists a sort of 'distributional' conflict between monetary and fiscal authorities on how to share the burden of stabilization.

Our results may provide a rationale for the traditional central bank's aversion for 'ex ante' coordination of macroeconomic policies. This reluctance was expressed forcefully in a recent speech by Otmar Issing, chief economist of the ECB (Issing, 2000): 'Not much can be expected from attempts to coordinate these macroeconomic policies ex ante…On the contrary, such attempts give rise to the risk of confusing the specific roles, mandates and responsibilities of the policies in question.' And later: 'if there is already an *efficient* initial assignment of responsibilities in place, which does take into account the individual policy-maker's objectives and actions, calls for policy coordination…would not be necessary. To put it simply, an efficient initial assignment of objectives and responsibilities will largely substitute the need for coordinated policies later on.'

As shown above, if fiscal authorities target an output beyond the natural level, under cooperation, an inflation bias will arise in equilibrium. This is likely to put off any incentive for policy coordination by an inflation-conservative central bank, whatever the possible gains from it in responding to shocks. However, if budgetary authorities only pursue cyclical stabilization, the Nash and the cooperative solutions are identical under zero shocks and no deficit or inflation biases arise in equilibrium. Hence, under no shocks, there are 'no risks' from cooperation for the central bank. Therefore, the benefits of coordination have to be assessed by looking at the response to shocks under Nash and cooperation. Our analysis points to gains from coordinating monetary and fiscal policies in response to shocks. If policy coordination is viewed as insurance against future shocks, there seems to be a good case for entering into a contract between monetary and fiscal authorities to provide an optimal response to shocks.

Obviously, this conclusion does not consider other factors such as the existence of 'transactions' costs of implementing coordination, or the fact that supply shocks – especially if long-lasting – should be dealt with via structural reforms and microeconomic adjustment rather than macroeconomic stabilization. To the extent that central bank's reluctance in engaging in coordination is justified by 'suspicion' on the real objectives of fiscal authorities, 'soft coordination' helping to understand each other's targets, identify the type of shocks, and achieve a common view on the output gap, would certainly be beneficial. It could also pave the way to stronger forms of coordination down the road.

The analysis in this chapter is subject to obvious limitations, starting with the extremely simplified structure of the model and policy preferences. We look at an a-temporal equilibrium and do not explore the dynamics of the response to shocks or to changes in policy preferences. For instance, an intertemporal trade-off may arise between inflation bias and deficit bias. Also, having chosen the interest-inclusive budget balance – instead of the primary balance – as a control variable has cut off an important channel of policy interactions. In the empirical section, the way in which the reaction functions of monetary and fiscal authorities have been derived deserves further investigation. Finally, as the analysis encompasses only one fiscal authority, one should be cautious in deriving direct policy conclusions for EMU.

Note

1. Directorate General for Economic and Financial Affairs, European Commission. The authors would like to thank Jacques Mélitz, Luisa Lambertini, Ralph Bryant and José Marin, as well as Bertrand Martinot and other Commission economists. The opinions expressed in this chapter belong to the authors only and should not be attributed to the European Commission. The usual disclaimer applies.
2. Some terminological confusion exists in the literature. Such fiscal behaviour is dubbed 'active' by Sims (1999), following the original contribution by Leeper (1991), or 'Ricardian' according to Woodford (1995). On the contrary, Leith and Wren-Lewis (2000) call such reaction function 'passive'.
3. One should, however, make a distinction between 'level' and 'direction' of the monetary stance. While monetary policy loosened over the retrenchment period, it remained basically cautious as confirmed by looking at the difference between actual and 'Taylor' interest rates. See OECD (1999a).
4. However, this is not true for all countries. As shown in European Commission (1999), tighter monetary policy has gone hand in hand with tight fiscal policy in Italy. This complementarity between the two policies is probably explained by the 'double convergence' – on budget deficit and inflation – that Italy had to accomplish to meet the Maastricht requirements.
5. See, e.g., van Aarle *et al.* (2000), Bennett and Loayza (2000) and Leitmo (2000).
6. Mainstream estimates indicate that the value of α is around 0.5 for the EU and EMU as a whole. However, it varies between 0.3 and 0.4 for the Mediterranean countries to between 0.8 and 0.9 for the Nordic countries; see European Commission (2000a), and Chapter 8 by Paul van den Noord. Other studies, such as that by Jacques Mélitz in Chapter 12, however, find considerably lower values of the automatic stabilizers (between 0.1 and 0.2).
7. A positive output gap target in L(FP) may also reflect the shorter time horizon of the governments relative to that of the central bank.
8. For a summary of the evidence, see Clarida *et al.* (1999) and Favero and Rovelli (2000).

9. A number of empirical analyses find that the weight of output stabilization in the reaction function of central banks in Europe is very low. For recent estimates, see von Hagen *et al.* (2001).

10. The expressions of the slope of FP and CB are, respectively:

$$\frac{(1+\phi_1\alpha)^2+\theta\,\phi_1^2}{\theta\,\phi_1\,\phi_2} \quad \text{and} \quad \frac{\phi_1\,\phi_2}{\beta\,\omega^2(1+\phi_1\alpha)^2+\phi_2^2}$$

The difference between the two slopes is always positive. This implies that an expansionary fiscal policy coupled with a restrictive monetary policy results in a higher budget deficit and a higher interest rate (instead of the opposite, as would be the case if CB were steeper than FP).

11. In equilibrium, the model does not feature an inflation bias because the monetary stance, in spite of interest rate smoothing, will be sufficiently tight to prevent the expansionary fiscal policy from endangering the inflation target. However, if e.g., there is a change in government preferences, during the path towards the new equilibrium interest rate, inflation can deviate from target.

12. If y appears explicitly in CB's loss function, demand shocks are still fully offset. However, supply shocks will imply a deviation of inflation and output gap from the target values reflecting the conflicting objectives of price and income stabilization. See Artis and Buti (2000b).

13. Clearly, the likelihood of shifting to a constrained regime depends on the medium-term deficit target of the fiscal authorities. If the latter are highly risk averse and want to avoid at all costs an 'excessive deficit', they may set a medium-term target which is able to withstand all shocks – regardless of their severity – without exceeding the deficit ceiling. This approach is behind the calculations of the so-called 'minimal benchmarks' which, on the basis of past business-cycle experience, allow a sufficient safety margin under the 3% of GDP deficit ceiling. See European Commission (1999, 2000a), and Artis and Buti (2000a and b).

14. This holds under normal values of the parameters. See discussion above on the special case of a higher fiscal stabilization resulting in an overall lower macroeconomic stabilization.

15. In fact, given the availability of the interest rate to stabilize output, the government can set d_s at its 'true' preference and not at the SGP-compatible level.

16. Notice that FP's reaction function is not directly affected by the supply shock. This implies that the original equilibrium under no shocks (E in Figure 13.3) remains the preferred position for the fiscal authority. Under more general assumptions on the IS equation or FP preferences (including an inflation term), FP's reaction function would shift to the right and so would the new Nash equilibrium. Obviously, the conclusions in the text remain unchanged.

17. It is easy to show that the Stackelberg solution entails values of the policy variables intermediate between Nash and cooperation. See Bennett and Loayza (2000).

18. For a description of the basic structure of the model and its parameter values, see Roeger, in't Veld and Woehrmann (2001). The version used here allows for overlapping wage contracts and sluggishness in prices with firms facing quadratic price adjustment costs per unit of output (see Roeger, 1999).

19. Since all variables in the model are defined in efficiency units, the growth rate of y must be interpreted as deviation from its long-run trend as defined by the growth rate of TFP and population.

20. Note that monetary policy does not target output at all.
21. The SGP has been interpreted by Allsopp and Vines (1996, 1998) as a 'commitment technology' by EMU members to bring a monetary relaxation which would reduce the costs of consolidation. As argued in European Commission (1999) and Buti and Martinot (2000), confirmation of the commitment to fiscal prudence contributed in triggering an accommodating monetary response by the ECB in the first year of EMU.

14
Central Bank Independence, Political Uncertainty and the Assignment of Instruments to Targets

Andrew Hughes Hallett and Nicola Viegi

14.1 Introduction

From the work of Alesina and Summers (1993) and Alesina and Gatti (1995), it has been accepted that there is no real statistical evidence to support the idea, associated with Rogoff (1985), that greater central bank independence produces higher output variability. It is usually argued that this is because central bank independence eliminates the uncertainty created by a polarized political system. Indeed, because political conflict produces an inefficiency in the determination of output and prices, the delegation of monetary policy solves the inflation bias problem by eliminating the *political* source of the macroeconomic instability.

However another explanation is possible. It may be that there is another policy instrument in play and that monetary and fiscal policies tend to move in opposite directions (Mélitz, 1997, and the contribution in Chapter 12 of the present volume). In that case monetary and fiscal policy would become strategic substitutes, with looser fiscal policy being used to stabilize output while tighter monetary policy is used to control inflation. In other words, the fact that we find lower inflation but no loss in output stability, may simply be due to the fact that a more active fiscal policy has been able to contain the rise in output variability.

At one level, this may just be an illustration of the consequences of policy assignments in economics, as shown in Tinbergen's work (Hughes Hallett, 1989). And further evidence for this 'strategic substitute' hypothesis appears in the work of Wyplosz (1999) and von Hagen *et al.* (2001). But it contrasts sharply with the results of Alesina and Tabellini (1987) who find that, with independent fiscal and monetary policies, fiscal policy will be forced to follow monetary policy in its stance – given that public expenditures would otherwise depend on monetary financing. Such a result would mean that central bank independence would have to produce a higher level of distortionary taxation and/or a lower level of national income on average. That would contradict the empirical findings cited above.

These conflicting results suggest that we need to re-examine the Alesina and Summers hypothesis and look for an alternative explanation of their results.[1] In this chapter we analyse the issue of monetary delegation in a world with multiple policy instruments (as in Alesina and Tabellini, 1987) and political uncertainty (as in Alesina and Gatti, 1995). We argue that central bank independence has two main effects. First of all it induces higher activism in the conduct of fiscal policy, in response to the lower propensity for monetary policy to counteract exogenous shocks. And secondly, where there is political polarization over the targets of economic policy, central bank independence resolves the political uncertainty in favour of the party more willing to use fiscal policy. This means that the median voter, who was previously indifferent between the two parties, would now choose the party with the highest propensity to expand fiscally because that would reduce the cost of having less output stabilization from the central bank. In other words, central bank independence would produce a system in which fiscal and monetary policies are assigned to different targets, and may follow different and potentially conflicting strategies. This may provide a simple one-to-one assignment of instruments to targets, and the possibility of conflicts similar to those analysed in Nordhaus (1994), Blake and Weale (1998) and Demertzis *et al.* (1999b). Or it may produce an incomplete assignment and a lower level of conflict. It all depends on the underlying economic structure.

The chapter is arranged as follows. In the following section we look at the effect of introducing fiscal policy in the standard Rogoff model. Then we analyse how this alters the choices faced by a median voter in a polarized political system, as introduced by Alesina (1987), Alesina and Rosenthal (1995) and Alesina and Gatti (1995). The chapter then concludes with some empirical observations which reinforce the theoretical argument that central bank independence is not 'neutral' with respect to the use of fiscal policy or the political process.

14.2 The Rogoff model with fiscal policy

14.2.1 The model

Consider an economy described by the following Lucas supply function, in which, by tradition, the level of output (defined as a deviation from its natural or full capacity level) is determined by the difference between actual and expected inflation, a random supply shock ε (with zero mean and finite variance σ_ε^2), and by the effect of distortionary taxes on output τ (Debelle and Fischer, 1994):

$$y_t = \pi_t - \pi_t^e - \tau_t + \varepsilon_t \tag{14.1}[2]$$

As is standard in this literature, the private sector moves first, signing wage contracts before the shocks have occurred and before the policies of the authorities have been implemented. Only the *expected* policy settings can be known. In the absence of delegation, the government will want to minimize the following loss function expressed in terms of inflation, distortionary taxes and output (Svensson, 1997):[3]

$$\min_{\pi, \tau} = \frac{1}{2}\left[(\pi_t)^2 + (\tau_t)^2 + \beta(y_t - k)^2\right] \tag{14.2}$$

The last term of (14.2) shows a possible source of expansionary bias in the objective function. The government wants to reach a level of output $k \geq 0$ that could be higher than the natural rate.[4] The parameter β is the relative weight given to the output objective: that is the indication of how 'conservative' the policy authority is, with a higher β showing a higher priority for output stabilization, and therefore a less conservative set of preferences. Finally, τ_t is defined to mean *net* tax revenues throughout – so that $\tau_t < 0$ signifies a fiscal deficit.

14.2.2   Discretionary policies

Substituting (14.1) in (14.2), minimizing the loss function with respect to the two instruments π and τ, and solving the system of first order conditions, one obtains:

$$\pi_t = \frac{\beta}{(1+2\beta)}[\pi_t^e + k - \varepsilon_t], \text{ and} \tag{14.3}$$

$$\tau_t = -\frac{\beta}{(1+2\beta)}[\pi_t^e + k - \varepsilon_t] \tag{14.4}$$

Solving (14.3) and (14.4) for rational expectations and dropping time subscripts, one obtains the following time consistent optimal level of inflation and taxation:

$$\pi = \frac{\beta}{1+\beta}k - \frac{\beta}{1+2\beta}\varepsilon \tag{14.5}$$

$$\tau = -\frac{\beta}{1+\beta}k + \frac{\beta}{1+2\beta}\varepsilon \tag{14.6}$$

and the following expressions for expected inflation and actual output:

$$\pi^e = \frac{\beta}{1+\beta}k \tag{14.7}$$

$$y = \frac{\beta}{1+\beta}k - \frac{1}{1+2\beta}\varepsilon \qquad (14.8)$$

The policy rules (14.5) and (14.6) show that the government will use a combination of both instruments to achieve its output and inflation objective and its desired level of stabilization of the shocks. This formulation introduces the traditional inflationary bias in the conduct of economic policies, as represented by the first term on the right-hand side of the policy rule (14.5).

From (14.5)–(14.8) it now follows that:

$$E(\pi) = \frac{\beta}{1+\beta}k, \qquad (14.10)$$

$$E(y) = \frac{\beta}{1+\beta}k \qquad (14.11)$$

$$Var(\pi) = \left(\frac{\beta}{1+2\beta}\right)^2 \sigma_\varepsilon^2 \qquad (14.12)$$

$$Var(y) = \left(\frac{1}{1+2\beta}\right)^2 \sigma_\varepsilon^2 \qquad (14.13)$$

$$Var(\tau) = \left(\frac{\beta}{1+2\beta}\right)^2 \sigma_\varepsilon^2 \qquad (14.14)$$

It is obvious that discretionary policy-making produces an inefficient outcome, in the sense that it does not reach zero inflation on average as the government would have liked. On the other hand, it does not reach the government's preferred level of k for output either. There is therefore a trade-off: we overshoot the inflation target, but undershoot the output target. And the degree of over- and undershooting is strictly related to the government's preferences for output stabilization. The larger is β, the more the government overshoots inflation and the less it undershoots the output target. Similarly a trade-off appears in variances. The larger is β, the higher the variance of inflation, and the lower the variance of output. Nevertheless, the fact that the policy authority cannot commit to zero inflation exactly reproduces the standard inflationary bias of economic policy adjustment highlighted by Kyndland and Prescott (1977), and formalized in a similar model by Barro and Gordon (1983).

14.2.3 Delegation of monetary policy

Following now the Rogoff argument, suppose that the government decides to delegate the conduct of monetary policy to an institution with more conservative preferences (with a preference parameter $\gamma < \beta$) than the society as a whole. However the government retains control of the fiscal instrument. Under this assumption the central bank will want to minimize the following loss function[5]

$$\min_{\pi} L = \frac{1}{2}\left[(\pi_t)^2 + (\tau_t)^2 + \gamma(y_t - k)^2\right] \text{ where } \gamma < \beta \tag{14.15}$$

while the government wishes to minimize the loss function (14.2), now using the only instrument remaining in its hands (i.e. taxation).

$$\min_{t} L = \frac{1}{2}[(\pi_t)^2 + (\tau_t)^2 + \beta(y_t - k)^2] \tag{14.16}$$

With this institutional specialization we obtain the following policy rules:

$$\pi = \frac{\gamma}{1+\beta}k - \frac{\gamma}{1+\beta+\gamma}\varepsilon \tag{14.17}$$

$$\pi = -\frac{\beta}{1+\beta}k + \frac{\beta}{1+\beta+\gamma}\varepsilon \tag{14.18}$$

and the following expected inflation and actual output:

$$\pi^e = \frac{\gamma}{1+\beta}k \tag{14.19}$$

$$y = \frac{\beta}{1+\beta}k - \frac{1}{1+\beta+\gamma}\varepsilon \tag{14.20}$$

Hence, from (14.17)–(14.20) it follows that:

$$E(\pi) = \frac{\gamma}{1+\beta}k \tag{14.21}$$

$$E(y) = \frac{\beta}{1+\beta}k \tag{14.22}$$

$$Var(\pi) = \left(\frac{\gamma}{1+\beta+\gamma}\right)^2 \sigma_\varepsilon^2 \tag{14.23}$$

$$Var(y) = \left(\frac{1}{1+\beta+\gamma}\right)^2 \sigma_\varepsilon^2 \tag{14.24}$$

$$Var(\tau) = \left(\frac{\beta}{1+\beta+\gamma}\right)^2 \sigma_\varepsilon^2 \tag{14.25}$$

As in the standard Rogoff analysis, delegation of monetary policy to a more conservative agent has produced a lower inflationary bias and lower inflation variability, but at the expense of no improvements in average output and a *higher* level of output variability.[6] Moreover the introduction of fiscal policy has changed the outcomes from those in the traditional literature. If $\beta \neq 0$, the government will always use taxation more vigorously to reduce the effect of shocks on output. Central bank independence should therefore be expected to induce a more active use of fiscal policy, a feature already noted in some of the literature (Hughes Hallett and Vines, 1993; Nordhaus, 1994).

14.3 Political uncertainty revisited

The previous analysis has simply incorporated fiscal policy into the Rogoff model, in a way not dissimilar from previous contributions. But as such it cannot explain the fact that the degree of central bank independence and the degree of output variability has not been correlated in the OECD countries – even if it does show that fiscal policy would have been used more vigorously with an independent central bank. To be more precise, our delegation model shows that output variability should be *higher* than otherwise with an independent central bank, whereas the empirical literature has shown that output variability appears to be unaffected by the degree of central bank independence. Hence fiscal policy must have been used more vigorously than our optimizing model implies it should have been. In other words, given that this lack of correlation is an important part of the evidence, our delegation models are going to have to explain why fiscal policy is actually used more vigorously than the optimal policies say that it should have been.

14.3.1 Electoral choices with an independent central bank

The answer to our question is going to lie in the political responses which emerge with an independently run monetary policy. To show this, we have to introduce fiscal policy into the Alesina and Gatti model of political polarization. This is a new departure in the literature. In the Alesina–Gatti model, two parties with different political preferences (expressed in terms of parameter β in (14.2)) coordinate before the election to the extent of selecting an independent central banker with preferences more conservative than those of the median voter. But in doing so they will have changed the nature of the choice faced by the electorate: the electorate will now have to choose the optimal fiscal policy they want, *given* the policy stance of the central bank. Formally, the two parties (D and R) have different and polarized preferences such that:

$$\min_{\tau} L_D = \frac{1}{2}\left[(\pi_t)^2 + (\tau_t)^2 + \beta^D(y_t - k)^2 \right] \tag{14.26}$$

$$\min_{\tau} L_R = \frac{1}{2}\left[(\pi_t)^2 + (\tau_t)^2 + \beta^R(y_t - k)^2\right] \tag{14.27}$$

with $\beta^D > \beta^R$. In the absence of central bank independence, and if the population either has preferences uniformly distributed between these two poles, or at least distributed symmetrically around them, the election will be decided randomly by the median voter with preferences equidistant from the two poles, i.e.:

$$\lambda = \frac{\beta^D + \beta^R}{2} \tag{14.28)[7]}$$

But suppose that before the election the two parties agree to appoint an independent central banker with preference parameter γ such that $\beta^R < \gamma < \lambda < \beta^D$.[8] What happens then, *after* the two parties have agreed to appoint this independent central banker? The elections still take place, but the choices faced by the median voter will have been changed by his loss of influence over monetary policy. The median voter now needs to choose β, and hence a government, to minimize the following expected loss function

$$\min_{\beta} L_{MV} = \frac{1}{2}\left[(\pi_t)^2 + (\tau_t)^2 + \lambda(y_t - k)^2\right] \tag{14.29}$$

subject to equations (14.17), (14.18) and (14.20). Inserting those expressions and taking expectations, we have

$$\min_{\beta} L_{MV} = \frac{1}{2}\left(\frac{\gamma^2 + \beta^2 + \lambda}{(1+\beta)^2}k^2 + \frac{\gamma^2 + \beta^2 + \lambda}{(1+\beta+\gamma)^2}\sigma_\varepsilon^2\right) \tag{14.30}$$

The voter therefore has to decide which one of the two alternatives gives the minimum losses as described by equation (14.30). Formally:

$$\min L_{MV} = \min \left[\begin{array}{c} \left(\dfrac{\gamma^2 + (\beta^R)^2 + \lambda}{(1+\beta^R)^2}k^2 + \dfrac{\gamma^2 + (\beta^R)^2 + \lambda}{1+\beta^R+\gamma)^2}\sigma_\varepsilon^2\right), \\[2ex] \left(\dfrac{\gamma^e + (\beta^D)^2 + \lambda}{(1+\beta^D)^2}k^2 + \dfrac{\gamma^2 + (\beta^D)^2 + \lambda}{(1+\beta^D+\gamma)^2}\sigma_\varepsilon^2\right) \end{array}\right] \tag{14.31}$$

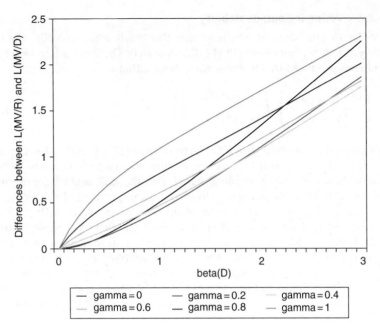

Figure 14.1 Numerical analysis of condition (14.32)

In particular the median voter would choose party D if and only if

$$
L_{MV/R} - L_{MV/D} = \left\{ \begin{aligned} & \left(\frac{\gamma^2 + (\beta^R)^2 + \lambda}{(1+\beta^R)^2} k^2 + \frac{\gamma^2 + (\beta^R)^2 + \lambda}{1+\beta^R + \gamma)^2} \sigma_\varepsilon^2 \right) \\ & - \left(\frac{\gamma^e + (\beta^D)^2 + \lambda}{(1+\beta^D)^2} k^2 + \frac{\gamma^2 + (\beta^D)^2 + \lambda}{(1+\beta^D+\gamma)^2} \sigma_\varepsilon^2 \right) \end{aligned} \right\} \tag{14.32}
$$

is positive. That is the choice which will determine the outcome of the election. We now consider how (14.32) varies when evaluated at the parameter values chosen by Alesina and Gatti: i.e. where, $k = 1$, $\sigma_\varepsilon^2 = 1$, $\beta^R = 0$ and where λ is defined by (14.28). Figure 14.1 shows the value of this function for different values of β^D and different degrees of central bank conservativeness γ.

Since $\beta^R = 0$, the values of β^D correspond to the degree of differences in the party preferences. Evidently, as the value of β^D (actually $\beta^D - \beta^R$) increases, electing the R party becomes steadily more costly for the median voter with preferences defined by (14.29) and (14.28).

14.3.2   Voting for output stability

In order to gain some insight into how this result arises, consider the two different policy components in (14.32) separately. On the one hand we have the losses produced by the exogenous shocks, that is:

$$\left(\frac{\gamma^2 + (\beta^R) + \lambda}{(1 + \beta^R + \gamma)^2}\sigma_\varepsilon^2\right) - \left(\frac{\gamma^2 + (\beta^D)^2 + \lambda}{(1 + \beta^D + \gamma)^2}\sigma_\varepsilon^2\right) > 0 \tag{14.33}$$

This inequality obviously holds for large values of β^D when β^R is fixed, whatever the values of γ and λ, since the median voter's preferences must be a positive function – say a simple weighted average of β^D and β^R, for example – of the preferences of each group in the political spectrum.[9] In that case the term on the left of (14.33) will be of $0(\beta^D)$ as β^D increases with β^R fixed, while the second term will be $0(1)$. As a result, the first term tends to infinity and the second to unity, as β^D increases without limit (γ, β^R remaining constant). Hence (14.33) holds for larger values of β^D at least; and the further the two parties are apart in terms of their preferences, the more the median voter will lose out in terms of stability if she/he chooses party R over party D. This is shown numerically in Figure 14.2, using the same parameter values as in Figure 14.1.

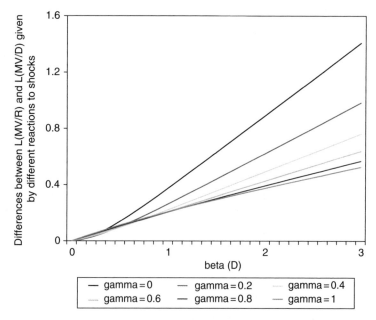

Figure 14.2   Numerical analysis of condition (14.33)

However, since we will need to know when (14.33) actually applies (and when it does not), we can add some additional but unexceptionable restrictions to show that (14.33) will continue to hold for all (rather than just some) values of $\beta^D > \beta^R$. Since $\beta^D - \beta^R$ by definition, we lose nothing in generality if we normalize β^R at zero, and take β^D to denote the degree to which β^D lies above β^R. Second, since the central bank is independent, we may apply Alesina and Grilli's result that, if making the bank independent is to guarantee a lower (at least not higher) rate of inflation on average, then the bank has to be at least as conservative as the median voter[10]: $\gamma \le \lambda$. Finally suppose the electorate's preferences are distributed symmetrically about β^R and β^D so that $\lambda = \frac{1}{2}(\beta^R + \beta^D)$, although the exact form and characteristics of that preference distribution remain unrestricted. In that case, it is easy to check that (14.33) now holds for all values of $\beta^D > \beta^R$.

14.3.3 Voting for higher/undistorted levels of output

On the other side of the comparison, the median voter will also benefit in terms of output levels if party D is chosen when:

$$\left(\frac{\gamma^2 + (\beta^R)^2 + \lambda}{(1+\beta^R)^2} k^2 \right) - \left(\frac{\gamma^2 + (\beta^D)^2 + \lambda}{(1+\beta^D)^2} k^2 \right) > 0 \tag{14.34}$$

But that inequality will hold, at least for larger values of β^D, for exactly the same reasons as (14.33) did: the first term is $0(\beta^D)$, but the second is $0(1)$, when β^R is fixed. Moreover, the terms in (14.34) are larger than the corresponding terms in (14.33) unless $k^2 < \sigma_\varepsilon^2$ by a significant margin, because $\gamma > 0$. That means (14.34) is more likely to hold for a wider range of β^D values than (14.33) is. In that case the more progressive fiscal authority – the one characterized by β^D rather than β^R – will be the one which arrives closer to the target output level k. In fact it is easy to check that this inequality also holds for *all* values of $\beta^D \ge \beta^R$, when the preferences are symmetric around β^D and β^R and when β^R is normalized at zero.[11] This is shown in Figure 14.3.

14.3.4 A summary: the impact of politics on economic policy

The upshot of these results is that creating an independent central bank directed at inflation control in a world of elected governments will produce a bias towards more left-wing governments – that is, governments which are more fiscally active and dedicated towards output stabilization. This was shown in inequalities (14.33) and (14.34) under certain restrictions on the distribution of the population's preferences; and also by (14.32) where it is possible for party D's greater success in providing higher levels of output to outweigh a smaller loss in output stability when (14.33) does not hold. That in turn implies a greater specialization in policy-making – if not an outright policy assignment – in which the central bank concentrates more on inflation

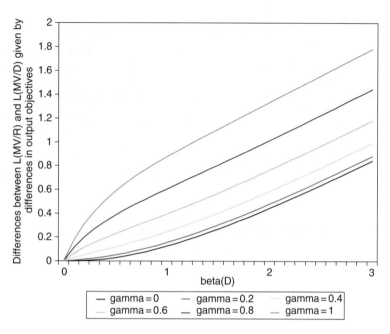

Figure 14.3   Numerical analysis of condition (14.34)

control, and governments more on output stabilization. This allows a more
targeted use of policy: with monetary policy taken care of by the central
bank, the electorate will demand more from fiscal policy for output stabilization purposes. And fiscal policy can provide that stabilization since it
does not have to worry about inflation so much. Conversely, monetary policy, freed of the need to stabilize output, can focus on inflation control. The
point here is that this is an *endogenous* development. And it will produce a
better set of outcomes for inflation (lower and more stable) and incomes
(higher and more stable)[12] – even if fiscal policy requires larger and more
variable deficits – compared to strict one-to-one assignments; and compared
to allowing each party to choose their fiscal and monetary policies; or compared to restricting the use of the fiscal (or monetary) instruments. Hence
the political process will create its own 'coordination' provided that it is not
restricted in terms of voting, preferences, or imposed assignments, or in
terms of using its policy instruments.

This is our main result. The fact that the political parties have chosen an
independent central bank has important consequences for the set of incentives faced by the electorate. Hence, political choices do not simply disappear
as they do in Alesina and Gatti. Instead they get transferred from monetary
policy to fiscal policy. What conditions (14.32), or (14.33) and (14.34), then
tell us is that the median voter, confronted with the fact that one part of

policy has been tied to the preferences of the central bank, moves 'to the left' as far as fiscal policy is concerned. That means the central bank is *not* neutral in terms of outcomes. In fact, such a regime will definitely produce lower inflation. But the effect on output will depend on how much the fiscal authority will be able to use its instrument, and on how much the electorate will ask them to do so.

14.4 Some empirical observations

The analysis in the previous section suggests that independence of the central bank should be associated with a change in the use of the fiscal policy. While central bank Independence would produce an increase in output variability, such variability may not actually materialize because fiscal policy is used more actively and because the electorate favours those who are willing to use it more. Thus, if our hypothesis is correct, a positive correlation between central bank independence and variance of deficits should be present. Previous empirical analyses have not looked at this issue. Instead they have looked at the relationship between the independence of the central bank and the *level* of those deficits (Parkin, 1987; Masciandaro and Tabellini, 1988; Grilli, Masciandaro and Tabellini, 1991, among others).

In order to examine that hypothesis, we have selected two indices of central bank independence and we looked at their correlation with the variance of primary deficits of 11 European countries, the US, Japan and Canada. The indices used are those of Alesina and Summers (1993) and the one constructed by Grilli, Masciandaro and Tabellini (1991).[13] They are both reported in Table 14.1.

Table 14.1 Two indices of central bank independence

	Alesina and Summers (1993)	Grilli, Masciandaro and Tabellini (1991): GMT
Austria	2	9
Belgium	2	7
Denmark	2.5	8
Finland	2	8
France	2	7
Germany	4	13
Italy	1.75	5
Netherlands	2.5	10
Spain	1.5	5
Sweden	2	5
United Kingdom	2	6
USA	3	12
Canada	2	11
Japan	3	6

We also use two measures of fiscal activism, one being the variance of primary deficit adjusted for cyclical components, and the second the variance of the overall primary deficit. In both cases we considered the period 1973–91, in order to avoid the aftermath of German unification which would have undoubtedly biased our results toward a positive correlation. Figures 14.4(a) and 14.4(b) show the correlation between the Alesina and Summers index and the two measures of variance of fiscal policy. A weak positive correlation is clearly evident, and more so when analysing the cyclical adjusted primary deficits.

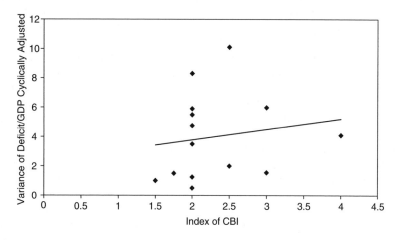

Figure 14.4(a)   Variance of cyclically adjusted deficit/GDP

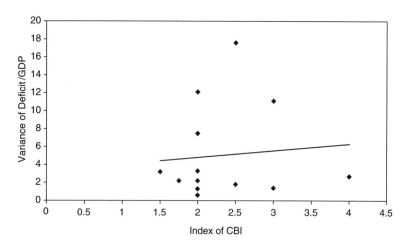

Figure 14.4(b)   Variance of deficit/GDP

These results suggest that the data may indeed reflect our hypothesis. Nevertheless figures 14.4(a) and 14.4(b) also show the results are highly sensitive to the measure of central bank independence in use. When using the GMT index the positive correlation disappears (see Figure 14.5a and b).

The fact that these two indexes, although similar in principle, give opposite results shows not only the very tentative nature of this kind of analysis, but also the low level of homogeneity among the indices themselves. Indeed, as Eijffinger and de Hahn (1995) point out, the correlations between the different possible indexes of CBI are very low. This is because each group of authors

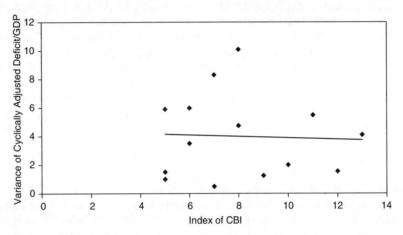

Figure 14.5(a) Variance of cyclically adjusted deficit/GDP (GMT Index of CBI)

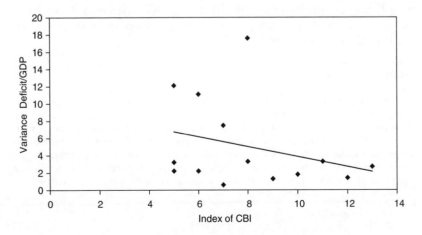

Figure 14.5(b) Variance of deficit/GDP (GMT Index of CBI)

puts weight on different concepts of independence (legal, political or economic); and also interprets the characteristics of each institution quite differently. On the other hand the factors influencing the variability of deficits are so many and diverse, that even finding a small positive correlation as indicated by the theory is a significant event in itself.

14.5   Conclusion

In conclusion, this chapter has shown that introducing fiscal policy into the traditional model of monetary policy delegation can change both the positive and the normative implications of the theory. From the positive point of view, the analysis shows that central bank independence produces a more extensive use of the fiscal instrument; and at the same time it changes, but does not resolve, the nature of the policy conflicts affecting the private sector.

Far from being neutral, the appointment of an independent central bank reduces the importance of inflation as a policy objective among governments and favours those political parties more willing to use the fiscal instrument to achieve other objectives of economic policy. Therefore central bank independence is not the instrument to solve any possible conflict between preferences: any differences over the preferred use of monetary policy are simply transformed into differences over how best to use fiscal policy. The point we make here is that the median voter, assured now about inflation control, would naturally prefer a more active fiscal policy.

The consequences of this institutional change are a more efficient assignment of instrument to targets, and a more polarized institutional setting in which the two policy authorities follow diverging policy objectives. The possibility of conflict between the authorities, as analysed by Nordhaus (1994), Blake and Weale (1998) and Demertzis *et al.* (1999b), therefore makes a real case for institutional safeguards; *and* for a stronger coordination between fiscal and monetary policies – if not between the different components of fiscal policy as well.

Appendix 14.A.1

In this appendix we show that the theoretical result that having a 'conservative' central bank shifts electoral outcomes towards the party with more expansionary preferences, is independent of the distribution of voters' preferences. The simplest way to verify this assertion is to perform the minimization of equation (14.30) in the main text with respect to the parameter β. That is to say each voter will want to exercise his or her vote in order to select the optimal value of β (the preference parameter for the government), given the preferences of the central bank, γ, and given his/her own preferences, λ:

$$\min_{\beta} L_V = \frac{1}{2} \left(\frac{\gamma^2 + \beta^2 + \lambda}{(1+\beta)^2} k^2 + \frac{\gamma^2 + \beta^2 + \lambda}{(1+\beta+\gamma)^2} \sigma_\varepsilon^2 \right) \qquad (14.A.1)$$

The first order condition for this problem is:

$$\frac{\partial L_V}{\partial \beta} = \left(\frac{\gamma^2 + \beta + \lambda}{(1+\beta)^3} k^2 + \frac{\gamma^2 + \beta(1+\gamma) + \lambda}{(1+\beta+\gamma)^3} \sigma_\varepsilon^2 \right)$$ (14.A.2)

Solving (14.A.2) will give an optimal value of β as a function of the conservativeness of the central bank and the preference parameter of each individual voter.

$$\beta^* = \beta(\gamma, \lambda)$$

First of all, consider the case in which there is no macroeconomic uncertainty. It easy to show that, with $\sigma^2 = 0$, the optimal level of β is:

$$\beta^* = \lambda + \gamma^2$$ (14.A.3)

Because $\gamma > 0$, (14.A.3) means that, as far as the achievement of output target is concerned, the optimal value of β for getting elected moves to the left once an independent (but not necessarily conservative) central bank is appointed.

But in the case in which there is no output objective (i.e. when $k = 0$), the solution to (14.A.2) will be equal to:

$$\beta^* = \frac{\lambda + \gamma^2}{1 + \gamma}$$ (14.A.4)

which shows the same leftward shift in the optimal choice of β if $\gamma \leq \lambda$ (i.e. when the central bank is dedicated to inflation control). Of course the actual choice of β will be some combination of these two solutions, and has to be obtained by solving the first order conditions (14.A.2). A closed form solution of this cubic equation is not possible, but we can approximate that optimal value of β by linear interpolation to yield:

$$\beta^* = w\beta_1 + (1-w)\beta_2$$ (14.A.5)

where

$$w = \frac{\sigma^2}{k^2(1+\gamma)^3 + \sigma^2}, \quad \beta_1 = \frac{\gamma^2 + \lambda}{\gamma + 1} \quad \text{and} \quad \beta_2 = \gamma^2 + \lambda$$ (14.A.5)

and we have used the fact that $1 + \beta_2 + \gamma = (1+\gamma)(1+\beta_1)$

Notice that $\beta^* > \gamma$ holds so long as $\gamma \leq \lambda$ or something a bit larger.[14] However the latter inequality is guaranteed in the appointment of an independent central bank designed to control inflation (Alesina and Grilli, 1992). Hence condition (14.A.5) shows that the median voter will always choose fiscal authorities whose preferences lie 'to the left' of the central bank. This means that the introduction of an independent central bank into a world of democratically elected governments will automatically produce and sustain relatively liberal governments, which attribute a high weight to output stabilization. This increases the likelihood of fiscal–monetary conflicts that lead to less effective policies.

Notes

1. The findings of Alesina and Summers are reinforced by the analysis of Cukierman *et al.* (1993), which extended the data set to include non-industrial countries, and does not find any correlation between central bank independence and output growth or output variability. However Crosby (1998) has argued that central bank independence is the product of low output variability, and not vice versa. As in Posen (1993), the causal relation is not from the institutions to the economy but from the economy to the institutions. It is the second branch of this interaction that we want to expose and analyse here.

2. Alternatively this relationship may be regarded as a supply side model with a new-Keynesian forward looking Philips curve for price settings (Roberts, 1995) – and may incorporate imperfectly competitive firms facing staggered wage–price contracts, and/or quadratic adjustment costs in the sense of Rotemberg and Woodford (1998). Further details on the microfoundations – including those which underlie the principal/agent ('multiheaded government') framework used here – will be found in Demertzis *et al.* (1999b).

3. Neither the supply function (14.1), nor the objective function (14.2), are a complete representation of the true structure and the true choices faced by the economic actors. However the decision to choose this framework has many advantages: it is the choice made in most of the literature (Alesina and Tabellini, 1987; Debelle and Fischer, 1994; Beetsma and Bovenberg, 1995, to mention just a few) in which a supply function like (14.1) is derived from profit maximization under a Cobb–Douglas technology, with labour as the only variable input and in which τ is equal to distortionary taxes levied on the revenues of firms (all in logs). Introducing taxes in this way allows us to compare our results with those of Rogoff, of Alesina and Gatti, and all the literature on central bank independence and accountability. Similarly, the objective function (14.2) assumes that the optimal value for both net taxes and inflation is zero, while there is a positive target for output, on the grounds that there are distortions in the economy (the result of either distortionary taxation made necessary by the need for social expenditures, or by the distortionary effects of wage bargaining when there is imperfect competition in the product or factor markets). In these cases government would try to counteract the distortions in output by means of its policy instruments. However, our model does not include any budget constraint. This is because the government's objective function, (14.2), contains the fiscal balance τ_t as an argument. That means the use of budgetary policies is penalized, and standard control theory implies a fiscal policy feedback rule which satisfies the necessary conditions for long-term solvency and the 'cash in advance' constraints (Canzoneri *et al.*, 2001).

   Since governments may always borrow on world markets, this specification endogenizes net fiscal expenditures and restricts all budgetary policies to be sustainable and financiable. The budget constraint therefore does not bind, and cannot affect our results, since all solutions are sustainable and financiable. The objective functions however are quadratic approximations to, and aggregates of, the individual welfare or utility functions where the aggregation is performed through the electoral process described in the next section.

4. Persson and Tabellini (1990) give a detailed discussion of this assumption, which drives all the literature on time inconsistency of optimal monetary policy since the contribution of Kydland and Prescott (1977).

5. The level of taxes appears in the objective function of the independent central bank in order to maintain a symmetric structure in the problem. But it does not affect the solution of the Nash game in any way.
6. For similar variability of shocks, (14.13) is clearly lower than (14.24) – given the assumption that $\gamma < \beta$.
7. The assumption of symmetrically distributed preferences is not essential for our argument that the independence of the central bank, and different institutional designs more generally, simply relocates economic and political distortions – but does not solve them. In fact, this result is independent of the particular probability distribution chosen, as we show in the appendix.
8 This is not an essential assumption. In the appendix we show that the same results, and the same inequality restrictions on γ, λ and the value of β (i.e. that $\gamma < \lambda < \beta$), will emerge from an elected government whatever the distribution of the preferences, and whatever the values of β^D and β^R, when the central bank's primary focus is inflation control.
9. Since, by definition, the preferences of the median voter must lie somewhere in between the preferences of the various political groupings, λ must show some positive (at least non-negative) responsiveness to shifts in the preferences of those groups; and a strictly positive responsiveness to shifts in the preferences of at least one of them.
10. Alesina and Grilli (1992).
11. Since this result does not require the 'restriction' $\gamma \leq \lambda$, it must hold more frequently than the corresponding result does for (14.33).
12. These results follow since a preference for the D party in (14.32), or (14.33) and (14.34), implies

$$E\pi = \frac{\gamma}{1+\beta^D} k, \quad V(\pi) = \left(\frac{\gamma}{1+\beta^D+\gamma}\right)^2 \sigma_\varepsilon^2$$

$$Ey = \frac{\beta^D}{1+\beta^D} k, \quad V(y) = \left(\frac{1}{1+\beta^D+\gamma}\right)^2 \sigma_\varepsilon^2$$

but

$$E\tau = \frac{-\beta^D}{1+\beta^D} k, \quad V(\tau) = \left(\frac{\beta^D}{1+\beta^D+\gamma}\right)^2 \sigma_\varepsilon^2$$

where $\beta^D > \beta^R$ in the two party case; or where $\beta^D > \beta$ in the dependent central bank and an 'average' government case; or where $\beta^D > \lambda$ and λ is the 'average' of the electorate's preference distribution.
13. There is a great variety of indexes based on very different criteria. The one constructed by Grilli, Masciandaro and Tabellini is based on the level of political and economic independence of each central bank. The one used by Alesina and Summers is an average of the GMT index, and the Bade and Parkin (1982) index is based only on political independence. A review of these and many other contributions can be found in Eijffinger and de Haan (1995).
14. Note that $\beta^* > \gamma$ remains true even if the central bank has the *same* preferences as the population at large ($\gamma = \lambda$). In fact $\gamma \leq \lambda$ is a particularly weak sufficient

condition for showing $\beta^* > \gamma$. The latter will continue to hold so long as $\gamma \leq 1$, or $\gamma^2(1 - w) \geq 1$, or $\lambda > [(1 - \gamma^2(1 - w))/(1 + \gamma(1 + w))]\gamma$ instead. The last two conditions allow γ to be considerably larger than λ and yet still have $\beta^* > \gamma$ – for example where k is large relative to σ_e, or where w is small because γ is large. We should therefore expect $\beta^* > \gamma$ in most cases. Finally (14.A.5) has a *unique* minimum between β_1 and β_2, since its second derivative remains positive throughout the interval $(0, 1/2(3\beta_2 + 1))$.

References

Agell, J., L. Calmfors and G. Jonsson (1996) 'Fiscal Policy when Monetary Policy is Tied to the Mast', *European Economic Review*, 40: 1413–40.

Agell, J., T. Lindh, and H. Ohlsson (1997) 'Growth and the Public Sector: A Critical Review Essay', *European Journal of Political Economy*, 13: 33–52.

Ahmed, S. (1996) 'Balanced-Budget Rules and Public Deficits: Evidence from the US States. A Comment', *Carnegie-Rochester Conference Series on Public Policy*, 45: 77–87.

Alesina, A. (1987) 'Macroeconomic Policy in a Two Party System as a Repeated Game', *Quarterly Journal of Economics*, 102: 651–78.

Alesina, A. and S. Ardagna (1998) 'Tales of Fiscal Contractions', *Economic Policy*, 27: 489–545.

Alesina, A. and T. Bayoumi (1996) 'The Costs and Benefits of Fiscal Rules: Evidence from US States', *NBER Working Paper*, No. 5614.

Alesina, A. and R. Gatti (1995) 'Independent Central Banks: Low Inflation at No Cost', *American Economic Review*, 85: 196–200.

Alesina, A. and V. Grilli (1992) 'The European Central Bank: Reshaping Monetary Politics in Europe', in M. Canzoneri, V. Grilli and Paul Masson (eds), *The Creation of a Central Bank*' (Cambridge and New York: Cambridge University Press).

Alesina, A. and R. Perotti (1995a) 'The Political Economy of Budget Deficits', *IMF Staff Papers*, 42: 1–31.

Alesina, A. and R. Perotti (1995b) 'Fiscal Expansions and Fiscal Adjustments in OECD Countries', *Economic Policy*, 21: 205–48.

Alesina, A. and R. Perotti (1995c) 'Fiscal Expansions and Adjustments in OECD Countries', *Economic Policy*, 21: 1–42.

Alesina, A. and R. Perotti (1996a) 'Fiscal Discipline and the Budget Process', *American Economic Review*, 86: 401–7.

Alesina, A. and R. Perotti (1996b) 'Budget Deficits and Budget Institutions', *NBER Working Paper*, No. 5556.

Alesina, A. and R. Perotti (1997) 'Fiscal Adjustments in OECD Countries: Composition and Macroeconomic Effects', *IMF Staff Papers*, 44: 210–48.

Alesina, A. and H. Rosenthal (1995) *Partisan Politics, Divided Government, and the Economy* (Cambridge, UK: Cambridge University Press).

Alesina, A. and L. Summers (1993) 'Central Bank Independence and Macroeconomic Performance: Some Comparative Evidence', *Journal of Money, Credit and Banking*, 25: 151–62.

Alesina, A. and G. Tabellini (1987) 'Rules and Discretion with Noncoordinated Monetary and Fiscal Policies', *Economic Inquiry*, 25: 619–30.

Alesina, A., R. Perotti and J. Tavares (1998) 'The Political Economy of Fiscal Adjustment', *Brooking Papers on Economic Activity*, 1: 197–249.

Alesina, A., A. Prati and G. Tabellini (1990) 'Public Confidence and Debt Management: A Model and Case Study of Italy', in M. Draghi (ed.), *Public Debt Management: Theory and History* (Cambridge University Press).

Allsopp, C. and D. Vines (1996) 'Fiscal Policy and EMU', *National Institute Economic Review*, 158: 91–107.

Allsopp, C. and D. Vines (1998) 'Macroeconomic Policy after EMU: The Assessment', *Oxford Review of Economic Policy*, 14: 1–23.

Andersen, T. (1997) 'Fiscal policy in the EMU and Outside', *Swedish Economic Policy Review*, vol. 4. no. 1 (Spring).

Angeloni, I. and L. Dedola (1999) 'From the ERM to the Euro: New Evidence on Economic and Policy Convergence among EU Countries', *European Central Bank Working Paper*, No. 4.

Arreaza, A., B. Sørensen and O. Yosha (1999) 'Consumption Smoothing through Fiscal Policy in OECD and EU Countries', in J. Poterba and J. von Hagen (eds), *Fiscal Institutions and Fiscal Performance* (Chicago: University of Chicago Press).

Artis, M. J. and M. Buti (2000a) ' "Close to Balance or In Surplus" – A Policy Maker's Guide to the Implementation of the Stability and Growth Pact', *Journal of Common Market Studies*, 38, 563–91.

Artis, M. J. and M. Buti (2000b) 'Setting Medium Term Fiscal Targets in EMU', Public Finance Management, 5: 34–57.

Artis, M. J. and B. Winkler (1997) 'The Stability Pact: Safeguarding the Credibility of the European Central Bank', *CEPR Discussion Paper*, No. 1688.

Artis, M. J. and W. Zhang (1995) 'Business Cycles, Exchange Rate Regimes and the ERM: Is There a European Business Cycle', European University Institute, Robert Schuman Centre, RSC No. 96/55.

Artis, M. J. and W. Zhang (1997) 'International Business Cycles and the ERM: Is There a European Business Cycle?', *International Journal of Finance and Economics*, 2: 1–16.

Artis, M. J. and W. Zhang (1998) 'The Linkage of Interest Rates within the EMS', *Weltwirtschaftliche Archiv*, 132: 117–32.

Aschauer, D. A. (1985) 'Fiscal Policy and Aggregate Demand', *American Economic Review*, 75: 117–27.

Aschauer, D. A. (1989) 'Is Public Expenditure Productive?', *Journal of Monetary Economics*, 23: 177–200.

Asdrubali, A., B.E. Sorensen and O. Yosha (1996) 'Channels of Interstate Risk Sharing: United States 1963–1990', *Quarterly Journal of Economics*, 111: 1081–110.

Auerbach, A. J. and D. Feenberg (2000) 'The Significance of Federal Taxes as Automatic Stabilizers', *NBER Working Paper*, No. 7662.

Bade, R. and M. Parkin (1982) 'Central Bank Laws and Monetary Policy', University of Western Ontario, Canada.

Bandt, O. De and F. P. Mongelli (2000) 'The Convergence of Fiscal Policy in the Euro Area', European Central Bank, *Working Paper*, No. 20.

Barro, R. J. (1974) 'Are Government Bonds Net Wealth?', *Journal of Political Economy*, 82: 1095–117.

Barro, R. J. (1979) 'On the Determination of Public Debt', *Journal of Political Economy*, 87: 940–71.

Barro, R. J. (1989) 'The Ricardian Approach to Budget Deficits', *Journal of Economic Perspectives*, 3: 37–54.

Barro, R. J. (1990) 'Government Spending in a Simple Model of Endogenous Growth', *Journal of Political Economy*, 98: 103–17.

Barro, R. J. (1991) 'Economic Growth in a Cross-Section of Countries', *Quarterly Journal of Economics*, 61: 407–43.

Barro, R. J. and D. Gordon (1983) 'Rules, Discretion and Reputation in a Model of Monetary Policy', *Journal of Monetary Economics*, 12: 101–21.

Barro, R. J. and X. Sala-i-Martin (1992) 'Public Finance in Models of Economic Growth', *Review of Economic Studies*, 59: 645–61.

Barro, R. J. and X. Sala-i-Martin (1995) *Economic Growth* (New York: McGraw-Hill).

Barry, F. and M. B. Devereux (1995) 'The Expansionary Fiscal Contraction Hypothesis: A Neo-Keynesian Analysis', *Oxford Economic Papers*, 47: 249–64.

Bartolini, L., A. Razin and S. Symansky (1995) 'G7 Fiscal Restructuring in the 1990s: Macroeconomic Effects', *Economic Policy*, 20: 109–46.

Bassanini, A., J. H. Rasmussen and S. Scarpetta (1999) 'The Economic Effects of Employment-Conditional Income Support Schemes for the Low-Paid: An Illustration from a CGE Model Applied to Four OECD Countries', *OECD Economics Department Working Paper*, No. 224 (Paris: OECD).

Baxter, M. and R. King (1993) 'Fiscal Policy in General Equilibrium', *American Economic Review*, 83: 315–34.

Bayar, A. H. (2001) 'Entry and Exit Dynamics of "Excessive Deficits" in the European Union', *Public Finance and Management*, 1: 92–112.

Bayar, A. H., A. Dramais, W. Roeger and J. in 't Veld (1997) 'Macroeconomic Effects of Fiscal Restructuring in Europe', in J.-Y.Hairault, P.-Y. Hénin, and F. Portier (eds), *Business Cycles and Macroeconomic Stability* (Boston: Kluwer Academic Publishers).

Bayoumi, T. and B. Eichengreen (1995) 'Restraining Yourself: The Implications of Fiscal Rules for Economic Stabilization', *IMF Staff Papers*, 42: 32–48.

Bayoumi, T. and B. Eichengreen (1997) 'Optimum Currency Areas and Exchange Rate Volatility: Theory and Evidence Compared', in B. J. Cohen (ed.), *International Trade and Finance: New Frontiers for Research. Essays in Honor of Peter B. Kenen* (Cambridge: Cambridge University Press).

Beetsma, R. (2001) 'Does EMU Need a Stability Pact?', in A. Brunila, M. Buti and D. Franco (eds), *The Stability and Growth Pact – The Architecture of Fiscal Policy in EMU* (Basingstoke: Palgrave).

Beetsma, R. and L. Bovenberg (1995) 'Designing Fiscal and Monetary Institutions for a European Monetary Union', *CEPR Discussion Paper*, No.1303, CEPR, London.

Beetsma, R. and H. Uhlig (1999) 'An Analysis of the Stability and Growth Pact', *Economic Journal*, 109: 546–71.

Bennett, H. and Loayza, N. (2000) 'Policy Biases when the Monetary and Fiscal Authorities Have Different Objectives', *Central Bank of Chile Working Paper*, No. 66.

Bernheim, B. D. (1987) 'Ricardian Equivalence: An Evaluation of Theory and Evidence', *NBER Working Paper*, No. 2330.

Bertola, G. and A. Drazen (1993) 'Trigger Points and Budget Cuts: Explaining the Effects of Fiscal Austerity', *American Economic Review*, 83: 11–26.

Besley, T. and A. Case (1995) 'Incumbent Behavior: Vote-Seeking, Tax Setting, and Yardstick Competition', *American Economic Review*, 85: 25–45.

Bini-Smaghi, L. and S. Vori (1992) 'Rating the EC as an Optimal Currency Area: Is It Worse Than the US?', in R. O'Brien (ed.), *Finance and the International Economy*, The AMEX Bank Review Prize Essays: In Memory of Robert Marjolin, Volume 6, pp. 78–104 (Oxford: Oxford University Press).

Bismut, C. J. (1995) 'Trends and Cycles in Government Revenues in France', mimeo.

Blake, A. P. and M. Weale (1998) 'Costs of Separating Budgetary Policy from Control of Inflation: A Neglected Aspect of Central Bank Independence', *NIESR Discussion Paper*, No. 133.

Blanchard, O. J. (1985) 'Debt, Deficits, and Finite Horizons', *Journal of Political Economy*, 93: 223–47.

Blanchard, O. J. (1992) 'Suggestions for a New Set of Fiscal Indicators', *OECD Economics and Statistics Department Working Papers*, No. 79.

Blanchard, O. J. (2000) 'Commentary', Federal Reserve Bank of New York *Economic Policy Review*, 6: 69–74.

Blanchard, O. and R. Perotti (1999) 'An Empirical Characterization of the Dynamic Effects of Changes in Government Spending and Taxes on Output', *NBER Working Paper*, No. 7269.

Blinder, A. S. and R. M. Solow (1973) 'Does Fiscal Policy Matter?', *Journal of Public Economics*, 2: 319–37.

Bohn, H. (1998) 'The Behaviour of U.S. Public Debt and Deficits', *Quarterly Journal of Economics*, 113: 949–63.

Bohn, H. and R. P. Inman (1996) 'Balanced-Budget Rules and Public Deficits: Evidence from the US States', *Carnegie-Rochester Conference Series on Public Policy*, 45: 13–76.

Bordignon, M. (2000) 'Problems of Soft Budget Constraints in Intergovernmental Relationships: The Case of Italy', Centre for European Integration Studies (ZEI) Working Paper.

Bradley, J., K. Whelan and J. Wright (1993) *Stabilization and Growth in the EC Periphery: A Study of the Irish Economy* (Aldershot, Brookfield, Hong Kong and Sydney: Ashgate, Avebury).

Bruneau, C. and O. de Bandt (1999) 'Fiscal Policy in the Transition to Monetary Union: A Structural VAR Model', Banque de France, *Notes d'Etudes et de Recherche*, No. 60.

Brunila, A. (1997) *Fiscal Policy and Private Consumption-Saving Decisions: European Evidence*, Bank of Finland Studies E:8.

Brunila, A. and C. Martinez-Mongay (2001) 'The Challenges for Fiscal Policy in the Early Years of EMU', paper given at the ECFIN workshop on 'The Functioning of EMU: Challenges of the Early Years', Brussels, 21–22 March 2001.

Brunila, A., M. Buti and D. Franco (2001) *The Stability and Growth Pact. The Architecture of Fiscal Policy in EMU* (Basingstoke: Palgrave).

Buiter W. H. (1998) 'Notes on a Code for Fiscal Stability', *NBER Working Paper*, No. 6522.

Buiter, W., G. Corsetti and N. Roubini (1993) 'Excessive Deficits: Sense and Nonsense in the Treaty of Maastricht', *Economic Policy*, 16: 58–100.

Buti, M. and B. Martinot (2000) 'Open Issues in the Implementation of the Stability and Growth Pact', *National Institute Economic Review*, 174: 92–104.

Buti, M. and A. Sapir (eds) (1998) *Economic Policy in EMU: A Study by the European Commission Services* (Oxford: Oxford University Press).

Buti, M., D. Franco and H. Ongena (1997) 'Budgetary Policies during Recessions. Retrospective Application of the Stability and Growth Pact to Post-War Period', *Recherches économiques de louvain*, 63: 321–66.

Buti, M., D. Franco and H. Ongena (1998) 'Fiscal Discipline and Flexibility in EMU: The Implementation of the Stability and Growth Pact', *Oxford Review of Economic Policy*, 14: 81–97.

Buti, M., D. Franco and L. Pench (1999) 'Reconciling the Welfare State with Sound Public Finances and High Employment', in M. Buti, D. Franco and L. Pench (eds), *The Welfare State in Europe*, chapter 1 (Cheltenham (UK): Edward Elgar).

Cameron, D. (1978) 'The Expansion of the Public Economy', *American Political Science Review*, 72, 1243–61.

Campbell, J. Y. and N. G. Mankiw (1989) 'Consumption, income and interest rates: Reinterpreting the time series evidence', *NBER Macroeconomics Annual* (Cambridge, Mass.: The MIT Press).

Campbell, J. Y. and N. G. Mankiw (1991) 'The Response of Consumption to Income: A Cross-Country Investigation', *European Economic Review*, 35.

Cangiano, M. (1993) *Financial Sector Taxation in Italy: Reform Proposals and Revenue Implications* unpublished mimeo, Fiscal Affairs Department (Washington: IMF).

Canzoneri, M. B. and B. T. Diba (1998) 'Is the Price Level Determined by the Needs of Fiscal Solvency?', *NBER Working Paper*, No. 6471 (Cambridge, Mass.: NBER).

Canzoneri, M. B. and B. T. Diba (2001) 'The Stability and Growth Pact: A Delicate Balance or an Albatross?', in A. Brunila, M. Buti and D. Franco (eds), *The Stability and Growth Pact – The Architecture of Fiscal Policy in EMU* (Basingstoke: Palgrave).

Canzoneri, M., R. Cumby and B. Diba (2001) 'Is the Price Level Determined by the Needs of Fiscal Solvency?', *American Economic Review* (forthcoming).

Chari, V. V. and P. J. Kehoe (1998) 'On the Need for Fiscal Constraints in a Monetary Union', Working Paper no. 589, Federal Reserve Bank of Minneapolis.

Cheung, Yin-Wong and Kon S. Lai (1993) 'Finite-Sample Sizes of Johansen's Likelihood Ratio tests for Cointegration', *Oxford Bulletin of Economics and Statistics*, 55: 313–28.

Chouraqui, J. C., R. Hagemann and N. Sartor (1992) 'Indicators of Fiscal Policy: A Reassessment', *OECD Economics and Statistics Department Working Papers*, No. 78.

Christiano, L. (1984) 'A Reexamination of the Theory of Automatic Stabilizers', *Carnegie-Rochester Conference Series on Public Policy*, 20: 147–206.

Clarida, R., J. Galí and M. Gertler (1998) 'Monetary Rules in Practice: Some International Evidence', *European Economic Review*, 42: 1033–67.

Clarida, R., J. Galí and M. Gertler (1999) 'The Science of Monetary Policy: A New Keynesian Perspective', *Journal of Economic Literature*, 37: 1661–707.

Cohen, D. and G. Follette (2000) 'The Automatic Stabilizers: Quietly Doing their Thing', Federal Reserve Bank of New York *Economic Policy Review*, April: 35–67.

Cooper, R. and H. Kempf (2000) 'Designing Stabilization Policy in a Monetary Union', *NBER Working Paper*, No. 7607 (Cambridge, Mass.: NBER).

Corsetti, G. and N. Roubini (1996) 'European versus American Perspectives on Balanced-Budget Rules', *American Economic Review*, 86: 408–13.

Cour, Ph., E. Dubois, S. Mahfouz and J. Pisani-Ferry (1996) 'The Cost of Fiscal Retrenchment Revisited: How Strong is the Evidence?', INSEE, *Document de Travail*, No. G 9612.

Cox, D. R. (1972) 'Regression Models and Life Tables', *Journal of the Royal Statistical Society*, Series B, 34: 187–220.

Crosby, M. (1998) 'Central Bank Independence and Output Variability', *Economic Letters*, 60, 67–75.

Cukierman, A., P. Kalaitzidakis, L. Summers and S. Webb (1993) 'Central Bank Independence, Growth, Investment, and Real Rates', *Carnegie-Rochester Conference Series on Public Policy*, 39: 95–140.

Dalsgaard, T. and A. DeSerres (1999) 'Estimating Prudent Budgetary Margins to Comply with the Stability and Growth Pact: A Simulated SVAR Approach', *OECD Economics Department Working Paper*, No. 216 (Paris: OECD).

Daveri, F. and G. Tabellini (1997) 'Unemployment, Growth and Taxation in Industrial Countries', *International Monetary Fund Seminar Series*, No. 28.

Debelle, G. and S. Fischer (1994) 'How Independent Should a Central Bank Be?', in J. C. Fuhrer (ed.), *Goals, Guidelines and Constraints Facing Monetary Policymakers*, Federal Reserve Bank of Boston, Conference Series, 38: 195–221.

Decressin, J. (1999) 'Regional Income Redistribution and Risk Sharing: How Does Italy Compare with Europe?', IMF, mimeo.

Demertzis, M., A. Hughes Hallett and N. Viegi (1999a) 'Can the ECB Be Truly Independent? Should It Be?', *Empirica*, 26: 217–40.

Demertzis, M., A. J. Hughes Hallett and N. Viegi (1999b) 'An Independent Central Bank Faced with Elected Governments', *CEPR Discussion Paper*, No. 2219.

Dixit, A. (2000) 'Games of Monetary and Fiscal Interactions in the EMU', Working Paper, Princeton, August.

Dixit, A. and L. Lambertini (2000a) 'Symbiosis of Monetary and Fiscal Policies in a Monetary Union', Working Paper, Princeton and UCLA, March.

Dixit, A. and L. Lambertini (2000b) 'Fiscal Discretion Destroys Monetary Commitment', Working Paper, Princeton and UCLA, August.

Dixit, A. and L. Lambertini (2000c) 'Monetary–Fiscal Policy Interactions and Commitment Versus Discretion in a Monetary Union', Working Paper, Princeton and UCLA, August.

Drazen, A. and V. Grilli (1993) 'The Benefits of Crisis for Economic Reform', *American Economic Review*, 83: 598–607.

Easterly, W. and S. Rebelo (1993) 'Fiscal Policy and Economic Growth: An Empirical Investigation', *Journal of Monetary Economics*, 32: 417–58.

Eichengreen, B. (1994) 'Fiscal Policy and EMU', in Barry Eichengreen and Jeffrey Frieden (eds), *The Political Economy of European Monetary Unification* (Boulder, Colorado: Westview Press).

Eichengreen, B. and C. Wyplosz (1998) 'The Stability Pact – More Than a Minor Nuisance?', *Economic Policy*, 26: 65–114.

Eijffinger, S. and J. de Haan (1995) 'The Political Economy of Central Bank Independence', *CentER Discussion Paper*, 9587, Tilburg University, The Netherlands.

Elmendorf, D.W. and N.G. Mankiw (1998) 'Government Debt', *NBER Working Paper* No. 6470.

Engen, E. and J. Skinner (1992) 'Fiscal Policy and Economic Growth', *NBER Working Paper*, No. 4223.

European Central Bank (1999) Monthly Bulletin, May, Frankfurt: ECB.

European Commission (1990) 'One Market, One Money', *European Economy*, no. 44.

European Commission (1996) '1996 Broad Economic Policy Guidelines', *European Economy*, no. 62.

European Commission (1999) 'Italy's Slow Growth in the 1990s: Facts, Explanations and Prospects', *European Economy – Reports and Studies*, no. 5.

European Commission (2000a) 'Public Finances in EMU – 2000', *European Economy – Reports and Studies*, no. 3.

European Commission (2000b) *The Contribution of Public Finances to Growth and Employment: Improving Quality and Sustainability*, Commission Communication, COM(2000) 846. Also published in *European Economy, Supplement A*, no. 1, January 2000.

European Commission (2001) 'Public Finances in EMU – 2001', *European Economy – Reports and Studies*, No. 3.

Evans, P. (1988) 'Are Consumers Ricardian? Evidence for the United States', *Journal of Political Economy*, 96: 983–1004.

Evans, P. (1993) 'Consumers Are Not Ricardian: Evidence from Nineteen Countries', *Economic Inquiry*, 31: 534–48.

Evans, P. and I. Hasan (1994) 'Are Consumers Ricardian? Evidence for Canada', *Quarterly Review of Economics and Finance*, 34: 25–40.

Evans, P. and G. Karras (1996) 'Private and Government Consumption with Liquidity Constraints', *Journal of International Money and Finance*, 15: 255–66.

Fatás, A. and I. Mihov (1998) 'Measuring the Effects of Fiscal Policy', INSEAD, mimeo.

Fatás, A. and I. Mihov (1999) 'Government Size and Automatic Stabilizers: International and Intranational Evidence', *CEPR Discussion Paper*, No. 2259.

Fatás, A. and I. Mihov (2001) 'Fiscal Policy and EMU: Challenges of the Early Years', paper given at the ECFIN Workshop on 'The Functioning of EMU: Challenges of the Early Years', Brussels, 21–22 March 2001.

Favero, C. and R. Rovelli (2000) 'Modeling and Identifying Central Banks' Preferences', mimeo (June).

Fiorito, R. (1997) 'Stylized Facts of Government Finance in the G-7', IMF, mimeo (October).

Flavin, M. A. (1981) 'The Adjustment of Consumption to Changing Expectations about Future Income', *Journal of Political Economy*, 89: 974–1009.

Frankel, J and A. Rose (1998) 'The Endogeneity of the Optimum Currency Area Criteria', *Economic Journal*, 108: 1009–25.

Friedman, B. (1981) 'Debt and Economic Activity in the United States', *NBER Working Paper Series*, No. 704, June.

Friedman, B. (1982) 'Money, Credit, and Nonfinancial Economic Activity: An Empirical Study of Five Countries', mimeo.

Friedman, B. (1987) 'New Directions in the Relationship Between Public and Private Debt', *NBER Working Paper Series*, No. 2186.

Friend, I. and M.E. Blume (1975) 'The Demand for Risky Assets', *American Economic Review*, 65: 900–22.

Fry, M. (1998) 'Macroeconomic Policy and the Negative Relationship Between Growth and Inflation', University of Birmingham, mimeo.

Fuente, A. de la (1997) *Restructuring Government Expenditure*, report prepared for DG ECFIN, European Commission, mimeo.

Fuss, C. (1999) 'Mesures et tests de convergence: une revue de la littérature', *Revue de l'OFCE*, 69: 221–49.

Galí, J. (1994) 'Government Size and Macroeconomic Stability', *European Economic Review*, 38: 117–32.

Gavin, M. and R. Perotti (1997) 'Fiscal Policy in Latin America', in *NBER Macroeconomics Annual, 1997*.

Giavazzi, F. and M. Pagano (1990a) 'Can Severe Fiscal Contractions Be Expansionary? A Tale of Two Small Economies', in O.B. Blanchard and S. Fischer (eds), *NBER Macroeconomics Annual, 1990*.

Giavazzi, F. and M. Pagano (1990b) 'Can Severe Fiscal Contractions Be Expansionary? Tales of Two Small European Countries', *CEPR Discussion Paper*, No. 147.

Giavazzi, F. and M. Pagano (1995a) 'Non-Keynesian Effects of Fiscal Policy Changes: International Evidence and the Swedish Experience', *CEPR Discussion Paper*, 1284.

Giavazzi, F. and M. Pagano (1995b) 'Non-Keynesian Effects of Fiscal Policy Changes: More International Evidence', Paper presented at the conference 'Growing Government Debt: International Experiences', Stockholm, 12 June 1995.

Giavazzi, F., T. Jappelli and M. Pagano (2000) 'Searching for Non-linear Effects of Fiscal Policy – Evidence from Industrial and Developing Countries', *European Economic Review*, 44: 1259–89.

Giorno, C., P. Richardson, D. Roseveare and P. Van Den Noord (1995) 'Potential Output, Output Gaps and Structural Budget Balances', *OECD Economic Studies*, 24: 167–209.

Glomm, G. and B. Ravikumar (1997) 'Productive Government Expenditures and Long-Run Growth', *Journal of Economic Dynamics and Control*, 21: 183–204.

Gordo, L. and P. Hernández de Cos (2000) 'The Financing Arrangements for the Regional (Autonomous) Governments for the Period 1997–2001, mimeo.

Graham, F. C. and D. Himarios (1991) 'Fiscal Policy and Private Consumption: Instrumental Variables Tests of the "Consolidated Approach"', *Journal of Money, Credit, and Banking*, 23: 53–67.

Graham, F. C. and D. Himarios (1996) 'Consumption, Wealth, and Finite Horizons: Tests of Ricardian Equivalence', *Economic Inquiry*, 34: 527–44.

Grauwe, P. De (2000) 'The Challenge of Monetary Policy in Euroland', paper presented at the 2000 Flemish Conference '*EMU: The Challenge*'.

Grilli, V., D. Masciandaro and G. Tabellini (1991) 'Political and Monetary Institutions and Public Financial Policies in the Industrial Countries', *Economic Policy*, 13: 341–92.

Haan, J. de, W. Moessen and B. Volkering (1999) 'Budgetary Procedures – Aspects and Changes', in J. Poterba and J. von Hagen (eds), *Fiscal Institutions and Fiscal Performance* (Chicago: University of Chicago Press).

Hagemann, R. (1999) 'The Structural Budget Balance: The IMF's Methodology', *IMF Working Paper*, 99/95.

Hairault, J. O. and F. Portier (1993) 'Money, New-Keynesian Macroeconomics and the Business Cycle', *European Economic Review*, 37: 1533–68.

Hall, R. E. (1978) 'Stochastic Implications of the Life Cycle–Permanent Income Hypothesis: Theory and Evidence', *Journal of Political Economy*, 86: 971–87.

Hall, S., D. Robertson and M. Wickens (1992) 'Measuring Convergence of the EC Economies', *The Manchester School*, vol. 60 Supplement (June): 99–111.

Hall, S., D. Robertson and M. Wickens (1993) 'How to Measure Convergence, with an Application to EC Economies', ESEM meeting, Upsala.

Hallerberg, M. (2000) 'The Importance of Domestic Political Institutions: Why and How Belgium and Italy Qualified for EMU', Working Paper, University of Pittsburgh.

Hallerberg, M., and J. von Hagen (1998) 'Electoral Institutions and the Budget Process', in K. Fukasako and R. Hausmann (eds), *Democracy, Decentralization, and Deficits in Latin America* (Paris: OECD).

Hallerberg, M. and J. von Hagen (1999) 'Electoral Institutions, Cabinet Negotiations, and Budget Deficits in the European Union', in J. Poterba and J. Von Hagen (eds), *Fiscal Institutions and Fiscal Performance* (Chicago and London: University of Chicago Press).

Hansen, L. P. (1982) 'Large Sample Properties of Generalized Methods of Moments Estimators', *Econometrica*, 50: 1029–54.

Haque, N. (1988) 'Fiscal Policy and Private Saving Behavior in Developing Economies', *IMF Staff Papers*, 35: 316–35.

Haug, A. A. (1990) 'Ricardian Equivalence, Rational Expectations, and the Permanent Income Hypothesis', *Journal of Money, Credit, and Banking*, 22: 305–26.

Haug, A. A. (1996) 'Blanchard's Model of Consumption: An Empirical Study', *Journal of Business and Economic Statistics*, 14: 169–177.

Hayashi, F. (1982) 'The Permanent Income Hypothesis: Estimation and Testing by Instrumental Variables', *Journal of Political Economy*, 90: 895–916.

Heller, P. and J. Diamond (1990) 'International Comparisons of Government Expenditure Revisited: The Developing Countries, 1975–1986', *IMF Occasional Papers*, No. 69.

Hellwig, M. and M. J. M. Neumann (1987) 'Economic policy in Germany: Was there a turnaround?', *Economic Policy 5*, 105–45.

Heylen, F. (1997) 'A Contribution to the Empirical Analysis of the Effects of Fiscal Consolidation: Explanation of Failure in Europe in the 1990s', Paper presented at the conference 'Public Deficits and Monetary Union', 27–28 November, Rome.

Himarios, D. (1995) 'Euler Equation Tests of Ricardian Equivalence', *Economic Letters*, 48: 155–63.

Hughes Hallett, A. (1989) 'Econometrics and the Theory of Economic Policy', *Oxford Economic Papers*, 41: 189–214.

Hughes Hallett, A. J. and P. McAdam (1997) 'Large Scale Fiscal Contractions in Europe: The Costs, Benefits and Likely Outcomes', manuscript, University of Strathclyde.

Hughes Hallett, A. and P. McAdam (1998) 'Large Scale Fiscal Retrenchments: Long-Run Lessons from the Stability Pact', *CEPR Discussion Paper*, 1843.

Hughes Hallett, A. and N. Viegi (2000) 'Central Bank Independence, Political Uncertainty and the Assignment of Instruments to Targets', University of Strathchyde.

Hughes Hallett, A. and D. Vines (1993) 'On the Possible Cost of European Monetary Union', *The Manchester School of Economic and Social Studies*, 61: 35–64.

Hume, David (1955) *Writings on Economics*, E. Rotuein (ed.) (London: Thomas Nelson & Sons Ltd).

Hüttner, B. (1996) 'Der Finanzausgleich 1997 und sein Umfeld', *Österreichische Gemeinde-Zeitung* 8, 11–16.

Hüttner, B. (1999) 'Österreichischer Stabilitätspakt, Maastricht Defizit und Länderhaushalte', *Das öffentliche Haushaltswesen in Österreich*, 40 (1–3): 93–114.

International Monetary Fund (1993) 'Structural Budget Indicators for the Major Industrial Countries', IMF *World Economic Outlook*: 99–103.

Issing, O. (2000) 'How to Achieve a Durable Macroeconomic Policy Mix Favourable to Growth and Employment?', speech at the Conference on 'Growth and Employment in Europe', European Commission, Brussels, May.

Italianer, A. and M. Vanheukelen (1993) 'Proposals for Community Stabilization Mechanisms: Some Historical Applications', *European Economy*, 5, 493–510.

Jacquet, J. and J. Pisani-Ferry (2000) *Economic Policy Co-ordination in the Euro Zone* (Paris: Conseil d'Analyse Economique).

Jappelli, T. and M. Pagano (1989) 'Consumption and Capital Market Imperfections: An International Comparison', *American Economic Review*, 79: 1088–105.

Johansen, S. (1995) *Likelihood-Based Inference on Cointegration in the VAR Model* (Oxford: Oxford University Press).

Jones, L. and R. Manuelli (1997) 'The Sources of Growth', *Journal of Economic Dynamics and Control*, 21: 75–114.

Karras, G. (1994) 'Government Spending and Private Consumption: Some International Evidence', *Journal of Money, Credit, and Banking*, 26: 9–22.

Katzenstein, P. (1984) *Small States in World Markets: Industrial Policy in Europe* (Ithaca: Cornell University Press).

Kell, M. (2001) 'An Assessment of Fiscal Rules in the UK', *IMF Working Paper*, No. 01/91.

King, R. and S. Rebelo (1990) 'Public Policy and Economic Growth: Developing Neoclassical Implications', *Journal of Political Economy*, 101: 485–517.

Kontopoulos, Y. and R. Perotti (1999) 'Government Fragmentation and Fiscal Policy Outcomes: Evidence from OECD Countries', in J. Poterba and J. von Hagen (eds), *Fiscal Institutions and Fiscal Performance* (Chicago: University of Chicago Press).

Kopits, G. and S. Symansky (1998) 'Fiscal Policy Rules', *IMF Occasional Paper*, No. 162.

Kormendi, R. and P. Meguire (1985) 'Macroeconomic Determinants of Growth: Cross Country Evidence', *Journal of Monetary Economics*, 16: 141–64.

Kremers, J. M., N. R. Ericsson and J. J. Dolado (1992) 'The Power of Cointegration Tests', *Oxford Bulletin of Economics and Statistics*, vol. 54, no.3: 325–47.

Krugman, P. (1993) 'Lessons of Massachusets for EMU', in F. Torres and F. Giavazzi (eds), *Adjustment and Growth in the European Monetary Union* (Cambridge, Mass.: Cambridge University Press).

Kwiatowski, D., P. C. B. Phillips, P. Schmidt and Y. Shin (1992) 'Testing the Null Hypothesis of Stationarity Against the Alternative of a Unit Root', *Journal of Econometrics*, 54: 159–78.

Kyndland, F. and E. C. Prescott (1977) 'Rules Rather Than Discretion: The Time Inconsistency of Optimal Plans', *Journal of Political Economy*, 85: 473–91.

Lambertini, L. and J. Tavares (2000) 'Exchange Rates and Fiscal Adjustments: Evidence from the OECD and Implications for EMU', typescript, UCLA.

Lamfalussy, A. (1989) 'Macro-Coordination of Fiscal Policies in an Economic and Monetary Union in Europe', annex to the *Report on the Study of Economic and Monetary Union in the European Community* (Delors Report) (Luxembourg: European Commission).

Lancaster, T. (1990) *The Econometric Analysis of Transition Data* (Cambridge: Cambridge University Press).

Landau, D. (1986) 'Government and Economic Growth in the Less Developed Countries: an Empirical Study for 1960–1980', *Economic Development and Cultural Change*, 35, 35–7.

Lao-Araya, K. (1997) 'The Effect of Budget Structure on Fiscal Performance: A Study of Selected Asian Countries', *IMF Working Paper*, No. 97/05.

Leeper, E. M. (1991) 'Equilibria Under Active and Passive Monetary and Fiscal Policies', *Journal of Monetary Economics*, 27: 129–47.

Leibfritz, W., D. Roseveare and P. van den Noord (1994) 'Fiscal Policy, Government Debt and Economic Performance', *OECD Economics Department Working Papers*, No. 144.

Leibfritz, Willi, John Thornton and Alexandra Bibbee (1997) 'Taxation and Economic Performance', GD (97) 107 (Paris: OECD).

Leiderman, L. and M. I. Blejer (1988) 'Modelling and Testing Ricardian Equivalence', *IMF Staff Papers*, 35: 1–35.

Leiderman, L. and A. Razin (1988) 'Testing Ricardian Neutrality with an Intertemporal Stochastic Model', *Journal of Money, Credit, and Banking*, 20: 1–21.

Leith, C. and S. Wren-Lewis (2000) 'Interactions between Monetary and Fiscal Policy Rules', *Economic Journal*, 110: 94–108.

Leitmo, K. (2000) 'Strategic Interactions between the Fiscal and Monetary Authorities under Inflation Targeting', mimeo, September.

Levin, J. H. (1983) 'A Model of Stabilization Policy in a Jointly Floating Currency Area', in J.S. Bhandari and B.H. Putnam (eds), *Economic Interdependence and Flexible Exchange Rates* (Boston: MIT University Press).

Levine, P. and A. Brociner (1994) 'Fiscal Coordination under EMU and the Choice of Monetary Instrument', *Journal of Economic Dynamics and Control*, 18: 699–729.

Levine, R. and Renelt (1992) 'Sensitivity Analysis of Cross-Country Growth Regressions', *American Economic Review*, 82: 942–63.

Lutkepohl, H. (1999) 'Order Selection in Testing for Cointegration Rank of a VAR Process', mimeo, Econometric Society Meeting, Santiago de Compostella, September.

Mackenzie G. A. (1989) 'Are All Summary Indicators of the Stance of Fiscal Policy Misleading?', *IMF Staff Papers*, 36: 743–70.

Martin, R. and M. Fardmanesh (1990) 'Fiscal Variables and Growth: A Cross-Sectional Analysis', *Public Choice (Netherlands)*, 64: 239–51.

Martinez-Mongay, C. (2000) 'The Long-Run Determinants of Government Receipts', in *Fiscal Sustainability*, Research Department, Public Finance Workshop (Rome: Banca d'Italia).

Martinez-Mongay, C. and R. Fernandez-Bayón (2001) 'Effective Taxation, Spending and Employment Performance', in M. Buti, P. Sestito and H. Wijkander (eds), *Taxation, Welfare and the Crisis of Unemployment in Europe* (Northampton, MA: Edward Elgar).

Martinot, B. (1999) 'Pacte de stabilité et efficacité de la politique budgétaire', mimeo.

Masciandaro, D. and G. Tabellini (1988) 'Fiscal Deficits and Monetary Institutions: A Comparative Analysis', in H. Cheng (ed.), *Challenges to Monetary Policy in the Pacific Basin Countries* (Dordrecht: Kluwer Academic).

Masson, P. R. (1996) 'Fiscal Dimensions of EMU', *Economic Journal*, 106: 996–1004.

McDermott, C. J. and R. F. Wescott (1996) 'An Empirical Analysis of Fiscal Adjustments', *IMF Staff Papers*, 43: 725–53.

Mélitz, J. (1997) 'Some Cross Country Evidence about Debt, Deficits and the Behaviour of Monetary and Fiscal Authorities', *CEPR Discussion Paper*, No. 1653, CEPR, London.

Mélitz, J. (2000) 'Some Cross-Country Evidence about Fiscal Policy Behaviour and Consequences for EMU', *European Economy, Reports and Studies*, No. 2: 3–21.

Mendoza, E., G. M. Milesi-Ferretti and P. Asea (1997) 'On the Ineffectiveness of Tax Policy in Altering Long-Run Growth: Harberger's Superneutrality Conjecture', *Journal of Public Economics*, 66: 99–126.

Molander, P. (1999) 'Reforming Budgetary Institutions: Swedish Experiences', in R. Strauch and J. von Hagen (1999), *Institutions, Politics and Fiscal Policy* (Boston: Kluwer Academic Publishers).

Mongelli, F. (1997) 'Effects of the European Economic and Monetary Union (EMU) on Taxation and Interest Spending of National Governments', *IMF Working Paper*, WP/97/93 (Washington, DC: International Monetary Fund).

Mongelli, F. (1999) 'The Effects of the European Economic and Monetary Union (EMU) on National Fiscal Sustainability', *Open Economies Review*, 10: 31–62.

Ni, S. (1995) 'An Empirical Analysis on the Substitutability Between Private Consumption and Government Purchases', *Journal of Monetary Economics*, 36: 593–605.

Nordhaus, W. (1994) 'Policy Games: Coordination and Independence in Monetary and Fiscal Policies', *Brookings Papers on Economic Activity*, 25, 2: 139–216.

Norregaard, J. (1997) 'Tax Treatment of Government Bonds', *Tax Notes International*, 15: 143–55.

OECD (1993) *Automatic Stabilizers: Their Extent and Role* (Paris: OECD)

OECD (1995) 'Taxation, Employment and Unemployment', *The OECD Jobs Study* (Paris: OECD).

OECD (1998) *Forces Shaping Tax Policy* (Paris: OECD).

OECD (1999a) *EMU Facts, Challenges and Policies* (Paris: OECD).

OECD (1999b) *Implementing the OECD Jobs Strategy: Assessing Performance and Policy* (Paris: OECD).

Orr, A., M. Edey and M. Kennedy (1995) 'Real Long-Term Interest Rates: The Evidence from Pooled-Time-Series', *OECD Economic Studies*, 25: 75–107.

Osterwald-Lenum, M. (1992) 'Practitioners Corner: A Note with Qualities of the Asymptotic Distribution of the Maximum Likelihood Cointegration Rank Test Statistics', *Oxford Bulletin of Economics and Statistics*, 4: 461–71.

Parkin, M. (1987) 'Domestic Monetary Institutions and Deficits', in J.M. Buchanan, C.K. Rowley and R.D. Tollison (eds), *Deficits* (Oxford: Basil Blackwell) 310–37.

Perotti, R. (1996a) 'Fiscal Consolidation in Europe: Composition Matters', *American Economic Review*, 86: 105–10.

Perotti, R. (1996b) 'Fiscal Policy When Things Are Going Badly', CEPII-DELTA conference on 'The Macroeconomic Effects of Fiscal Adjustments', Paris, September.

Perotti, R. (1999) 'Fiscal Policy in Good Times and Bad', *Quarterly Journal of Economics* 114: 1399–436.

Perotti, R., R. Strauch and J. von Hagen (1998) *Sustainable Public Finances* (London: CEPR).

Persson, T. (2001) 'Do Political Institutions Shape Economic Policy?', *NBER Working Paper Series*, No. 8214 (Cambridge, Mass.: NBER).

Persson, T. and G. Tabellini (1990) *Macroeconomic Policy, Credibility and Politics* (London: Harwood Academic Publishers).

Persson, T. and G. Tabellini (1999) 'The Size and Scope of the Government: Comparative Politics with Rational Politicians', *European Economic Review*, 43: 699–735.

Persson, T. and G. Tabellini (2000) *Political Economics: Explaining Economic Policy* (Cambridge, Mass.: MIT Press).

Persson, T. and G. Tabellini (2001) 'Political Institutions and Policy Outcomes: What are the Stylized Facts?', mimeo.

Phelps, E. (1994) *Structural Slumps: The Modern Equilibrium Theory of Unemployment, Interest, and Assets* (Cambridge Mass.: Harvard University Press).

Philipps, P. C. B. and M. Loretan (1991) 'Estimating long-run Economic Equilibria', *Review of Economic Studies*, 58: 407–36.

Pisani-Ferry, J., A. Italianer and R. Lescure (1993) 'Stabilization Properties of Budgetary Systems: A Simulation Analysis', *European Economy*, 5: 511–39.

Posen, A. (1993) 'Why Central Bank Independence Does Not Cause Low Inflation: There is No Institutional Fix for Politics', *AMEX Bank Review*, 40–65.

Poterba, J. M. (1996) 'Budget Institutions and Fiscal Policy in the US States', *American Economic Review*, 86: 395–400.

Poterba, J. and J. von Hagen (1999) *Fiscal Institutions and Fiscal Performance* (Chicago: University of Chicago Press).

Ram, R. (1987) 'Warner's Hypothesis in Time-series and Cross-Section Perspectives: Evidence from 'Real' Data for 115 Countries', *Review of Economics and Statistics*, 69: 194–204.

Ribe, F. (1995) 'Structural Fiscal Balances in Smaller Industrial Countries', IMF *World Economic Outlook*, May: 108–11.

Roberts, John (1995) 'New Keynesian Economics and the Phillips Curve', *Journal of Money, Credit and Banking*, 27: 975–84.

Rodrick, D. (1998) 'Why Do More Open Economies Have Bigger Governments?', *Journal of Political Economy*, 106: 997–1032.

Roeger, W. (1999) 'Output, Prices and Interest Rates over the Business Cycle', *Zeitschrift für Wirtschafts -und Sozialwissenschaften*, 119: 57–98.

Roeger, W. and H. Ongena (1999) 'The Commission Services' Cyclical Adjustment Method', *Indicators of Structural Budget Balances* (Rome: Banca d'Italia).

Roeger, W. and J. in't Veld (1997) 'Quest II: A Multi-Country Business Cycle and Growth Model', *DG ECFIN Economic Papers Series*, No. 123 (Brussels: European Commission).

Roeger, W., J. in't Veld and D.I.A. Woehrmann (2001) 'Some Equity and Efficiency Considerations of International Tax Competition', *International Tax and Public Finance* (forthcoming).

Rogoff, K. (1985) 'The Optimal Degree of Commitment to an Intermediate Monetary Target', *Quarterly Journal of Economics*, 99: 1169–89.

Rose, A. (1999) 'One Money, One Market: Estimating the Effect of Common Currencies on Trade', *NBER Working Paper*, No. 7432 (Cambridge, Mass.: NBER).

Rotemberg, J. J. (1982) 'Sticky Prices in the United States', *Journal of Political Economy*, 90: 1187–211.

Rotemberg, J. J. (1996) 'Prices, Output and Hours: An Empirical Analysis Based on a Sticky Price Model', *Journal of Monetary Economics*, 37: 505–33.

Rotemberg, J. J. and M. Woodford (1998) 'An Optimisation Based Economic Framework for the Evaluation of Monetary Policy: An Expanded Version', *NBER Working Paper*, 233, NBER, Cambridge, Mass.

Roubini, N. (1995) 'The Economics of Fiscal Bondage: The Balanced Budget Amendment and Other Binding Fiscal Rules', manuscript, Yale University.

Roubini, N. and J. D. Sachs (1989) 'Political and Economic Determinants of Budget Deficits in the Industrial Democracies', *European Economic Review*, 33: 903–38.

Sala-i-Martin, X. (1997) 'I Just Ran Two Million Regressions', *American Economic Review*, 87: 178–83.

Sargent, T. and N. Wallace (1981) 'Some Unpleasant Monetarist Arithmetic', *Quarterly Review of Minneapolis Federal Reserve Bank*, 5: 1–17.

Seater, J. J. (1993) 'Ricardian Equivalence', *Journal of Economic Literature*, 31: 142–90.

Sefton, J. A. and J. W. In't Veld (1999) 'Consumption and Wealth: An International Comparison', *The Manchester School*, 67: 525–44.

Shigehara, K. (1995) 'Commentary' on Paul Masson and Michael Mussa 'Long-Term Tendencies in Budget Deficits and Debt', in Federal Reserve Bank of Kansas City Symposium, *Budget Deficits and Debt: Issues and Options*.

Sims, C. A. (1999) 'The Precarious Fiscal Foundations of EMU', September.

Sørensen, P. B. (ed.) (1997) *Public Finance in a Changing World* (London: Macmillan).

Sørensen, P. B., L. Wu and O. Yosha (1999) 'Output Fluctuations and Fiscal Policy: US State and Local Governments 1978–1994', *CEPR Discussion Paper*, No. 2286.

Stein, R., E. Talvi and A. Grisanti (1999) 'Institutional Arrangements and Fiscal Performance: The Latin American Experience', in J. Poterba and J. von Hagen (eds), *Fiscal Institutions and Fiscal Performance* (Chicago: University of Chicago Press).

Stienlet, G. (1999) 'Institutional Reforms and Belgian Fiscal Policy in the 90s', in R. Strauch and J. von Hagen (1999) *Institutions, Politics and Fiscal Policy* (Boston: Kluwer Academic Publishers).

Strauch, R. (1998) 'Budgetprozesse und Haushaltsdisziplin – Eine Analyse der U.S.–Amerikanischen Staaten', dissertation, Bonn.

Strauch, R. and J. von Hagen (1999) *Institutions, Politics, and Fiscal Policy* (ZEI Studies in European Economics and Law) (Boston: Kluwer Academic Publishers).

Sturm, R. (1998) 'Finanzpolitik am Ende oder vor der Wahl? Akteure, Instrumente und Blockaden in der Finanzpolitik', in U. Andersen (ed.), *Der deutsche Steuerstaat in der Finanzkrise* (Schwalbach: Wochenschau Verlag).

Sutherland, A. (1997) 'Fiscal Crises and Aggregate Demand: Can High Public Debt Reverse the Effects of Fiscal Policy?', *Journal of Public Economics*, 65: 147–62.

Svenson, L. E. O. (1997) 'Optimal Inflation Targets, Conservative Central Banks, and Linear Inflation Contracts', *American Economic Review*, 87: 98–114.

Tanzi, V. (1998) 'The Role of Government and the Efficiency of Policy Instruments', in *Public Finance Reform in Asia Pacific*, pages 73–86, EDAP Joint Policy Studies, No. 2, (Seoul: Korea Development Institute).

Tanzi, V. and J. King (1995) 'The Taxation of Financial Assets : A Survey of Issues and Country Experiences', *IMF Working Paper*, No. 95/46.

Tanzi, V. and H. Zee (2001) 'Taxation and the Household Saving Rate: Evidence from OECD Countries', forthcoming in *Banca Nazionale del Lavoro Quarterly Review*.

Taylor, J. (1993) 'Discretion versus Policy Rules in Practice', *Carnegie-Rochester Conference Series on Public Policy*, 39: 195–214.

van Aarle, B., A. L. Bovenberg and M. Raith (1995) 'Is There a Tragedy of a Common Central Bank? – A Dynamic Analysis', Tilburg University, mimeo.

van Aarle, B., J. C. Engwerda, J.E.J. Plasmans and A. Weeren (2000) 'Monetary and Fiscal Policy Design under EMU: A Dynamic Game Approach', *CESifo Working Paper*, No. 262.

van den Noord, P. (2000) 'The Size and Role of Automatic Stabilizers in the 1990s and Beyond', *OECD Economics Department Working Papers*, No. 230 (Paris: OECD).

Velasco, A. (1999) 'A Model of Endogenous Fiscal Deficits and Delayed Fiscal Reforms', in J. Poterba and J. von Hagen (eds), *Fiscal Institutions and Fiscal Performance* (Chicago: University of Chicago Press).

Virén, M. (1998) 'Do the OECD Countries Follow the Same Fiscal Rule', Government Institute for Economic Research, Helsinki, *Vatt Discussion Papers*, No. 186.

von Hagen, J. (1992) 'Budgeting Procedures and Fiscal Performance in the European Communities', *ECFIN Economic Papers*, No. 96 (Brussels: European Commission).

von Hagen, J. (1997) 'European Experience with Fiscal Initiatives: Fiscal Institutions, Maastricht Guidelines, and EMU', typescript, University of Bonn.

von Hagen, J. (1998) 'European Experiences with Fiscal Initiatives: Fiscal Institutions, Maastricht Guidelines, and EMU', in T. Courchene and T. A. Wilson (eds), *Fiscal Targets and Economic Growth* (Kingston: J. Deutsch Institute).

von Hagen, J. and I. Harden (1994a) 'Budget Processes and Commitment to Fiscal Discipline', *European Economic Review*, 39: 371–9.

von Hagen, J. and I. Harden (1994b) 'National Budget Processes and Fiscal Performance', *European Economy Reports and Studies*, 3: 311–418.

von Hagen, J. and I. Harden (1996) 'Budget Processes and Commitment to Fiscal Discipline', *IMF Working Paper*, WP 96/78.

von Hagen, J. and R. Strauch (1999) 'Tumbling Giant: Germany's Experience with the Maastricht Fiscal Criteria', in D. Cobham and G. Zis (eds), *From EMS to EMU* (Basingstoke: Macmillan).

von Hagen, J., A. Hughes Hallet and R. Strauch (2001) 'Budgetary Consolidation in EMU', *DG ECFIN Economic Papers*, No. 148 (Brussels: European Commission).

Woodford, M. (1995) 'Price Level Determinacy Without Control of a Monetary Aggregate', *Carnegie-Rochester Conference Series on Public Policy*, 43: 1–46.

Wyplosz, C. (1999) 'Economic Policy Coordination in EMU: Strategies and Institutions', *ZEI Policy Paper*, B11.

Zaghini, A. (1999) 'The Economic Policy of Fiscal Consolidations: The European Experience', *Banca d'Italia Working Paper*, No. 355.

Zee, H. H. (1997) 'Taxation and Unemployment', *Tax Notes International*, vol. 14, no. 3: 225–54.

Zeldes, S. P. (1989) 'Optimal Consumption with Stochastic Income: Deviations from Certainty Equivalence', *Quarterly Journal of Economics*, 104: 275–98.

Index